RECONSTRUCTION OF THINKING

AXIOLOGY OF THINKING series

Reconstruction of Thinking

ROBERT C. NEVILLE

STATE UNIVERSITY OF NEW YORK PRESS
Albany

Published by
State University of New York Press, Albany

© 1981 State University of New York

For information, address State University of New York
Press, State University Plaza, Albany, N.Y., 12246

Library of Congress Cataloging in Publication Data
Neville, Robert C.
    Reconstruction of thinking.
    Bibliography: p. 329
    Includes index.
    1. Thought and thinking. I. Title.
B105.T54N48   128'.3   81-5347
ISBN 0-87395-494-7   AACR2
ISBN 0-87395-495-5 (pbk.)

For
Richard Perry Neville
1909–1973

Contents

Preface

The new fields of psychobiology, sociobiology, and artificial intelligence have focused attention upon ways in which thinking is a function of nature and natural processes. This serves as a timely corrective to the generally nonnaturalistic conception of thinking in modern Western culture. But essential to thinking also is a host of cultural contributions; thinking is an artifact, a range of historical phenomena. An apocalyptic destruction of civilization would eliminate the conditions for thinking in most of the forms we recognize. That we think at all requires culture, and how people think differs from one culture to another. Furthermore, the understanding of a culture's basic modes of thinking involves historical understanding of how it developed from modes of thinking in its cultural antecedents. The scientific focus may obscure the importance of the fact that thinking is concrete only in historically relative cultural contexts, and that our own culture's modes of thinking themselves have a history. If the exclusive scientific orientation were right, if thinking in its basic modes were only a natural product as understood by natural sciences, then there would be no point in making a critical historical appraisal of our own culture's conceptions of thinking.

Because thinking is a range of cultural and historical artifacts, however, not only might thinking have been different from what it is, it *has* been different, and today differs from one culture to another. Furthermore, by understanding how basic modes of thinking have evolved historically, we can see that some of the means of changing them are now at our disposal and that among the processes which affect the evolution of thinking are those we can influence. Therefore, it becomes extraordinarily important to appraise the drift of our culture's thinking, to identify ways of affecting that drift, and to conceive of alternate directions in which it should be encouraged. That we have some measure of control over value-laden processes makes us responsible for them. This "moral" intellectual consideration is the context for the following project.

This book begins a systematic philosophic examination and reconstruction of conceptions of thinking. As the first chapter explains, the extraordinary success of the European Renaissance in combining qualitative and quantitative modes of cognition in a unified model of thinking in mathematical science unfortunately obscured the roles of valuation in thinking. The aim here is to construct new conceptions of thinking that distinguish and bring into perspective some of those roles for valuation. Indeed, the thesis of this book is that elemental processes of human behavior, those of imagination, seize upon natural stimuli and thereby establish human experience within natural, causal interactions; these processes are synthesizing activities that value diverse influences according to norms.

In what sense is there a foundation for human experience? Western epistemology has been plagued by the claim that experience ought to enjoy some foundation in knowledge that is supposed to be incorrigible and certain. But there is a prior question. How can we even think about foundations for experience if all our thinking takes place within the confines of experience? In Part 1 of this volume, an effort is made to address the question of foundations, explaining something of the philosophic work necessary to raise the question and presenting the principal thesis that thinking is founded in valuation, which first appears in imagination. Part 2 then develops a reconstructed conception of imagination.

Imagination is not the only dimension of thinking, nor is it the only one where valuation plays important roles. At the very least, interpretation, theorizing, and the pursuit of responsibility are dimensions of thinking, each with unique valuational components. This volume, therefore, introduces a larger study, a series entitled *Axiology of Thinking*, for which five major parts are projected. Part 1, "Foundations," and Part 2, "Imagination," make up *Reconstruction of Thinking*. Part 3, "Interpretation," Part 4, "Theory," and Part 5, "Responsibility," are yet to come. Chapter 1 of this book, however, discusses the contours of the entire project as presently envisioned.

It may be helpful to some readers to understand the relation of the present book to my earlier ones. *The Cosmology of Freedom* aimed to develop a naturalistic, participationist social theory on the basis of a conception of experience arising from process philosophy and pragmatism. In that book, however, the conception of experience was developed mainly by supplementing the categories used by Alfred North Whitehead, the genius of process philosophy, in areas he had left undeveloped, and by rejecting certain basic notions in process thought. *Creativity and God* was a direct discussion of certain elements of process philosophy that I believe should be rejected. The present book begins to supply a more thorough and fundamental theory of experience than that sketched in *The Cosmology of Freedom*. *Soldier, Sage, Saint* attempted to illustrate the thesis that the valuable aspects of human character are those achieved by instantiating ideals, not the aspects that develop naturally or by socialization. The present project seeks to lay the groundwork for arguing that case, not merely illustrating it, because the bearing ideals have on life is, in part, a function of valuation in thinking. *God the Creator* was a metaphysical essay whose theory of identity or determinateness argued that *to be* is to be a harmony; the thesis of the essay was that a harmony is contingent and therefore must be created if it is to be real. A more profound issue, and one that remains to be pressed, is understanding the normative character of harmony. Although Chapter 3 of *The Cosmology of Freedom* discussed the issue, the discussion there was limited by an inadequate theory of valuation in experience. This book begins to redress that lack.

It may seem that *Reconstruction of Thinking* is a systematic continuation of earlier work, but to me the discontinuities are more striking. I now realize that those earlier essays presuppose a more revolutionary stance toward modern philosophy than they explicitly took. Two factors blinded me to the pressing need for revolutionary reconstruction in philosophy. One was that I thought John Dewey had already carried it out in his *Reconstruction in Philosophy* and that I had digested it. True, Dewey did argue correctly for the intimate involvement of valuation in thinking of all kinds, and he did so on a naturalistic base similar to that constructed here. Dewey, however, did not carry out the reform of categories necessary for his proposed reconstruction. Left with their old categories, philosophers paid him lip service but unwittingly returned to business as usual. The second factor was that I half-believed that the construction of systematic categories is indeed a premodern philosophic enterprise and that Dewey's reconstruction was consistent in not reconstructing the systematic categories. Without admitting it explicitly, I then conceived my own systematic philosophy as a defense of a method out of time. Now I have come to see that the development of a systematic philosophy as a postmodern cultural artifact is just right. *Reconstruction of Thinking* is self-consciously historical in my attempt to position it in relation to the diverse modes of philosophy needed in the present. There is a deliberate rejection of the a-historicism of analytic and phenomenological philosophy, of cognitive science, and of the poststructuralism of Foucault and Derrida. To see the need for a revolution, however, and to set oneself to work, do not by themselves accomplish the task. I have no illusions (or at least not many) about the extent to which this book carries out the proclaimed sea change in which the old patterns become unfamiliar and things seem naturally to belong in new arrangements. Nevertheless, the concern for *foundations* is self-referential in this volume, as the first chapter amply illustrates.

ACKNOWLEDGMENTS

Many people have been important in the writing of this book. Five in particular have pushed me again and again to think more deeply and to dare a more radical vision: David Hall, Beth Neville, Jay Schulkin, Paul Weiss, and David Weissman; each employed a unique combination of personal example and browbeating to do the pushing. Marcia Aufhauser, Richard Bernstein and Carl Resek read the earliest draft; Paul Weiss, George Allan, Paul Kuntz, and Donald Sherburne read the latest draft; and Jay Schulkin read all the drafts. They effectively form the public within which the book was written. I have also benefited enormously from conversations with and criticisms from Thomas J. J. Altizer, Patricia Athay, Robert S. Brumbaugh, Antonio de Nicolas, Richard Gard, Christopher George, Patrick Heelan, Dick Howard, Don Ihde, Donald Kuspit, Peter Manchester, Marie-Suzanne Niedzielska, Sungbae Park, Andrew Reck, Charles Sherover, Michael Simon, John E. Smith, Judah Stampfer, William Sullivan, Alexander von Schönborn, George Wolf, and Kuang-ming Wu. Finally, I thank the State University of New York at Stony Brook for the sabbatical year during which most of the thinking for this project was done.

The publication of this book is due to the tenacity, encouragement, and particular helpfulness of William Eastman, director of the State University of New York Press, to whom I am especially grateful. Beth Neville designed the cover.

The book is dedicated with love and thanks to my father, Richard Perry Neville, whose unpublished book, "This Backward World," I have sought to comprehend in these pages.

Centerport, New York
February, 1981

RECONSTRUCTION OF THINKING

PART 1
FOUNDATIONS

1

Foundational Issues of Thinking

AN HISTORICAL CRISIS IN THINKING

The Renaissance Synthesis

Two ideals of thinking have dominated Western civilization since the classical period of Greece. The importance of discerning and classifying the *qualities* of things was demonstrated by the Milesian philosopher-scientists, by the sophists, and by Aristotle (384–322 B.C.E.). Aristotle's celebrated analysis of scientific knowledge distinguished four modes of analysis that might be sought in answer to the question, Why is a thing what it is?: What form is it? What is it made of? What is it for? What made it? This analysis is still attractive today, although it is rarely applied to objects of the physical sciences. Associated with Pythagoras (b.570 B.C.E.) and Plato (c.428–347 B.C.E.) is the other ideal, namely, that the most rational form of understanding is mathematical. If things can be *quantified,* the internal perspicacity of ratios and proportions in a mathematical articulation of things seems the ideal paradigm of rational understanding. With the integration of the quantitative thinking of mathematics and the qualitative thinking of observation and practice, the world could be grasped intelligently and viewed as being harmonious.[1]

The development of mathematical science during the European Renaissance seemed to be the first step toward integrating qualitative and quantitative thought. Beginning with physics, the integration has been applied to chemistry and is currently revolutionizing biology. Even the social sciences are struggling to give themselves a mathematical form through statistical studies.

In an important sense, however, the great stride taken in the Renaissance was a misstep, for the conception of mathematical science excluded rational thought about the values of things. Mathematical science knows things as facts and therefore thinks of the world as a totality of facts. The debate about the true nature of a *fact*, of course, began early and has not ceased today; but rational thinking according to the general ideal of mathematical science is other than rational valuation. Events of valuing may be treated as facts, and scientists may value their methods, visions, and discoveries. Valuing, however, is a different kind of thinking from rational knowing which accords with the ideal of mathematical science.

Mathematical science is definitely *not* the integrative ideal the Greeks had in mind. For them, thinking of all kinds involved appreciation, valuing, and being reasonable about both the intrinsic and the extrinsic worth of things. In general, the ancient Greek approach to experience—whether during the archaic, the classical, or the Hellenistic period—was thoroughly aesthetic. Aristotle, for instance, argued that no substance lacks a purpose or final cause; this gives each thing a value for the universe and often for human affairs. In knowing a substance, then, one could at least appreciate it. Plato, who spoke so eloquently for the higher rationality of number and proportion, called his highest category the form of the Good. He argued that the just purpose of knowing is not the contemplation of truths for their own sake but the guidance of social and personal life toward greater value. Neither Plato nor Aristotle would have recognized his ambitions in the work of Newton.

The dramatic shift during the Renaissance was not limited to the world of science. Around 1599, Shakespeare could represent the Aristotelian confidence that integrating values are intrinsic to nature apart from forcible ordering by human will.[2] Here is the Archbishop of Canterbury's advice to the king in *Henry V*, Act I, Scene ii:

> I this infer,
> That many things, having full reference
> To one consent, may work contrariously.
> As many arrows, loosed several ways,
> Come to one mark; as many ways meet in one town;
> As many fresh streams meet in one salt sea;
> As many lines close in the dial's centre;
> So may a thousand actions, once afoot,
> End in one purpose, and be all well borne
> Without defeat.

Shortly afterward, in 1601 or 1602, he could have Ulysses explain the weakness of the Greeks with the modern claim we associate with Hobbes, that things fly apart or debase themselves without the direct control of the leader. Consider *Troilus and Cressida*, Act I, Scene iii, where Ulysses concludes his jeremiad on lost leadership:

> Then everything includes itself in power,
> Power into will, will into appetite;
> And appetite, an universal wolf,
> So doubly seconded with will and power,
> Must make perforce an universal prey,
> And last eat up himself. Great Agamemnon,
> This chaos, when degree is suffocate,
> Follows the choking.

Failure of the Synthesis

The historical realities of interest here are less the accomplishment than the development of the ideal constructs of mathematical science. An ideal construct selects certain elements of its subject as being important and then articulates them as existing in some ideal relationship. Mathematical science is an ideal construct (or rather, a whole family of ideal constructs) of what cognitive experience *ought* to be. No scientist's actual cognitive experience has ever fully conformed to the ideal; nor has it even come close. The ideal has merely been a guide to the development and practice of science.

If an ideal construct is powerful within a culture, it serves to legitimate or de-legitimate various elements of actual experience. Mathematical science—a powerful, ideal construct indeed—has legitimated those elements of experience that lend themselves to scientific interpretation or that foster the development of science. Thus, within our experience we have come to view as real those things that might be knowable according to some conception of mathematical science, while prizing the approaches to knowing that lead to science.

The regulative force of the ideal construct of mathematical science has contributed largely to the impoverishment of the conception of knowledge in areas having to do with value, particularly political theory, ethics, and aesthetics. Generally speaking, in all areas, the approach to the values involved has become increasingly harder to classify as cognitive, because the ideal construct of mathematical science dictates another meaning for cognition.

In political theory, for instance, our situation is still dominated by realpolitik and by managerial "pragmatism," for which the search for political values is dismissed with the phrase "the end of ideology"; even the revolutionary humanism of the contemporary Frankfurt school calls political debate a process of "will formation," not one of cognitive discovery of the best policy.[3] In industrialized countries, ethics is regarded by most lay people, and by many philosophers as well, as noncognitive valuation.[4] Even aesthetics is often made a function of feeling *in contrast to* knowledge.[5] Of course, many factors besides the reign of mathematical science enter into this, including the development of national states and of liberal political ideology, the rise of the bourgeoisie, and the serendipitous making of scientific discoveries. These and other factors are needed to account for mathematical science's rise to dominance. Yet Ludwig Wittgenstein (1889–1951), the Viennese-British philosopher, summed up the attitude of many theorists of knowledge when he wrote:

> All propositions are of equal value. The sense of the world must lie outside the world. In the world everything is as it is and happens as it does happen. *In* it there is no value—and if there were it would be of no value. . . . Hence also there can be no ethical propositions. . . . It is clear that ethics cannot be expressed. . . . (Ethics and aesthetics are one.)[6]

However, mathematical science as a conception of thinking is *only* an ideal construct, an abstraction from life; it presents a truly absurd picture of experience if interpreted otherwise. The pragmatists Charles Peirce (1839–1914), William James (1842–1910), and John Dewey (1859–1952)—all scientists—showed that actual thinking experience is shot through with values and valuing.[7] Process philosophers, beginning with the revolutionary metaphysician of the twentieth-century Alfred North Whitehead (1861–1947), have provided comprehensive theoretical visions that reinforce this.[8] And the phenomenologists Edmund Husserl (1859–1938), Martin Heidegger (1889–1976), and Maurice Merleau-Ponty (1908–61) began the systematic description of the basic dimensions of experience that demonstrate qualities for the understanding of which mathematical science simply would be inappropriate.[9] In their common experience, people live within a world every bit as structured by the values of politics, morals, and aesthetics as the ancient Greeks averred, though perhaps with less coherence than in the Apollonian vision.

If, however, the picture provided by the ideal construct of mathematical science is indeed valid, as the whole picture rather than one idealized abstraction, then a higher-level theory must be provided and justified, one that shows the scientific ideal to be more appropriate than all others for interpreting the whole of experience. This has not yet been done in a way that does not beg the question of the legitimacy of the universal extension of the scientific construct.

A Reconstruction

The failure of the Renaissance synthesis to do justice to the still pervasive experiential sense of value and of valuation calls for a new start to be made. A comprehensive conception of thinking as basic as the Renaissance synthesis itself is needed, a conception that maintains the advantage of the Renaissance integration of qualitative and quantitative thinking while also including valuative thinking in the various modes exhibited by experience. The conception of thinking needs to be reconstructed at its foundations.

To say, though, that the conception of thinking "needs" to be reconstructed masks a serious problem. It assumes, without argument, that there *are* values amenable to cognitive grasp, that valuation is a legitimately cognitive part of thinking, that the scientific ideal has but partial applicability, and that its claim to set the standard for thinking is misplaced. None of these points has been proved. What if there is no valuational knowledge? What if moral values cannot be grounded? What if art is *mere* illusion? What if there is no unitary nature of human life, no transcendental principle of unitary consciousness, no ideal of spiritual perfection worth pursuing? The only genuine proof of these or other valuations would have to be a long-range construction of a new conception of the foundations of thinking, one that succeeds in legitimating the value aspects of prima facie experience where the ideal of mathematical science failed.

Should it be the case that the defense of values is misplaced and that mathematical science is the best and only defensible ideal construct for thinking, there is no need for reconstructing the conception of thinking. There is only the need for interpretation of the implications of the situation to which the scientific ideal has led. This is the line taken by the contemporary French "deconstructionist" philosophers Michel Foucault and Jacques Derrida.[10] They see the "destructuring" of the older conceptions of thinking as an unmasking of nostalgia for a lost dream of unified thinking. Yet their line of argument itself rests within the same dilemma of thinking as the project of reconstruction, namely, that the need for a defense of values presupposes an unjustified position transcending the ideal construct of mathematical science. The deconstructionists' version of the dilemma is that if values *are* defensible, then the conception of thinking, by means of which they interpret the present situation, is too narrow for that fact to be recognized. This, too, is an issue that cannot be decided in advance of an attempt to comprehensively reconstruct the conception of thinking.

There is an irony that lends this situation drama while, at the same time, providing the clue to reconstruction. The heady success of the Renaissance integration of qualitative and quantitative thinking fostered the easy assumption that *thinking is founded in reason*. Modern philosophy, from Thomas Hobbes (1588–1679) and René Descartes (1596–1650) through David Hume (1711–76) and the greatest of modern philosophers, Immanuel Kant (1724–1804), may be understood as exploring the foundation of thinking in reason, as well as reason's limits. Georg Hegel (1770–1831) made a magnificent case for reason, in its many forms, as both the foundation and the capstone of thought, culture, and cosmos. The grand Hegelian synthesis could not be sustained, however. Søren Kierkegaard (1813–55) showed that if reason is thinking's foundation, then in certain crucial ways reason alienates thinking from life. Karl Marx (1818–83) argued that thinking is founded not in reason but in material conditions of existence about which those who believe in the ultimacy of reason must do so in bad faith. Sigmund Freud (1856–1939) reinforced Marx's attack on the integrity of rational consciousness by showing that there is a darker "reason" in the unconscious which, when detected, gives the lie to rational pretensions. Friedrich Nietzsche (1844–1900) summed all this up by declaring the bankruptcy of Western rational culture, declaring it to be weak, self-alienating, and fraudulent. His proclamation of the death of God was a dismissal of reason as the foundation of thinking and culture.

The irony of the critique of reason doubles back on mathematics itself. One of the great advantages of the quantification of quality in the Renaissance synthesis was supposed to be the pure foundational certainty of mathematics. The American mathematician Morris Kline, however, recounts the following:

> Creations of the early 19th century, strange geometries and strange algebras, forced mathematicians, reluctantly and grudgingly, to realize that mathematics proper and the mathematical laws of science were not truths. They found, for example, that several differing geometries fit spatial experience equally well. All could not be truths. Apparently mathematical design was not inherent in nature, or if it was, man's mathematics was not necessarily the account of that design. . . . It is now apparent that the concept of a universally accepted, infallible body of reasoning—the majestic mathematics of 1800 and the pride of man—is a grand illusion.[11]

If even mathematics suffers a fate similar to that of the Hegelian synthesis, how can reason be the foundation of thinking?

Yet if reason is not the foundation, where does this leave the ideal construct of mathematical science? If cognition is supposed to be only science, and science is ungrounded reason, is our experience at best only the will to power, arbitrary and thoughtless? Existentialists and romantic critics, with considerable warrant, read the twentieth century as fulfilling Nietzsche's prophecy. The noble ideals of science too often do seem groundless, and the true reality of science may be its manifestation in ugly and arbitrary technology: gas chambers, nuclear bombs, environmental rape, economic exploitation. The self-referential difficulty with this interpretation, however, is that it is too rational for its own case. Its argument presupposes the tight logic of historicist prophecy: for the prophetic mind, history has a thread of internal necessity and the unity of a dramatic story. If, however, rationality is indeed undermined, then so is the drama of history. If, on the other hand, there is a hidden reason replete with norms, according to which historicist prophetic criticism can be made, then the fall of contemporary life into arbitrary, mindless savagery is not the whole, even of its own story.

An alternate interpretation of the contemporary situation will not come from another look at history alone. Rather, it requires a new look at thinking itself. One may read the works of such deconstructionists as Foucault and Derrida as a new examination of thinking, with a new interpretation of the significance of twentieth-century culture. For the most part, though, their examination of thinking merely shows the results of the mathematical scientific ideal to be what they are. Instead of the usual nostalgic longing for modes of thinking that predate the collapse of consciousness-centered rationality, they call for an acknowledgment of thinking's destructured form and a celebration of this form.[12] This is merely to accept the implications of science for thinking, not to rethink thinking at its foundations. They turn Nietzsche's negative critique into positive assertion and ask that we be happy about it.

In summary, two major components form the historical crisis of thinking. One component is that the forms of thinking legitimated by the influence of the mathematical paradigm of science tend to exclude a critical acknowledgment of the cognitive dimensions of valuation and the normative nature of values themselves. This constitutes an absurd dissonance between our experience of thinking and the experience of life. It is the "problem of value." The second and more critical component is that the very rationality of the grand conception of reason in mathematical science has been undermined by various critiques of consciousness. To separate legitimate reason from justified valuing leaves reason's technological powers afloat on the capricious sea of arbitrary will. Purely technological reason is hardly reason. This second component of the crisis forces the issue of value, not in a theoretical but in a practical way. The crisis in thinking is a profound turning point for our culture.

The dramatic, apocalyptic response of prophesying the collapse of culture and the deconstructionist response of acquiescing in the belief that fragmented factual thinking is thinking's true nature—both are shallow. Neither examines the foundations of thinking itself. The question is, Can a profound response be made? Can thinking be examined at its foundations? Or is thinking, in fact, as shallow, as "factual," as has been urged? The answer cannot be determined in advance of the attempt to make a profound response. If the following chapters are successful, the answer is yes: *esse* proves *posse*.

VALUATION

An Axiological Hypothesis

The clue to reconstructing the conception of thinking is that one need not assume that thinking is founded in reason or that, if reason's foundation is faulty, there is no foundation. A contrary hypothesis is that thinking is founded in valuation. Valuation, in several related senses, underlies both qualitative and quantitative thinking and their integration. Valuation supplies and justifies the norms that guide thinking to be rational when it is; therefore, valuation, in several senses, is the foundation of reason. Whenever reason is a function of false consciousness, it is founded on a deeper valuation, as when the psychological meaning of consciousness is determined by a primary libidinal process or when ideologies about social order mainly express hidden interests in maintaining or overthrowing economic controls. A proper understanding of the role of valuation, made possible by a reconstruction of the basic conception of thinking, would effect an integration of valuative with qualitative and quantitative thinking. It would also explain why the attempt to ground thinking in reason has failed, interpreting that failure not as a dramatic death of God and decline of the West, but as a mistake. Finally, it would provide guidance for addressing, thoughtfully and intelligently, the practical *problem of value*.

The hypothesis that thinking is founded in valuation requires for its development what philosophers call "axiology," the philosophic study of values. Of course, values are not phenomena that float into view, stimulating a "philosophy of values" to study them. Rather, it will be argued that values should be conceived of as the universal character of everything. Axiology, therefore, is the study of things with regard to their value dimension. An axiology of thinking is a study of the various roles of value in thinking.

A study of thinking is itself an exercise in thinking; a study that questions the foundations of thinking has undermined the solidity of its own starting point. Thus, in a sense, every comment about thinking—every analysis, every thesis—is issued with a promissory note that its own viewpoint will, in the end, be justified. And, of course, it never is, for the end of thinking never comes. The most that can be hoped for is that the plausibility of the general vision of thinking in the axiological expression will grow with the successive accumulation of detail. In this kind of axiological study of thinking, the strategy is quite the opposite of that which tries to conform the argument to the accepted canons of thinking within the mathematical ideal construct of science. In his recent book, *Reason and Morality*, Alan Gewirth, a philosopher at the University of Chicago, attempts to deal with the problem of value by employing dialectical arguments that adhere to the norms of deductive and inductive logic.[13] The security and sense of steady progress in such approaches as Gewirth's, however, are undermined whenever basic questions are asked.

The general axiological hypothesis that thinking is founded in valuation is novel in some senses and a continuation of old programs in others. It is novel in focusing attention on the role of value in the most foundational issues. This contrasts, for instance, with phenomenology's positivistic claim that the foundational issues are best understood by getting down to what simply "appears." It contrasts also with the hypothesis that foundations are reached through the investigation of language. The axiological hypothesis is novel, too, in its selection of foundational issues, as well as its particular theses about them. The hypothesis is a vision of its own, responsive to a set of problems interpreted in ways peculiar to itself.

In several senses, however, the axiological hypothesis is not new, and its antecedents lend it momentum. Even in the "modern" period, many philosophers have been uncomfortable with the separation of valuation from legitimated thinking and with the view that thinking is based exclusively on reason. Hume, for example, may be read as attempting to develop a theory of thinking as perception that integrates the sense of understanding he thought reflects science with the valuation involved in passion and morality. His difficulty was that his theory of perception was too simplistic to articulate the integration of the valuations with the thinking actually found in experience. Kant, too, with his conceptions of practical reason and judgment, attempted to save valuational thinking from being reduced to a scientific knowledge of mere fact, as would be the case if thinking were based exclusively on scientific reason and its transcendental superstructure. Like Hume, however, Kant lacked a cosmology of thinking that would have allowed him to appreciate the continuity of valuation with scientific reasoning. He ended by specifying separate senses of thinking for practical reason and for judgment that were vulnerable to being "de-legitimated" by the dominance of the scientific ideal construct. The axiological hypothesis presents a cosmology of thinking that achieves Hume's and Kant's goals without separating valuative from cognitional thinking.

Even in presenting an integrative cosmology of thinking, the axiolog-

ical hypothesis is not new. It arises from certain clues laid out by Charles
Peirce and followed by James, Dewey, and Whitehead. Our contemporaries
Paul Weiss, Charles Hartshorne, and Justus Buchler mine the same field
today.[14] The naturalistic orientation involved in an interest in a cosmology
of thinking is shared by such heirs of the linguistic tradition in philosophy as
Hilary Putnam, Saul Kripke, and, most especially, Stephen Toulmin. The
naturalistic bent of this speculation is reinforced by experimental psychologists, for example, Paul Rozin.[15] The great phenomenologist Max Scheler
(1874–1928) developed the conception of value as fundamental to all thinking; such contemporary phenomenologists as Don Ihde provide descriptions
of experience so continuous with the studies of William James as to lend
verification to the naturalistic theories of the pragmatic-process tradition.[16]
The writings of David L. Hall, in the philosophy of culture, show how
issues as broad as "the problem of value" hang on fundamental conceptual
structures of the kind that are at stake in the axiology of thinking.[17] Viewed
correctly, the enterprise of the axiology of thinking resonates with a great
many other programs in philosophy, science, and culture, while at the same
time putting them in a new and unusual light.

A Problem of Foundations

The most problematic element at the beginning of the axiological
hypothesis that thinking is founded on valuation is the very concept of
"foundations." Like the terms "reason" and "valuation," "foundation" and
its cognates have been used historically in several senses, and perhaps none
is satisfactory.

The Cartesian tradition down through Husserl, for instance, sought
foundations for thinking in the sense of a sure, certain starting point on
which the edifice of thought could be built. This "quest for certainty,"
however, was adequately criticized by John Dewey in his book of that
name, and it is not the sense of foundations intended here.[18] The axiological
hypothesis is precisely that— an *hypothesis* about the foundational elements
of thinking. It is subject to modification by considerations appropriate to
that level of hypothesis.

Various moralists have used the notion of foundations in the sense of
justification. A moral judgment, an argument or a paradigm of reasoning, is
founded on whatever justifies it. In an extraordinarily subtle way that interprets justification as dialectically advancing on internal contradictions,
Hegel developed the master conception of "reason" or "spirit" as the foundation of life and culture, as well as of thinking. Foundation, in this sense,
depends on what it founds rather than supports it, as in the case of

certainty.[19] The very meaning of justification, however, presupposes a family of concepts that relate justifying norms to their objects. In Hegel, for instance, this had to do with the achievement of coherence that (re)establishes the unity of consciousness in the context of a negative dialectic. Since the axiological hypothesis questions the very bearing of value on things, "justification" is not basic enough.

For the axiology of thinking, the foundations are the most general structures of experience, those that are illustrated in all experiential activities. Foundational issues are those that question those basic structures. Discussions of thinking fail to be foundational when they do not reflect a calling into question of these basic structures. In particular, the axiological hypothesis proposes that the basic structures of experience involve valuing in various ways. The foundational issues are those having to do with the adjudication of this hypothesis over against alternatives that restrict valuing to a special kind of thinking or that reduce valuation to a nonnormative activity.

This conception of "foundations" is closely tied to the conception of the importance of philosophical cosmology, for it is cosmology that makes it possible to articulate the level of generality regarding the conceptions of thinking that can be called foundational.[20] In certain respects, the cosmology of thinking can be likened to what Kant called "transcendental" or "critical" philosophy; it is a view of things which shows how thinking is possible. However, unlike a transcendental theory—which begins with the assumption that certain kinds of thinking are normative, and goes on to argue that the higher-level theory which shows why these kinds of thinking are normative is itself a necessary condition—a cosmology presents itself only as an hypothesis. Its plausibility is measured by a host of subtle logical, empirical, historical, and dialectical considerations by which any hypothesis stands judged—scaled to the breadth of appropriate generality. In certain other respects, this conception of foundations is similar to the attempt to understand such "basic" features of thinking as taste and motivation through laboratory studies of animals and human beings. Unlike experimental psychology, however, which frames its hypotheses in accord with what can next be investigated most fruitfully, philosophical cosmology must relate the hypothesized foundational structures of thinking to the main categories of the most sophisticated, subtle, and highly developed thinking. The plausibility of the axiological approach to foundational issues comes from the capacity of the approach to make possible an envisionment of the full contours of experience through its hypothesis, rather than through experimental confirmation of a primitive aspect of thinking that may mislead understanding of the achievements of culture. Ideally, experimentally manageable hypotheses become congruent with philosophically rich ones.

Some thinkers have attacked the idea of seeking the foundations of thinking. Usually, the object of their attack is the quest for certainty or the quest for ultimate justification, neither of which is the sense of foundational issues of concern here. Other thinkers follow the lead of Nietzsche in claiming that thinking has no foundations in the sense of basic structures illustrated in all thinking activity. The force of this claim comes partly from the historicist supposition that the foundations of thinking are those elements which are actually operative, consciously or not, in forming the thinking of a certain period. Throughout the modern period, for instance, thinking was informed by certain structures of rationality as its basic structures, and these were insufficient for the task. Therefore, thinking *no longer* has a foundation, according to that view. In answer to this, it may be pointed out that, if thinking is thoroughly valuational, and if the values of reason in any form (mathematical, dialectical, analytical, or whatever) are only a subset of the larger class of values normative for thinking, then the other values may have informed thinking as norms all along, although they are unacknowledged because mathematical science has provided the chief ideal construct. Further, the valuational foundations of thinking are not merely the actual pursuits, conscious or unconscious, of the various norms of thinking; rather, they are the relationships between the norms and the activity called thinking precisely because it is measured by those norms. In other words, the foundations of thinking are the general structures of experience, not the historical experience itself. Particular historical thinking can be discerned only with a cosmology of thinking in hand, whether it is acknowledged or hidden.

The attack on foundational thinking can be renewed at a different level. To speak of general structures of experience that can be put together in a coherent hypothesis may suppose a unity to thinking that it simply does not have. The art and culture of our age reveal a pervasive fragmentation. The various sciences reveal the regularities and knowable features of experience to be discrete, relative to special, separated methods and instruments of research, and not to have the forms that lend themselves to comprehension as part of either unified experience or the "human drama." Even the discipline of history finds its appropriate expression to be descriptions of systems, arrays of data, and reflections on instruments of research—not the form of story in which personal life has meaning and unity. Therefore, to seek a foundational hypothesis about thinking is to search nostalgically for a unifying myth when the reality is that things are simply fragmented, destructured.[21]

The attack on foundational thinking assumes that philosophy is not logical work in its own right. On the contrary, cosmology is an example of positive philosophic work. A foundational hypothesis, of course, should be genuinely coherent and consistent, applicable to appropriate areas of experience and adequate to the elements of experience in which it is supposed to be illustrated. Any genuine objection to a cosmological hypothesis about the foundations of thinking can be registered in objection to its coherence, consistency, applicability, or adequacy. That is the way to object to any empirical hypothesis. One cannot object to the process of bringing unity to the conception of subject matter by constructing hypotheses without rejecting the notion of hypothesis in all its uses. It is precisely because of the strength of certain scientific hypotheses that one might have confidence in "knowledge here" fragmentally disjoined from "knowledge there." If a comprehensive, unifying hypothesis about the foundations of thinking is illegitimate, then, in fact, it cannot be constructed; any attempt to construct it would have to sin egregiously against consistency, coherence, applicability, or adequacy. On the other hand, if such an hypothesis can be constructed, the argument that it is impossible is foolish. Again, *esse* proves *posse*.

The hope that one can determine in advance whether a basic philosophical enterprise is possible is sheer vanity. What can be determined, and what is shown here as determinable, is that it is possible, and legitimate, to make the attempt. The only objection that can be made to making the attempt must be registered as a specific objection to a claim made in the attempt itself. The serious question of the possibility of examining the foundations of thinking must be postponed until the examination itself is presented.

A FOUNDATIONAL HYPOTHESIS

The general claim of the axiological hypothesis is that thinking is founded in valuation. The content of the hypothesis is not specified in that claim, however. What are the foundational structures of thinking, and how are they valuational? The following is a provisional sketch of the axiological hypothesis. It suggests that the basic structures of thinking appear in four dimensions: imagination, interpretation, theory, and responsibility.

Imagination

Of the various natural processes of human life, experience is distinguished by virtue of involving a synthesis of otherwise merely causal components into a unity whose parts potentially have a meaningful relationship to each other. The most elementary form of this is synthesis of the components into a field that serves as a background for focused attention. As Kant showed in the *Critique of Pure Reason*, this elementary synthesis can be analyzed in three ways: as grasping a manifold into unity, as reproducing steps for moving from one component in the field to others, and as unifying the potential movement with form. Following Kant, this synthetic activity is called imagination, and the dimensions of experience having to do with elementary synthesis may all be labeled imagination. This use of the word *imagination* faithfully reflects a dominant strain in philosophic tradition, although such use is considerably broader than the common use of the word to mean "fictional fantasies" or "inventive thoughts that do not represent reality." In the philosophical use of the word, all thinking—including assertions about reality, theories, and the reflective taking of responsibility—presupposes imaginative synthesis as its experiential context.

One way of answering the question why imagination or experiential synthesis occurs is to point out that when it does occur, *experience can express the value of beauty*. The contrast between background field and foreground focus of attention is the elementary form of beauty. The gathering of otherwise merely causal components of human processes into imaginative experiential synthesis is thus a primary form of valuation. In fact, it employs valuation in a primary sense to constitute the field of experience. Chapter 5 explores this in detail.

The reference to beauty remarks on the contrast between the background field of experience and the focal points of attention. To constitute experience as having focal points is to give experience the form of perception. Perception does not necessarily mean "true" perception, although the Western philosophic tradition has sometimes used the word that way. At the level of imagination, the question of the truth or falsity of experiential elements does not arise. Rather, *perception*, as it is used here, means the organization of experience so that objects or events stand out as identifiable against a background of experiential elements. This is to constitute experience in such a way that, at least at a minimal level, it is beautiful in the sense of containing a harmony contrasting focal objects against a field. The form of this contrasting harmony can be analyzed (following Whitehead) in terms of the depth of experience produced by synthesizing the background with vagueness and triviality and by synthesizing the focal points with narrowness and width. Indeed, this analysis is a formal analysis of beauty in a highly general sense. Perception at the imaginative level, then, involves the valuative synthesis of experiential components so as to produce a formal harmony of objects against background, exhibiting some degree, however minimal, of experiential depth, of beauty. This is discussed in Chapter 6.

To experience objects in a field is to have experience in the form of a rudimentary world. In fact, part of the elementary meaning of experience, it will be argued, involves transforming otherwise merely causal components of process into elements felt as being in and constituting a world. As it is with perception, the question here is not whether the world of experience is the "true" world; the question of truth does not have to arise in the mere having of experience in the form of a world. Within the dimension of imagination, the question concerns the form of the world as such.

The nature of form itself is the central issue concerning the constitution of experience as appearance in the world. To be sure, the notion of form is employed to make sense of synthesis, since the field must have a synthetic form. It is employed to make sense of perception as a formed focus against a background. Form itself can be analyzed as a mediating factor between sheer multiplicity, from which imaginative synthesis arises, and sheer beauty as the value of synthesis. Neither sheer multiplicity nor sheer beauty alone can be experienced nor even made intelligible; but this only proves, among other things, that the elementary form of experience is indeed a structured harmony that combines both. Prior to a *formal* axiology articulating a theory of value (which is provided in part in Chapter 3), little can be said that is persuasive about the normative status of value in form. It is apparent from what has been said, however, that because imagination gives form to experience, structures are described using such value words as *harmony*.

The discussion of form in Chapter 7 deals centrally with the connection between the concrete particularity of "an experience" and the universality of the form that structures the experience but which also could structure other experiences. The mediating element that is both particular and universal is the element in experience that can be called an image. An image is the form by which imagination synthesizes its components into experience. It is that selection of components whose integrated presence allows the other components to be present in the synthesis, either as background or as focal elements. An image is thus normative for a particular synthesis. Another manifold could be integrated if it had similar elements whose presence together would enable the rest of the components to cohere. The universality of an image lies in the importance of its form in integrating a manifold, even though the material in which the image is wrought differs from one manifold to another. Imagery, therefore, involves universality and "importance." If an experience has form, as it must, then it has an image, which, if an ingredient in other experiences, can be called by the generic word *imagery*.

The analysis of imagination as the elementary dimension of thinking thus involves the development of a theory of form. The theory presents form as the expression of beauty in a determinate manifold. At this point, the claim to making a *foundational* analysis of thinking can be appreciated, since it is indeed difficult to get behind the concept of form itself. Furthermore, the "fact-value dichotomy" is undermined, because even the "form of facts" is shown to express value.

The references above to the natural processes of human life from which experience arises reflect the concept that the axiological hypothesis is embedded in a naturalistic cosmology. Its cosmology of thinking is but a subset, or specialization, of a larger cosmology of nature. Imaginative intentionality, interpretive reference, theoretic vision, and the reflective pursuit of responsible life are all built upon natural causal elements which, at levels below that of the complexity of experience, are merely causal. At the experiential level, they are specialized forms of causality. The terror of existence rests upon the vague apprehension—brought to consciousness by death and suffering—of nature's blind forces only barely humanized by fragile forms of experiential causality. Religious imagery addresses this terror.

Before the question of the truth of experiential claims can be raised, it is necessary to ask about the relation of the imaginatively constructed experience of the world, subjectively considered, to the elements in the causal process that the experience might be "about." The question is, how does experience in the form of world *engage* the world? Engagement is founded precisely on imagery, since it is the imagery which experience employs that determines which causal elements can be sustained as components within the world of experience and which must be excluded simply because they do not fit the imaginative synthesis.

With the discussion of imagery, the implicit distinction between the subjectively considered world of imaginative construction and the objective world of elements collected into experience may be abandoned. The practical experiential question is whether one's imagery allows something to be experienced, and if so, how. With the question of imagery, the whole of experience, no matter how sophisticated, complex, or subtle, may be brought to philosophical attention insofar as it is a matter of formed imagination.

Here, the issue of responsibility is raised for the first time. Can one be responsible for one's imagery, in order better to engage the world? This is a difficult question to answer. At one extreme, it is clear that one's imagery is the precondition for any reflective thought that might be responsible. At the opposite extreme, it is clear that artists and other "heroes of the imagination" do indeed create new images that allow the world to be experienced differently, perhaps better. Experiential techniques of psychology and religion, particularly the latter, enable people to increasingly take control of their world-forming imagery. To some extent, then, experiencing the world with imagery is a kind of valuation, a choice of beautiful form over which one has control and for which one takes responsibility. The control of imagery, however, is more basic than intellectual or moral control; rather, it has to do with primitive engagement with life, with taking responsibility for the form of the world, not for forming things within the world. Insofar as it is culturally institutionalized, this sense of responsibility is religious.

Interpretation

Beauty is the dominant norm for the valuations involved in imagination, and truth is the analogous norm for interpretation. Interpretation is a triadic synthesis that takes the form of judgment. It involves reference to an object and the assertion of the meaning of the object. Charles Peirce's theory of signs was the landmark investigation of interpretation. Truth is the norm for interpreting well.

The first element of interpretation is meaning, hermeneutics. One may ask whether this or that is the true meaning of an intention. The question is independent of whether the original intention is true or false in reference to its object. Hermeneutical theory has a complex, involved history in European thought. One result is that the hermeneutics of meaning is not merely subjective introspection but an objective, potentially public discipline. The hermeneutical theory of the "truth of meaning" gives currency to the ancient idea that concepts, and not merely assertions, have validity. Some meanings are good, and others are not, because good meanings are true of real intentions. The issue to be addressed here is now natural things can have intentional structures.

The question of meaning is related to the second element of interpretation, reference. Interpretations assert meanings as referring to objects. Judgments are true or false in the sense that, in some way, they correspond to the world. Yet the correspondence cannot be construed as a simple mirroring of the world, Rather, it must be construed as a real or a potential outcome of a *critical* process. The very meaning of the correspondence involved in assertive interpretations includes reference to the process of criticizing the interpretation, as well as to the object of the interpretation. Again, Charles Peirce originated this line of thought with his theory of the infinite community of mutually correcting investigators. The difference between a naive imaginative view of the world as "this way," and the interpretive assertion that the world "really is this way," is the underlying supposition of the possibility of asking, "Is it really this way, or is it perhaps some other way?" This, in turn, presupposes a community of interpreters, for the relation between the potential questions and the answers is public.[22] One can, of course, conduct a dialogue with oneself, but that is a special instance of general dialogue. Interpretation is meaningful only as a form of dialogue.

The interpretive assertion of a fact includes the claim that, in a certain context, the totality of experience is best, or with justifiable worth, grasped using this factual form. That is, the interpretation involves asserting that the meaning of experience fulfills the value of "truth" for experience in a particular context. This means that the world, as referred to in the interpretation, is best, or justifiably, experienced with the interpretation's meaning.

One of the most important kinds of interpretation is the assertion of what is a right and what is a wrong action. In the case of morality, interpretation is assertion about the best way to "experience" the world, as referred to where the meaning is not a contemplative one but a practical activity. Logic's duality of true or false is a species of the same normative applicability of truth as morality's right or wrong. Valuational reference in morality can be seen as inseparable in kind from valuational reference in "mere cognitive assertions."

Interpretation involves not merely true or false assertions in the context of presupposed community criticism, but, as its third element, knowledge of the truth as well. Knowledge is an interpretation asserted of the world with good warrant. Although one's interpretive knowledge inevitably is freighted with theoretical elements, knowledge is not limited to asserting the truth of theories. A person can know that he or she feels pain, that it is or is not raining, that wanton killing is wrong, without asserting that a particular theory is true. Valid warrants for knowing differ enormously in kind and degree of plausibility. Making a claim to knowledge, however—even knowledge of a value-neutral fact, if there is such a thing—*includes reference to evaluations of the warrant with which the interpretation is made.*

As is remarked above, the very possibility of raising the question of the truth of assertions presumes that interpretation presupposes the public form of dialogue. It is difficult to say whether the normative features of the community come before the normative features of interpretation, or vice versa. What is clear is that they go together, and the axiology of thinking is perforce a social theory. Individuals are social animals insofar as they engage in self-criticism or reality-testing. Whereas at the end of the discussion of imagination, responsibility means taking control of one's imagery, making engagement with the world as "beautiful" as possible, the discussion of interpretation leads to a normative theory of society for allowing life to be as "true" as possible.

Although the norm of truth applies to thinking (and its problematic is to be approached through the professional philosophers' concerns with meaning, reference, verification and so forth), it is apparent from the above that there is a metaphysical theme to the discussion. In contrast to beauty, which is embodied in degrees approaching disorder at the minimal end, truth is a dyadic value, expressed in such oppositions as true or false and right or wrong. Where we speak of partial truths, it is in the sense of "true in these respects but false in those." As philosophers from Plotinus (205–270 C.E.) to Peirce have pointed out, the dyad is the mark of existence: opposition, separation, over-againstness. This has to do with the existential requirement broadly interpreted, that a thing have a definite identity, that it be itself and not some other thing. There are many meanings of "existence," but they all involve assertion of at least partial definiteness. Things can be called "true" when they have their own definite nature in contrast to being something else. Thinking can be called true when it interprets the truth of things, including people and their thinking. Whereas truth reflects a dyadic situation, however, interpretation requires a triadic one, namely, that of interpretive dialogue. This suggests that the peculiar "existence" of thinkers as interpreters involves the dyadic element of cleaving to the norm of truth in the context of dialogue. People cannot exist as interpreters without triadic discourse; this is the determinate nature of interpretive thinking and the condition for making claims to truth. It is yet one more affirmation of the intrinsically social nature of human life. On the other side, interpretation becomes fakery when the process of discoursing and sharing meaning loses sight of the brute dyadic character of the norm of truth. Like Hegel's "spirit" and perhaps even Peirce's infinite community, the conception of interpretation as dialogue is subject to the temptation to be satisfied with pallid communication. Interpretive dialogue is a precondition of the possibility of assertion, even for the possibility of raising the question of the difference between subjective experience and the real world. It cannot, however, be authentic interpretation without being true.

Theory

A central contention of the axiology of thinking is that theory is an essentially different dimension of thinking from interpretation. The Greek root of the word refers to "seeing," to "envisioning." The elementary function of theory can be understood as envisionment, as grasping the subject, the world, or experience within one view. As envisioned, the various components of the subject about which theorizing takes place are brought into unity. Their characteristics are understood in reference to each other, the relations between them are manifested, and the theoretical grasp of them constitutes some kind of coherence in the mind of the theorizer.

Unity in vision cannot be understood merely as a coordination of parts. Rather, it consists of ordering parts so that what is important stands out, to the comparative neglect of what is trivial. Formal structures present the "important" as focal. Unity is intrinsically valuational in employing discriminations of the important from the trivial, which abstract out formal structures. In contrast to coordination, unity has to do with ordering vision in terms of the relative importance of things. By highlighting and ordering experience with important elements, the trivial elements can be included within the vision as present but trivial.

This is not to say that a theory presents a mystical vision of all things blended into one. Rather, a theory has certain elementary principles that may be understood either individually or together, in abstraction from the materials they unify. Theorizing may involve appreciating some of the subject matter in light of theoretical principles. It may involve elaborating theoretical inferences. In all respects, however, theorizing has to do with grasping, appreciating, coming to terms with a multiplicity by virtue of theoretical form. The means for the envisionment of a field is abstract form, theoretical structure.

It is only within the dimension of theory that formal logic becomes an interesting topic. Formal logic supposes an arena of discourse within which one may speak in "well-formed formulas." The distinction between a well-formed statement and an ill-formed one is that the former has a theoretical form, but the latter does not. Formal inferences can be made only within the structure of a theory defining well-informed formulas.

Neglect of this point has worked unbelievable mischief in twentieth-century philosophy, which has generally been enthusiastic about formal logic. In fact, most philosophic disputes are not about logical implications within a theory but rather about the validity of theoretical presuppositions themselves. To insist, as has often happened, that the disputation take place within a language of formal logic is covertly to smuggle in theoretical commitments which themselves are the implicit subject of the disputation. When objection is made to this procedure, the response frequently is that the discussion must be "clear," that only adherence to logical form can bring clarity. This, however, merely reinforces the point that logical form takes place *within* theoretical commitments, for the clarity required is the clarity of logical form, of what Descartes called "simple essences." Of course, this begs some of the most important questions twentieth-century philosophers have disputed. Most such questions require great care in juggling formal theories so as not to prejudice the case. They must be approached by comparing theories with each other and with areas of evidence, with critical experimentation. Most actual philosophical discussion is dialectical in the sense Aristotle condemned, namely, as discussion to arrive at the truth that does not follow logical deductive or inductive principles. The "truth" arrived at in philosophical discussion is not the validity of inference, since that validity can be true only on the hypothesis of the formal theory providing the inferential rules and "formation." And it is *that* theory which is so often at issue. Stephen Toulmin has done a great service in calling attention to the wide variety of essentially historical, rather than logical, considerations that go into justifying why the critical community gives up one theoretical view for another.[23] Formal logic is philosophically important only within the narrow range of drawing out the structure and implications of theoretical premises and indicating what they mean for envisioning phenomena.

This is not to say that logic is unimportant, however; logic does indeed allow for envisionment, for the unity of experience in terms of the important. Unity is the transcendental value for theorizing. It is not the same value as truth, for it is possible that a theory provide a unified vision of its subject matter and that vision still be false. In fact, many philosophers would say that, strictly speaking, all our theories are false, although some are less so than others. In light of this common recognition of the falsity of theories, the difference between unity of thinking and truth should be appreciated.

Within the public dialogue of interpretation, theories themselves are often treated as assertions about whose truth or falsity inquiry · is made. Physicists have been interested not only in whether it is true that the light reflected from Mercury when it passes behind the sun can be seen "before" it should be seen, given the sizes and speeds of the bodies, but whether Einstein's theory predicting the perihelion of Mercury is true. Philosophers are interested not only in approaching the theoretical visions of the speculative theorists but also in ascertaining which of them better interpret the world. Theories can always be interpreted as meanings which, when asserted, refer to their subject matter. This, however, is the use of theory for purposes defined by the value of truth; it is not the appreciation of theory for the value of the unity of envisionment. Whitehead commented that it is more important for theories to be interesting than it is for them to be true.

It is impossible to separate theories from interpretations. Not only are we interested in which theories are true interpretations (or not false), but nearly all of our interpretive assertions—all the discourse of the community, assertive or not—involve terms structured in theoretical form. To explicate the meanings of many terms, it is necessary to parse their formal connections within theories. Much of the disputation involved in dialogue has to do with uncovering the uses of terms that reflect hidden theoretical commitments. This all derives from the historical consideration that language has long been affected by vast networks of theories. Again, however, this is not to reduce theories to the concerns of truth. Although one might need to explicate a political theory in order to determine whether the policies of one nation are inimical to the welfare of another, and although knowing whether the theory is true might help determine the policy, debate about the truth of the *interpretation* of the policy is not the same as concern for the *truth* of the theory. Also, whether a theory is true is not the same as whether a theory is, in fact, an interesting, unified vision of its subject matter.

It is remarked above that a theory might provide a unified vision and still not be true. In this light, Ptolemaic astronomy was just as much a theory as was Copernican. According to formal criteria, however, some visions are more unified than others. The Copernican theory is more elegant, more "theoretical," than the Ptolemaic. This reveals, as Platonists have long pointed out, that certain norms of formal unity are implicitly appealed to if we express preference for one theory over another when both norms are adequate to account for the known phenomena and when they are equally applicable to experience. To understand theorizing, then, it is necessary to look beyond the express content of theories to the norms presupposed in their construction and appealed to in their evaluation. This is what Plato meant, in part, by "dialectic."

Once the question of truth is raised, envisionment of a subject matter is intended to be something more than merely private experience. To envision something is to grasp the *real* objects of vision and integrate them in a unified experience of what is important. Envisionment, therefore, requires real engagement with the world, not disengaged fantasy. Theorizing takes its rise from imagination. A theory begins as an "image" of its subject matter. The image is formally transformed into well-formed theoretical structures embodying the norms of formal unity. The image is also "criticized" by interpretive processes that assess its truth. For a theory to be a successful envisionment, it needs some warrant that it truly engages its subject matter. Such a warrant makes an appeal to experience, if not to critical experiment, intrinsic to theorizing.

From the critical standpoint of the community of investigators, however, all theories are false, or at least partial. Is there then no successful envisionment? In a sense, no, and in a sense, yes. Any theoretical vision is, at best, an hypothesis subject to being improved on if it is not clearly superseded; in this sense, any theory is unsuccessful as envisionment. In another sense, though, a theory can be considered with respect to its existential role for the thinker or for the community of thinkers. In that case, its role is to constitute thinking experience as formally unified and important, provisional and shifting but formally unified. In this formal unity, the value is not merely for making true assertions. In fact, the concern for unity may get in the way of ascertaining truths that cannot be integrated with any theory at hand. Rather, the value in formal unity is an existential one of constituting the thinker as a presence in the world. Put another way, it constitutes experience as a world for thinking. Just as imagination constitutes experience in and of a world, theorizing constitutes this experience, with the added dimension that the thinker takes responsibility for the unity of the world. A world cannot be experienced except as a partially ordered unity. Only by virtue of a theory can a thinker take responsibility for that unified experience, particularly for the truth of the unity. A theory is essentially an image of what is important in its subject matter, indeed, for the world as generalized, for which cognitive responsibility can be taken because of the formal structures that can be analyzed, tested, and grasped clearly. As Socrates demonstrated to Thrasymachus in Plato's *Republic*, one cannot take responsibility for the interpretations of political life—that justice is the interest of the stronger and that injustice pays better than justice—without a formal theory. Lacking a theory, Thrasymachus fell prey (wolf that he was) to silly logical contradictions.

The role of theory in responsibility calls attention to responsibility itself, which is the fourth dimension of foundational issues for thinking.

Responsibility

The cosmology of thinking that lies at the heart of this axiological hypothesis represents thinking as a family of activities intrinsically related to values. That is, imagination is what it is because, to some degree, it embodies beauty. Interpretation is what it is by virtue of the relevance of the value of truth. Theory expresses the unity of envisionment. These and related values define thinking in its various modes.

Part of being a subject who thinks, therefore, is being *obligated* by the values that are norms for thinking. The character of obligation is an extraordinarily difficult topic to consider with sophistication, for obligation is neither a state of affairs that has value nor a value to be embodied. Rather, it has to do with the relation of thinkers as subjects of experience to the values that are normative for thinking. One difference between a "mere thing" and a "person" is that, whereas the thing actualizes certain values and perhaps could actualize greater ones, a person subjectively faces values as obligations. In terms of what is indicated above, human processes are thinking activities not only because they embody beauty and other values but because they are the kinds of processes that *should* embody them. Part of the subjectivity of being a thinker is that where imaginative beauty is possible, it ought to be realized to the greatest degree. Where truth is applicable, it should be justified by being applied. Where vision is possible, it should be as unified, true, and engaged as possible.

The relationship of thinking experience to obligation constitutes the state of being responsible. "Responsibility" is an analogical word used in many related senses, which are discussed in Chapter 4. Generally speaking, to be responsible means to engage in the kind of activity that is under obligation. The activity can be expressed in terms of the value of goodness. There are many norms in various contexts that obligate thinking experience, but whether one does what one is obligated to do determines the extent to which one is "good." Goodness is not a separate value alongside the others so much as it is a specially transcendental value. It is the value of fulfilling obligations or of being responsible. Although the content of one's "goodness" is determined by the particular obligations attendent on nature, character, and station, the general character of goodness consists of being responsible to obligations as such. This is the crucial insight—or something approaching it—expressed by Kant in his famous discussion, in *Foundations of the Metaphysics of Morals,* of the "good will" and of acting for the sake of duty rather than for the particular attractiveness of one's goals.

How is the goodness of responsibility related to thinking? In one sense, a person's responsibilities extend far beyond thinking well. Obligations to the beauty of experience, to truth, to unified visions and the rest, exist alongside equally important obligations to relate to other people with love, respect, and justice, to produce worthwhile goods, to fulfill the diverse obligations of citizenship, to occupy an ecological niche as well as one's particular place in history, and develop personal virtues and spiritual perfections. One's goodness consists generally in fulfilling obligations in all these areas, and more. It would be foolhardy to suggest that the norms of thinking occupy a preeminent place within the content of goodness. Further, the array of particular responsibilities varies from person to person.

In another sense, goodness is peculiarily related to thinking. It is by virtue of thinking that people have obligations rather than simply being things with values that might be improved upon. In a logical sense, prior to fulfilling one's obligations to children, for instance, is the obligation to engage one's children well with imagination, to interpret them and their situation truly, and to envision well the context in which one is related to them and their prospects. The responsibility of thinking well in all dimensions is a precondition to acting or being "with responsibility" in broader contexts, for the normative activities of thinking are what define a subject as having those obligations in the first place. The normative activities do not define the content of the obligations so much as they define the possession of them.

The axiology, then, may reexamine the previously mentioned values in thinking from the standpoint of the moral subject, as matters of responsibility. As Chapter 4, "Responsibility, Norms, and the Social Reality of Thinking," indicates schematically, this adds the dimension of responsibility to all other dimensions of thinking. Put another way, every act of thinking not only has imaginative, interpretive, and theoretical elements but also dimensions of responsibility.

Regarding each dimension of thinking, the questions of responsibility can be put: Does this thinking have the best character, and is it about the most important, relevant things? These questions may be answered in the attendent case by considering the particular circumstances—the ages and personalities of one's children, for instance. The question, however, indicates the peculiar relationship of thinking to responsibility, namely, that thinking well is an elementary requirement necessary for taking up one's responsibilities.

This interpretation of responsibility bears the marks of moral rigorism. It implies that how one thinks and what one thinks about are not merely hypothetical postulates but obligations. We often excuse ourselves by saying, for instance, "I don't understand my child"; our responsibility, however, is to have attained that understanding in the best way possible. The statement is merely an excuse. One might say: "Theoretical contemplation is not my cup of tea—you need an expert"; but it is irresponsible, particularly and in general, not to have a critical grasp of the world in which one acts and occupies a place. Even one's images make a difference. Some images that structure the world, because they are disengaging, are evil, and one is under obligation to perfect imagination.

Expressing the point in a crude, classificatory way, religion deals with being responsible in imagination, politics with being responsible in interpretation, knowledge with being responsible in theory, and the full-fledged enterprise of philosophy as being responsible regarding responsibility itself. True, this is a very large view of philosophy. Most professional philosophers deal with only parts of the philosophic task of being responsible, yet most philosophers would admit that there is no philosophical justification for setting smaller limits to one's philosophic task, only the practical limitations of time, energy, and wit. Even the necessity of living the "philosophic life" is recognized by most philosophers. This large sense of philosophy has profound roots in the traditions of the West, as well as India and China; it is what the world of nonphilosophers rightly expects of philosophers.

STRUCTURE OF THE ARGUMENT

It is now possible to state how the argument of this study is structured. This chapter has presented the problem of values in thinking as calling for a reconception of the foundations of thinking itself. Thinking should be "founded," in a special sense of the word, not on reason but on valuation. The ideal construct of mathematical science is inadequate as a complete paradigm for thinking. How thinking is founded on valuation may be spelled out with respect to each of four foundational issues: imagination, interpretation, theory, and responsibility. The hypothesis for an "axiology of think-ing" was sketched.

Chapter 1 is an exercise in the art of philosophical imagination, con-juring up an initial articulation of the problem of thinking and values and presenting hypotheses for solving the problem. The hypotheses have been presented without giving relevant alternatives. Little has been said to justify them. In the special sense of "image" discussed above, however, this chap-ter presents images for engaging the problem of reconceiving thinking.

It is remarked earlier that the way to raise foundational issues is through philosophical cosmology. That kind of philosophical argument, however, is rarely practiced these days. Most philosophers, if they think of it at all, would say it is a fruitless venture. Therefore, in order to engage directly the foundational issues in cosmology, the philosophic enterprise must be explained and justified against the standard objections. That is the task of Chapter 2. Then the cosmology operative in the axiology of thinking must be presented. As a cosmology, it deals with affairs of nature that far transcend thinking; but the cosmology must be expressed in terms that make thinking explicit. Chapter 3 does this, preparing the way for each subse-quent chapter to elaborate the cosmology in specific detail relative to its topic. The philosophic function of Chapter 3 is to present a cosmological theory that will allow the diverse dimensions of thinking—imagination, in-terpretation, theory, and responsibility—to be envisioned together. It pre-sents the metaphysical theory of value as well.

Chapter 4 continues the development of the theory so as to address questions of value in thinking, beginning with a discussion of the knowledge of values and a defense of axiology itself. Then the four norms for thinking mentioned in the original statement of the hypothesis—beauty, truth, unity, and goodness—are defined with some care, in terms of the cosmology and theory of value. This is still merely a definition, or articulation, of theory; it is not proof. Justification of the values and of the claims made about them will be given in the following chapters by showing them to be operative in the various dimensions of thinking. The definition of values and of the norms for thinking, however, makes it possible to say more exactly what responsibility consists of and what this means for the philosophical responsi-bilities of getting to the foundations. The incorrigibly social nature of re-sponsibility is again brought out, but this time it is shown to require an equally incorrigible location of responsibility in individuals.

The four chapters of Part 1 thus exhibit in appropriate ways the four main dimensions of philosophic thinking one would expect from the axiolog-ical hypothesis: the engaging creation of images, critical interpretive asser-tion, theoretical envisionment, and a dialectic of philosophic responsibility. The chapters also provide an introduction to the discussions of each dimension of thinking. Apparently diverse in topic and method, they move the discussion down to the foundational issues where an axiology of thinking can begin its positive argument. They do this with a systematic rhythm: first, creating images to engage an enormously complex problem; second, placing the discussion in the community; third, presenting the relevant theory; and fourth, backing up and justifying the values guiding the discussion with a dialectic of responsibility.

Part 2 of this volume and parts 3, 4, and 5 that are to be written later take up the major foundational issues, imagination, interpretation, theory, and responsibility, respectively. The chapters of each part deal with problems as they arise, according to the nature of the issues. If one squints so as to blur the details, one can observe that in each part, the first chapter focuses mainly on the imaginative aspect of the topic, the second on the interpretive, the third on the theoretical, and the fourth on either the responsibility or the valuation as such. Still squinting, one can observe that in each chapter the first section is an imaginative phenomenology or presentation of the problem with a suggested response; the second is a discussion of major options within the philosophic or cultural community; the third is an elaboration of the cosmology for the topic at hand; and the fourth is a reflection on the values and responsibilities involved. One should not read these chapters with squinted eyes, however, since it is not the methodological rhythms but the details of the argument that are important. The reader should avoid the false sense of understanding that sometimes comes when the rhythm of argument is grasped without the content.

The architectonic rhythm does suggest alternate ways of reading, however. This book is written to be read in the rhythm described here, reconsidering issues and proposals from different angles and with increasing complexity, each section deliberately placed at a distance from its neighbors. The generally interested reader can read only the first section in each chapter and still derive a coherent account both of the book's presentation of the problems of reconstructing thinking and of its positive suggestions. The reader would then need only a tolerance for the lack of transitions and a trust that when technical terms appear, they are defined and defended elsewhere. Similarly, a general reader might want to read the fourth section of each chapter, because these provide a continuous commentary on the moral or cultural aspects of thinking as defined through the reconstruction. The second section of each chapter is a commentary on the bearing of reconstruction on the important figures in the history of philosophy and in the contemporary situation, often with a dialectical defense of the reconstruction's methods or content. Perhaps only philosophers will want to read the second section of the chapters as a continuous narrative; readers not interested in the critical place of the reconstruction may skip these sections. It is suggested that those few readers who are devotees of cosmology can read the third sections in order, although this approach is unrelentingly abstract. If the axiological hypothesis about thinking has some merit, the best way to think about these matters is simultaneously from the view of the four approaches. Although it has become philosophically fashionable since Kant to emphasize the temporal or successive quality of thinking, the reconstruction reveals a spatial quality in which several logically different processes necessarily go on together. The rhythm of each chapter in the present book is a temporal compromise designed to represent this spatial quality.

2

Cosmology and Its Sources

If philosophical cosmology is the intellectual instrument for the reconstruction of thinking, it needs to be examined in its own right. This may seem paradoxical. If cosmology is a form of thinking, and thinking is to be reconstructed, how can one examine it in advance of the reconstruction? Some readers, therefore, may wish to skip this chapter and move on to the cosmology itself in the next. But whether or not cosmology is a proper philosophic tool is likely the first point at which most contemporary thinkers critically engage the project of the reconstruction of thinking. Thus it needs to be addressed in these introductory chapters as the focal question for the critical community.

Four main questions are asked. The first is, What is philosophical cosmology? "The Nature of Cosmology" will address this in terms of both cosmology's form and its role in intellectual life. The second question concerns whether philosophical cosmology is a respectable and justifiable philosophic enterprise. Since most of the contemporary, professional, philosophic world would reject philosophical cosmology as such, that is the most direct, forceful, and perhaps terminal engagement of the community with the project of reconstructing thinking. The second section, "Critique of Cosmology," takes up this debate.

The next two questions arise from a different angle of questioning. Whereas most contemporary philosophy is "modernist," in the sense of cutting itself off from the history of thought, on the one hand, and finding its own intelligibility and value solely within itself, on the other, a reconstruction of thinking is essentially "postmodernist."[1] That is, its intelligibility and value come from its being an historical project, one that attempts to alter culture. It has little significance as "pure philosophy" justified by a "style"; nor is it premodern, in the sense of being traditional or determined by history. Rather, a reconstructing cosmology appropriates historical resources for itself, attending to their own characters, insofar as these can be discovered, and to their value for reconstructing thinking.

From this angle, the third question about cosmology is, Does it have a decisive historical source or inspiration? The third section, "Plato and the Cosmology of Thinking" argues that the cosmology of thinking has just such a source in Plato. Today, however, what aspects of experience should a cosmology of thinking be attentive to, that have been neglected or even masked by their Greek origins? The fourth question, then, concerns the directing of philosophical responsibilities regarding cosmology. "Aristotle and the Task of Cosmology" deals with this question in a discussion of Aristotle, his relation to Plato, and his influence on the tradition of *praxis*; the chapter ends with a discussion of Chinese philosophy as an alternate source for cosmology.

THE NATURE OF COSMOLOGY

Philosophical cosmology has two essential moments. The first is the attempt to frame a broad system of categories in terms of which, with supplementary bridging interpretations, every item in the world can be represented as an illustration. This system must be extremely abstract. It is generally empirical in the sense that, besides being formally consistent and coherent, the system must, when properly supplemented, provide an interpretation of everything in the world while excluding that which is not found in the world. Philosophical cosmology, however, should not be viewed as empirical in any sense that would imply that it can easily be tested by critical experiments. Rather, the aim of philosophical cosmology is to single out the *important* features of the world. The main test of whether it accomplishes this is to determine that our broad experience verifies what the cosmology says about the importance of various things. And, of course, like any theory, cosmology points out potentially important things that we might not have noticed. The problem of verifying judgments of importance will be addressed here only with the circular remark that cosmology ought to give an account of how to make judgments of importance. No cosmology can be more than a tentative hypothesis. This moment of cosmology was brilliantly executed by Alfred North Whitehead, the greatest philosophical cosmologist since Aristotle; his system is the main inspiration for contemporary philosophical cosmology.[2]

The second moment of cosmology, largely neglected by Whitehead, is the movement from the abstract system to particular phenomena, showing how those phenomena, in fact, can be interpreted in terms of the system.

Only if this is done is it possible to gain a theoretical perspective on the phenomena that is directly connected to theoretical perspectives on other phenomena. Further, this theoretical perspective must be broad enough to allow interpretation of our value-experience, as well as interpretation of the experience of those disciplines that tell us about feeling, spontaneity, and judgment—the main themes of a cosmology of thinking. Whitehead engaged in the cosmological move from the abstract to the specific only in dealing with the microentities and macrostructures of the universe, and then only incidentally to illustrate the general theory. To deal with thinking, we need a "mesocosmology," cosmology made specific to affairs on the scale of human life. Of course, mesocosmology would be just another theory of human affairs if it were not integrated with microstudies and macrostudies through abstract cosmology. By virtue of abstract cosmology, however, mesocosmology has access to the most minute and the grandest experiences our esoteric sciences have made available to us.

Cosmology can be understood in terms of the contrast between images of the world and formal schemes abstracted from these images. A cosmological theory is a formal scheme for which one takes intellectual responsibility. The categories of images and schemes will take on additional technical significance in Part 2, "Imagination," where they are defined as elementary and necessary factors in "having a world."

Images

One of the most significant ways human beings differ from other animals is in the larger amounts of information they handle. As Kenneth Boulding has pointed out in his beautiful study, *The Image*, the difference occurs chiefly because human "patterns" for handling information are more complex and efficient.[3] This is not to say that other animals lack patterns and must handle information bit by bit. The bird outside the window has a pattern that lets it handle all the information involved in getting to South America and back every year. There is no reason to suppose the bird keeps all that information in mind at once; it does not have to remember much or to think far ahead. Its information pattern, however, allows it to respond to landmark information when it comes along and, when the need arises, to recall past information filed and forgotten. Despite its capacity for long-range flight, the bird cannot handle much history or philosophy; if a North American human traveler wished to go to South America, the requisite information could be handled easily with a travel agent and an American Express card. Human information patterns handle so much information because their structures are articulated with symbols that give experiential access to

highly diverse behaviors. The more comprehensive of these patterns are projections of what the world is like, images of the world or its significant
parts.

An image is the horizon in terms of which our definitions of its contents makes sense. It is like a mental picture of the rough outlines of the
world: it handles information by giving each datum a position relative to the
rough outlines. But the visual metaphor of "picture" is too narrow, because
a world image also has an historical dimension. The structure of historical
elements of an image may be significant stories—for instance, the adventures of Moses or the American Revolution—or it may be a mental picture
of a page from a history book with a chronological chart. Perhaps even
"structure" is the wrong word to use in describing images, becames images
also sort bits of information in terms of their relative importance. An image
lets us handle an item of information as being more important than some
others, less important in some contexts, and important instrumentally for
other values. An image includes a value system, although "system" may
connote too formal an arrangement. Most important, there are many levels
of images, from basic geometries of perception to styles of clothing by
which we unconsciously categorize people in social classes.[4]

Our image of the world articulates our sense of spatial arrangements at
many levels. Most medieval Europeans believed that the world is flat. The
Renaissance realization that it is round altered the general European image
of the world in ways that affected nearly everything. That we have now seen
pictures of the earth from space has altered our own image. Our sense of
geographic space depends on our world image. A parochial person can locate items of information in his cr her own neighborhood with precision;
things outside the neighborhood are merely located "out there." Most sophisticated Americans can locate spatial information precisely about North
America, Korea, Vietnam, Western Europe, and the Middle East. They also
have a general outline of the geography of South America and Africa, even
if they cannot locate the smaller countries. They can handle information with
spatial precision about Tokyo but not about Tashkent.[5]

Our sense of temporal dating is also a function of our world image.
Primitive or unsophisticated people can deal precisely with information
within the limits of living memory; beyond that they must switch to mythical time or to no time at all.[6] Most sophisticated Americans can locate information as "before civilization" (a [pre]historical time block within which
we have difficulty locating things as "earlier" and "later"), as relative to
Egyptian, Greek, and Roman history, as falling somewhere in the Dark
Ages, or as dated in modern history about which we have a numerical chron-
ology ("dates"). If, however, we do not know how the Han empire was

related to Egypt, Greece, or Rome, we do not know when the empire existed.

Spatial and temporal elements are closely interrelated. We can locate information about the Roman empire with spatial and temporal precision, but when and where was the Parthian empire?

The value dimensions of a world image are even more complex. In the first place, an image determines whether a bit of information is worthy of being dealt with at all; because of our selective attention, most information is screened out of consciousness. Then the image gives importance to each bit of information, over and above any importance or value it might carry on its face, because the image "places" the information in our experience.

We can have many images—one for the cosmos, one for our daily lives, another for our families and careers. If our view of the world is coherent, we have only one image for each domain of life, and these images are related to each other consistently, completing something that resembles a whole. Sometimes, however, the images relative to certain domains are incommensurable with, and irrelevant to, those of other domains. Even more striking is the fact that people can have different, conflicting images governing the same domain of information. This leads to a confusion of experience. When the conflict concerns the more comprehensive images, those images beyond that of local scale, the confusion can become a general disorientation of life.

A bit of information, or "message," is practically meaningless by itself. Alone, this bit is perhaps better thought of as a sound, a smell, an excitation of the optic nerve, or an electrochemical event in the brain. By virtue of an image, a message can be related meaningfully to other messages, including the afferent messages of actions. Although the image itself is largely made up of messages, it does not function as a message but as the connector of messages. An image for intellectual thought is like a leading principle of logic. The aesthetic elements of an image guide the process of anticipation. In general, an image provides the habits of thought that enable us to handle one message in terms of others.

There are two important considerations about messages in terms of their relation to images. On the one hand, the message is handled by the image relative to other messages; in this sense, the image is the preliminary condition for meaningfulness. On the other hand, the message itself may alter the image. Perhaps every message alters somewhat the image receiving it, at least to the extent that it confirms or subverts the relations suggested. Some messages simply do not fit the available images, however. If they are sent insistently enough, they demand alteration of old images or construction of new ones. All this supposes that messages are not *completely* uninterpreted when they come to images; they have elementary meaningfulness from prior images or from interpretive contexts of sense and body feeling too primitive and unsymbolic to be called images.

Images can be analyzed only partially as symbol systems composed of beliefs about important relations. "Beliefs" is too narrow a term; it connotes only intellectual symbols. Images also contain patterns for relating emotional feelings, aesthetic qualities, the vectors of forces, and tastes. Furthermore, image patterns involve a contrast between focal and background elements, and only the former can appear as beliefs or as objects of belief; Part 2, "Imagination," will argue this in detail. To handle information, images need not have "true" elements, just accepted or believed ones. So images include myths without raising the question of their literal truth. The question of truth is raised regarding an image when it *fails* to function with respect to certain information. If information does not demand the truth of an image, at the very least, it demands accord between the image and the source of the messages.

In terms of practical importance, images provide our individual and group senses of identity, inheritance, destiny, and moral orientation. They give us places in the world, our sense of values, and our habitual attention to responsibilities. From the standpoint of comprehensiveness, there is nothing of greater practical interest than our society's image of the world. Under some circumstances, of course, it is not necessary to pay attention to the image directly, since it is presupposed in all other thinking. In the twentieth century, however, Western society has received many messages pointing out the incapacity of generally accepted images to engage life appropriately.

Schemes and Cosmological Theories

Strictly speaking, an image is not an intellectual construct. Although intellectual messages play a role in the formation of an image, feelings, aesthetic perceptions, art inventions, and the memories of pleasures and pains probably play more important roles. An image is closely related to a scheme, and a scheme is the intellectual abstraction of an image for which one can take intellectual responsibility.[7] As an abstraction, the scheme is too lacking in emotion to handle the messages of life directly. The advantage of a scheme is precisely that it is an intellectual abstraction, a product of imagination working *on* images, and thus it is open to criticism. With an improved scheme in hand, it might be possible to guide culture to the construction of a fully fleshed-out image. An intellectual scheme is the lever, subject to disciplined human control, by which society's images can be moved.

That we can take intellectual responsibility for a scheme means at least three things. First, we can take responsibility for determining that the beliefs or categoreal assertions in the scheme are true. Second, we can take responsibility that the messages interpreted in the scheme are properly assessed. Whereas the first deals with the truth of the scheme, the second deals with the validity of its functioning. And third, we can take responsibility for altering the scheme in accordance with new messages. That is, the scheme should have a built-in self-criticism mechanism, by virtue of which it seeks out unfamiliar messages to test itself and invokes new imagination when it has to be changed.

A scheme whose alleged domain of reference is a "world," is a *theory*. Insofar as it is self-conscious and intends to define itself comprehensively, it is a cosmological theory.

The most important logical feature of cosmological theories is that their crucial concepts are vague, and thus they themselves are vague. This claim derives from the logical theory of Charles Peirce.[8] A concept is vague if the objects it specifies cannot be identified without further information. This implies that a vague theory is not illustrated by items in the world without intermediate theories saying how the items are illustrations. A general concept is different; *generality* means that the concept applies to any of its objects indifferently and that one knows from the concept what the objects are. In the phrase "all men are mortal," everyone knows what the general concept of a man is, and they can say to whom the word *mortality* is being applied in any case. A vague concept, on the other hand, requires more information than is supplied in the concept itself before it can be used to deal with particular things.

A vague concept or theory is subject to specification in a variety of ways. The specifications cannot be deduced from the theory precisely because the theory is vague in the ways that need to be specified. There can be alternate specifications of the same theory, exclusive of each other. *The theory is true as vague if there could be some true specification of it.* It is true as specified only if the specification in question is true. It is false as specified if the specification in question is false, even though it may, in itself, be true as vague.

The cosmological theory presented below is claimed to be true as vague. The grounds for this are, first, that it is perspicuously consistent and coherent and that it is applicable and adequate. In this case, *applicability* means that there is no part of it that cannot be specified by means of at least some claims arising out of experience or out of some intellectual discipline. If some part of the theory finds applicability in only one discipline, and that discipline later proves spurious, the claim of applicability must be suspended temporarily. Since only *possible* specification is required for vague truth, another exemplification might be found. If there is some actual and respectable discipline exemplifying the theory, then a prima facie case is made for applicability. Adequacy, here, means that there are no claims made by any respectable disciplines that cannot be interpreted by the theory. Some of these disciplines may turn out to be spurious in the long run, and the interpretation of their claims would be supererogatory; this would not lead to inapplicability in the theory, however, unless the elements required to interpret the spurious discipline find no applicability elsewhere. New disciplines will arise, no doubt, and old disciplines will make new claims; the cosmological theory may turn out to be inadequate to what it cannot anticipate. Thus claims for adequacy must be most tentative here; every philosophical system has been proved inadequate. A cosmological theory, however, should make provision for its own alteration.

Like nearly all claims for truth, the claim that "the cosmological theory is true as vague" is merely hypothetical. This recognizes that it may later turn out to be inapplicable or inadequate, or even inconsistent or incoherent. That the truth is hypothetical, though, does not mean the theory is just a guess or that any other theory is just as good. The claim is that, given our present state and direction of knowledge in the various disciplines, the theory is true. Aside from attacking consistency and coherence, the only legitimate attacks on the theory are those centering on the interpretation and significance of specifying disciplines.

To cite vagueness as a philosophical virtue doubtless seems perverse, because philosophers are trained to prize precision. Most of our ordinary categories, however, are vague rather than general, and it is an advance in precision to recognize where and how this is so. The category "book" is intrinsically vague, for instance, and is specified by lower-level conventions far more relative to historical fashion than the category itself. Aristotle's writings are called books, although contemporary writings on scrolls (the medium in which Aristotle's products were "published") would not be called books. We have no good conventions for deciding whether comics, pamphlets, government budget print-outs, and the like, are books. Among philosophical categories, for instance, "substance" can be determinately contrasted with its logical alternative, "event"; but because Aristotle, Descartes, Spinoza, Leibniz, and Kant had mutually exclusive (or at least quite different) specifications of "substance," the category itself, insofar as it is common to them, is vague. We cannot classify anything particular as a substance unless we have *some* philosopher's version of what substance is specifically. Cosmologies contain both vague categories and routes for specifying them both within philosophy itself and through extra-philosophical experience.

The strategy here regarding cosmology is to present a cosmological theory claimed to be vaguely true. It will be used in detail to interpret imagination, interpretation, theory, and responsibility. Then, in the examination of cosmological theory itself in Part 4, entitled "Theory," several of the important intellectual disciplines will be discussed as specifications of the theory, the sciences as one family of specification and the humanities as another. The validity of the disciplines on their own terms will be assumed, although the claims they make as to their relations with each other will be in question.

The benefits of this strategy are several. First, the disciplines are all related to a single common language, that of the cosmological theory; the disciplines are illustrative specifications of the cosmology. This kind of relation is different from *reducing* the disciplines to a common language; therefore, it avoids that kind of totalitarianism. If the disciplines cannot be related to the theory as exemplifications, this says nothing against the disciplines, only against the adequacy of the theory.

Second, it is possible to suggest what each discipline by itself contributes to our knowledge of the world. When the discipline must be its own judge, it must limit itself to saying that this is how the world looks when investigated with this particular method. When the discipline specifies the cosmological theory, however, its information is taken outside its own limits and interpreted in terms of how it fills in the larger vision of the world. The larger theory, of course, is only an hypothesis in its own right, yet it is one of much larger scale. Furthermore, the larger theory is an abstraction of a concrete *image* of the world, in terms of which practical action is oriented. Therefore, representation of the discipline as a specification of the theory expresses its information in practical terms ready for moral action.

Third, it is possible to exhibit, in terms of the theory, whether the claims of the various disciplines are equivalent, complementary, contradictory, or mutually irrelevant. Each discipline specifies the theory its own way; some of the ways are alternative, and some are not. There is no possibility, however, of determining through this process which discipline is correct; that is an empirical contest not to be decided by reference to the theory. The function of the theory is to represent what the various disciplines contribute, consistently or not, to an overall conception of the world and to human life.

The move from the language of "scheme" to that of "theory" is a significant one. The language of theory is appropriate on two general counts: indicating its development and indicating its function. A theory is a scheme that has been rendered into a form for which someone can take responsibility. For instance, the scheme extracted from an image is expressed in verbal concepts with definitions, with more or less explicit connections with other theories, with the experience of testing theories, and with a sense for how the theory is related to the reality expressed in the image. At the very least, a scheme deserves to be called a theory when the person holding it is aware that it is a *way* of grasping the world. Although it is perhaps abstracted from an image (theories can be constructed in many ways other than abstracting them from images), a theory has the world—or a part of it—as its object. A theory is a scheme that has been developed as a way of taking responsibility for an image. As to function, a theory may have any number of functions, from the technical to the contemplative. An essential function of a theory, in this meaning of the term, is that it is a way of envisioning the world. That is, through the theory its object can be comprehended in one "look." When its object is the whole world, as is the case with cosmological theories arising from taking responsibility for world images, the "look" is a contemplative grasp of the world.

Willy-nilly, we have an image of the world—or rather, several unconnected ones—for which we ought to take intellectual responsibility. Doing so leads through the foundational issues regarding thinking. Here is the need, therefore, for a cosmological theory.

CRITIQUE OF COSMOLOGY

The claim that philosophical cosmology is a necessary condition for addressing foundational issues is by no means undisputed. Although cosmology is respectable in the American tradition of systematic philosophy, it is not appreciated by most continental thinkers or by most philosophers in the Anglo-American tradition. Because the critique of cosmology from various strands of transcendental philosophy is a major theme of later chapters, the position of continental thinkers is not discussed here. The critique most often leveled by analytic philosophers, however, is much more sharp, direct, and ready to dismiss the entire cosmological enterprise. That critique, in several of its nuances, is the topic here.

The general critique of philosophical cosmology, as that discipline is defined here, has not been explicit. Most professional philosophers simply do not have a serious understanding of twentieth-century cosmology (as contained in the views, for instance, of Whitehead, Hartshorne, Weiss, Justus, Buchler, or David Weissman). The reason for this is that they believe "real" philosophy excludes speculative thinking of the sort involved in cosmology. This is usually discussed by means of attacks on "metaphysics" or speculative theorizing. Since the nonprofessional philosophic public has the right to assess these in-house debates, several of the critical arguments are considered as they might be thought to bear on cosmological theory as it is defined in the section "The Nature of Cosmology."

The First Argument: Philosophical Presumption

The first argument, and perhaps the argument most often lodged, is that philosophers should not be so presumptuous as to think they can speak systematically about the cosmos. Unless cosmology is to be mere empty play with words, it must arise out of a range of erudition impossible in the modern age. To engage in cosmology without this erudition is plain arrogance.

To this attack on philosophical character and motive, it is enough to admit that systematic philosophy is very difficult. Indeed, it requires far more general culture and erudition than is required for modernist philosophy, which conceives of itself primarily as "method"; method—in the form of standard moves, logical analysis, the use of counterexamples, and so forth—can be taught to undergraduates and can be used to define "professional competence." The background required for systematic philosophy is much more extensive. But to tackle the very difficult is a mark of courage rather than arrogance—unless one overrates one's results! The critic may rejoin that this remark misses the point. The difficulty with philosophical cosmology is that, to master all the fields, one is required to know in a responsible way what a theory of the world ought to be about, and this is existentially impossible. Whereas Aristotle could write a *Physics* and a *Metaphysics* comprising, organizing, and building on front-line knowledge in just about all fields of his day, today there is simply too much to know. We must be specialists; comprehensive knowledge is virtually beyond our grasp.

The reply to this more important criticism is to call attention to the distinction made in the preceding section, "The Nature of Cosmology," between vagueness and generality. A general claim (or theory) is one that, although it applies to a universal class, does so in a way that determines which concrete phenomena it refers to. By contrast, a vague claim is one that requires further specification before it determines any concrete phenomena. "All human beings are mortal" is a general claim. "All the people of whom I am now thinking are left-handed" is vague, requiring further specification of those of whom I am thinking. For the most part, scientific theories are intended to be general, not vague, referring to entities alleged by the theories as concrete phenomena. This is a difficult subject, however. Cosmological theories, in the sense discussed here, are deliberately vague, requiring a move from the theory to experience to specify them through more empirical methods. What this means in reply to the objection of the critic is as follows. A philosophical cosmologist's "specialty" is the dialectical construction of the vague theory, related to alternate theories and made applicable to the world through various routes of specification. The cosmologist, on the other hand, need not master all domains of knowledge, precisely because cosmology itself is vague. Even those areas of knowledge through which the cosmologist specifies the vague theory need be grasped only to the extent required for specification. True, to gain systematic balance requires considerable erudition, but the very vagueness of the theory and its need of specification invites practitioners of other forms of knowledge to engage cooperatively in the specification. This is a concrete example of the requirement of interdisciplinary organization in philosophy.

The Second Argument: Metaphysics as Nonsense

The second argument of the critic is sharper, namely, that if philosophical cosmology is anything more than the cosmology that physicists study, it is metaphysics, which is not true philosophy.

In reply to this, it is necessary to discuss just what metaphysics is supposed to be. For the great critic of metaphysics, Immanuel Kant, metaphysics was supposed to be a nonempirical discipline that determines its objects a priori. A cosmological theory, however, is hypothetical, not a priori. For such rationalists as Gottfried Leibniz (1646–1716) and our contemporary, Charles Hartshorne, metaphysics is the study of the conditions that would obtain in any possible world. Philosophical cosmology is *not* this, because it intends to lay out the generic traits of the existence of *this* world. For certain British idealists, metaphysics is the study of some logical implications of the characteristics of the world as a whole. A philosophical cosmology is not a logical implication for which the world is a premise, however. Rather, it is a speculative hypothesis in which the relation between it and the world has to do with the applicability and adequacy of representing what is important, coherently and consistently. In the scholastic tradition, metaphysics is the "science" of what was taken to be an Aristotelian sense of "inducing" to the first principles of things. Philosophical cosmology, by contrast, is no more an inductive implication than it is a deductive or dialectical one. It is an hypothesis that allows envisioning the whole; there may be many such hypotheses. Grounds for choosing among alternative cosmological theories are not inferential relations between the empirical world and the theories. In these bad senses of metaphysics, philosophical cosmology is not metaphysics, and the critical objection does not apply.

The Third Argument: Empirical and Nonempirical

But this leads to a third objection from the critic. The legitimate ways of doing metaphysics are careful to respect the distinction between the empirical and the nonempirical, it is said. For Strawson, for instance, metaphysics is an empirical discipline whose data base is the ordinary use of language. Philosophical cosmology, however, seems to be metaphysics that confuses the distinction between the empirical and the nonempirical, setting forth speculative hypotheses that are more general than those that can be tested in any critical scientific experiment or that can be illustrated conclusively in the accepted use of language, with the same empirical warrant being claimed.

This is a serious objection. It can be answered by referring again to the vagueness of philosophical cosmology. If there were no way in which the basic cosmological concepts could be made specific with respect to empirical data, the cosmology would not be empirical. If it can be specified, it can be shown as having empirical applicability and adequacy. Of course, this does not prove that it is "true"; but scientific theories have similar limitations. There are various informal dialectical criteria for judging cosmological theories. In a sense, the most comprehensive test of a cosmology is whether it guides, enlightens, and enriches life when lived with, supposing that its empirical specifications are employed in common and professional life and that the aesthetic components of its vision are appropriately felt. This larger sense of empirical testing should not be confused with the more formal senses in which scientific theories are tested. As will become clear in the discussion of theory in Part 4, "Theory," a cosmology is not intended to be a superordinate theory replacing theories of less generality; nor is it to have more primitive explanatory power.

The Fourth Argument: Lack of Clarity

The fourth objection of the critic follows from the third argument. If a cosmological hypothesis is empirical only by virtue of further specifications to its vague assertions, then it must be unclear. At the least, philosophy should be clear.

The reply to this is both no and yes. No, cosmology need not be unclear, insofar as it expresses the sharp distinctions between alternate cosmological claims and categories; nor do cosmologies need to be unclear in the ways specified by concrete experience. Yes, they are unclear insofar as they are vague. For instance, if one asks for an example of an "actual occasion" or an "eternal object," to mention some of Whitehead's categories, none can be given. Any empirical object would have to illustrate *all the other categories, too*; otherwise, the theory would not be properly applicable.[9] This is very frustrating to philosophers, who like to employ refutation by counterexamples: if anything is a counterexample to a cosmological theory, everything should be. To illustrate a cosmology empirically requires building intermediate models that specify the vague cosmological categories, and that complicates the issue with the problem of the validity of the specifying experience or discipline.

The Fifth Objection: Misuse of Words

The fifth objection is more serious than those that have been answered by appeal to the logical distinction between generality and vagueness. It is that insofar as cosmological questions are not those of empirical science, they arise from a misuse of words. This is not merely a logical point but an interpretation of philosophy and its role in life. The perspective deserves extensive quotation from Ludwig Wittgenstein, who advanced it in his influential *Philosophical Investigations*.

109. It was true to say that our considerations could not be scientific ones. . . . And we may not advance any kind of theory. There must not be anything hypothetical in our considerations. We must do away with all *explanation*, and description alone must take its place. . . . The problems are solved, not by giving new information, but by arranging what we have always known. Philosophy is a battle against the bewitchment of our intelligence by means of language.

116. When philosophers use a word—"knowledge", "being", "object", "I", "proposition", "name"—and try to grasp the *essence* of the thing, one must always ask oneself: is the word ever actually used in this way in the language-game which is its original home?—

What *we* do is to bring words back from their metaphysical to their everyday use.

122. A main source of our failure to understand is that we do not *command a clear view* of the use of our words.—Our grammar is lacking in this sort of perspicuity. A perspicuous representation produces just the understanding which consists in "seeing connexions". Hence the importance of finding and inventing intermediate cases.

123. A philosophical problem has the form: "I don't know my way about".

124. Philosophy may in no way interfere with the actual use of language; it can in the end only describe it.

For it cannot give it any foundation either.

It leaves everything as it is. . . .

133. It is not our aim to refine or complete the system of

rules for the use of our words in unheard-of ways.

For the clarity that we are aiming at is indeed *complete* clarity. But this simply means that the philosophical problems should *completely* disappear. . . .

494. I want to say: It is *primarily* the apparatus of our ordinary language, of our word-language, that we call language; and then other things by analogy or comparability with this.

655. The question is not one of explaining a language-game by means of experiences, but of noting a language-game.[10]

It is an answer to Wittgenstein on one level to point out the following. A language game is concretely and immediately used in an activity, and philosophical cosmology is an activity with a long history of wrestling with basic questions. Democritus, Plato, Aristotle, Aquinas, Scotus, Locke, Descartes, Spinoza, Leibniz, Kant, Hegel, Peirce, Whitehead—all developed languages for their cosmological activity that are sufficiently related to one another to be in intelligible continuity, yet different enough to express basically different visions. Philosophical cosmology constitutes a rather close-knit family of language games that resemble each other. Whereas the languages of philosophical cosmology may not be ordinary for the average person, they are ordinary for the host of people who engage in philosophical enquiry. One should no more insist that that activity be reduced to the cosmological prejudices of the average person than that the language game of a baseball broadcaster be reduced to that of the kinesiologist. To turn Wittgenstein's remark in paragraph 655 around, the (family of) language games of philosophical cosmology should be noted and played by those who are interested; they should not be explained in terms of experiences of misusing language or of being bewitched by it.

Wittgenstein's argument, however, operates on a deeper level than this. It expressed his firm conviction that some kinds of activity, with their language games, are genuine, and that philosophic activities dealing with cosmological or metaphysical issues are not. What lies behind this conviction? If Wittgenstein had ever engaged in sustained criticism of Aristotle's theory of the four causes, or Scotus's doctrine of haecceity, or Leibniz's theory of monads, he might have shown that their speculations were indeed spurious activities that came from confusing the language of other activities. Wittgenstein did not do this; indeed, he may have been innocent of any systematic, serious cosmological philosophy. Instead, he discussed such fragmented metaphysical or cosmological statements as "This is how things are" (paragraph 134) or "Sensations are private" (paragraph 248), isolated from responsibly developed philosophic visions in which they might make sense. Perhaps he thought that philosophic statements by themselves should be intelligible. Philosophic statements, however, no less than statements about baseball, make sense only when their language game is understood.

Perhaps Wittgenstein's conviction came from a failure to note a subtle distinction that may be registered within his own theory of language games. Within any activity involving speaking, the utterances may have one, or both, of two functions. One function is to advance life "within the game"— for instance, if telling a story, to narrate the next incident; if moving with the preacher, to clap and shout "Amen!"; if calling for the next stone, to say "Slab!" (Wittgenstein's example). The other function is to enjoy the game itself, to feel the form of life, as expressed in the utterance. For example, some narrations not only tell the story but call attention to being in the world of storytelling. Some *amens* celebrate hearing the word of God itself; even *slab* can be pronounced so as to evoke awareness of the orientation of the world through building. The first function may be called "interpretation," following Peirce (although Wittgenstein, in his *Investigations*, wanted to restrict the word *interpretation* to a smaller domain; compare paragraph 201). The second function may be called "envisioning." Envisioning occurs when the world image, of which the language game is a partial expression, itself comes into focus and the world presented is possessed as a whole.

Envisioning, in contrast to interpretation, is a phenomenon Wittgenstein himself recognized. In *Philosophical Investigations*, philosophy is supposed to produce such clarity that the language game itself is "noted." The distinction he drew between "explaining" and "noting" (paragraph 655) is precisely that between interpreting further and envisioning—enjoying with a complete immediacy of wholeness. Wittgenstein made this point early in his writings. The discussions of the "world" at the beginning and end of the *Tractatus* reflect his view that a grasp of the world as such is ineffable, or "mystical," but for all that, genuine.[11] This is the envisioning function, in contrast to what can be said and shown of the world, which is the function of interpretation.

Wittgenstein, along with many other professional philosophers, was committed to the view that philosophy is the solving of puzzles, the removing of difficulties. He thought that if he could show us how to use our language so that the difficulties were removed, philosophy's goals would be fulfilled. The great contribution of Western philosophy to culture, however, has not been the solving of puzzles—most puzzles have become culturally irrelevant, or they have not been solved at all—but the creation of new ways of asking questions. Rather than eliminating questions, philosophy has created new conceptual perspectives that allow new forms of probing, that make things problematic which without philosophy could be taken for granted. Philosophy's constructions increase the angles of vision in which things can be seen and inquired about. Whereas the philosophical constructions, often cosmologies, may, out of internal incoherence or silliness or ultimate impotence, fail to raise good questions, they are not faulty simply in raising new perspectives for understanding. In this, philosophy is a cultural achievement on a par with art or science. To argue, as some think- ers do, that philosophical constructions are superfluous if experience can be talked about coherently without them is like saying art is superfluous be- cause we can see things without it or that science is superfluous because nature works whether or not we understand it. Wittgenstein's advocacy of what he called the "therapeutic" task of philosophy, to the exclusion of all others, makes sense only as a modernist phenomenon. Outside the context of cultural modernism, it is crude anti-intellectualism.

Moreover, the moral point that Wittgenstein seems not to have seen is that we have a responsibility to use the language games we do use. Lan- guage games can be modified, as they are all the time. There are valuational issues, not only within language games but concerning language games as whole imageries. Wittgenstein spoke, though, as if language games were uncriticizable. For him, to criticize a language game from the outside could only be to play a different language game. He seemed to come closest to dealing with the responsibilities of language games when he wrote (in para- graphs 81 and 100–105 of the *Philosophical Investigations*) of logic as an ideal; but he disparaged this logic as a normative ideal.

That we can be responsible for our language games or for our images of the world is not an obvious truth. One can see how someone from Witt- genstein's modernist cultural background could think that the greatest re- sponsibility is merely to be clear about what we say, regardless of its value or the value of the language game or form of life in which statements are made.[12] The way to argue that we do have normative responsibilities in this matter is to display them. The axiology of thinking aims to present an im- age, an interpretation, and a theoretical vision of thinking that displays its responsibilities.

Assuming for the moment that the case can be made for the claim that we are responsible for having the best images or language games possible, and that this makes sense, the argument for the possibility of cosmology can be restated. Our language games, like our images (of which the language games are linguistic elements), provide a primordial sorting of information, a valuation of what is important, a framework for orienting ourselves toward the world. The images are diverse; they are perhaps contradictory, com- plementary, or an overlapping compromise. Life is richer and more concrete than any one image or language game because we can move from one image or game to another, *and because we know this*. It is thus possible to ask whether our images do well by life. Do they make the important connec- tions? Do they highlight the important messages? Do they provide the best orientations? The only way to answer these questions is to bring the images to consciousness and formulate them in whatever terms are necessary for their worth to be recognized. This is what is meant by asking a foundational question. It is also the process of transforming images into theories; the formal elements of theories urge unity, coherence, comprehensiveness, and so forth. The testing of images as such—not just this image or that one, but simply the best ways to image the world—is philosophical cosmology. An image explicitly brought to attention is a vision; a responsible vision is a cosmology.

PLATO AND THE COSMOLOGY OF THINKING

Having sketched the intended structure of a philosophical cosmology, and having defended that intention against contemporary critics, it is appropriate now to put the project in an historical context. The conception of philosophical cosmology has its analogues in India and China, but it is the direct heir of Greek thought. The ancient Greek philosophers, of course, did not have a cosmology in just the sense described above, but they did have views on thinking and its role in nature and society. Plato's theory about these matters is an inspiration for the cosmology of thinking developed below.

Although Plato wrote in response to an intellectual and political situation already formed, he was the first philosopher in the West to address the diverse faculties of thinking in a systematic and fundamental way. One of the best statements of his view is the discussion of the "Divided Line" in the *Republic*, Book 6, 509f.[13] (See Figure 1.) Plato's basic claim is that there are four general classes of cognition, which are distinguished by the kind of normative claims they can legitimately make, and that this distinction is a major source for approaching the foundational issues in the reconstruction of thinking.

The first class is cognitions of discrete objects, objects considered with respect to no larger context. These objects—"images"—could be wrenched from a more concrete experience by abstraction, as copy artists do when they paint representational pictures. The images could be items of folk wisdom, quoted as proverbs apart from a meaningful context. They could be reflections of natural objects in other media, for example, the reflection of shoreline trees in a lake. Or they could be the imaginative invention of artists, agents, or thinkers, considered only as the imaginative product without reference to the situation for which they might be imagined. The only kind of normative claim intrinsically appropriate for images is the immediate value they show on their faces after analysis. From the standpoint of imagination alone, an image cannot be said to be true of, or valuable for, a world

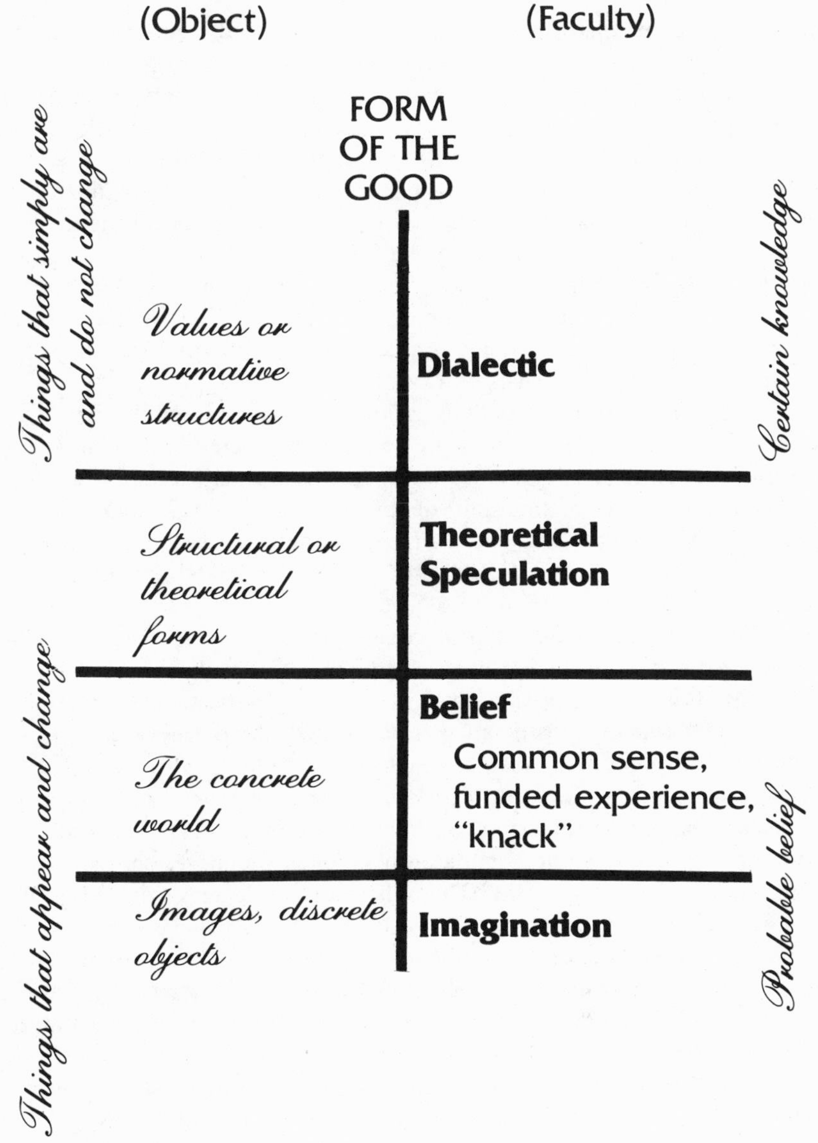

(Object)   (Faculty)

FORM
OF THE
GOOD

Things that simply are and do not change

Values or normative structures | **Dialectic**

Certain knowledge

Structural or theoretical forms | **Theoretical Speculation**

Belief

The concrete world | Common sense, funded experience, "knack"

Things that appear and change

Images, discrete objects | **Imagination**

Probable belief

Figure 1

larger than itself. (Plato's objection to artists, expressed in many places, was that they were taken to be teachers of larger things.) On the other hand, an image has a kind of internal, immediate, formal integrity that can be felt intuitively; the discursive expression of that immediate worth moves beyond the intuition. All human novelty comes into the world through imagination.

In this sense, for Plato, imagination and art were indispensable to human creativity and advance (see *Phaedrus* 245a).

The second class of cognitions has as its object the concrete world of experience organized according to conventional categories and beliefs. We move through the world on the basis of "funded experience," to use John Dewey's phrase. We develop a knack for dealing with things, without having theories of how they work. Of course, such commonsense beliefs are no more probable than is warranted by the experience out of which they arise. We do not doubt them unless experience disappoints our expectations or, somehow, a conventional value comes into question. The normative claim proper for common sense is simply that it *is* funded experience subject to previous error and future change of conditions.

The third class of cognitions is logical deductions or theoretical inferences. These inferences have as their object mere conceptual forms, speculatively entertained. The deductions themselves are certain, for Plato, indicating only the relationship of premises and conclusions. Certain though it is, theoretical or speculative thinking by itself, entails nothing about the concrete world of experience except the limits of logical possibility.

The fourth class—dialectical cognition—consists of questioning the justification, or worth or presupposed norms, of other kinds of cognition. By *dialectic* is meant stepping up to ask for the justification of some other claim. Then, when the justification is discovered, the process is used to ask about the presuppositions of *that*. Dialectic, therefore, moves through the other domains of cognition. It might, on the first level, ask of an image, for instance, whether it is plausible as a representation in a larger context. Putting aside its face value or its attractiveness, does the image represent something valid in a larger context? Thus, dialectic would move the image into the second level, the commonsense world, in which its connections with the rest of life are revealed. What, though, is the validity of common sense? Here, dialectic must make a different move; it must offer a theory that can show why a belief might be true (or false), then test the theory. This means moving to the third level of the line to produce a theory. Then, however, the theory must be related to the experiential world as an hypothesis. Dialectic, therefore, moves from common sense to science by way of speculative theory. A theory becomes an hypothesis through its relationship to the world; it is then evaluated using inductive methods. What about the suppositions of the theoretical structure as such? This is not a question about a true relation between the theory and the experiential world, but one about the norms of theories considered by themselves. Apart from their hypothetical truth or falsity, theories are distinguished by their degree of wholeness, their coherence, their elegance, their self-referencing capability, and so forth. These normative concepts are the only kind of "objects" dialectic has to itself; otherwise, it deals with the relative normative status of other forms of cognition.

Plato's conception of the divided line reflected his larger concern to discover whether there is any way to justify value claims on the social level. The sophistic thinkers, of course, had denied that there is such a way, arguing, instead, that the function of thinking is successful persuasion. Plato's analysis of the relationship between thought and society was at the heart of his philosophical conception, for he believed that the conventionalism of the sophists rendered meaningless all claims that any society, or polity, is better than another. Recognizing that moral and social values cannot be identified as mere facts—and yet not wanting to admit that they are mere arbitrary conventions, as some sophists taught—Plato invented the notion of the form of the Good, whose primary property is to be normative (*Republic*, Books 1, 4, and 6; *Protagoras*; *Philebus*). Plato's epistemology was his attempt to show how the Good can be known in relation to change, involving hypothetical structures of theoretical forms that might be used to measure the ratios of process (*Republic*, Book 7; *Meno*; *Theaetetus*; *Sophist*). His cosmology was an attempt to acknowledge both the chaos—or unlimitedness, of process, on one hand—and the pure, unchanging integrity of value, on the other, as well as how the chaos and integrity combine to produce relatively stable order in the world of experience (*Phaedrus*; *Timaeas*; *Philebus*). His ethics-politics attempted to show how critical, normative judgment can be exercised by the analytical and speculative skills of dialectical thinking, considering one hypothesis after another and discerning which formal or empirical properties make one hypothesis superior to another (*Republic*; *Statesman*).

Despite the opinions of such polemicists as Karl Popper, Plato was an incorrigible pluralist in his view of the world, the first major Western thinker to believe that a "thing" is actually a "society" or a "social ordering" of component things.[14] This is expressed in the Platonic view that a form is a structure that makes it possible to think of certain otherwise disparate things as a unit. A person is a society of desires, of reasoning powers based on knowledge and art, of habits of discipline. This means that the relationship of the components of a person or a substance are to be construed in metaphors of social interaction rather than in metaphors of placement in space or of mechanical dynamics. In the political sense, a society has diverse essential functions—including production, decision-making, and regulation and enforcement mechanisms—none of which can be reduced to another.

Plato described injustice in terms of the usurpation of the function of a part of society or of a person by another. For Plato, thinking has both immediate qualities and instrumental purposes. At one level, thought may be described as in the "Divided Line" in terms of imagination, effective discrimination and habit, theorizing in several of its forms, and reflective philosophic understanding of presuppositions, including a conception of the whole of things (*Republic*, Book 6, 509–11). At another, instrumental level, thought has the function of guiding life. Reason should guide each person's life, while, at the level of the state, social embodiments of the best reason should be at the helm. The most important point here, however, and one that is often missed by critics, is that the instrumental property is the more essential: thinking is at the service of the entire "society of parts," in both personal and civic life. The immediate qualities of thinking often are more pleasurable than the task of ruling. In such areas of knowledge as statecraft and philosophy, many skilled thinkers prefer to remain aloof, reasoning that by doing so they will be freer to think well. Just as the person who has ascended from the cave (in Plato's famous allegory) would have to be dragged back down and forced to rule the captives (*Republic*, Book 7, 517c), so the philosophers and the rational part of the soul must be forced by the disciplinary elements to rule. Although interest in thinking is among the legitimate interests of life (hence, thinking is not *merely* instrumental), the essential *role* of thinking is to order the whole of life according to proper discriminations and wise choices.

What exactly is the role of reason for Plato? Social engineering? Plato's conception of the nature, powers, and content of reason is one that emphasizes discernment of all the variables in a changing and pluralistic situation. Reason appeals to its imagination of norms to invent patterns that make the best of the changing kaleidoscope of things. It directs the art of well-timed activity that adjusts the countless small factors which keep affairs as near the ideal as possible (*Statesman*; *Philebus*). For Plato, there was no form of the *human*, no ideal common to all individuals. All persons must discern for themselves what is uniquely best for them. Did Plato believe that there is an ideal state? The utopian state described in the *Republic* is based on the premise that people are essentially appetitive (*Republic*, Book 2, 369b), which, it turns out, is true only of one class of people. Within this ironic parody of the economic-man theory, Plato introduced the soldiers as "watchdogs" (Book 2, 375a). The rational rulers (Book 3, 415a) appear under the metaphor of base metals—nonhuman images, because, in this parody, essential humanity is merely appetitive. The dialogue goes on to argue (Book 4) that not only are there very different kinds of people, there are different elements within each person. *The Republic* concludes with the Myth of Er (Book 10, 618), in the midst of which Socrates provides the following editorial comment, summarizing the point of the dialogue:

> Here, it seems, my dear Glaucon, a man's whole fortunes
> are at stake. On this account each one of us should lay aside all
> other learning, to study only how he may discover one who can

give him the knowledge enabling him to distinguish the good life from the evil, and always and everywhere to choose the best within his reach, taking into account all these qualities we have mentioned and how, separately or in combination, they affect the goodness of life. Thus he will seek to understand what is the effect, for good or evil, of beauty combined with wealth or with poverty and with this or that condition of the soul, or of any combination of high or low birth, public or private station, strength or weakness, quickness of wit or slowness, and any other qualities of mind, native or acquired; until, as the outcome of all these calculations, he is able to choose between the worse and the better life with reference to the constitution of the soul, calling a life worse or better according as it leads to the soul becoming more unjust or more just.[15]

Would this conception of the relation of reason to life and society lead to a totalitarian polity with philosophers in charge? No, it would not. Philosophers could be totalitarian only if their process of rational goal-setting were discontinuous with the process of governing. Just as Platonic reason rules the spirit and appetites by persuasion, so it must rule the state by persuasion or be false to itself. Plato devoutly wished that philosophy be persuasive enough to be politically effective, but he was highly pessimistic about the possibility. Surely society would not stand for a philosopher at its helm! The reason for this seeming impossibility, one that so depressed Plato, is that society as he knew it simply could not be persuaded by reason; it prefers the flattery of tyrants. The precondition of rule by philosophical persuasion is that the populace be educated to respond to persuasive ideals, hence Plato's "political activity" as founder of the Academy. Where persuasion fails, reason must abdicate; it cannot call in the soldiers.

Unfortunately, the disastrous tragic fault in Plato's vision is that, when reason abdicates, there is nothing left but the soldiers. When the rationally wise are not persuasive rulers, rule falls to those expert only in power and control, the military, and after them, the economic agents. When reason fails to direct one's personal life, the direction, by default, descends upon the habits that organize personality by the power of aggression, or upon the unorganized siren call of desires. Tragic as this vision is, Plato thought it to be descriptively accurate, and it may be.

Nevertheless, a critical vision ought to construe things so as to reveal points of access for making the best of things. Plato's take-it-or-leave-it vision betrays a petulant perfectionism. Perhaps reason may be conceived of in such a way as to reveal a way to influence affairs when one is not completely in charge. This would require, in a cosmology of thinking, a more straightforward, mediating link between rational thinking and the control thinking Plato assigned to the military. Can valuation be that link?

In summary, Plato's protocosmology of thinking addresses two main issues. The first issue concerns the basic dimensions of thinking. Plato's solution was given in his discussion of the Divided Line, although, of course, he greatly refined numerous points in other dialogues. The second issue concerns the relation of thinking to human nature and society. Here, Plato's solution was his "social" theory of persons and society, according to which thinking is the guiding principle. Both concerns must be registered in a contemporary cosmology of thinking. The cosmology developed below is a remote offspring of Plato's own answers.

As critics have noted, Plato's conception of thinking as a *principle* for guidance does not make thinking the *agent* of guidance. When reason fails, both people and society become unjust. When reason fails on Plato's ground, it must retreat and when that happens, Platonism becomes mere ineffectual idealism. A contemporary cosmology of thinking, therefore, must wed thinking as a principle for guidance with the agency for guidance, thus integrating Plato's reason with what he called "spirit."

ARISTOTLE AND THE TASK OF COSMOLOGY

Aristotle stood in striking contrast to Plato, although he too was within the philosophical posture of the ancient Greeks. Instead of construing activity on the analogy of a social process of ordered but quasi-independent elements, Aristotle construed activity as the essential property of a unitary substance. This view involves both a more "solid" conception of natural objects than Plato's social ordering of otherwise chaotic elements and a more unified, agent-oriented conception of activity. Although Aristotle and Plato agreed that the defining context of human action is the *polis*, their differences over the nature of activity and substance led them to answer differently questions about the relation of thinking to values.

Thinking, for Aristotle, was an essential activity of a person. The modes of thinking are correlative to personal virtues. According to Aristotle, a person is a hierarchical layering of functions, not an interacting harmony of social elements (*De Anima*, Book 2). Nutrition and consciousness of sense perceptions are necessary conditions for the functioning of rationality, but rationality is an improvement on nutrition and consciousness, or sentience, because it is closer to self-sufficiency (*De Anima*, Book 3, 7; *Nichomochean Ethics*, Book 10). The activities proper to mankind include *poesis* (the making of products for the sake of the products) and *praxis* (those activities whose principle value lies in the excellence of their own performance). Because *praxis* is more self-sufficient, needing no justification beyond itself, it is better than *poesis*.

Aristotle divided logical thinking into two kinds (*Nichomochean Ethics*, Book 6), the first of which is practical reasoning, whose end it is to direct or judge other activity. Many of Aristotle's greatest insights occur in the discussions of the subtle interaction of social forms and logical reasoning that produces moral virtue and practical wisdom. Theoretical knowledge is *useful* in the more complicated practical deliberations about making things (*poesis*) and about regulating personal and social conduct (*praxis*). Theoretical knowledge as such is the second kind of logical thinking. Its end is simply knowing, whatever the practical purposes to which it is put. Because theoretical knowledge is held to be its own end, it is more self-sufficient and thus better than either practical knowledge or the practical use of theory. The highest activity associated with theoretical knowledge is not investigation or deductive movement from premise to conclusion but the contemplation of truths as such. The importance of this point merits extensive quotation.

> If happiness is activity in accordance with virtue, it is reasonable that it should be in accordance with the highest virtue; and this will be that of the best thing in us. . . . That this activity is contemplative we have already said. . . . For, firstly, this activity is the best (since not only is reason the best thing in us, but the objects of reason are the best of knowable objects); and, secondly, it is the most continuous, since we can contemplate truth more continuously than we can do anything. . . . And the self-sufficiency that is spoken of must belong most to the contemplative activity. For while a philosopher, as well as a just man or one possessing any other virtue, needs the necessaries of life, when they are sufficiently equipped with things of that sort the just man needs people towards whom and with whom he shall act justly, and the temperate man, the brave man, and each of the others is in the same case, but the philosopher, even when by himself, can contemplate truth, and the better the wiser he is; he can perhaps do so better if he has fellow-workers, but still he is the most self-sufficient. And this activity alone would seem to be loved for its own sake; for nothing arises from it apart from the contemplating, while from practical activities we gain more or less apart from the action. (*Nicomachean Ethics*, Book 10, chap. 7, 1177a12–b4)[16]

Contrast this view of contemplation as the supreme happiness of man with Plato's lament that the contemplative life is the least evil way of surviving a situation in which justice in political life is impossible.[17] For Plato, philosophers may perfect their thinking, but they are unfulfilled as people if their thinking cannot be used in the service of a just life in a just society. For Aristotle, thinking is perfected only when the thinker is able to transcend social needs and engage in contemplation. From a metaphysical point of view, this difference is reinforced by Plato's view that value lies in that which measures or harmonizes plurality so as to produce order. The more harmonious the order, the better; it is an aesthetic conception. For Aristotle, however, value is conceived of structurally, as being self-sufficient, the completion of actuality, so that no potential is left and nothing is needed. Substances need support for existence, but they are perfected alone. Because Aristotle defined value in nonvalue terms, his account could not be of help in a foundational reconstruction of thinking in an axiology; something like a Platonic account of value is needed.

This interpretation of what is important in Plato and Aristotle differs sharply with that of Richard J. Bernstein, whose *Praxis and Action* is the most astute historical essay to date on the roots of the problem of thinking and society. Looking at the notion of *praxis* through the eyes of the left Hegelians, including Marx, he emphasizes Aristotle's use of it in distinction from *theoria*, where it

> signifies the disciplines and activities predominant in man's ethical and political life. These disciplines, which require knowledge and practical wisdom, can be contrasted with *theoria* because their end is not knowing or wisdom for its own sake, but doing-living well. When we add that for Aristotle, individual ethical activity is properly a part of the study of political activity—activity in the *polis*, we can say that *praxis* signifies the free activity (and the disciplines concerned with this activity) in the *polis*.[18]

Bernstein's interpretation deemphasizes Aristotle's point that the primary virtue of man is contemplative activity—a pure *praxis*, one as nearly free from external need as possible—an activity that is *supra*-social. The remaining meaning of *praxis* is embedded within social activity, and Bernstein focuses on three contemporary philosophic movements that attempt variously to define philosophy in terms of action and its transformatory effect—namely, Marxism, existentialism, and pragmatism. These three stand in contrast to the view expressed by Hegel—and before him, Aristotle—that philosophy or theory (thinking's approach to perfection) aims to understand the world as finished fact, not to guide or transform it. Analytic philosophy, Bernstein concedes, is closer to the Hegelian view than are the others because, although among its most interesting contributions is the analysis of the *concept* of action, the analysis is for the sake of understanding, not for doing-living well in a social or political sense.

The heritage Bernstein thus calls down from the Greeks (for some reason, he does not discuss Plato as part of the background of the problem of *praxis*, thinking and society) carefully distinguishes between theory and *praxis*, with the latter being more pertinent to thinking and society. Thinking is thus construed on the model of *an agent performing an action*, an agent liable to moral assessment. Logic, said Charles Peirce, is that species of ethics that applies to thinking. There is an undeniable truth in this: thinking is, *among other things*, an action, and it has many modes of moral value. Insofar as thinking is an action, either as judging or willing, it is analogous to speaking.

Thinking, however, also allows one to assimilate the influences of the world, to take it in, a point neglected in the *praxis* emphasis. It has an aesthetic moment, in the Greek sense of perceiving or "bringing through" into oneself. Thinking *feels*, and feeling is not the same as acting. If the action paradigm is employed, in which thinking is understood to be an action of judging or willing, then feeling appears in distorted form as an intuition of a brute given, as Peirce would say, a "first representation" or a potential premise. In this form, critics of the "myth of the given" are correct in rejecting it.[19] But why should the aesthetic moment be translated into what the action paradigm of thinking says of it? Why not incorporate feeling on its own terms into an understanding of thinking?

Besides acting and feeling, thinking also has a moment of creative assemblage, working what is felt into the actions it takes. This internal spontaneity does not obey the logical rules that order finished judgments—it is an "argument," according to Peirce, not an "argumentation"—yet it lacks the passivity or absorptive quality of feeling. Peirce called this aspect of thinking "musement," and it is the part of thinking given the most thorough analysis by Whitehead, who also emphasized feeling, or "prehension."[20] That Whitehead and process philosophy do not appear among Bernstein's interesting positions obscures *this* element of thinking by a heavy emphasis on thinking in connection with *praxis*.

The absence of a proper sense of feeling and spoıtaneity is often cited as being at the heart of the problems posed by the scientific construct of thinking. In a culture that seems to stress the outreach of thinking in intentional judgments, feeling and spontaneity tend to be isolated from thoughtful life. Feeling is popularly taken to be subjective, too private, a matter merely of taste. Yet when its importance to life is recognized, as, for instance, it is by psychologically-oriented people, it is often romanticized dangerously out of proportion. Spontaneity also tends either to be ignored (hence uncultivated and stifled) or to be celebrated as the special province of genius. Thinking that lacks healthy components of feeling and spontaneity is difficult to relate to the social life in which these missing components are so important. The cosmology of thinking developed in the following chapters includes a precise definition and analysis of feeling and spontaneity.

To the extent that control is on the cultural agenda of the West, judgment, that part of thinking most amenable to control, is the most often noticed, the best rewarded, and the most disciplined. This has not always been true of the West. Plato was much concerned with the education of taste and with the social nurturing of creativity. He was careful not to reduce these to the executive reason so central to his vision of human thinking, but he did indicate that the education of the nonrational elements of the soul should be directed by reason and that a well-education person is one whose passions and spirit follow reason's dictates. Plato's conception of the rational part of the soul is generous regarding both its aesthetic and ecstatic components, yet he likened the aesthetic and erotic passions to horses that need a driver (*Phaedrus*). He introduced into Western history the following themes: that the most important characteristic of thinking is that it be true or moral; critical dialectic sets the conditions for personal integration; and anarchic feeling and spontaneity should be transformed into "good acts" of thought.

The responsibility of a contemporary cosmology of thinking is to be sensitive to the importance of feeling and spontaneity as well as to judgment. The difficulty is that the Western tradition has formed a cosmology with an extraordinary bias toward judgment. A contemporary cosmology, therefore, even if it is heir to Plato's theory of the dimensions of thinking and to his theory of thinking as a principle of guidance, must be genuinely revolutionary regarding the Western tradition.

Chinese Variations

China provides a much more fertile field than the West for harvesting a culture rich in the ways of feeling and spontaneity. The fundamental concept of Chinese culture, antedating and surviving philosophic texts, is that of the Tao. *The Yellow Emperor's Classic of Internal Medicine (Huang Ti Nei Ching Su Wen)*—attributed to Emperor Huang Ti, who was alleged to have lived from 2697 to 2597 B.C.E., (and which was written probably around 1000 B.C.E.)—employs the notion of the Tao as the ultimate reality that manifests itself in yin and yang when in movement.[21] The Tao was conceived of at once as ultimate reality containing all distinguishable things, as the most "real" reality, as the reality manifest in the most veridical experience.

It is misleading, however, to speak of a *concept* of the Tao, as if the Tao were conceived in a judgment. Rather, one feels or intuits the Tao. Sometimes the Tao is said to be discovered in a sudden enlightenment. This experience and its object can be conceptualized, and the spiritual path to the experience can in a sense be taught; but conceptual knowledge of the Tao does not bear the appropriate cognitive relation to it. One must find the Tao in feeling the universe in a certain "true" way and in feeling oneself in the process of moving with the universe. The concept of Tao cannot be separated from the enlightened experience of Tao, and that experience includes feeling and creativity as well as conceptualization.

In his remarkable book *Creativity and Taoism*, Chang Chung-yuan exposites the basic meaning of the Tao in terms of two phrases, the "invisible ground of sympathy" and the "immeasurable potentialities of creativity."[22] The first phrase refers to a fundamental ontological condition: each thing contains within it the entire universe. To be is to contain the universe. That is part of what it means to be a manifestation of the Tao. *Sympathy* is taken literally. A thing contains the universe by "feeling with" the universe. To bring this "feeling with," or sympathy, to full consciousness requires the enlightenment of an Immortal. Once enlightened, however, a person is supposed to appreciate this sympathy as being quite ordinary.

The Tao is not static "being" but a flow, an ever-changing "becoming" of elements, often described as interactions of the polarities, yin and yang. Although each present moment is in sympathy with its world, its own nature is to be spontaneous, not necessitated by the world it feels but a fresh reaction upon it. There is something of an asymmetry in the temporal flow of the Tao.

Chang Chung-yuan points out in numerous contexts the similarity of the Tao with the nature of process as described by Whitehead. He did not, however, sufficiently draw out the correspondence between the "invisible ground of sympathy" and Whitehead's concept of "feeling," the existential act by which the past is taken up into a present occasion as a component of its present nature. A present reality *is* the "prehension" of the entire world that exists as available to be "prehended." It is a prehension that integrates the elements of the world in a concrete, individual reality with an individual perspective. Whitehead also called his prehensions "feelings." His view is responsive to the need mentioned above to emphasize feeling.

Chang's phrase, "immeasurable potentialities of creativity," refers to the spontaneity by which each thing—or better, "event"—creates itself. He describes it in the following way:

> Lao Tzu says: "Tao never acts, yet through it nothing is undone. . . . All things create themselves" (*Tao Teh Ching*, chap. 37).
> Whitehead explains this concept of self-creativity in Western terms: "Creativity is without a character of its own. . . . It is

the ultimate notion of the highest generality at the base of actuality. It cannot be characterized because all characters are more special than itself. But creativity is always found under conditions and described as conditioned." (*Process and Reality,* p. 47)

This is what the Taoist would refer to as self-creativity. We can only see creativity in its manifestations, only as conditioned. "*Tao* never acts, yet through it nothing is undone." "Changes take place by themselves, without movement; things reveal themselves, without display." To be free from the confusion of external conditions, to be rid of the perplexities of life, to be fully charged with primordial creativity, is to attain *Tao.*[23]

The spontaneity of a thing's own existence, or the happening of an event, is consistent with its sympathy with the world: an event is made of the world it takes in, a coordination of sympathies. The *way* it takes in and coordinates its sympathies with the world, however, is its own being, its present and spontaneous existence. An event is self-causing, even though the material from which it causes itself is given in sympathy. In the Tao, the sympathy of connection and the spontaneity of immediate existence are inseparable.

The concept of the Tao makes some direct suggestions regarding values in thinking. They stem from the concept of "nonaction" (*wu-wei*). Realizing the nature of the Tao, a person is true to this realization by cultivating nonaction. Neither still nor motionless, nonaction, rather, is action that does not involve force against other parts of nature. It is in perfect sympathy with the environment, yet is spontaneous, as the sudden brush strokes of the calligrapher are in complete harmony with the subject yet are completely original and idiosyncratic. The cry of a baby or a spontaneous expression of emotion or insight are in tune with the Tao (*Tao Teh Ching*, chap. 55); words that argue or provide reasons in expectation of controversy are not (chap. 81). Knowledge requiring study and extension of oneself beyond an environment with which there can be conscious sympathy is dangerous (chap. 56). Benevolence is a natural emotion, but calculation of benevolence supposes an opposition of right and wrong (chap. 38). Any social organization requiring cooperation that might turn to competition is contrary to the Tao. A ruler contravenes the Tao in attempting to impose order or justice (chap. 48); a ruler in accord with the Tao lets things happen, bringing order by controlling the line of retreat (chaps. 29, 30). Thinking should be visionary and empathetic but not theoretical (chap. 41), full of surprises but not cunning (chap. 47), expressive of the principles of life but not instrumental or administrative (chap. 49).

This is a difficult philosophy with which to run an empire, and the Confucianists developed a counterpoise to the Taoists regarding the Tao.

Confucianism recognized that whatever the virtues of natural sympathy and spontaneity, civilization requires constant attention to the distinction between right and wrong. The distinction between the "Superior Man" and his inferiors was of great importance, consisting largely of the former's being more serious about the virtues of humanity, righteousness, propriety, and wisdom. The Confucianist Mencius developed a brilliant moral theory based on the view that these virtues stem from innate perceptions of people, indeed, from an innate sympathy (*Mencius* 2A:b). Although perhaps he does not take in the whole of the cosmos, a Superior Man has an innate sympathy with the morally significant aspects of the human sphere. The seriousness with which a Superior Man is supposed to pursue these virtues was explicated as a matter of sincerity. In Confucianism, sincerity is a state of personality in which there is a translucency in the connections between one's inner heart, cultivated to be tranquil, and one's outer actions, made morally responsive to the "ten thousand things" in the world. A person's inner heart should show in the person's outer actions (*The Doctrine of the Mean*). Indeed, through the thinking concerned with cultivation of one's own character, a person might affect the world. The *Great Learning*, attributed to Confucius, says:

> When things are investigated, knowledge is extended; when knowledge is extended, the will becomes sincere; when the will is sincere, the mind is rectified; when the mind is rectified, the personal life is cultivated; when the personal life is cultivated, the family will be regulated; when the family is regulated, the state will be in order; and when the state is in order, there will be peace throughout the world. From the Son of Heaven down to the common people, all must regard cultivation of the personal life as the root or foundation.[24]

In practice, the Confucian conception of thinking relative to society emphasized cultivation of personal authenticity through arts and letters. Instead of believing, with Plato, that reason guides through persuasion, or, with Aristotle, that practical reasoning and *theoria* lead to consensual deliberation, the Confucianists emphasized the exemplary force of thinking: the virtue of the rulers whose lives are thoughtfully lived should trickle down by imitation to ministers and people. Filial piety and respect for superiors provide the motive force for imitation. A person is supposed to attain human strength, excellence, and virtue by absorbing those qualities from people earlier or higher.

Alas, in practice, domination of society by the character of leaders too often displayed the downward tendencies Plato described in Book 8 of *The*

Republic, rather than the ideals the Confucianists ascribed to the ancients. Confucianism, then, was subject to two attacks, one from the Taoists and one from the legalists. The legalists, concerned with effective government and the universal application of laws, advocated the use of reward and punishment as the primary force of government. Not only were reward and punishment considered more important than exemplary reason, but the scholars, or literati, were derided as argumentative and ineffective, and enlightened rulers were supposed to ban books and records.[25] The more contemplative Taoists advocated withdrawal from important affairs and delighted in poking fun at certain pompous Confucianists whose self-righteous seriousness was a fine subject for sport. On a more systematic level, the Taoists criticized the Confucian emphasis on exact description and naming. Related to sincerity, the "rectification of names" was a Confucian ideal for personal life, scholarship, and statecraft. The Taoists argued, however, that *all* names and descriptions distort; the perspectival surface of things which can be named is not the Tao. The Confucianists were thus committed unwillingly to both ineffectiveness and superficiality. Their conception of thinking and its relation to society became idealistic, in the pejorative sense, tolerable when little depended on it but dangerous in times of stress. This created a vacuum in social thinking that was filled successively by magical Taoism and by Buddhism.

Through the development of Neo-Confucianism in the Sung and Ming dynasties, the remarkable feat was accomplished of synthesizing the principal intentions of Taoism, Buddhism, and ancient Confucianism. In agreement with the more contemplative Taoists (in contrast to the Taoist magicians), Neo-Confucianism elaborated a systematic cosmology. This allowed for an interpretation of human life as a focal element in the cosmos, whose distinguishing mark is the presence of *li*, a cosmic moral principle that also determines the structure of things. With the Buddhists (and Taoists, who were reinforced in this by Buddhism), the Neo-Confucianists advocated a careful, systematic cultivation of the personality, with special attention paid to meditative insights and realizations. With the Confucianists, all this was made relevant to the problems of social life. Although philosophy was not to be limited to studying the human sphere, as Confucius urged, it *at least* had to study human nature and society. The Neo-Confucianists carefully criticized Buddhism and Taoism for their inattention to the problems of civilization and social life, and most were sympathetic to attacks on Buddhist and Taoist monasticism, which drained people from the work force, the tax rolls, and the army.

The contribution of Neo-Confucianism to the problem of thinking can be focused in terms of a dispute between its two greatest figures. The Sung philosopher Chu Hsi (1130–1200 C.E.), the greatest and most original of the synthesizers, emphasized that thinking of all worthwhile sorts rests on "the investigation of things," a phrase from the ancient *Great Learning* quoted above. By "investigation of things" Chu Hsi meant the discernment of "principle" in outer things and in oneself. It provides the foundation for—and, in fact, results in—the cultivation of the will, mind, and personal life. In his early days, Chu emphasized the investigation of outer things by examination of texts and observation; later he emphasized the discernment of principle within the self. His philosophy has been called "rationalistic" because the objectivity of knowledge provides the foundation and guide to moral, or personal, development.

The Ming philosopher Wang Yang-ming (1472–1529 C.E.) agreed with Chu on most points, but Wang disagreed seriously about one doctrine. Arguing that the investigation of things is likely to be corrupted if the will and the inner mind are not first rectified, he rearranged the order of items in the *Great Learning*, putting sincerity of the will first. This was in accord with the older text that Chu Hsi had altered.[26] Wang put equal emphasis on the need for perception and action in the proper preparation of the mind, saying that neither insight nor action will be correct if the inner heart is not ready. He developed the concept of the heart-mind as the inner spontaneous source of life. The cosmic principle within the heart-mind is that which opens up the principles of external things to knowledge, as well as the principle that guides proper moral action. Indeed, he argued that fully to know an external thing is to act properly with respect to it, to will it according to its own principle.

Wang's conception of thinking stressed sympathy. With the early Taoists, he believed that one's heart-mind sympathetically contains the world, being one body with the world. This is experienced most easily in quiet repose; but that is not the only or even the most authentic, source of participation in cosmic principle. The source is best discovered through concrete action. Wang, a great general, statesman, and administrator, was not only a Confucian model but an effective agent in bringing what he considered the "order of heaven" to the affairs of mankind.

For the Neo-Confucianists generally, society greatly needs careful, considered thinking, in matters both of exemplifying excellence and making policy. Like Plato, they argued that thinking is instrumental to life; but more than Plato, they stressed the need—within thinking—for a sympathetic, cultivated feeling of things, a meditative appreciation of the world. They believed thinking's ideal response to feeling is a spontaneous surge of the heart that issues in action formed by concrete principle, action that might be verbal, decision-making, war-waging, calligraphic writing, or the quick

painting of a bamboo shoot. The Neo-Confucianists emphasized that thinking should be grounded in aesthetic and practical experience, deeply
appreciated.

Plato and Aristotle need not be the only cultural and intellectual
sources for a contemporary cosmology of thinking. Ours is a time when the
Chinese tradition is also available. Its importance for a reconstruction of
thinking lies in three main points. First, it expresses an entire culture that
has integrated fact and value, and our cosmology can be assessed with regard
to whether it faithfully acknowledges this achievement. Second, our cosmology can be assessed similarly, according to its sensitivity to the importance
of feeling and spontaneity in Chinese culture. Whereas Western culture has
subordinated feeling and spontaneity to judgment, Chinese culture has not.
Third, the Chinese philosophical systems provide categories by which a cosmology can be sensitive in these areas, and a cosmology of thinking can
employ them where appropriate. In particular, the doctrine of Wang Yang-
ming, that heart-mind involves moral discernment at its core, can support
the general contention that thinking is based on valuation. Furthermore,
Wang's notion that knowing and acting are somehow one is a doctrinal
counter to Aristotle's separation of theory from *praxis* and to Plato's spe-
cializing of reason to the point that it easily loses its grip on things. Western
culture has stumbled over the limitations in Plato's and Aristotle's views,
but the old ideas of China provide paths around them.

3

Axiological Cosmology

There is no way to avoid an abstract, detailed, disciplined discussion in the construction of a cosmological theory. The discipline of philosophical cosmology is as difficult in its way as that of physical cosmology. It requires familiarity with a style of thinking different from both critical essays and dialectical argument. Critical essays begin and remain with terms whose initial meanings are familiar; cosmology begins by attempting to define new basic categories that promise philosophical advancement precisely because of their novelty and their escape from patterns defined by familiar categories. Dialectical philosophical arguments, especially those written for journals, posit reasons for one's philosophical opponents to change opinions; cosmology, by contrast, attempts to offer a new way of thinking or theorizing, and its arguments have the general form, not of inference according to logical rules, but of explicating hypotheses by analogies and metaphors that become new technical terms. Once explicated into clear-cut categories and principles, a new cosmological theory allows its terms to be defined relative to one another and its assertions to be deduced internal to itself.

Reading a cosmological theory for the first time can be like reading the rules of a game before actually playing it. Then one rereads and thinks about the assertions as if one were playing the game, practicing thinking according to the rules. Learning a cosmological theory can also be like learning a language—unfamiliar, discomforting, and unintelligible except when translated fragment by fragment into an already known language. The very intent of new cosmologies, however, if not new languages, is to say things that cannot be said in other terms. This becomes apparent when one becomes familiar with its texture and idioms. After a while, the new rules of thinking, the new language, become a perspective on the world from which it is possible to see things otherwise invisible.

Expecting a cosmology to "make sense" early on, to relate to common experience, or to be illustrated in familiar terms can be a mistake leading to frustration and anger. Strictly speaking, if a set of categories is abstract enough to be a cosmology, it is illustrated by everything and, therefore, not significantly by anything. Explanatory examples distort the cosmology by being more specific than is warranted. To relate cosmology to experience requires going beyond vague categories to specifying carefully those categories in describing other things. The rhetorical development of cosmological categories moves from the initial abstract statements to greater application to various aspects of thinking. If one does not become at ease with the abstractions, however, applying them to more specific matters will seem needlessly technical and jargonistic. Repeated reading and moving from the specific to the abstract will provide that ease; then the description of a specific matter in the technical cosmological terms will seem a pleasurable advance in knowledge, a grasping of new connections rather than obscuration. The long-range usefulness of the cosmology is that when it has provided descriptions of many specific matters, the coherence of its categories allows comparison of specific areas. In turn, this helps identify what is fundamental or most important in all the areas studied.

The cosmology to be used in the reconstruction of thinking is introduced in this chapter and is developed in detail where it is needed below. The section "Cosmological Categories" defines the basic categories and the units of thinking for a cosmological theory of occasions. The section "The Body, Nature, and Society" specifies these to the topics indicated in the title. A metaphysical theory of value is necessary to define the axiological character of the cosmology; this is the topic of the section "A Metaphysics of Value." The last section, "Cosmology: Norms and Good Thinking," relates the value theory to thinking.

COSMOLOGICAL CATEGORIES

The basic cosmological concepts of the axiological position here are those originated by Whitehead as amended in the notes or the text.[1] The purpose of this discussion is to introduce the concept of "occasions" and show its revolutionary impact on the concept of causation in order to provide a naturalistic vision of thinking.

Occasions

The most unusual element in this cosmology, compared with common sense, is that its basic unit of existence is conceived of as an occasion. The significance of this can be seen by contrasting it with the position it denies. Both our common sense and most philosophical cosmologies (excepting the process tradition stemming from Whitehead) agree that substances, not occasions, are the basic units. As we usually think of it, a substance is concrete and has a continuous identity. It undergoes a career relative to things around it; and it can change internally in some respects, although not "substantially," without ceasing to be what it is and turning into a different substance. In a substance, identity and continuity derive from the stuff or matter of which it is made, while change derives from different forms which the matter assumes at different times. A substance is unique and individual because of its own matter, even if it shares the same forms and qualities of other things.

By contrast, in the cosmology presented here, the basic unit is an occasion—not a substance but a happening. This is a radical change in conceptual foundations, a point which will be stressed in the following chapters. There are two ways of analyzing an occasion. We can ask, What happened? Answers to this question depict the occasion as a thing, a concrete determination of the world. This line of questioning leads to accounting for the same phenomena that substance-philosophies stress: definite data. On the other hand, we can ask how the occasion happened. Answers to this describe how the occasion came about, even how the occasion felt to itself as it was happening and before it became a past fact. Phenomena accounted for here include those dear to existentialists and to others who object to treating life and decisions as mere things. These two approaches to occasions lay the conceptual groundwork for many of the distinctions related to thinking that are made below in this book.[2] A word of caution here: such terms as *occasion* are defined technically, not according to commonsense meanings. Most commonsense meanings are substantialist in their philosophical commitments and can be trusted only at introductory phases.

Let us begin with a technical definition. An "occasion" is the prehending of the world into a harmonious, definite individual. (Although that sentence is semantically meaningless in a substantialist model, it is acceptable in a process model.) "Prehension," like "occasion," is a relatively primitive term in the cosmology and is also a radical reversal of usual modes of thought. To say that an occasion prehends something is to say that it grasps, or takes in, that other thing as part of its own being. The very "stuff" of an occasion is the set of finished prior occasions separately prehended and harmonized as a unique, new occasion. The *reality* and *essence* of an occasion is its unification of its many prehensions of the various things in its past into one internally harmonious prehension of the world as a whole. Because most things in the world cannot be synthesized in the same individual, they must be "eliminated"; the process of elimination is the heart of harmonization.

This conceptual scheme reverses the commonsense view that substances are internally fixed and are grasped by other things only externally. The popular view of knowledge is that a known thing is represented in the knower by an idea, with the object outside and the representation inside. The difficulty with this view comes in comparing the two to check the truth of the idea.[3] In the present theory, an occasion "knows" by including the object known in its own being, modified only by being made compatible with the other things prehended. In substance theory, the usual view of causation is that one substance imparts force and direction to another, although what the force is and how it works on that view is mysterious. In the axiological cosmology, causation consists in the cause becoming a conditioning component in the internal harmonization of the effect; its energy stems from the requirement that it be taken into account, and consists in the antecedent occasion to which the harmonizing occasion must conform. Prehension is general to all natural causations. Only some prehensions are cognitive: electrons prehend, but they do not think.

Two points illustrate the revolutionary significance of Whitehead's conception of "occasions prehending." The first is a reversal of the usual conception of *agency*. In the substance view, we imagine that the earlier thing—the cause—is the agent producing the later thing—the effect. Even in theories of reciprocal causation (the head causing a depression in the pillow, for instance), the agent is the actualized thing which imparts actuality to the potential thing. Within the axiological cosmology, however, action takes place only in the present. It is the emerging occasion that acts. Precisely because they have completed their processes of becoming fully actual, past occasions can no longer act and cannot be agents causing the effect. In this sense, the emerging occasion is self-creating. On the other hand, since self-creation consists in an occasion's making a unitary, definite individual out of the factual entities of past occasions which it prehends, the past occasions are "causes." The past occasions are the sources of the emerging occasion; because of that, they limit what the emerging occasion can become. Although an emerging occasion might combine its prehended initial data into novel patterns, it must work with the occasions given. Axiological metaphors of causation, then, center on an emerging occasion's taking up, or grasping, or prehending, or feeling its past. The metaphors have a dual character, referring, on the one hand, to the creativity involved in combining the past occasions, and on the other, to the limitations imposed by past occasions.

The second point of significance for the axiological cosmology is that the causal relations between an occasion and its past conditions are explicated in terms of articulating the patterns in the environment out of which the occasion arises. This contrasts with the rhetoric of the substance theory, which suggests looking in the environment for the thing that is the cause. The structures of the environmental patterns, the ecosystems of which the emerging occasion is a part, are the crucial factors for the axiological cosmology. Since the emerging occasion itself plays various roles in patterns and systems, physical causation may be analyzed in abstraction from particular occasions as patterned interplays among systematically interrelated things.

With these general remarks about the cosmology, the discussion may proceed directly to the cosmology of thinking.

Units of Thinking

As a first hypothesis in the theory, let us suppose that the most rudimentary structure in any occasion in which thinking takes place involves the following.

The first is the grasping of an object: objects may be included within the occasion of thinking even if they are not consciously thought or intended. The objects in such an occasion are its primary contents and material.

The second hypothesis is that there is the actual activity of grasping objects; the occasion in which objects are thought adds something new, in addition to what was in the objects apart from the occasion in which they are thought. Except for antecedent thinking, which existed prior to the occasion in question, the activity of thinking in the occasion is spontaneous. Although the result of thinking possibly might be predetermined by the character of the objects thought, the existential reality of thinking them is new. Spontaneity may range from mere repetition of objects in the new occasion to highly creative rearrangements and reconstructions of objects, in order to produce a genuinely new thought.

The third hypothesis is the intention that is thought in the occasion. Comprised of the objects grasped, by the spontaneous activity of thinking, the thought occasioned in the occasion is the result. After the occasion, we identify the occasion by the thought it contains: "My thought then was *that she was here*." By imaginatively projecting ourselves into the occasion as it was happening, the result is the object to be thought as an intention. Intentionality is guidance of the occasion to its intended result. A completed occasion of thought is a concrete actuality which itself is ready to be an object for a subsequent occasion of thinking. Thus objects play two roles for any occasion of thinking: past objects are given as what Whitehead called "initial data," and objects are the intended thoughts which would satisfy the activity of thinking within the occasion. A thought which is the intentional outcome of one occasion may be an initial datum for another occasion. If a thought is a pure perception, its initial data and intended objects are the same, or they are similar.

Nothing in this hypothesis implies that an occasion of thinking goes on within a thinker who is substantially separate from the objects prehended or intended. Rather, this hypothesis is part of a larger cosmological view (discussed below), according to which enduring thinkers are themselves composed of both thinking occasions and other kinds of occasions. In this hypothesis, an occasion of thinking is more primitive than a thinker who thinks. Although the significance of this is developed below, certain features are readily apparent, which, because they present thinking as a component of nature, bear on the reconstruction of the concept of thinking.

The First Feature. Among these features it is apparent that, first, an occasion of thinking entails an intrinsic and natural connection between whatever objects are thought and the private contributions of the moment. In the rudimentary structure of a thinking occasion, a real, initial object is given. While the spontaneous activity of thinking might make an imaginary duplicate of the object and employ the duplicate in its intended resulting thought, the real object is initially present in the occasion. If the initial object is itself a thought, it is initially present just as it resulted from the occasion in which it was originally thought; if the initial object is a physical thing or a social phenomenon, it is also initially present as physical or social.

This hypothesis may seem strange to those accustomed to viewing an act of thought as confined to a thinker. If an object is something other than the thinker—a house, for instance—then it would seem that not the house itself but only a representation can be in the thinking. The representation theory has given rise to the insurmountable difficulty of judging whether the thinker's representation corresponds to what it is supposed to represent. It has led some theorists to suppose that there is no real object, only an ordered set of representations. It should be noted, however, that the representational view itself is just one hypothesis about thinking—that it takes place within a thinker who is separate from at least some objects and who, therefore, must reproduce them. The hypothesis presented in this book—that thinking consists of occasions of thinking—is an alternative, which is not to be judged by presupposing the representativists' hypothesis to be common sense.

The Second Feature. Because each thought intended in an occasion becomes a potential datum for future occasions when the occasion has become a past happening, it is subject to two universal norms, namely, that each thought necessarily exhibits the characteristics and conditions of thinkability (that is, each must not only be intendable but also thinkable, in the sense of being able to enter a future thinking occasion as an initial datum), and that each thought must in principle be judicable according to the relevant norms of good thinking, whether or not it approximates these norms. The norms vary with the kinds of thought involved and the context of thinking. Because the norms are universal (as is argued below), the factual character of a finished occasion of thinking is ineluctably public. Even if the thoughts are not expressed in a public medium, and even if the thinker does not recall them, in this hypothesis the form of a finished thought has the potential for entering later thought; hence, in principle, it is measurable according to the norms of thinking.

The Third Feature. It follows from the discussion of the previous two features that thinking is simultaneously a subjective act and an objective worldly act, two distinguishable aspects of the same process of spontaneously working initial data into intended thoughts. The spontaneous activity in a thinking occasion is immediately what it is. Receiving external influences only in its initial data, an occasion of thinking cannot be influenced directly by contemporary occasions. Nor can a thinking occasion influence other occasions until it is over and its definite thoughts enter future occasions as initial data. The happening of an occasion is private.

Still, the initial data of an occasion comprise objects in the real, past world, not mental reproductions of an external world. The occasion of thinking is continuous with other events in nature. In this hypothesis, *nature* has a significance to the thinking occasion somewhat different from what it has in most other hypotheses. Its initial objects include not only physical things but past thoughts as well; the past thoughts may be expressed not only in symbolic artifacts such as speech or print, but also in states of the nervous system. From the standpoint of linguistic physiology, it is difficult to say how a past thought enters as thought when its physical nature is a state of the brain. Similarly, it is difficult to say how a past thought enters a thinking occasion when its physical nature is an auditory perturbation of the air or marks on a page. In part, the difficulty is empirical, in finding out how the mind works. More interestingly, the difficulty stems from philosophically conceiving of what it is to be mental and also physical. We will return to this point shortly.

Despite the immediacy of spontaneity, its products—the thoughts that occur in an occasion of thinking—enter the resulting environment and must be formed with the potential for doing that. It may be said, then, that an occasion of thought results from the objects that go into it and that it is constrained in its intention by the requirement that it find a place among objects in a future world. This hypothesis presents thinking as a cosmological event, as a happening within nature, not as a mental event continuous only with other mental events and merely reflective of nonmental events.

The Fourth Feature. The fourth feature is an hypothesis about a thinking occasion that is a specification or subclass of the larger hypothesis which is similar to that presented by Whitehead about *all* occasions in nature. According to the Whiteheadian hypothesis, every occasion takes its rise by prehending previous occasions as its initial data; it spontaneously integrates these data by sorting, selecting, and combining them according to the occasion's unique subjective form; and, it satisfies its own existential demand to issue in a definite, individual, concrete happening by objectifying the results of its spontaneous integration. For Whitehead, "mentality" meant the special contributions made by the subjective process of integration to the initial physical data. Thus each occasion begins with an initial physical pole, moves through a mental pole of subjective integration, and issues in a new physical reality.

There is a difficulty with Whitehead's use of the word "mentality." Since there is considerable continuity of thought, among the most important objects taken in as initial data must be previous thoughts. In fact, most thinking involves not one occasion but a series of thinking occasions. The antecedent thinking occasions may be taken in naturally as elements of antecedent physical occasions; they are the mental, or "thought," elements in these occasions. Whitehead called this kind of prehension "hybrid" because, although its object is physical, what is prehended is the mentality that went into its physical construction. That is to say, some of the objects among the initial data of a thinking occasion are the prior occasions' thoughts; thinking, or mentality, involves continuity from thought to thought. As will be argued later, Whitehead's hypothesis is correct in claiming that the beginning and end of each occasion is a natural state that presents features, some of which are best described in physical terms, while others are best described in mental terms.

In the larger cosmological view, a thinking occasion is an occasion like any natural one, except that in the thinking occasion, mental elements are important. An occasion in a stone may have some mentality, in Whitehead's sense, because there is minimal spontaneity in the integration of its stony predecessors among its initial data into its own intended stony nature. But there is little spontaneous novelty and, therefore, little mentality. Insofar as we know, occasions in stones do not keep thoughts from prior occasions among their initial data, nor are they available to future stone occasions as thoughts. Thus the continuity we experience in real thinking is foreign to them. The complexity of human social context and the human nervous system enables occasions in human beings sometimes to exhibit great novelty and continuity of thought from one to the next. In human beings, a continuity of mind is such that occasions in the nervous system, and perhaps elsewhere, are important for *both* their physical interrelations *and* their semantic ones. We assume this to be true in experience and believe it to be implausible only when we think about what physical and mental things are supposed to be according to some theory in which they are separate substances.

The Fifth Feature. Because thinking occasions are those *natural* occasions in which thinking assumes great importance, thinking occasions have physical components and arise from the web of physical relations in which they occur naturally. This was asserted above in noting that physical things are among the initial objects of thinking occasions. The importance of the point is that there is a continuum within occasions, reaching from elements which plainly are physical in the commonsense view to those which are mental. Since thinking is the experience of the occasion from within the spontaneity of its occurring, awareness ranges from the sort whose objects are already intellectually formed with symbolic meanings down to the kind of "physical feel" one sort of "meat" has for its impinging tissues. Toward the physical pole, the language of feeling oneself "caused" is more appropriate than the language of "meaning" because physical objects have less the character of signs. Within the larger cosmological hypothesis, thinking must be construed as a special kind of being caused (initial objects) and causing (intention). This hypothesis is able to account for and legitimate a far wider range of awareness than is possible in theories of representative thinking, in which all objects of thought must have the cognitive structure of representations.

The Sixth Feature. The sixth feature or hypothesis differs significantly in one important point from that typical of the phenomenology of Edmund Husserl (that is, apart from the controversial claim that Husserl's view is an hypothesis rather than a phenomenological description or a transcendental deduction). For Husserl, all acts of thought are intentional, possessing their objects by intending them. Objects are possessed by thought only through being intended. By contrast, for the present hypothesis, there are two modes in which a thinking occasion possesses objects: as initial data and as intended result. The objects possessed in the former mode are those which are transformed and objectified in the latter mode. There is no material of thought which does not find objectification in intentional form. All thought is intentional insofar as it can be an object for later thought; thus all self-conscious thought is intentional—or, in the language of the preceding chapter, all thought involves judgment. Thinking also bears the subjective marks of its origin in some initial objects which do not have the form of intended thoughts. There is a physicality to thinking that may be ignored by paying attention to objects solely in the sense in which the occasion intends them. The occasion also can feel itself being caused by objects, and sensitivity may inform the intended thought with feelings of physical emergence. This is the root of the cosmology's account of feeling, in contrast to judgment. *What* a nonintentional object feels like among initial data cannot be thought *about* except by being transformed into intentional form, into a sign. But the intentional thought that does this should give expression to its feeling of physical origin. Whitehead's theory of objects, described above as the two modes in which objects enter occasions of thought, is the decisive point of difference between the interpretation of experience in process philosophy and that in the phenomenological tradition. Because objects entering as initial data establish occasions of thinking continuous with other natural processes, from the process perspective, Husserl's move from the natural to the transcendental standpoint has little special philosophic significance. If it is insisted on, the move is a denaturing mistake.

BODY, NATURE, AND SOCIETY

The presentation of the hypothesis in the previous section may have given the impression that the world consists of objects. In one sense, this is accurate, each object being an occasion in which certain prior objects are objectified in a new way. However, a grab bag of objects does not make a world.

The objects presented as initial data to occasions, including presentation to thinking occasions, come organized in various structures. For example, if a painting is presented with some objects on the left side and some on the right, the left-right arrangement is included among the initial data of an occasion that experiences the painting as a complex object. If the occasion begins not only with the painting among its initial data but also focuses attention on it—that is, *intends* the painting—then the occasion is, at least in part, one in which the painting is perceived. To be a true perception, the painting as a complex intended object must be seen as having its left parts on the left and its right parts on the right. Of course, the intention of the occasion could focus on something other than the painting; in that case, the painting would be relegated to the background of experience or excluded altogether.

Occasions of an individual's experience always take place within the human body. This means that among the initial data of any occasion are the other bodily occasions organized in the normal patterns of physiology. One may perceive a car going by; the perception is an intentional thought. However, entering the perceptive occasion are the organized structures of the body which influence the thought of the car. The perception takes visual form because of the optic system, and auditory form because of the auditory system. If the car goes by close to the body, its vibrations affect the bones, its wind touches the skin and perhaps affects one's balance, and a slight perturbation of temperature is felt. In theories of representative cognition, this situation would be explained by saying that the car itself, with its component occasions, does not directly enter the perceptive occasion but is represented by visual, auditory, and other sensa which substitute for it. In the present theory, however, this paradoxical deletion of the perceived object is unnecessary. The car is among the initial data, and so are the occasions in the body which themselves have been affected by the car. To think of the car in an intentional way requires integrating many of these initial objects.

If every past object in the world presented itself democratically among the initial data of a thinking occasion, the confusion would be impossible! The only way the occasion could come to some definite intentional result would be to exclude from its intention nearly all the initial data. Objects do not present themselves democratically, however. The objects in the body have orders of dominance. By organizing the world of objects according to their visual, auditory, and other sensory effects, the order of the world is made manageable in thought. Although bodily perceptions are more varied and subtle than we pay conscious attention to, they are vastly simplified compared with the democratic welter of real occasions. The value of sensory initial data lies in their transparency. Through our customary ways of integrating sensations among our initial data, it is possible to intend the car with focused attention. The customary organization of experience reflects the dominance of the organization of objects or occasions within our bodies. It is not enough to say that the same car can be perceived by two people because it is the same car; they also need similar bodies with similar sensory experience. Without that, they could not integrate their experience so as to have similar perceptive intentions of the car, although the same car would enter both people among their initial data.

The continuity of experience through a chain of thinking occasions also depends on the relative stability of bodily structure. As William James pointed out, part of the way by which I feel previous thoughts to be mine is by feeling their kinetic sense to be continuous with my present kinetic feeling. I feel my present thought taking place within my body, and I felt my past thoughts take place within the same body. Even though the occasions of my body that I feel as immediate are different from those in my body an

hour ago, it is the continuity of the organization of the body that is important, because it is that organization which gives the integration of data its
typical dominant forms.

The limits of an occasion's spontaneity are set by the possibilities for
it inherent in the environment from which it arises. The world presents itself
as structured in various specific ways, and the occasion must cope with
those structures. Furthermore, the various structures of the world tend to
endure, however briefly, and even when they change in relationship to each
other, those enduring structures do so in ways that are reinforced by their
mutual interdependence. The world is highly systematic, although perhaps
not as systematic as to be rigid in mechanism. Consequently, the occasions
occurring in much the same place tend to be presented with much the same
sort of initial data; such occasions tend to solve the problem of their integration in much the same way. Stony occasions, for instance, tend to be repeti-
tive. The richer and more organized the environment out of which an occasion arises, the more possibilities that exist for spontaneous variation.

As the subjective process of integration gains sufficient complexity for
intentional thinking, resolution of the occasion aims not only at its own
immediate integration but also at some effects in the future. The intentional
object of most thought is not merely the thought itself in its material immediacy, but the thought as leading to some further meaning, some interpre-
tant; or the thought as the initiation of action carried out by the organized
physiological systems of the body. When an occasion aims at the future, it
must subject itself to a further limitation on its spontaneity: the future must
tolerate its results. It must limit itself to what is compatible with the likely
continuities of the systematic arrangements of nature, society, and the
semantics of thought. Indeed, one can imagine few thinking occasions in
which intention does not build into itself a fitness for further effects. Thinking, like the action of a moving arm, must comport itself in such a way as to
observe, conform to, and intentionally make its mark in the future world
that provides its context.

Some occasions of thought differ significantly from occasions of arm
movements precisely because the thoughts have few noticeable physical consequences outside the brain. Reverie, musement, idle speculation—all are
kinds of thinking that require continuity between many thought occasions
themselves but do not greatly conform to semantic structures beyond themselves. Perception, description, explanation, deliberation, evaluation, and
emotions all take form with some reference to large-scale, meaningful structures. Intentional thoughts which are purposive and initiate overt action conform even more to the environing systems of the world. To the extent that
thoughts intend consequences—more thinking or overt action—which are

meaningful when measured by norms but which do not necessarily embody those norms, thinking intends to be logical.

Phenomenologists and process philosophers have shown that thinking is much richer than the mere interpretation of signs according to grammars of surface and deep structures. Most thinking, however, is *also* the interpretation of signs; thus, thinking takes place within the social context in which signs arise. People learn to think because they engage in social interactions which provide them with signs and habits of interpretation as initial data. Thinking requires culture, and culture requires society. Thinking is a process within which society itself is directly present. Seen from this perspective, the question of whether there are "other minds" is absurd. Clearly, my mind includes other minds—and vice versa. Although I can invent signs of my own to some degree, and although all my signs are affected by being thought in the context of my unique body, my signs are largely inherited social signs, and I intend meanings for them which abide within the horizon of the social community's various signs.

Thinking is not an activity performed by a thinker; rather, a thinker is comprised of continuous and semantically connected occasions of thought that take place within a broad social context. Indeed, it is the steadiness and enduring quality of culture in the society that provides much of our sense of personal continuity: not only do my past thoughts feel like mine because of my body, they feel like mine because of the particular history of my thinking as it recognizes things within the sign system of the community.

This section has attempted to relate the basic categories of the cosmology of thinking to recognizable items in our world, to the human body, to nature, and to society. This could be done only with general examples here. A more direct argument could be made only if the cosmology were expressed in terms of specific theories of human physiology, of natural processes, and social structure. Nonetheless, what has been said is enough to give the cosmology some applicability.

The crucial category for the axiological cosmology—namely, value—has not yet been introduced. For this we must turn to a discussion of metaphysics.

A METAPHYSICS OF VALUE

Whereas cosmology deals with the generic traits of this world, metaphysics has been described as the study of the traits that would be exemplified in any possible world.[4] A preferable characterization is what metaphysics is the study of determinateness: any world would have to have some identity, and identity is being determinately one character rather than something else. The features that accrue to determinateness can be called transcendental in keeping with Western medieval usage; they must be exhibited in any determination. Vagueness is an attribute of cosmology (as Chapter 2 points out) and of metaphysics as well; in fact, cosmology is a specification of metaphysics to the traits of *this* world. Although some contemporary philosophers use the word *ontology* to mean study of the basic kinds of existence, here that study is covered by the terms *metaphysics* and *cosmology*. Thus, *ontology* can be reserved for its older meaning—the study of why anything determinate exists. The question of value, as conceived of here, is metaphysical because it is a transcendental property of anything determinate.

This use of "transcendental" differs from that common in contemporary philosophy, which derives from Immanuel Kant. For Kant, the chief problem of knowledge was whether the thinking of a subject could include necessary knowledge of external objects. If the object is external in the sense that it transcends experience, then knowledge of it is "transcendent," and Kant said we have no such knowledge. However, if the object conforms to the conditions for entering experience, and if we know those conditions, we can know the object as appearance through those conditions. Kant used the word "transcendental" (not "transcendent") to describe the conditions for an object's appearing in experience. The study of those conditions is transcendental philosophy.[5] There is no necessity, however, to share Kant's assumption about the privacy of thinking and the consequent transcendent character of external objects.[6] Rather, objects are external and objective but naturally available to enter the experience of knowers. Metaphysics proceeds through dialectical reflection on how things must be in order to have determinate character (this is not to suggest that determinate things are determinate in all respects).

As a preliminary consideration it may be observed that any determinate thing must be complex. It must contain some conditional features by virtue of which it is related to and different from other things; it must also contain essential features by which it has its own perspective in terms of which it can be different. Without conditional features the thing could never be "this" rather than "that"; part of being determinate is having some kind of otherness as a constituent part of the determinate character. Without essential features it would be impossible for the thing to have the self-standing by which it could be *other*.[7] Since metaphysical claims should be specifiable in any possible world, they may be made plausible by specification to an Aristotelian cosmology as well as to the axiological cosmology. In Aristotle, the essence in the formal cause of a substance constitutes its essential features, whereas the material, efficient, and final causes are the conditional features.

Only because the material, final, and efficient causes connect the substance with other substances does its formal cause have to be expressed in a way that relates to other substances. By contrast, in the axiological cosmology, feelings of past occasions are the conditional features, and the contributions of the feeling occasion to the integration of what it feels are its essential features.

The complex of conditional and essential features is a harmony, whether it be the substantial harmony of an Aristotelian substance or the physical objectification of a processive occasion. The harmony integrates not only the conditional and the essential features, but also the conditional features with each other and the essential features with each other. A harmony is an *achievement* of having things together which would be separate without the harmony, or which would be together in a different way with another harmony. This achievement is a value. If the harmony is achieved without loss of the achievements of otherwise separate components, it is a net gain. (For reasons to be discussed, it is a matter of indifference here whether the net gain is a gain in reality or a gain in value.)

Is not a harmony a value, however, in a stronger sense than merely achieving additional togetherness? Is it not part of our common aesthetic sense that a harmony is *good*, all else being equal? Furthermore, do we not say that an arrangement of things is better if it is more harmonious? The greater the harmony, the greater the value. The argument here is an appeal to our common experience of responding to perceived harmonies. It makes sense to think "the greater the harmony, the better" only when one can imagine an alternate way by which a comparable set of components might be harmonized with greater or lesser harmony. Perhaps few things have alternate ways in which they can be harmonized, and probably we fail to imagine most that can be. However, the value that is appreciable in a harmony about which we can think of greater or lesser alternative harmonies, is also appreciable in a harmony without alternatives. In that case, appreciation is not *e*valuative in the sense of being compared with imagined alternatives; it is valuative. We may neglect noting that our response is valuative, because that noting is a further interpretation beyond the direct appreciation.

What are the factors in harmony determining why some ways of harmonizing components are more harmonious than others?[8] There are two principal factors in the structure of a harmony—complexity and simplicity. Complexity is the diversity of kinds of things included within the harmony; it is subject to degrees, and the minimal degree is homogeneity. Simplicity is the character of organization within the harmony whereby the togetherness of components constitutes a new reality within which the components are harmonized. Observed from the standpoint of the new reality, simplicity is the character by which the highest integrating principle contains or generates the multitude of components. There may be many levels in a harmony, each creating new realities that enter as components in yet higher realities. Simplicity, too, is subject to degrees, and the minimal degree is conjunction. A harmony is more harmonious to the degree that both its complexity and its simplicity are increased. A high degree of complexity and a low degree of simplicity would yield a low-level harmony of diverse things integrated merely by conjunction, with little difference being made to the components by virtue of their togetherness. A high degree of simplicity with a low degree of complexity would yield great self-reflection or self-reference but dull homogeneity. The structure of any harmony exhibits a certain degree of complexity and a certain degree of simplicity. Is it true that when we imagine better and worse ways of harmonizing the components of a harmony, we do so by imagining alterations in either complexity—removing or adding certain kinds of components—or simplicity—altering the ordering principles so that components are removed from relation to or brought into new relations with each other?

This discussion employs a distinction between the de facto harmony of a thing, imagined alternate harmonies, and ideal harmonies. The de facto harmony is the nature of the complex as it is. The imagined alternatives are ideas about alternate harmonies, although as products of the imagination they are highly abstract. An imagined harmony is an alternative only to certain abstract features of a concrete thing, unless the de facto harmony in question is itself abstract—as, for instance, a theory is. An ideal harmony is a maximal way of harmonizing the components. Whether or not the ideal harmony is imagined depends on the cleverness of the imagination. Presumably most ideal harmonies are glimpsed abstractly and at a confusing distance. That there are maximal ways of harmonizing components is presupposed by the fact that there are degrees of harmony. There need not be only one maximal harmony, however, since there may be many variations in complexity and simplicity that are merely trade-offs with the intensity of harmony. Thus, many equally good ideals may exist for a given set of components.

We must be careful to distinguish between a real ideal harmony and a conception of that ideal. In common speech, frequently we mean the *conception* when we speak of ideals. To prevent this confusion, a more technical term may be introduced for the real ideal harmony. As Plato did in the *Statesman*, we may call real ideal harmonies "normative measures." This phrase points out that the ideal is a normative way of measuring the components of a harmony. In Plato's discussion, normative measures are not so much objects of thought as "knacks" that good statesmen have for harmonizing the components of the state.

A normative measure takes its form from the manifold it is to measure, from the set of components it harmonizes maximally. Without components to harmonize, the normative measure would not be constrained to have one structure rather than another. A normative measure, therefore, presupposes the plurality of an actual world to which it is relevant. Whitehead hypothesized a realm of universal forms apart from occasions; these forms are "eternal objects" and constitute the possibilities for structuring the actual occasions. However, his theory of eternal objects is inconsistent with axiological cosmology, not only in failing to emphasize the normative character of the objects (except insofar as they are subjectively aimed at), but also in attributing to them prior reality independent of the actual world. Whitehead said that the eternal objects are, in themselves, indeterminate; this suggests that they are nothing. Whitehead also said they achieve determinateness by being graded in the divine mind. Yet what would God have to grade if they were intrinsically indeterminate? If all determinateness comes from God, why not say God creates the determinate eternal objects?[9] Even this would suppose that the eternal objects gain their determinateness solely with reference to each other. Although this might be a possible world, from our cosmological perspective it seems simpler to say that eternal objects are merely normative measures which take their form from measuring the actual components presented, and from the natures that each of the other eternal objects has by its own measuring of actual data.

Plato and Whitehead were both correct in noting that normative measures are, in a sense, eternal. The intrinsic relationship normative measures bear to the passing flow of actual things is to be normative—that is, ideal—for them. Whether a normative measure is, in fact, actualized depends on various cosmological causal factors and does not affect the "eternal" fact that it is ideal or normative for the things to which it is relevant. Whether a normative measure is *relevant* to the world is a temporal factor, because relevance depends on the existence of those things for which it is the measure. But it is eternally true that for certain components, this measure is a normative harmony.

Conceiving of normative measures in relation to the changing world is an extraordinarily complex problem. Alternate harmonies are discussed above for a *given* set of components. Yet what determines the membership of a given set? In certain moral situations some definite set of components may be specified as given. But in trying to imagine what the normative measure for a situation might be, it must be remembered that one way to vary a harmony is to vary its complexity; this means that harmonies differ by what they include or leave out. A major question in deliberating about normative measures, therefore, is how to group components so that this or that normative measure is relevant. Because of the eternality of the normativeness of these measures, however, the problem is an objective one. That is, if there are highly diverse ways of grouping the potential components for a variety of normative measures, there may be a grouping that maximizes the harmonies of all. A *concept* is a way of mentally grouping various components whose combination is valuable because of a normative measure. The "real" identity of things comes from the normative measure of which their de facto harmony is an approximation.

The metaphysical question of identity can thus be stated with respect to the notions of value involved. A thing's de facto identity is its de facto harmony. Its identity, therefore, has a de facto value, a value that is appreciated when the thing is felt. The de facto identity is intelligible only as an approximation of the structuring of the thing's components according to its normative measure. The nature of the approximation is determined by the various cosmological causes that go into its actualization; this approximation can be understood, in part, by grasping the cosmological causes. The approximation's integral nature as a harmony, however, is fully intelligible only the reference to its normative measure. As the next section demonstrates, a description of a thing is a function not only of the values directing inquiry but also of recognizing the achieved de facto value in the thing. The difficulty in describing the actual thing lies in discerning the natural joints of what to describe—where to speak of electrons and where of tables and chairs, where to talk about historical movements within civilizations. The "where" questions are seen to depend on discerning the objective normative measures for the historical process relative to the interests of inquiry. If the world were fully rational, the normative measures of all things would be coherent in their juxtaposition, overlapping, and mutual determination; it is doubtful, however, that the world is rational.

From this highly abstract, metaphysical perspective, the falseness of a distinction between facts and values is apparent. The factual character of something is its de facto harmony, its way of embodying normative measure in its components. The value of something is its de facto harmony considered as a harmony. The degree of its value is a function of how closely it approximates its normative measure. The degree to which its value is appreciated in an evaluative way depends on how successfully one imagines its normative measure as an ideal for comparison.

Value or goodness can be seen as a transcendental property of everything determinate. Every determinate thing has a de facto value *as* a de facto harmony. Each thing also has a real, ideal value as its normative measure; this may or may not be distinct from its de facto value. Each thing is subject to being conceived of with a value description, which relates the thing's components to its normative measure through the interests guiding inquiry. Finally, the normative measure of each thing can be described, albeit lamely, by developing an ideal construct. The ideal construct picks out from a welter of elements in process those things which are important for making certain normative measures relevant. Thinking, for instance, can be described—as it is in the next chapter—through ideal constructs in such a way that its various components are presented in relation to their normative measures. The normative measure can then be described as a norm. Each dimension of thinking—imagination, interpretation, theory, and responsibility—has different, though related, norms because they present different components as being important.

COSMOLOGY: NORMS AND GOOD THINKING

The development of an axiological cosmology of thinking is intended to show the involvement of values in thinking. Now the focus will be on norms, or ideals, for thinking itself. The rationale for this stems from a peculiarity of thinking—namely, that it should be *good* thinking to be called thinking at all. Not all thinking is good thinking. Nonetheless, we identify it as thinking because it seems to be appropriately measured (and perhaps condemned!) by the norms of good thinking. The concept of thinking has built-in reference to norms for good thinking. This reference to norms is involved in any concept. As a stipulative definition, let us use the word "rationality" to refer to that characteristic of thinking in which it is defined by norms for excellence in thinking. The norms for thinking are "norms of rationality." This does not imply that there is only one norm of rationality or that several norms are integrated to form a system which defines rationality; it implies only that the norms for thinking are any norms which measure the excellence of the kind of thinking in question.

Does not this definition of rationality contradict the fundamental thesis of this study? It is said at the beginning of this book that thinking is not founded in reason, but in valuation; however, now it is said that thinking is defined by rationality, by reference to norms for excellence in thinking. A crucial distinction needs to be drawn between reason and rationality, although the distinction is merely stipulatory with respect to the use of the words. Reason is thinking which has the intention of being justified self-reflectively; it applies only to thinking as judgment, which, in the West, has been the nearly exclusive concern for excellence in thinking. As Freud, Marx, and Nietzsche have shown, judgment's intention of self-reflective justification is undermined by qualities that can be analyzed in terms of feeling and spontaneity, qualities which reason views as bestiality and unlimited will. Rationality, on the other hand, comprehends whatever norms may apply to feeling and spontaneity, as well as those of judgment. Certain processes of human life are called thinking because they are measurable by norms of rationality. It is precisely because these various human processes involve valuation that they are measured by the norms of rationality. Although the relationship of process and norm has yet to be demonstrated—this task begins in Chapter 4—the point is that thinking is identified because it can be appreciated relative to one or more norms for thinking.

In objection to this, one might argue that Descartes, for example, wanted to distinguish mental substance from corporeal substance and listed a group of mental acts that are "mere" actions without reference to norms. His list includes doubting, understanding, conceiving, affirming, denying, willing, refusing, imagining, and feeling (*Meditations,* 2). Of these, the first seven involve the intentionality of being correct and appropriate. In doubting, for example, we mean that the object is doubtful and that the context is right for doubting it. Imagination, in Descartes' sense of the faculty of feigning objects, is better or worse insofar as it embodies an appreciable coherence and unity; and as distinct from perception or memory, imagination is normatively measured insofar as it is novel or inventive. Feeling, too, is better or worse to the extent that it conveys its source—be it endogenous or exogenous—into awareness with some sensitivity, straightness, or purity. (Whether the feeling is good is another matter—consider a toothache!)

This stipulative definition might be objected to on the ground that rationality applies to the products of thinking—for instance, ordered propositions—rather than to the process of thinking itself. Stephen Toulmin makes an excellent case for the opposing point of view, however, in his *Human Understanding.* If, by *rationality,* we mean the conditions under which thought should be pursued or abandoned, the thoughts themselves, no matter how systematic, constitute only part of the matter to be measured by rationality's norms.[10] The norms also apply to the thinking process of pursuing or abandoning.

Exactly why the concept of thinking makes implicit reference to norms is a complex metaphysical question, which it is premature to address here. For heuristic purposes, however, it is helpful to hazard a general answer to the question. As Kant remarked, conceptions are the ways by which we unify the manifold of our experience; they are rules according to which the plethora of things can be ordered. To bring coherence and order to a manifold means to select certain items and relationships as more important than others. Those items and relationships are identifiable because they are already an ordering of a lower-level manifold. Some of the reasons for valuing certain aspects of experience as important stem from the interests of the process of thinking itself. Conceding even the psychological hypothesis that thinking is nothing more than a specialized kind of adaptive behavior, the general long-range interests of the thinking process are served by discerning the aspects of experience that are *really* important, ranked by various kinds of importance. To conceive of different acts of thinking, as Descartes did, is to pick out certain aspects of the process of experience important to regard as going together, and going together in such a manner as to relate to other things in certain ways. Descartes' analysis of doubting, for instance, lays bare his view of the real and important interconnections of the features of doubt, and relates doubt to knowledge, to moral practice, and to a host of other aspects of the process of experience.

It has been prevalent in twentieth-century philosophy to commit the "fallacy of mere description." This is the mistaken assumption that a description can be devoid of the influence of selective values. Even when one says of a red barn that it is red, the importance of its *color* is selectively operative. The proposition "the barn is red" can be regarded as merely descriptive only by abstracting it from the process of describing and by considering it as an abstract truth. But "the barn is red" is only a shorthand summary of the descriptive process of selecting color as an important value and identifying the barn's color. One of the most pernicious results of the fallacy of mere description is the false advertisement of a "fact-value" problem. There are no mere "facts," although morality is clearly concerned with whether factual situations are as good as they should be, or whether they can be kept from getting worse. Another result of the fallacy is misunderstanding science as the investigation of facts. Recent developments in moral philosophy and in the philosophy of science have exposed the paradigms according to which values are presupposed in selectively conceiving of the facts. There seems to be no way of guarding against this fallacy except by reflecting continuously and responsibly on the values which the process of thinking brings to what it thinks about, and by a criticism of those values in light of what can be sustained as genuinely valuable.

A nearly opposing fallacy prevailed in nineteenth-century philosophy. The fallacy can be called the "fallacy of disguised idealization"; it arises out of the following situation. For various purposes it is important to develop ideal constructs of things and processes. For instance, in analyzing moral deliberation, philosophers might consider the problems of deliberation and the norms that make deliberation good and then construct the image of a person employing these norms to address the deliberative problems. In discussing the relationship between moral deliberation and aesthetic judgment, the philosopher may speak of moral deliberation in the sense of the ideal construct in order to keep the moral aspects "pure," in contrast to ideally pure aesthetic considerations. Max Weber analyzed this process with respect to the conceiving of social behavior in his concept of the ideal type.

Ideal constructs are useful and perhaps necessary to philosophy, but they become involved in fallacies when philosophers disregard the difference between their ideal status and the real state of affairs to which they bear an ideal relationship. Actual states of affairs rarely embody ideals as they appear in ideal constructs; even when they do, they also embody a great deal more. The ideal construct of the "free, critical individual" may obscure the evidence, for instance, that the freedom is based on an evil class structure and that the criticism is really the pursuit of narrow interests. The ideal construct of the proletarian worker may, in turn, obscure the pettiness and bourgeois aspirations of actual proletarians.

Ideal constructs are at a higher level of simplification than descriptions with selective norms. One using such ideal constructs to bring out logical relations with other ideal constructs must safeguard against confusing them with descriptions of actual states of affairs. Such confusion is the fallacy of disguised idealization.

The basis for an ideal construct of rationality is the conception of thinking as a series of occasions that take in objects, spontaneously order and integrate them, and objectify them as a new entity to be taken in by others. It is possible to conceive of the potential deficiencies of each aspect of that process and to determine how they might be overcome in order to render each aspect as excellently as possible. The ideal construct summing all aspects can be called rationality.

The notion of rationality is too general to be useful by itself, precisely because it contains a miscellany of norms. At one time or another, the excellence of nearly every aspect of thinking has been identified with rationality, unfortunately to the exclusion of other important aspects. Insofar as the cosmological theory provides a unified vision of things, the notion of rationality will be reconstructed and given definite meaning as the theory presented in this book succeeds in integrating the many aspects of thinking—each according to its relevant norms—in a unified, ideal construct. An imprecise meaning of rationality is simply that it is good thinking. More restricted meanings would provide inappropriate orientations.

Rationality, for instance, might be associated with a sense of thinking as mind that stands opposed to bodily nature and action and opposed, therefore, to public social interactions. This was Descartes' theory according to some interpreters. Because of the naturalistic cosmology on which the present conception of thinking is based, however, thinking must be conceived of here as part of a natural process, continuous with activities identified more practically as physical and publicly available in social interactions.

Rationality might also be associated with the "measured" and "ordered" in thinking, with due proportion, as its Latin root, *ratio*, connotes. If so, the ideal of rationality might well be opposed to the ideal of plenitude, of Dionysian frenzy, of the deliberately irrational that is in more authentic communication with the elemental forces of the universe and of the creative muses. This former sense of rationality is what Heidegger saw as the perversion of authentic thinking (and human existence) which began with Plato and Aristotle. It is difficult to dissociate this specialized use from a broad meaning of the term. If thinking, however, is construed in accordance with the cosmological theory indicated above, then one of its intrinsic aspects is the taking-in of objects as initial data. Here lies the manifold for thinking's norms to measure. Given proper emphasis, this aspect should guarantee that the integrating construct of rationality will include the infinite plenitude of the "unrationalized" world, the unmeasured frenzy of letting nature's forces move through one's being, the conformation of one's self to a wilder nature than can be intended by human artifice. The taking-in of objects is at the opposite pole in a thinking occasion from objectifying them intentionally; moreover, it is possible that a thinking person would subvert the initial plenitude of experience, making it a narrowly rational intention. It is necessary in every occasion to make a response to the plenitude of initial data that will achieve a unified intention which satisfies the existential requirements for the occasion's actually happening; this is the thought's de facto value.

An "irrational" Dionysian frenzy satisfies those conditions as much as a measured Apollonian response does. The difference between Apollo and Dionysus is that the former selects as important those elements of the initial plenitude which fit some ongoing, continuous scheme of thinking—one characterized perhaps by linear logical inference or at least by a sense of propriety through time. Dionysus responds selectively instead to those elements of the plenitude that present themselves most forcefully at the moment, without regard for the demands of linear propriety. Both responses are possible, according to the cosmological theory's conception of thinking. The question is, which is better, and under what circumstances? Or, in what ways should the Apollonian and Dionysian extremes be mixed, purified, or tempered with each other?

If that question of integration is answered solely from the standpoint of the Apollonian mode, then rationality is defined in a narrow sense, which begs the question of how to integrate the two. (There is little chance of dominance by the Dionysian mode because that perspective exhibits little interest in integration. Despite that flaw, the Dionysian mode is seductive in its purity.) The historical dominance of the Apollonian mode has often been associated with a conception of rationality demanded by society. Societies, particularly hierarchical ones, seem to demand regular, ordered, well-balanced thinking.

The attempt to forge links between rationality and sociality, therefore, is in danger of giving too much weight to the narrowly rational Apollonian side. To counteract this danger, it is necessary to make a two-fold response.

On the one hand, it is important to pay close attention to the unique nature of the norms measuring the "taking-in" aspect of experience in contrast to those of the objectifying aspect, as well as those of the spontaneous aspect. On the other hand, society must be ordered with particular care to make room for those aspects of rational existence that encompass the relatively unmeasured frenzy that responds to the immediate forces of the past.

Creativity is an irrational faculty which Plato likened to madness. Is it genuinely irrational? Only in the narrow sense that it does not proceed from premises according to rules, and that it requires spontaneity. The cosmological theory supports a conception of thinking that stresses spontaneity. Spontaneity is involved in the selection and integration of initial data. Are its norms identical with those of the objective results it produces? Not necessarily, because the subjective, spontaneous process of integrating data is the very life of thinking itself, whereas the finished products of an occasion are the thoughts that are thought—and, more broadly, the deeds done and the stances taken. As the ideal construct for thinking which includes spontaneity, rationality would have to embody those norms dealing with the subjectivity of the process of life.

One final point needs to be made, a point which casts the metaphysics of value in a new light. To call a value a harmony may connote something attractive. Yet we know aesthetically that harmony often involves contrast, disjunction, discord; aesthetic elements can often perfect themselves by standing in opposition to one another rather than in some higher unity. In the sphere of interpretation, a good judgment sometimes is one that rejects, that opposes; in moral interpretation it is sometimes appropriate to go to war. As the verse in Ecclesiastes says, for everything there is a season. The opposition between Apollonian and Dionysian elements in rationality dramatizes the point that harmony means togetherness, though not necessarily pleasing togetherness. The basic connections in a harmony are dyadic, not triadic. A harmony is simply a "contrast" with value.

The argument of this section may be summarized as follows. Rationality is stipulatively defined as good thinking—the ideal or set of ideals for thinking considered in its most inclusive sense. It has been suggested that all thinking refers to ideals or norms. One indication of this referral is that thinking is selective; thinking about kinds of thinking identifies those aspects of thinking worthy of selection. If this is true, there is no such thing as "mere description," especially no such thing as thinking, merely described. On the other hand, even if the barest description is value-laden, description is still different from the analysis of ideal constructs regarding things—ideal constructs that depict what properly functioning rationality would be in various situations, relating rationality to other aspects of experience, which are also conceived of through ideal constructions. This book interprets rationality as an ideal construct broad enough to encompass the ideals for most aspects of thinking. Assuming that rationality is associated only with good judgment, it is necessary to show how it can be associated as well with the Dionysian or Taoist sense of the immediacy of the plenitude of being and with the sense that creativity transcends "rational" limits. It is argued that the cosmological theory within which thinking is conceived of treats both the taking-in, or feeling, aspect of thinking and the spontaneous aspect on their own terms and with their own ideals. The ideal construct of thinking, therefore, deals with feeling, spontaneity, and judgment according to their norms.

4

Responsibility, Norms, and the Social Reality of Thinking

What is it to be a thinking person? The steps taken so far toward the construction of an axiological cosmology preclude certain common ways of answering this question. Thinking, here, has been characterized through norms; thus there is no simple way of *describing* persons in the act of thinking. Rather, we must describe how they fare regarding their responsibilities toward these norms. Furthermore, if thinking is to be characterized in terms of thinking occasions rather than thinking activities of personal agents, then the ordinary substance-attribute model cannot display the connections between thinking and the other activities of life.

The clue to the question—What is it to be a thinking person?—lies in the concept of responsibility. This concept is central to understanding both thinking and being a person. As is indicated in Chapter 3, the reconstructed conception defines thinking according to the norms for thinking well. These norms involve criticism of each mode of thinking other than responsibility—that is, imagination, interpretation, and theorizing; they also involve recursive consideration of the norms for good thinking within responsibility. They govern those aspects of thinking well that are implicated in various human activities, which themselves are not primarily thinking.

The reconstructed conception of responsibility in thinking suggests that to be a person at all is to be responsible. Whereas all natural things exist in value-laden contexts such that what they are and do makes a difference to the worth of the environment, persons face the value-laden context in such ways that the worth of what they can do puts them under obligation. While the interconnection of values in the context, relative to possible outcomes, constitutes the content of objective obligation, responsibility is the subjective way by which those obligations bind persons. Unlike other natural things, persons are responsible for the worth of what they do, and this makes what they do *actions* rather than mere motion.

The range of personal responsibility is defined by the range of actions open to people. Thinking is merely one kind of responsibility. For this reason, a discussion of responsibility as a fundamental dimension of thinking is only a partial approach to responsibility and to being a person. Moral, political, religious, and aesthetic experiences are also important responsibilities, yet even this list is merely a crude classification of the multifarious activities of life that are obliged by values. Responsibility also undercuts the distinction between individual life and social life. Responsibility as specified in thinking vaguely applies to the other specifications of responsibility. Thus responsibility in thinking can indicate—at least in outline—what it is to be a thinking person. The section entitled "The Theoretical Program" addresses this topic.

Our needs in the present chapter are as follows. If responsibility is defined in terms of values that turn possibilities into obligations, then the abstract discussion of values in Chapter 3 must be made more specific. What are the values of things and of possibilities? How do we know what they are? Although these questions are, of course, premature in light of the proposed reconstruction of thinking, the theme implicit in them can be set forth here. This is the point at which to pose the critical question about the axiological focus of the cosmology. If this strategy is mistaken, or if this particular axiology is a vastly wrong way to carry out the strategy, then the approach to responsibility will be undermined. The second section, "Critique of Axiology," takes up this critical question.

The theoretical center of Chapter 4 is to set forth in preliminary fashion the norms for thinking in general. The principle for the array of norms comes from three essential components of the cosmology of thinking: feeling, spontaneity, and judgment. The values hypothesized in Chapter 1—governing such foundational dimensions of thinking as beauty, truth, unity, and goodness—are shown to be normative for judgment. The naturalistic embodiment of thinking, beyond its intentional character, is indicated by the relationship of these norms for judgment, as well as others governing feeling and spontaneity. The theoretical display of norms in the third section, "General Norms for Thinking," provides a perspective from which to understand the role of thought in life with a sense of wholeness (the topic of the fourth section, "The Theoretical Program"). This, in turn, sets the stage for a detailed examination of imagination in Part 2.

EPISTEMOLOGY OF VALUE

The discussion of value in Chapter 3 is metaphysical, with an application to cosmology. The root of the question of value in our time, however, is experiential. Is the affective aspect of our experience what it seems? Can it be trusted? Few would deny that our common experience is laced through with evaluations, but many have come to suspect that the aspect of appreciation is a subjective overlay on a neutral, objective world even when we are in agreement in trusting our value responses. The reasons for this skepticism are mainly epistemological. A metaphysics of value, therefore, is not plausible without an epistemology of value.

Three questions must be posed, questions that are interconnected. First, what value does a thing have? Second, how is this value recognized? Third, what is there about a thing that gives it value?

The first question is empirical. A thing's value is a composite of all the values of its components as they are modified by the way in which they are harmonized. Identifying the components and the harmonizing modes is empirical inquiry. The harmony may increase or diminish the values the components would have separately, or the harmony might be the condition for the very existence of the components. Most likely, the components are modified in different ways, some gaining and some losing by being harmonized.

The second question, though more controversial, is also empirical. A *harmony* is something whose integrity must be grasped simply and intuitively, according to the metaphysical hypothesis stated above. Either the viewers recognize that something hangs together, or they do not. Of course, many preliminary steps are necessary for intuition. These steps must be recognized for what they are, and the structures in the overall harmony must be identified and analyzed. The linguistic clues available are often both unsubtle and misleading; valuing must break through this barrier. In addition, people often have expectations that mislead them about the way in which things are harmonized, as well as about the function of the things' components. Further, it is difficult to establish a context in which something can be appreciated for itself or in which its connections with other things can be perceived accurately in appreciating it. But once these misleading visions are brought under control, the grasp of the harmony must be intuitive.

The questions of how and why this is so are explored in many ways in this book. The claim about intuition of harmony does accord with our experience, even though it is apparent only in the breach. How often do we have the experience of suddenly seeing something in a new light and saying "Aha!"? This insight is merely clarification of a context or recognition of a component or structural feature heretofore neglected. Good art and literary criticism have important functions in providing analytical categories that allow a thing's harmony to be apparent. In ordinary experience, without the "Aha!" sense of grasping a harmony, an appreciation of a value is still there, at least in feeling; but we usually do not recognize the value until the question of value is raised. We realize we were expecting something when the shock of disappointment hits; we then ask whether something has the value we assume it has. This, then, raises the question whether our feeling of value is accurate, and the question is transferred from uninterpreted feeling to the level of the truth of interpretations of value.

The third question—what is there in a thing that constitutes its value?—is addressed in "A Metaphysics of Value" in Chapter 3. The claim in that section is that what constitutes a thing's value is its harmony. A formal analysis of harmony focuses on complexity and simplicity. That analysis is an empirical one in yet another sense. In the short run, it is to be entered into by a philosophical dialectic of the sort found above, in which the implications of such conceptions as determinateness are analyzed; dialectical considerations can also be used to compare the answer proposed with other answers. An honest dialectic must be open to the possibility that assessment of the answer might go the other way. In the long run, however, the question should be asked and answered through experience. Is it the case that when we make value judgments, an element of intuitive recognition enters in? Is this the way harmonies are grasped as harmonies? Is it, in fact, harmonies that we are grasping in value experience? Do we, in fact, distinguish among them according to variations in complexity and simplicity? Does this understanding help us get at the values of things we once thought to be opaque, which were resistant to analysis? This book intends to answer enough of these questions positively, in enough contexts, to make the overall theory plausible.

This discussion of value may better be put in perspective by relating it to the process of occasions discussed in Chapter 3. Every occasion begins with the feeling of previous occasions, which includes the feeling of the occasions' de facto values. Each occasion objectifies some of what it feels in its own satisfaction. Satisfaction is its own harmony, or value and consists of the objectified portion of its felt objects and its own essential contributions by which they are harmonized. If the occasion involves significant thinking, potential satisfaction may be envisioned while in the process of achieving the satisfaction (this is discussed in subsequent chapters). The satisfaction envisioned is its own ideal conception. Single occasions do not constitute ordinary human experience, but a sequence of occasions could involve awareness of an ideal considered relevant to the way in which each constituent occasion contributes to the structure of the sequence. For instance, if the sequence is one of thinking the sentence "snow is cold," the early occasions that make up the thought of *snow* have a bare, vague glimpse of the semantic unity of the sentence—so bare that there sometimes is a sense that a sentence can be finished many different ways within the limits of the anticipations at the beginning. Nevertheless, we rarely would think of *snow* without thinking of it as part of a larger sentential unity. Just as there are values moment by moment, there are values that measure larger processes, for example, *thinking* a sentence. There is a de facto value in thinking "snow is cold" in a given context, and there are normative measures about what is worthiest of thought in that context, measures which may or may not include the thought "*snow is cold.*"

That there are normative measures for processes (which there must be if they are in any way harmonious) means that the process of events is obliged by norms. Events have a natural ideality that is trivial in most contexts because the way things happen is determined largely by antecedent conditions. Situations occur, though, in which the outcome of an event is open to control by some constituents with the capacity to imagine the normative measure. Most human events fall into this category. Where the outcome is subject to control, normative measures relevant to the process become *obligations.* In general, persons are obligated to achieve the best in situations where they can exercise a degree of control. Specific normative measures provide specific obligations. Acknowledgment that they do, however, does not provide an analysis of just what an obligation consists of, nor does it show how obligations are related to specific agents with the obligations, or how obligations are related to enjoyment, suffering, praise, blame, reward, or punishment. In general, with certain important exceptions having to do with the just distribution of obligations and with obligations of prior commitment, a person has the obligation to bring the best out of a situation in which what the person does determines the value of the outcome. The theory of value provides the terms for identifying what the "best" consists of.

CRITIQUE OF AXIOLOGY

The above theory of value has the status of an hypothesis. The first, and most obvious, objection to the theory is that it or any theory of value is irrelevant because it has no subject matter; there are no real values for which a theory may account, hence neither obligations nor responsibilities. The illusion of value in experience, according to this objection, is to be accounted for, and explained by, theories other than value theories.

Values as Theoretical Subject Matter

As simple as the objection of irrelevancy is, it is, nevertheless, profound. How does one go about proving the existence of real values?

Suppose one were to try to prove their existence deductively. The premises from which the conclusion follows would beg the question, for they must be part of a theory that acknowledges real values. We cannot prove the legitimacy of value theory by showing that the legitimacy follows from a theory that implicitly contains a theoretical commitment to values.

Suppose one tried to prove the existence of real values by deducing their existence from a theory widely accepted on other grounds. For instance, theoretical physics viewed as a progressive history is widely believed to be well grounded. It is assumed that, in its future development, theoretical physics will better explain what present physics has explained. It is sometimes pointed out that the development of theoretical physics, or even its state at any given time, presupposes that there are real values—namely, those of inquiry. Scientists must believe in the pursuit of truth, clarity, logical rigor, public articulation, and the integrity of the scientific community. Therefore, it is argued, to do science is to presuppose the reality of at least certain basic traditional values. If not exactly deductive, this argument is sometimes taken as logically coercive.

The most the argument proves, however, is that scientists believe in—or function as if they believe in—the values of inquiry. The argument does not prove that the scientists should operate this way or that their belief in inquiry is legitimate. If elaborated, the argument might show that science is impossible without the orientation of these values; but this would not prove that science should be conducted so that these values are acceptable; it would merely give what Kant disparaged as a hypothetical justification for the value of inquiry. Scientists might, in fact, engage in science only because they like it, not because it is worthy of pursuit. If scientists could be brought to dislike the pursuit of science, they would abandon their practical acceptance of the value of inquiry. At any rate, the opponent of value theory would point out that the dialectical connection between science and the values of inquiry can be explained not by value theory but by sociology of knowledge, that is, by a theory that explains how beliefs influence cognitive experience.

Instead of arguing from some theory to a legitimating subject matter for value theory, one might argue inductively from experience, beginning with the observation that people report that they find some things more valuable than others, that they behave as though their actions were selectively oriented toward things they prize, and that they deliberate about the relative merits of things. If this experience is taken at face value, then the world does contain values to which people respond, and value theory is thus legitimated.

An opponent might answer that this proves only that people believe there are values and that they act as though there were. This experience should not be taken at face value; the value of the belief is a subjective projection onto factual experience. We might answer, in return, that this objection would be fatal if applied to both scientific observation and value experience. "The photographic plate shows streaks where we expected beta particles to be." "Oh, you mean you say you see streaks there; that doesn't prove there are streaks!" The first speaker could point out that everybody in the room can check whether there are streaks. There is no such unanimity

about values, however. It is precisely the *public* character of scientific inquiry, in contrast to value inquiry, that makes real the subject matter of
scientific inquiry, which, in turn, makes scientific theory legitimate.

John Dewey and others have defended the reality of values by turning
this argument around. In concrete, as opposed to merely theoretical, inquiry
about values, the issues are equally as public as they are in science. Yet this
argument fails as an inductive argument for values, for its crucial feature is
not demonstration that values are found in experience but that value-
experience should be taken at face value. One might argue that everything
should be taken at face value until substantial reasons are lodged for interpreting it as being other than what it seems, but that would be an inductive
argument.

One might also argue that we know intuitively that values are real.
That is, the structure of experience is such that people evaluate things; if
people deny that what they are doing is evaluating, then they are not describing experience correctly. To appreciate that experience as anything
other than evaluation would require falsifying the inner content of the experience itself. Such an appeal to the immediacy of evaluation is in some
ways valid, but the question Peirce made famous must be pressed here: Is
the judgment that a given cognition is intuitive itself intuitive or inferential?
If it is intuitive, is the judgment that it is so also intuitive? Ad infinitum? Or
if the judgment is not intuitive, does not the identification of intuitive moral
judgments become fallible and, therefore, not proved? Although these questions by no means refute the claim that value judgments are in some sense
intuitive, they do raise doubts about the matter sufficiently that one cannot
claim it has been proved that values are real.

However, have we not asked a false question in wondering whether it
can be proved that values are real? It makes sense to ask whether it can be
proved that electrons are real, because the reason for thinking they might be
real is that they are implied by a physical theory. But there is no such theory
suggesting that there are values. Rather, values are pervasive elements of
experience, occurring in many forms. Whatever one finally makes of their
true status, the diversity of responses to values is even greater than the
responses to physical theories.

Thus, the question is how one should *interpret* the value elements of
experience, not whether they are there. Perhaps one should interpret them as
systematic illusions, perhaps not. The only way to resolve the question of
the philosophic interpretation of value elements in experience is to present
and defend an interpretation of them against alternate interpretations. This
suggests that the four dimensions of thinking discussed in Chapter 1 all
make partial contributions to the interpretation of value, none sufficient in
itself and no combination conclusive. The value elements must be articu-

lated as imaginatively and artfully as possible, in terms of their implications, connections with other elements in experience, and meanings relative to various systems of interpretation. The elements must be represented in a theoretical scheme that articulates their properties. They will also need to be related to the various responsibilities of life, particularly the responsibilities having to do with philosophic thinking.

Only with a multidimensional approach to the philosophical interpretation of values can we hope to assess the real nature, if any, of values. Furthermore, if such an assessment is given, any reductive elimination of values will have little plausibility. If it is argued that only facts are real, that values are not facts and that values are, therefore, not real, it still is only a *theoretical* claim that only facts are real. If the integrity of our imagination, the hurly-burly of concrete life, and our reflective sense of responsibility present values as real elements, the theoretical argument against them becomes weak. If a more comprehensive theory can be developed—as is attempted here—that would account for both the value elements of experience and the phenomena that lead us to the limited view that only facts are real, the reality of values can be attested.

Dewey's Critique

The second major objection to the theory of value is that while values constitute real subject matter to be understood, they cannot be understood in the form of this axiology. A good value theory should differ from the theory presented. This objection takes various forms, depending on the alternative theory one has in mind.

Consider the objection made from the standpoint of John Dewey's *Theory of Valuation*, a view close to the one presented here.[1] For Dewey, the initial, important distinction made in value theory is the distinction between prizing something and appraising the act of prizing. Appraisals are made with de facto ends in view by weighing both the means used to attain them and their consequences. The means required to attain something we prize might be too costly in terms of other things we prize; thus we reevaluate the original end as "desirable but not worth the cost." According to Dewey, to say that a given end itself has value is to make a false abstraction. Its value is always conditioned by the larger context of experience of which it might be a part. To abstract an end in view from the larger context of experience is to represent the end falsely as something we *merely* prize; we would merely have a valuational *attitude* toward it, and that is not normative. When viewed in the larger context, however, the end is normative because, in terms of means and consequences, there are reasons for appraising it as we do.

Dewey's criticism of the theory of value would go something like this. Being so formal, it is abstracted from experience; things are represented as values apart from their living connections with means and ends. Therefore, there are no grounds for appraising alleged values, and claims about values being normative must be reduced to mere appeals to intuition. The argument against intuition is that a proposition such as "I intuit x to be worth M" amounts to no more than "I prize x as being worth M," which is a non-normative, factual statement.

In answer to Dewey, two main points need to be made. The first is that, although Dewey's theory does not contain a formal account of value as harmony, it should. The relation between means, ends, and further consequences is complex. Deliberative alternatives differ according to the means employed, the ends realized, and the consequences. According to Dewey, in deliberation we imagine these alternatives and, when choosing well, choose the one that brings the most of what we prize, after our prizings that rank the alternatives have been altered by the way in which the components of the alternatives are combined. But this is comparing harmonies, which is just what is accounted for in the metaphysics of value. In *Human Nature and Conduct,* Dewey expressed the point in terms of imaginative comparison; in *Art as Experience* he expressly made it a matter of aesthetic judgment. His analyses of consummatory experiences in *Experience and Nature* and *The Quest for Certainty* show how such experiences are harmonies of antecedents and consequences. Dewey's failure was that he did not move back one more reflective step and ask about the structure of harmony, inquiring why consummatory experiences are valuable. His contribution was to show in detail how we come to value these experiences and to describe the experience of valuing. Without studying the matter formally, however, one can always argue that Dewey left this problem unexplored.

The second point to be made in reply to Dewey is that we can accept his requirement that values be articulated in the broad scope of experience. On the one hand, the theory of value is only a small part of any adequate treatment of value, and Dewey's kind of treatment is a necessary supplement. On the other hand, the analysis of value as harmony or normative measure is sufficiently abstract and vague (in the logical sense) to allow for exemplification in Dewey's description of experience. Among the components of a concrete harmony are the means and consequences of arranging affairs harmoniously, as well as all the required and de facto environmental conditions. With regard to the four dimensions of thinking mentioned in Chapter 1, Dewey's great strengths lay in imagination, interpretation, and responsibility. His weakness was a failure to take theoretical obligations seriously, based on his fear that formalism would come to replace concrete experience with an ironic reduction of value-laden experience to the abstractions of "facts." The axiological theory helps correct this weakness.

Hartman's Critique

A logical axiologist such as Robert S. Hartman would make the opposite criticism of the theory of value from Dewey—that it is not formal enough or that it does not allow forms to remain sufficiently stable for the formal analysis of value situations. In *The Structure of Value*, for instance, Hartman attempts to present a theory in which the value of a thing is a measure of the extent to which it fulfills its concept.[2] Within this theory it should be possible to develop a formal logic for comparing values with the precise operations of adding, subtracting, multiplying, and dividing them. Although admittedly primitive at this stage, the program of such a formal axiology is to make valuation into an exact science. The metaphysics of value sketched above, however, is insufficiently formal because the form of any harmony is a function of two elements that cannot be formalized. The first element is the form of normativeness as such, which is indeterminate except insofar as it is expressed as a measure of a given multiplicity. Without the ability to formally grasp this indeterminate form, there will always seem to be something arbitrary about formed values. The second element is even more upsetting to a formalist—namely, the multifariousness of the multiplicity to be measured by a normative measure. A normative measure depends for its form on what it is given to measure. Although the form of each item given is also a valuable measure, the actuality or givenness cannot be derived from normative measure alone. The Yale philosopher Robert S. Brumbaugh calls this the "principle of plenitude" and points out that form is somewhat alien to the burgeoning of existence, that life is formed but is not reducible to its form.[3] Consequently, the force of any formal axiology must be limited. It can be true only insofar as the forms at hand remain descriptive of the pulse of existence.

In response to Hartman's point of view, it must be said that a sufficiently formalized axiology of the sort he envisions may simply be impossible. If values and valuation are indeed expressible in a purely formal way, they would have to be cut off from both the foundations of life as found in the form of normativeness and the plenitude of life found in its creative process. Stated another way, if cosmological and metaphysical considerations obstruct the project of formal axiology, it is the latter that is cast into doubt. At least, this would be so if the cosmology and metaphysics were well grounded. The mere hope that value theory can be formalized on the model of the foundations of logic is not enough to guarantee success, since, from a considered metaphysical point of view, reality might not be isomorphic with form.

On Hartman's side, however, remains the claim that we do make comparative evaluations. As Dewey argued successfully, when pressed we can spell out the reasons for the results of comparisons. Thus, for the range of comparative evaluations it should, in principle, be possible to state the formal connections. There is nothing in the axiological cosmology, however, that would militate against this. The only limitation would be in evaluative thinking and speaking, where appeals to metaphor, to unexpressed but elicited feelings, to a variety of other conceptual devices that do not "say" things logically or even "show" them in a demonstrative sense, which nonetheless bring into our intelligent life the nonformal elements of the normativeness of norms and the plenitude of creativity.

Perhaps the strongest critical point that can be made from the opposite extremes of Dewey and Hartman is that the middle ground of the theory of value is unproductive. It may be too detached from experience and too lacking in the formal power of abstractions. However, a metaphysical theory of the kind developed above does not stand alone. It is worthwhile only insofar as it can be developed and made specific with regard to concrete matters by way of cosmology and the disciplines that deal with values. Our discussion returns, therefore, to spelling out values in thinking.

GENERAL NORMS FOR THINKING

An occasion of experiencing is a unitary process by which the occasion comes to be a completed happening arising from its initial data and issuing in a definite experience that can be grasped as a complex fact by subsequent experiences. This is the cosmological hypothesis. The initial data are objects that previously were occasions or arrangements of occasions in their own right. They do not exist in the current occasion except as they are involved in the process of being integrated into the new definite occasion; they cannot be treated alone. We can examine an occasion with respect to its function of taking in objects as initial data. Let us call this function *feeling*.

An occasion is a set of feelings, each feeling having its own object as an initial datum. Each feeling is involved in the process of being integrated with other feelings in the occasion, forming as an outcome with them a single, definite, complex feeling. The form of feelings, therefore, is determined not only by the objects that begin as their content but also by the processive requirements of being integrated with each other within the subjective life of the occasion; this latter can be called "subjective form." The resultant complex feeling is called a *feeling* insofar as it is the remainder of those initial objects objectified by the occasion for subsequent occasions.

From the beginning, the process of the occasion can be analyzed with respect to its *forward* look toward satisfying the requirements of integration, rather than its "backward" look toward feeling. Insofar as the satisfaction of an occasion involves thinking, the process can be called an "intention." Feeling and intentionality are converse functions of the same process in a thinking occasion, each identified by its own kinds of norms.

What is meant by "identifying the functions of a process by norms"? A *norm* is a way of measuring or organizing a multiplicity. In this case, multiplicity is a process of experience; the way of measuring may be called a function. If a process has two functions, it is organized so as to exhibit— or be measured by—two norms. It functions well insofar as it achieves the norms. The norms for a process are related to the concepts appropriate for analyzing it. If the process has two functions, each identified by the relevance of a norm, then there are two sets of concepts for analyzing the process, one articulating each function. If feeling and intentionality are two functions of the same experiential process, then there are two norms or complexes of norms that measure the process. Also, there are concepts of intentionality and concepts of feeling that articulate the process. The concepts of either can be related through systematic, theoretical interdefinition; but the concepts of one cannot be reduced to or translated into the other, and they may not be mutually reducible to a single conceptual scheme of the same grade of specificity.

What does it mean, however, to say that the same process can have two or more functions? Clearly there are examples of this, but what is the analysis? The difference between functions is relative to the difference between respective norms. The norms differ by virtue of differences in what they measure. Because a norm harmonizes the values of things, the difference consists of differences in the value of the things measured. For instance, the norms of feeling measure the objects felt in experience with regard to the values those objects have on their own as constituting the environment out of which the experience arises. By contrast, the norms of intentionality measure the objects felt in experience with regard to their values as components in the world or environment that results from the experience. Broadly, the norms of feeling have to do with being faithful to the origin of experience; the norms of intentionality have to do with the achievements of experience, including the achievement of a definite, satisfactory experience itself. The single process of experience has value with respect to its origin. It has value—a different value—with respect to its achievement; a conceptual analysis of its functions demonstrate this. Each function can be broken down into subfunctions according to the way in which values are relevant in the feeling process and according to the way in which other values are relevant in intentionality.

There is, therefore, a method of theoretical analysis to be used regarding the norms for thinking. Where the process of thinking can be analyzed into functional components, it will be seen that each component has a relative integrity, consisting in the fact that it is good for its own constituents to be together in certain ways. Recognition of this involves noting that such ways enhance certain values in the constituents of the components that are not enhanced when those constituents are part of other components of the process. The intrinsic value of a thing felt is enhanced when the feeling is sensitive; but the intrinsic value may not be enhanced when the thing is subordinated to a merely instrumental role in an intention, in which case, its *instrumental* value is enhanced. If the norms of feeling alone were recognized, the object's instrumental value would be neglected, and vice versa. Western culture has tended to recognize norms of intentionality to the exclusion of those of feeling, with the result that the instrumentality of things is overemphasized. Reacting against this, some romantic critics have recognized the norms of feeling to the exclusion of those of intentionality, with the result that the origins of experience are sentimentalized. As will be seen, there are also norms of spontaneity, reflecting a third basic function of thinking process, equally irreducible to norms of either feeling or intentionality (see Figure 2). That the norms for thinking are morally relevant can be demonstrated by showing that we possess some control over how the components express them; we are therefore responsible for cultivating them well.

The following discussion separates the various components of feeling, spontaneity, and intentionality and shows what is valuable in structuring the functions with those components by pointing out the values the components exhibit. An analysis of the components is derived from the cosmology of thinking, which has not yet been examined in detail; nor has it been justified. The analysis of thinking in the remainder of this book does just that, giving increasingly specific content to the bare categories employed here.

Norms of Feeling

Following the structure of the axiological cosmology, the norms of feeling can be thrown into two broad categories, conformation and inclusion.

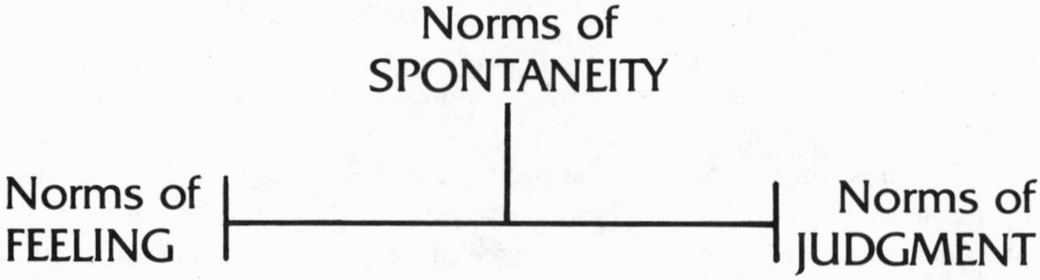

Norms of
SPONTANEITY

Norms of | | Norms of
FEELING |———————————|———————————| JUDGMENT

Figure 2

Conformation Norms. Conformation norms are those that apply to all feelings in an occasion, regardless of which feelings are selected for objectification in the final result and regardless of which are deemed important. In fact, the conformation norms apply to the feelings as a group, no matter how they are grouped. If there were no conformation norms, it would be pointless to ask how well the feeling of an item in experience conforms to the item in its own subjective context. There are two main conformation norms—the norm of *embodiment*, reflecting the occasion's arising out of the environment, and the norm of *energy*, reflecting the force of the occasion's inheritance from the environment.

Norm of Embodiment. The norm of embodiment directs that the experience within the occasion be appreciated as occurring within a bodily physical context. Stated more formally, the process of integrating the diverse feelings should arrange the feelings so that those of the proximate physical environment are retained as a background for all other feelings. The feelings of the body, which embody the experience as a whole, need not themselves be objects of attention; they should, however, be present in an arrangement of feelings such that if the final intention of the occasion is to direct attention to them, they could be appreciated as the embodying context.

The reasons why this embodiment is normative for feeling are as follows. The embodiment is faithful to the real situation of thinking; thinking is an aspect of a much larger process, most of which is not only described scientifically as physical but is experienced as that. We may suppose that unthinking occasions observe the norm automatically. Only thinking occasions, whose capacity for narrowly focused intentions allows them to introduce radical discontinuities between feelings of their physical context and feelings of signs, have an obligation to observe the norm which they might not fulfill.

Another reason why embodiment is normative is that embodiment is necessary for the appreciation of continuity from occasion to occasion required for discursive thinking. The sense of a continuing body is crucial to the sense of continuing thinking or personal identity. Yet another reason why the norm is worthwhile is that physical connections are the medium through which we can think about remote things. Without a cultivated sense of embodiment, one's experience might seem to be that of a disembodied Cartesian soul, however false this might be to the true situation of thinking. With such a cultivated sense, however, the Cartesian experience should not be taken seriously except as an exercise. The phenomenologists—particularly Merleau-Ponty, in *The Phenomenology of Perception*—have demonstrated that, to some degree, embodiment always forms the background of experience. The interesting question is, how is this sense cultivated?

If embodiment is a relevant norm for feeling, then it must be obligatory without necessarily being achieved in full. Thus some way to *cultivate* embodiment should be conceivable. Embodiment cannot be made the direct object of attention, because attention is an element of intentionality, looking away from feeling as such to the integration of feeling. Experience, however, *can* have a sense of embodiment as a background within intention. It can cultivate this sense by focusing attention on certain kinds of experience in which the background is unusually perspicuous.

Indian and Chinese cultures have developed elaborate techniques for cultivating this sense. Indian yoga, for instance, involves methods of attaining postures and focused attention on body areas that make awareness and control possible where they are usually not.[4] Kundalini yoga involves focusing attention on directing a flow of energy, or energy feeling, from the genital area along the backbone, passing through specific centers of attention called "chakras" and emerging through the top of the head (or top of the mind, as the experience has it). Meditational Buddhism—for example, Zen—cultivates embodiment not only through postures for meditation but also through an attempt to obliterate focused attention, with the remainder being merely the background in which one's embodiment is continuous with the world.

The esoteric forms of Taoism are similar to Kundalini yoga, although they are more complex in terms of energy.[5] According to Taoism, ching, associated with sexual energy, has its center near the genital area and circulates up along the backbone in meditation, across the top of the head, and down the front line of the body, returning to its center. Ch'i, the energy of life and movement, a kind of "esoteric breathing," is centered just below the navel and can be directed by the mind, or it itself can elicit awareness in every movement and metabolic process. Shen, a form of mental energy centered in the middle of the head, is capable of identification with distant things. In the course of Taoist meditation, the ching circulates up and around the perimeter of the body and is then felt to rise in the center, joining the ch'i and thence the shen. Circulation of the three combined energies throughout the body perfects the sense of embodiment, not only with one's own body but with the cosmos. Such fulfilled meditational experiences are rare, but their pursuit involves the methodical cultivation of embodiment.

Perhaps the most sophisticated, yet adaptable, discipline is t'ai chi ch'uan, the slow-moving Chinese exercise.[6] It not only cultivates extreme attention and control of the body but also, through the necessity of balance, a fine sense of the physical environment. Some Chinese claim that in its advanced forms, t'ai chi ch'uan turns focused attention to emptiness, as in Zen Buddhism, and feels its movement to be the natural movement of ch'i. It can be a kind of moving Taoist meditation, as described above.

Cultivation of embodiment is not unknown in the West. Sometimes it is explicit in "physical education." In the West, however, it has become closely associated with performance and thus tends to be limited to experts. To put the problem more exactly, because embodiment requires a high degree of discipline and cultivation, if it can be relegated to the experts, it ceases to be everyone's obligation.

Norm of Energy. The norm of energy directs that the experience within an occasion appreciate the ways in which the experience is the result of a variety of forces. We not only feel ourselves embodied but we also feel ourselves to be the result of physical and mental forces. On one hand, it may seem like coercion on our part to conform to the past, whereas, on the other hand, we *are* the forces that have come down to us in the present. The energy of the world is now, in part, focused in our own experience. Stated more formally, the process of integrating the diverse feelings in an occasion should arrange the feelings so that there is an appreciated background continuity between the energy in the physical processes inherited from the past and the subjective experience requiring intention.

The reasons why being energized is a norm for feeling are similar to those for embodiment. First, it is the true situation of thought. In a sophisticated, scientific sense, the physical structure of embodiment is merely an alternate way of analyzing a set of energies. Energized, feeling can be problematic only for beings whose intentions are capable of drawing attention so far away from the sense of energy that discontinuities are introduced, which make thinking falsely abstract. Like embodiment, a sense for one's energies is essential to the continuity of thinking and to the sense of connection with the distant natural world.

Cultivation of a sense of one's energies is similar to that for embodiment. In fact, the description of the methods of cultivating embodiment make explicit mention of the various forms of energy. True, the esoteric Eastern disciplines are bound to a cosmology apparently at odds with modern science. Effective as these disciplines are, perhaps modern science can suggest supplementary disciplines for cultivating a sense of energy and embodiment.

Embodiment and energy together are norms for the background of experience, providing a fundamental sense of continuity with the world and with inner location and drive. Although this background need not be a matter of conscious attention in all experiences, it still ought to function as a background in providing a natural, or worldly, orientation for thinking in its more refined and semantic modes. Otherwise, the experiential differences between ways of conforming to the world are neglected.

Inclusion Norms. Inclusion norms, in contrast to conformation norms, apply to feelings insofar as feelings function in the process of integration with each other to present their objects. Inclusion norms apply to the way in which objects are incorporated in the integrative process. The two main inclusion norms for feelings are *sensitivity* and *purity*.

Norm of Sensitivity. The norm of sensitivity directs that the experience within an occasion retain as much as possible of what is important in the object felt. The problem for sensitivity arises in the following way. Each object felt is present in its entirety as an initial datum in the occasion. The requirement that it be integrated with all the other feelings, however, may necessitate that it be entirely negated in the process, that only parts of it be maintained in feeling, or that it be substituted for or altered by something else. The norm of sensitivity requires that the most valuable elements in the objects be given the highest priority within the integrating process. If integration is a question of keeping object A or object B, the norm of sensitivity says that, all else being equal, the decision should be based on what is most important in A compared with what is most important in B. Of course, all else is never equal; there are many other feelings in the occasion that might be more compatible with the object of lesser value. If integration is a question of abstracting certain elements of an object while negating the rest, the more important elements should be kept; if the problem is one of alteration or substitution, the new representation should express what is most valuable in the object rather than what is most valuable in other elements. The norm of sensitivity compares the value of objects entering experience with the intentional interest in achieving a satisfactory unity. The norm insists that the value of these objects be taken into account in defining satisfaction or in establishing the value of intentional judgment. Because there are ways to harmonize experience that involve respect for the value of felt objects, as well as ways to neglect them in favor of treating objects with instrumental intentionality, the norm of sensitivity is applicable.

The stipulation that objects have values that can be felt—indeed, that are necessarily felt as initial data—is one of the more controversial elements of the hypothesis being presented. Although the hypothesis is defended piecemeal in this work, it can be suggested now, abstracting from the vast networks of organized nature and dealing only with single occasions as objects, that an object's value is the value it achieves in its own satisfaction. That is, an occasion integrates many initial data, forming a coherent, individual, complex, final feeling. This feeling must satisfy all the demands of coherence and include as its content what remains of the objects in its initial data. The value is the sum of the remaining values of the initial data, plus the value derived from satisfying the demands of coherence and the value gained by the individual parts of the occasion by virtue of being combined in a unique way of satisfying the demands of coherence. This is a circular definition; the value of the thing includes the sum of the values of its parts. The extra value of the parts is derived from the way in which the parts are combined. That the circular definition is not conceptually vicious is difficult to demonstrate; that it is what one expects from the cosmology is obvious, however. One occasion feels the value of its predecessor, which is the sum of the values of the predecessor's predecessors as uniquely combined, and so on. Whatever the theoretical difficulties, experientially, it seems to be the case that we feel the world as having a multitude of values, that this feeling is different, though inseparable, from our reaction to the feeling.

The reasons for sensitivity being a norm of feeling are, first, that this multiplies the value of the world by a factor of whatever value is appreciated in feeling, and second, that the value of the experiencing occasion is thereby enhanced. When the norm of sensitivity for feeling is slighted, the valuational aspects of intentional judgment are hollow to the same extent. The extreme view of this deprivation is the case where people perceive the world as consisting merely of facts, that the only value in life is that contributed by the intentional aspect of thinking. Value becomes not natural and real but merely volitional, arising from the intention's spontaneity. In less extreme views, a slighting of the norm of sensitivity in feelings results in counterfeit appreciations of value. One may know from other sources that a bouquet is beautiful and utter appreciative comments. Without sensitivity in feeling, however, the experience is mere sentiment, not a feeling specifically for the bouquet. Indeed, experience can be organized so that sentiments function in place of truly sensitive feelings. This leads, however, to denial and, when the missing feeling has an important function, ultimately to neurosis.

Like the other norms for feeling, sensitivity cannot be addressed directly. It can be approached only indirectly and negatively by careful criticism of one's faculties for valuing, to determine whether the values are based on genuine feeling or on sentiment. This approach is closely connected to cultivation of the norm of purity.

Norm of Purity. Purity as a norm for feeling determines that as far as possible, the experience within an occasion respect the integrity of the objects felt. Whereas sensitivity emphasizes the appreciation of the greatest value in things, purity emphasizes the existential value of things themselves, according to their integrity, an integrity which, however, might not allow for facile division into the valuable and the trivial. Whether purity is an important norm in specific experiences depends on the integrity of the objects experienced. For example, persons have such a supreme integrity or integration that we say they have infinite, immeasurable dignity and worth. A person consists of many networks of structured occasions, however; probably none of the subsystems or occasions within a person approaches the degree of integrity of the person as a whole. Purity of feeling is closely allied with respect, although respect is a characteristic of intentions. As Kant pointed out, in the case of human beings, respect demands that they be treated as ends in themselves, never as means only; their organs and thoughts though, can often be valued legitimately merely as means. Aesthetics also provides examples of a special need for purity of feeling. The ideal connoisseur is a person who can apprehend a work of art without distorting its integrity. Although the work is integrated with the rest of the connoisseur's experience, and because it is simplified, altered, and interpreted within that experience, all modifications of the original feeling about the work must somehow respect integrity. To appreciate the world's value and beauty requires that we maintain a *feel* for it, in addition to maintaining a certain purity while experiencing it.

The value of purity as a norm lies in its fixing on the role of individuality in the nature and worth of things. Together with sensitivity, purity describes the condition necessary for excellent aesthetic appreciation insofar as it is distinct from aesthetic judgment. In his *Critique of Pure Reason*, Kant cited the concept of the "aesthetic" in its proper sense as the study of original feeling or the "taking-in" of the world. Because Kant considers aesthetics transcendentally—that is, as setting the conditions for the possibility of scientific knowing—and because his understanding of scientific knowledge was mechanistic, he neglected the value element of the term *aesthetic*. He thereby reinforced the tradition that "intuition" actually concerns matters of fact that are exclusive of values. Kant cast the old association of "aesthetic" with art into categories radically discontinuous with more straightforwardly cognitive experience.

Purity and sensitivity in feeling are cultivated only through indirect criticism of the results they have in the satisfactions or intentional judgments of experience. People can examine their intentional experience for distortion and perversion, and they can practice "looking again." Furthermore, there is a role for the authority of masters with sensitive and pure feeling, although it is difficult to tell just who has that mastery. Purity and sensitivity of feeling is not the same as accurate perception, since perception is a matter of intentional judgment; but they are involved in perception, and inappropriate neglect of them can be detected there.

In sum (see Figure 3), the norms for feeling are those that deal with the conformation of experience to the world and with the valued inclusion of the world into experience. The norms of conformation are embodiment and energy; those of inclusion are sensitivity and purity.

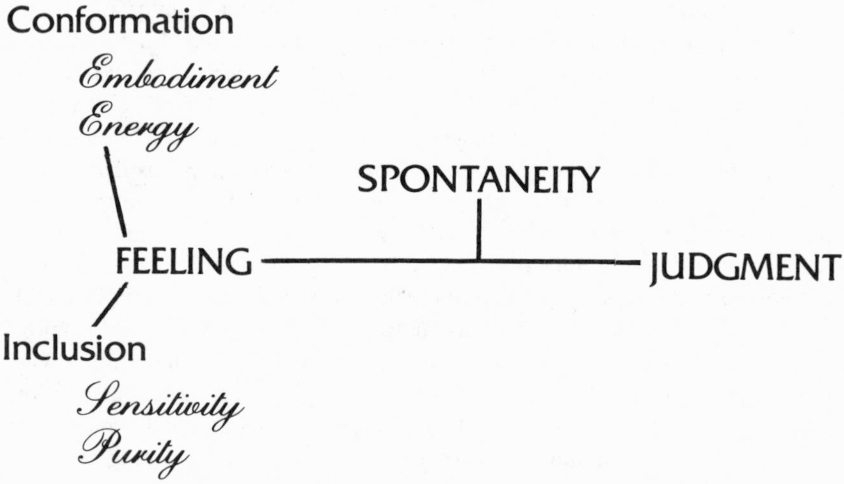

Conformation

Embodiment
Energy

SPONTANEITY

FEELING —————————————— JUDGMENT

Inclusion

Sensitivity
Purity

Figure 3

Norms of Spontaneity

The unitary process within an occasion of experience moves from initial data to completed satisfaction; the satisfaction of a thinking occasion involves intentional judgment. Although the initial data are moved in their various configurations, this moving is spontaneous. "Spontaneity" sometimes connotes the production of a novel effect completely disconnected from the environment. The spontaneity in an occasion of experience, however, according to the cosmological hypothesis, is hedged from behind by having to consist in rearrangements of *given* data and hedged from before by the existential requirement that the occasion must attain coherence and definiteness if it is to come into full existence. Spontaneity is the process by which the occasion itself comes into existence. It provides both the sense of life and existence itself. Spontaneity is a moving of data which has subjective awareness; when spontaneity ceases with the completion or complete existence of the occasion, that occasion's awareness also ceases. Spontaneity is the process by which the norms of feeling and the norms of judgment are themselves realized.

Furthermore, spontaneity has its own norms. Referring to the feelings it integrates, spontaneity's norm is *novelty*. Referring to its intentional goal, the norm is *relevance*. And referring to the subjective existential process itself, the norm is *presence*.

Novelty. Novelty as a norm for spontaneity directs that the process of experience within an occasion allow as much novelty as possible in the production of subjective form. Novelties are new patterns for integrating initial data—new in the sense that the patterns are not among the initial data. By itself, novelty makes no reference to whether the new patterns are relevant to the overall integration of the occasion. Merely novel patterns might not succeed in being actually thought, although their presence during the occasion provides a subjective sense of richness and an objectified judgment that carries its form, however faintly, into the history of the entire development of the occasion.

In theoretical terms, the limits for novelty in an occasion are set by the structure of the environment out of which the occasion arises and by the environment to which it must conform in order to exist successfully. At the minimum, a natural occasion may be so constrained by its environment that the only ways for it to integrate its initial data are by repeating the patterns of certain environing past occasions. For instance, an occasion within a rock is limited to the few patterns typical of rock-occasions. At the maximum, an occasion may have an environment that, simultaneously, has simplified the distant occasions, making much of the world accessible and felt with sensitivity and purity, and that tolerates numerous ways of assembling the world in various new postures. An occasion within the nervous system of a human being, for instance, can organize its world by simplifying sensations and yet can initiate a wide variety of alternate, consequent neural processes. Furthermore, occasions within human experience are sensitive to the subjective mental life of previous occasions, making possible continuous, conscious thought—a possibility we doubt rock-occasions enjoy. We may suppose that all thinking occasions range toward the maximum extreme of novelty. Because the degree of novelty in human experience depends on the stability and regularity of the bodily environment (as well as the relative stability of symbol systems), the norm of novelty applies to thinking occasions, but not to all natural occasions.

In experiential terms, novelty in patterns of integration marks the degree to which the subjective process of an occasion's coming into existence has a zest or intrinsic energy of its own, apart from its past and future. The degree of novelty marks the intensity of existence, even when most of the novel patterns are eliminated from the final intentional result. When a series of occasions encompassing a simple deliberative procedure results in a judgment that was expected from the first, that deliberative experience is more vital if it is filled with a high degree of novelty among the patterns that present themselves for potential integration.

Novelty in spontaneity is not to be confused with imagination, although it is a crucial ingredient in imagination. Imagination is an intentional matter, whose form is a judgment. Spontaneity is the producing of the various stages in the coming-to-be of an occasion, each stage exhibiting many patterns, only the last of which satisfies the demands of definite existence with a single unified pattern. Only the last stage is a judgment. Therefore, the novel patterns which do not survive the process to take a place in judgment never are objects of intention. However, their presence is felt as enrichment or vitality in the subjective process of coming-to-be.

There are two reasons why novelty is a norm for spontaneity. The first has already been expressed as a kind of aesthetic quality—a vitality or zest—in the process of experience. The second is the pragmatic reason that only novelty in the process of experience makes possible diversification and improvements in the world. To be sure, novelty can make things worse as well as better, and diversity can lead to destruction and chaos as well as to pluralistic enrichment. Control over which novelties are objectified is a matter of intention, not of spontaneity.

Because spontaneity is not intentional, there can be no intentional control of novelty. A person cannot will to have more novel thoughts, although it is possible to put oneself in situations where one's intentional behavior tolerates a wide range of novelty, succeeding to the objective stage of experience. A person can also develop sensitivity to the feeling of richness and zest in experience, to the tone of relaxation and freedom. "Lateral thinking," as de Bono uses the term, exhibits this. Training in Oriental calligraphy and Taoist or Zen painting also provides contexts for identifying this feeling.[7] The freshness of a master's painting of a bamboo tree involves sensitivity and purity of feeling as well as a physical embodiment of and participation in the tree's energy. It involves great aesthetic clarity in the intended brush strokes; it also involves a relaxation of intention by admitting countless novelties in applying the brush to paper. What should be cultivated is not the novel brush strokes—which are intentional objectifications of experience—but the feeling of relaxation and acceptance of novelty. That the novelties of potential pattern are relevant for being expressed in the "judgment," or brush movement, exemplifies the norm of relevance.

Relevance. Relevance is a norm for spontaneity which directs the process of experience to include patterns for integrating initial data in a pattern satisfying the conditions for existence. Novelty which arranges a few of the components of an occasion in a new way does not necessarily bear on whether that arrangement is potentially compatible with everything else that must be integrated. If the initial data in a thinking occasion comprise only a large finite set, there still is an inconceivable number of possible combinations of each pair, each triad, each tetrad, and so on. The chance that a finite process of integration would find a way of fitting them together in a single definite new entity is extraordinarily slim. Musing on this, Charles Peirce pointed out, there must be a built-in attunement of the process of thinking to the thoughts necessary for existence.[8] Relevant novelties must be produced simultaneously, relevant to potential objectification in the pattern of the whole judgment. The norms of intentionality direct what relevance consists of. These norms are various. The norm for spontaneity dictates that it produce relevant novelties.

The chief reason that relevance is a norm for spontaneity is seen by reflecting on two extreme situations. The first, mentioned above, is novelty with no relevance; the process of experience would not advance toward any intentional resolution. The second is the absence of novelty, and relevance is comprehended from the data felt; that is, only previous patterns of intention are available. In this extreme case, experience would have no novelty. Since the mere repetition of occasions by habit can hardly be called human experience, certainly not consciousness, relevant novelty is necessary for the adventurous quality of human experience.

Like mere novelty, relevance can be cultivated only indirectly through the practice of those intentional modes of experience in which it is highly active. Those modes mentioned for mere novelty are applicable here. One tries to sense the kind of intention that maximizes relevant novelty in experience, minimizing both habitual thinking and indecision. Getting a sense for relevant novelty is something like learning through biofeedback how consciously to control one's blood pressure. One cannot will blood pressure to go down like willing a hand to go down. But by observing what it feels like when blood pressure goes down, and then intentionally rehearsing those changes to occur, blood pressure indirectly is controlled. Within any single occasion of thinking, the sense of either mere novelty or relevant novelty is a feeling of a previous occasion in which the intentional outcome embodies novelty.

Presence. Presence is a norm for spontaneity, determining that the process of experience include a sense of the immediacy of its own happening within the subjective form with which its intentional judgment is clothed. The experiential expression of this norm is conveyed when we say that someone conversing with us is "present." To be present is not necessarily to have the immediacy of the experience at the focus of attention—indeed, that mediation of the immediacy as an intentional object may ruin the immediacy. Attention is a function of the intentional aspect of experience. Nor is presence merely the felt objects in the process of being integrated with embodiment, energy, sensitivity, and purity; one way to lose presence is to lapse into the things felt. Rather, presence is the sense that the spontaneous activity of integration is the existential character of the occasion of experience itself. This sense can be part of the tone by which intentional judgments are expressed. Little is more frustrating than talking with someone who is paying attention to the conversation and is familiar with the subject matter but who neither listens nor speaks with the sense of being directly engaged in the conversation. To be present is to identify oneself as the one whose intentions are expressed. Just as embodiment and energy are ideals that orient feeling as a background for intentionality, presence orients spontaneity as a background, or tone. It may be helpful to use visual metaphors—background and foreground—for feeling, and an aural metaphor—tone—for spontaneity.)

Presence is a norm for human experience but not necessarily for the occasions of nonhuman or subhuman things. In one way, nonhuman things simply cannot help being present, in the sense of being immediate. In another way, what is important for the world in nonhuman things are the feelings or objects they objectify, not the sense of their own presence. Presence is important for people, however, because it is achieved by personal effort and because it has a role in person-to-person encounters and in the peculiar relation of a person to himself or herself required to be self-possessed. This is not the place to spell out the complex ideals for human relationships; but reflective experience indicates enough value in being personally present in one's own experience to warrant mention of the ideal.[9]

Cultivating presence is more difficult than cultivating other ideals. Like the other ideals mentioned, presence must be approached indirectly. Like the cultivation of sensitivity and purity, presence is developed through criticizing the conditions that would lead one not to be present. People dwell in the intentional future, lapse into the felt past, and hide behind atemporal images of themselves; thus they are not present. But what future, what past, and what images? And why do people flee from the present? These are questions that each person must answer individually, yet they all are part of the general quest for self-knowledge. In the West, self-knowledge has been approached dialectically and psychologically. In the East, it has been part of the discipline of losing attachment to the ego, which is viewed as an obstruction to free action and mind.

Figure 4 summarizes the norms for spontaneity.

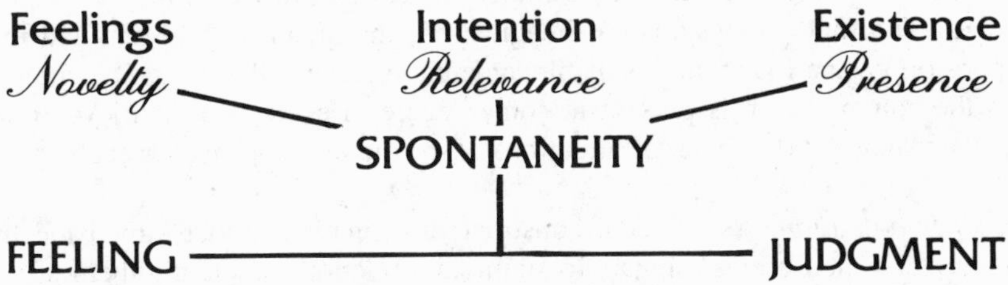

Feelings   **Intention**   **Existence**
Novelty ————   *Relevance*   ——*Presence*
                                  |
                         SPONTANEITY
                                  |
                                  |
FEELING ——————————————————————— JUDGMENT

Figure 4

Norms of Judgment

The preceding section observes that feeling and intentionality are converse functions of the process by which an occasion comes to be. Intentionality is the drive of an occasion to integrate its data into a coherent whole, satisfying the existential requirements for becoming an existent thing. The outcome of an occasion can be called its "satisfaction," because, in Whitehead's usage, the result is what satisfies the conditions for coming into existence. The satisfaction of an occasion is a complex harmony. It may contain many levels of integrated feelings. All natural occasions express integrated physical feelings; some, whose feelings grasp thoughts, express these thoughts. The latter are thinking occasions. The integration of a satisfaction may not distinguish the levels clearly, however. There is no sharp line between physical and mental contents. As the capacity of awareness is sharpened—through biofeedback for instance—elements that were once regarded as physical without mental properties, can be integrated with thoughts according to their own mental signification. If people were fully aware, they would have thoughts in their fingers and toes. "Intentionality" can be limited to that part of the process of seeking satisfaction in which the satisfaction involves meaningful awareness. The merely physical parts of the satisfaction, those without meaningful awareness, embody the creative urge, but they need not be called intentional. It must be remembered that the boundaries of intentionality are unclear.

As contemporary phenomenology urges, the intentional field includes foreground and background elements, in diverse modulations and relationships. The architectonic thesis of the axiology of thinking specifies four principal dimensions of the intentional field, according to which various objects are arrayed or disposed in the foreground and background, according to which they are related, and particularly according to which they are evaluated. The four dimensions are imagination, interpretation, theory, and responsibility: the four families of fundamental issues for thinking. Depending on the context, each is present to some degree in every occasion. Any one of them may be the focus of attention. Also, there are norms for each.

Imagination. As an ideal construct, imagination is that dimension of judgment which brings things into significant relation by relating them all to some pattern—an image—which has formal integrity. The image may have any number of sources: for example, the received culture, novel spontaneity, or the form of judging. There are many kinds of mediation it may perform, from the subconscious to the symbolic mediation found in creative thinking. On the most profound level, one's imagination is what grounds one's most fundamental relationship to the world. Types of images are too numerous to list. Anything with formal integrity, to which two or more other things are related, can function as an image. It is important not to assume too static a view of images: their integrity lacks the precision we demand of explicit beliefs and theories, and, like dreams, they can glide through changes according to their own imaginary integrity. If it has the right integrity, any kind of cognitive element can function as an image. This includes interpretations, critical judgments, theories, and responsible activities; in other words, the other dimensions of judgment can be adapted to imaginative use.

Images per se need not be true or false. (If images are also assertions, then it is good if they are true; that, however, is an extra–imaginative concern.) Nor must images per se have the kind of unity which theories have, allowing one to understand explicitly the routes of connections between things. Rather, images have an integrity that brings things into relation functionally, albeit mysteriously from the standpoint of explicit understanding. (If the images have a theoretical structure, then their unity should be precise and explicit; that, too, is an extra–imaginative matter.)

The chief norm of images per se is *beauty*. Beauty is the aesthetic norm of formal integrity, and some of its characteristics are explored in Part 2. Images, however, do not occur in experience per se but in imaginative

mediating functions in judgment. An additional norm for imagination, therefore, is *responsibility* for its mediating functions. For purposes of preliminary discrimination, this responsibility can be divided into that which is
intrinsic to imagination and that which is extrinsic. The intrinsic responsibility of imagination is to provide authentic mediation. This is most important
(perhaps *only* important) on the general level where imagination relates one
to the world. Imagination can provide the context for genuine engagement
with the world, or it can produce images for alienation. Art, philosophy,
and science, as well as politics and economics, all produce images that lead
to engagement or alienation. Even in their dimension of image-making,
apart from their claims to truth, images are measured by the moral norm of
responsibility intrinsic to imagination, that of mediation through authentic engagement. The extrinsic responsibility of imagination is to produce
images that are true if they make assertions, theoretically unified if they present visions, and moral if they define responsibility. As Plato pointed out,
perhaps overstating the case, poets must be judged as moralists if their poetry is to be used as moral teaching.

Interpretations. Interpretation, as an ideal construct, is that dimension
of judgment that predicates or asserts the character of something. This is the
usual meaning of *judgment* in logic. There are many types of judgments,
and scarcely any brief representation of their forms would apply equally to
all. By interpretation is meant as broad a range of types of judgment as
Peirce meant in his theory of interpretation. He defined a situation of interpretation as one in which something functions as a sign of an object that
warrants a meaning (another sign) to be asserted of an object. Even hypothetical assertions are interpretations in this sense. Most, if not all, thinking
occasions involve interpretations in which something is asserted, either of
the world or of the experiencing occasion itself. Interpretation is an essential
ingredient of intentionality; an interpretation fulfills an intention.

Speaking generally, it is possible to distinguish cognitive from moral
interpretations. In cognition things may be interpreted according to nonval-
uational categories, according to their worths, or according to the obligation
their various values place on various potential actors, including the inter-
preter. Moral interpretations are like Aristotle's practical syllogism, in
which the conclusion is not merely a cognitive proposition, but the beginning of the moral action. Because the intentional elements in a thinking
occasion are embedded in a larger set of physical elements, and often tightly
integrated there, most cognitive interpretations influence a person's comportment that bears on action.

The chief norm of interpretation is *truth*, which has many modes,
depending on the assertion involved. It is possible for truth to be defined

solely in terms of the isolated subject and predicate, regardless of the wider meaning and context. For instance, the judgment "*a* is *b* or *not b*" is necessarily true in an abstract sense. Another norm for interpretation is responsibility. The intrinsic responsibility of interpretation is that it be appropriate and relevant for the situation, that one get not only truths but the important truths. Unfortunately, most formal studies of interpretation, or hermeneutics, or even logic, have neglected the importance of *importance* in interpretation. In order for interpretation to be responsibly true, the imaginative element in the judgment must be intrinsically responsible; that is, one must be engaged properly to get at the important truths. The extrinsic responsibility of interpretation is to be not only true, important, or appropriate, but also theoretically perspicuous where the interpretation has theoretical implications. Since most important truths have theoretical implications, they should be framed in such a way as to make them perspicuous. This demands that the judgment be expressive of a theory, which is another dimension.

Theory. Theory, as an ideal construct, is a dimension of experience which presents a vision of its subject matter through an integral conceptual structure and which provides explicit cognitive connections between all parts. A theory allows one to make connections between elements in experience that may otherwise seem to have no connection or to make no reference to one another. In this, it is like imagination. Whereas imagination merely makes the mediation, theory unifies vision with a structure that can itself be examined and criticized. Like imagination, a theory needs formal integrity; unlike imagination, its integrity exhibits logical structure. It abstracts from the plenitude of its subject matter to articulate its important structural elements.

The norm of theory is *unity*, in a complex meaning of that word. By exhibiting unity and nothing more, a theory presents a coherence to the experience it affects. Beyond unity, however, the intrinsic responsibility of theories is to organize the intentional aspects of experience into a coherence, wholeness, and richness that makes thinking fully authentic. What Aristotle called contemplation (as quoted in Chapter 2) is a crucial and extremely valuable component of thinking, although possibly not as superior to other components as he thought. In order for theory to fulfill its intrinsic responsibility, it should be true; otherwise, contemplative experience would not be congruent with the world out of which it arises and on which it leaves its mark. To determine whether a theory is true requires interpreting it. In order to be true, importantly true, theory must be couched in the terms of proper imagination, engaging the world. The extrinsic responsibility of theory is that it guides actions according to what is truly important in light of the whole. This means two things. First, it means to direct responsible behavior. Behavior always presupposes a vision of how things are and what is worthwhile, theory should provide this vision. Second, it means to provide a special critical context for judging interpretation. One way to assess the truth of an interpretation is to see if it makes sense theoretically within a theory, which itself has already been interpreted critically and found plausible.

Responsibility. Responsibility, as an ideal construct, is that dimension of experience according to which the world is affected, for good or ill. To be responsible is to have an obligation to affect the world for the best, whatever that might be; to act responsibly is to fulfill that obligation, in that context. Responsibility can be analyzed in terms of its integration with the other dimensions of judgment or in terms of its consequent effects. Responsibility, in the former sense, can be called *dialectic*, and in the latter, *morality*. But these two cannot be separated, because what is experienced internally is what is felt within the subsequent world. Dialectic is a moral responsibility. Moral behavior must be dialectical in order to be responsible. The conjunction of morality and dialectic is what makes thinking ineluctably social in its norms and practice.

On the dialectical side, responsibility has several features which are noted above: imagination should function to enhance engagement, interpretation should aim at *important* truths, and theory should unify one's thinking. Dialectical responsibility is thus a component of the other dimensions of judgment. But what is an engaging rather than alienating image? What lines of interpretation are the truly important ones? What is genuinely visionary thinking? Dialectic must answer these questions imaginatively, with a sense of the important issues, and with a true and appropriate vision. Thus dialectic (or morally responsible thinking) involves an unending stepping up to raise critical questions on all levels. Plato's image of the ladder of hypotheses is apt (*Republic*, Book 6, 511b).

There does seem to be a subject matter unique to dialectic besides bringing responsibility to imagination, interpretation, and theory. All of the other forms of critical inquiry involve norms. Norms even exist for what constitutes a theory: norms of wholeness, consistency, coherence, adequacy, and applicability. What *is* a norm? Although cognitively we have access only to particular norms, the intrinsic responsibility of dialectic is to grasp what makes norms normative. This can be expressed only in theories which have hypothetical status at best. Expressing this dialectical grasp of normativeness is not the same as possessing it. It is possessed as a dimension of judgment in which values are appreciated as authoritative, relative to their context. Therefore, an intrinsic part of dialectical responsibility is considering the variety of contexts in which things are measured by norms thereby becoming familiar with the felt authority of resident and obligating values. This point is consonant with Plato's discussion of the role of dialectic in the training of the philosopher-king who must know the sciences, appreciate the form of the Good, and spend time in minor administrative posts in order to discover how norms function in life (*Republic*, Book 7, 522–41).

A dialectical understanding of what things are, of what they are worth, and of what one ought to do, is a necessary, although insufficient, condition for morality. It is necessary, first, because only a being who has the obligation to be dialectical can have moral obligations and, second, because only dialectically informed action is moral action. A machine or a moron with no obligation whatsoever in dialectics can perform an action with a morally good effect. Since this is done without any intent to be moral, the *action* cannot be called a moral action, although its consequence is moral. There are many degrees and kinds of responsible moral behavior. A person can simply want to do good and, without knowing how or why, do it. This, however, is not being as fully responsible as the person who does good, knowing that it is good and why it is good, in what contexts, and according to which approvable justifications. Furthermore, since the environment in which one acts most consistently and most often is oneself, one is responsible for the dialectical development of one's own character, building a character that has a backlog of dialectical deliberation, attuned to the world, and critical. One's character is not the only environment, or even, in some contexts, the most important one. The entire social environment is the arena in which responsibility is exercised. Not only is one responsible for one's subsequent effects in society, but society provides the resources for one's being responsible. Therefore, one has an added obligation of influencing society to better provide those resources for responsibility in oneself and others.

Dialectical understanding of what to do is not a sufficient condition for morality; one must perform the moral action. How often do we know the better yet choose to do the worse! Freedom of choice sustains an infinite gap between knowledge and action, however we try to bridge it. Responsibility, therefore includes not only the dialectical ordering of thinking but the actual integration of the thinking with the physical components of experience, with the result that the dialectic is expressed in action. To know what is better and to choose to do what is worse is intentionally to construct one's experience with a discontinuity between deliberative and physically efficacious elements. This, of course, is unintelligible if one's experience is construed exclusively in terms of cognition or in terms of physical action. With a proper cosmology, however, it is possible to see ill will for what it is: an intentional discontinuity between dialectical understanding and action, which otherwise is a continuum within any occasion of experience. If responsibility were not a dimension of intentional judgment, it would not be possible to say that one is still responsible for doing something bad when one knew it was wrong. Theories of the devil are attempts to conceive isolated components of the self as areas for which one is not responsible despite one's actions.

The norm of responsibility is goodness. From the standpoint of personal character in which one is judged by one's intentional life (in contrast to one's impersonal worth as ballast in the world), one must be responsible in order to be good.

Figure 5 summarizes the norms of judgment.

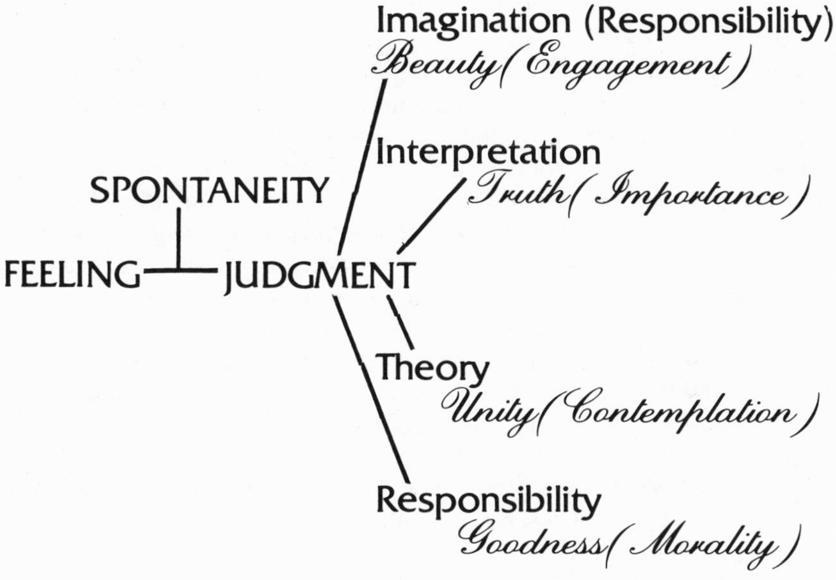

Imagination (Responsibility)
Beauty (Engagement)

Interpretation
Truth (Importance)

SPONTANEITY

FEELING──JUDGMENT

Theory
Unity (Contemplation)

Responsibility
Goodness (Morality)

Figure 5

The Theoretical Program

It is possible to represent diagramatically (Figure 6) the various aspects of experience and norms just discussed. Feeling, spontaneity, and judgment are the three principal aspects of the process within an occasion. Labels in roman typeface refer to their main orientations or dimensions, and labels in italics are the respective norms, according to the hypothesis presented.

An important distinction should be made between feeling and spon-

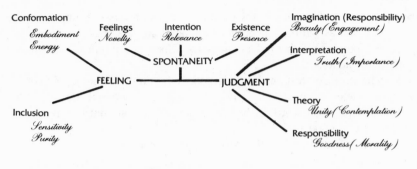

Figure 6

taneity, on one hand, and judgment, on the other, with regard to the social reality of thinking. Feeling (although not its objects, apart from being felt) and spontaneity take place within the subjective process of the occasion's coming-to-be. They are not objective public realities which enter into reciprocal social relations except insofar as they are expressed in judgment. Judgment, the intentional outcome, is a public expression, although the process of arriving at the judgment is subjective. An occasion's satisfaction, including its judgmental elements, is a public fact with consequences. Even in the continuity of thought within an individual, unexpressed in words, each moment expresses its judgment for a subsequent thinking moment; each thought is public for the next thought. Indeed, the flow of thought of which we are aware is a complex chain of thoughts connected by their objectivity for one another.

Another reason is apparent now for judgment's being the focus of attention in Western philosophy. Judgment is the only aspect of thinking that is involved directly in society. The involvement of feeling and spontaneity in social interaction can only be indirect, mediated through judgment. As to feeling social reality, one merely feels others' judgments. As to expressing feelings socially, one does so only through making public judgments. Spontaneity is utterly private.

If the hypothesis about thinking that has been described is accurate, then the aspect of thinking that must be *re*constructed in order properly to conceive human rationality in light of human sociality is the judgmental aspect—namely, imagination, interpretation, theory, and responsibility. Western treatment of knowledge has traditionally dealt with these concepts, although responsibility has seldom been included with the others since the time of the ancient Greeks. The aim of the present program, however, is to treat these topics as part of a larger theory of thinking that includes feeling and spontaneity. The axiological cosmology expresses the aspects of thinking emphasized by the Chinese as well as by the Europeans. On the basis of such a cosmology, it is possible to reconstruct the rationality of imagination, interpretation, theory, and responsibility.

RESPONSIBILITY

The Social Character of Thinking

Plato, Aristotle, and the sophists in the West and the Taoists and Confucianists in China—all understood thinking to be a social activity however problematic its form. Similar observations could be made about other traditions. The impact of technology, the clash of cultures, the relative breaking up or totalizing of political authority, and the increasing narcissism of "high" culture place enormous demands on thinking.

Yet, in our time, thinking has come to be viewed as a private matter, except in circumscribed areas. "Private" usually means that one can think as one likes—that is, irresponsibly—as long as the results of that thinking do not directly harm others. For thinking to be public, it must be judged responsibly according to public criteria that can be applied in the public community. Under the constraint of the ideal construct of mathematical science, those criteria have been limited to the logic of science and cognate disciplines. In morals, politics, and matters of cultural taste, thinking is usually construed to be private and, therefore, not subject to the demand of responsibility. Responsibility, if it is asserted at all, is reserved for the overt expression of thinking in those domains. We hold people responsible for immoral acts, not for bad moral judgment; for unjust deeds, not for inept political understanding. We believe that if some matter of value judgment is a matter of taste, then the phrase "to each his own" applies, without any responsibility assigned.

The major thrust of Kant's work was not merely to justify a demand for certainty but to reverse what he saw as the increasing privatization of thinking. No one, not even Hume, seriously doubted the public objectivity of natural science: scientists could be called to responsibility by checking their mathematical reasoning and their experimental results. Kant's strategy for accounting for this was unique and, he thought, generalizable to other areas of thinking, thus rescuing them from privatism. According to Kant, scientific knowledge is possible because objects, to be experienced, must conform to a transcendental structure of mind. Scientific thinking is public because, in principle, all people can think according to the logic of a transcendental mind. How is morality possible? Although perhaps never actualized, it is possible, said Kant, because people can conform to a transcendental law—the categorical imperative—which makes *willing* autonomous and free. Furthermore, only autonomous willing is moral. How is aesthetic judgment possible? It is possible, said Kant, because of a transcendental structure of feeling that apprehends finite and infinite aesthetic quality, and it is public because all people can share in it.

Kant's treatment of theoretical science, morals, and aesthetic judgment in his three *Critiques* is profound and brilliant, but a transcendental argument is a dangerous enchantment for the sorcerer's apprentice. For example, Kant argued that there is no way by which God can be given to human experience through the senses; therefore, metaphysical knowledge of God is impossible. Challenging this, Rudolf Otto argued that because many people do experience God and give similar accounts of the experience, there must be a transcendental a priori structure of the mind for mystical experience. If we accept that, then *any* alleged object of experience can be justified as being determined by an a priori transcendental faculty of mind.

Kant's strategy ultimately fails because the concept of a transcendental structure to which one conforms in order to gain publicity and objectivity stands in the way of checking up. Trust in the publicity of judgment comes only when there are ways of checking up, indirect or biased as they are by the difficulties of exact replication. To make one's thinking public requires inviting others in to check up, and making oneself as vulnerable as possible. Transcendental structures are too impersonal to be inviting and vulnerable. Kant is often credited with justifying objectivity through subjectivity. It would have been better, however, if he had justified the integrity of public thinking by cultivating the fulfillment and presence of persons. Persons are individual people, not transcendental structures.

The dilemma of private thinking can now be seen in a new light. It is possible to check up in mathematical science; the scientific community has expressed outrage at the irresponsibility of those who alter their figures or falsify their experimental observations. But how does one check up in matters of value judgment? Good judgment in scientific matters focuses mainly on mathematical ability and an understanding of the relevant instruments, and judging the elegance of scientific reasoning requires a certain aesthetic ability. By contrast, good judgment in matters involving value requires taste and discernment resulting from years of experience; it often requires sensitivity to the subtleties of affections; it requires profound acquaintance with the objects being judged as well as with the contexts in which they might exist, especially the context in which they are judged. In short, good judgment regarding the worth of things requires a depth of experience and erudition that cannot easily be specified in advance. How can there be any community check on thinking which deals with value, without handing over legitimating responsibilities to a self-selecting clique claiming wisdom in these matters?

The dilemma is one of authority, in two meanings. On one hand, those with the authority to "check up" on others exercise political authority; in science, this involves funding, granting of prizes and degrees, and controlling opportunities for research. On the other hand, authority refers to the kind of expertise that should be respected for checking up. In science, it is knowledge mainly of the conceptual apparatus and the instrumental hardware. Scientific expertise can be largely demonstrated by an examination. Compare this with authority in the system of the Indian yogis. In this system one is expected to spend many years under the supervision of a master to develop levels of experience inaccessible to those without similar training. Documentation of yogic expertise can come only from the approving word of a master who cannot communicate the criteria used to those not adept. The experience of a yogi is much closer to the experience we would require of someone who is adept at the experiential judgments involving subtle values. Yet, in Western society, far from being thought authoritative in scientific experience, the yogic experience is often thought to be private because it can be expressed only to those who are adept.

If thinking about matters of value is understood as public, it will have to be construed as taking place within a community that can hold thinking to its intrinsic responsibilities. This means that the concept of the responsibilities of thinking is essentially bifocal.

First, responsibility is the value that is normative for the way the activity of thinking relates to various values experienced. Dimensions of this kind of responsibility were presented in the section "Theoretical Program." Here, responsibility defines what it is to be an ideal thinker in an experienced world with values in it.

Second, responsibility makes thinking a public activity with special obligations to invite comment, to disclose the inner workings of thinking, and to be vulnerable. The reason for this is that responsibility is not a possession of the thinker, but a norm which obligates thinking, irrespective of the thinker. Since a norm obligates the one whose standing it is to meet it, it is the added obligation of the thinkers to form the community and to act in such a way within the community to correct the process of thinking. Although one may be the immediate locus of thinking, one's whole social milieu is the context in which thinking can be done well. In the long run, there is no such thing as "Plato's" thinking or "Kant's" thinking. There is the thinking which surrounds the writings of Plato and Kant. During their lifetimes, Plato and Kant were the subjects of this thinking. Since they are no longer subjects, this is no longer true. Thinking, in this sense, is a social matter.

The Individual Locus of Responsibility

In another sense, however, responsibility is ineluctably an individual matter. Those obliged by norms are not necessarily identical with the domain of things measured by the norms. Although norms may apply to the activity of a group or to an aspect of social activity such as thinking, *the subjects obliged by norms can only be individuals*.

The individuality of responsibility is perhaps an unhappy state of affairs. If there are norms, for instance, for a political group, it would seem to be appropriate for "the group" to be responsible. For the group as a whole to be responsible the group would have to be an individual, inclusive of the reality of its members. But people in any social group have aspects of their lives which are not completely expressed in their group roles. Furthermore, because of norms other than those governing the group, the individuals may have responsibilities that conflict with group responsibilities. Thus, it is a problem for them to react responsibly to the conflict between their group responsibilities and other responsibilities. Because the individuals have "extra-group" responsibilities, the group cannot be seen as an individual. Nor is it possible to take an office within the group and grant it complete responsible political authority. The fact that individuals have extra-group responsibilities means that the authority within the state cannot bind them completely. Political authority is, therefore, only positive authority, authority posited by the members of the state and dependent on their sufferance. It is logically impossible to alienate responsibility. One can delegate responsibility, but one is still responsible for what one's delegate does.

Applied to the social process of thinking, this means that every individual is responsible for his or her own thinking. Although there can be some delegation of responsibilities, division of labor according to expertise, and so on, ultimately the responsibilities for thinking with beauty, truth, unity, and goodness rest with individual thinkers.

The initial statement of this hypothesis is necessarily incomplete without a cosmology of responsibility. Following is a brief account of what responsibility means within the larger cosmological theory, an account that intends to clarify what we mean by responsibility in ordinary deliberations.

It will be recalled from Chapter 3 that within the cosmological theory an actual occasion comes to be by the integration of previous occasions as felt into a new unity. The value of the occasion is the value of the unity it attains, which may repeat the value of a previous occasion, diminish the summary values of what it integrates, alter them, or enhance them. Some occasions may have more than one option for integrating themselves. This is not significant, except in the case of occasions complex enough to have mentality and to imagine the array of options. Such occasions of human experience are described fully in the following chapters, but let us imagine here that we are dealing with such occasions. In this cosmology, the root meaning of responsibility is that an occasion has the obligation within its own process of integration to actualize the best harmony. This lies at the heart of obligation: to come into existence as well as possible. The word *responsibility* refers to the fact that the objective worth of a potential outcome puts an agent in the position of having better and worse choices. *Obligation* refers to this same fact from the perspective of the agent who is obligated. Within the occasion itself, there is an identity of the act of coming into existence and the result attained. The result attained has an objective value of some sort. The act of coming into existence approaches that value subjectively; to face that value as the object of intention is to be obliged by it as a responsibility.

The argument is more complex when we are dealing with responsibilities for actions that extend beyond a momentary occasion. Most serious responsibilities are of this kind. May we say that an occasion is obligated to cause the best remote result possible? The following elements make the situation under consideration more complex than the case in which an occasion is obligated to make the best of itself. First, the remote effect is not wholly a consequence of the allegedly responsible cause. The effect is conditioned by a range of causes and the effect itself may have some options for its actualization. The difficulty we have in accomplishing what we want testifies to this democracy of causal control. Therefore, the antecedent occasion in question can be only partially responsible at best for the remote effect. (We commonly distinguish degrees and respects in which an agent can be held responsible for an effect.) Second, although it may seem obvious that a thing is responsible for its own good, there is no similar obvious connection between a conditioning cause and a remote effect.

Let us deal with the second complex factor first. Is there anything in the inner constitution of an occasion that obligates it to make its remote consequences the best possible consequences? We may answer that question by asking what it is in an occasion that obligates it to make itself the best possible. It is conceivable, of course, that the cosmological theory could be structured to hypothesize that an occasion simply comes to some possible unity, denying that there is any value element involved. But this would not explain sufficiently what it is to be a structured unity. A structured unity is a compresence of the components structured; this is a value. Furthermore, it would not explain the affective feelings deep in our experience. To resolve this, the axiological cosmology says that each integration consists in realizing a value. It follows, then, that where there are options between possible harmonies, it is better that the better harmonies be realized.

What obligates an occasion to make itself the best possible is that differing values distinguish the various ways it has of acting. Its own existential reality as a subject consists in part in deciding its own form of harmony. When the decisions involve differing values, the decisions are obligated. This also refers to cases in which the decisions have remote consequences. Qualified by the fact that remote consequences have other causes, an occasion may face the point of deciding which option determines greater or lesser values. If an occasion has two options, one of which is better than the other, the better choice is to choose the better option. That is to say, the occasion has an obligation to choose the better because the actualization of the better depends on that choice. This is what is meant by obligation, in the cosmology and in common experience as well.

This point illustrates the cosmology's category of *essential features*. Essential features determine the form by which data from the past are harmonized. Some essential features—those of inherited character—derive from the past. Others—those of spontaneity—derive from the immediate moment. Essential features emerging from the future are the obligations of an actual occasion to do the best. That the immediate activity of coming into existence may determine whether the future will be better or worse implies that some choices are better than others. This implication is essential for determining the moral quality of the present occasion. Essential features emerging from the future are not coercive; they do not mandate that the occasion choose the best. Our experience is quite the contrary. However, they determine the moral qualities of the occasion; they determine what the occasion ought to do and measure how well the occasion fulfills its obligations.

Our discussion here speaks of individual occasions as if they were significant moral beings. This is an abstraction, of course. Only enduring individuals with developed minds are significant moral beings, and these are complex groupings of occasions. More precisely, what we call "moral individuals" are groups of occasions whose connectedness reflects in part the demands of obligation. For a single occasion to have an obligation toward the future, for instance, requires that it be grouped with many other occasions that it can dominate as a body with which to act, occasions that provide it with the past thoughts necessary for decisions, and so forth. (These connections are explored in the following chapters.) Many of a person's most important obligations are toward the future occasions of his or her own life, making those occasions more fit to handle responsibilities. The reason a person is obligated to do the best is that this is the best thing to do, that responsibility is the existential reality of facing alternatives of differing value.

The other complexity in speaking of obligations toward remote consequences is one of dependent co-origination. The future event is the consequence of innumerable conditions apart from any particular agent. Nevertheless, the laws of nature ensure that proximate actions can have partially predictable remote consequences. Furthermore, some factors are far more important than others. It is often undeniable that the worth of the future depends in specifiable ways on how a given agent chooses. Therefore, it may be said that the person is obligated with regard to that element of the future.

Responsibility may now be characterized in the following way. If a person is causally related to the future, in such a way to have the potentiality of making a difference in worth, and if the person has the potential of choosing how to affect the future in relevant respects, then that person has the responsibility of doing the best. Or, from that person's standpoint, the choices are obligated ones. Whether, in fact, the person chooses to fulfill responsibilities determines whether the person has the achieved character of being responsible. This is responsibility in a different sense, however; one may have responsibilities and fail them, thus being—in the sense of achievement—irresponsible.

Perhaps it is now clearer why only individuals have responsibilities and why groups do not. What we *mean* by a moral individual is the structure of occasions that, together, make moral responsibility possible. *Personhood* may be defined by the special norms that must be fulfilled in some measure for human moral responsibility to be present. A political group, or any other group of persons, cannot be the subject of responsibility (except in obvious, derivative ways) because its structure cannot be personal. A personal structure requires domination of most elements by the decision-making elements in a way that would be sheer tyranny in the interpersonal realm.

Individuation through Participation

The account of responsibility in individuals presents a different view of individuals from that stressed in individualistic philosophies. The individualism of the liberal political tradition, for example, supposes that persons are identified by what they own—first their own bodies and then their transferrable property. The individualism of the utilitarian moral tradition supposes that the human moral character is egoistic, that people act, and ought to act, for their own personal advantage, that broader humanitarian moral precepts must be justified by showing them to be to everyone's advantage.

The axiological position, however, does not fit either the liberal or the utilitarian conception. Rather than having their identities shaped by ownership, in the cosmological theory persons are identified by the range of responsibilities by which they are obligated. That is, people are "essentially" what they must be to have the various responsibilities by which they are obligated. Instead of defining responsibilities by the motive of self-interest, the cosmological theory defines responsibilities causally and normatively. People are responsible for situations in which their potential activity can make a difference; normatively, they are responsible for making a difference for the better. To define individuals in terms of responsibility rather than ownership or personal interest is to define them through participation in their environment, participation that itself has norms.

Most human responsibilities are for shared activities, for such social processes as thinking. Although responsibilities fall on individuals who are obligated, these are responsibilities for affecting social reality for the best. In the main, these responsibilities cannot be met by individuals acting separately, because the causes would be too far removed from the social reality to be affected. Therefore, the pursuit of social responsibilities is a complex process of social interaction. Normative social theory is the study of the norms that any society ought to express in order that the individuals participating in it can fulfill their own social responsibilities. The topic of this study is somewhat narrower than that—namely, the ways by which various kinds of thinking exhibit norms and how thinking is given responsibilities by values in experience.

Thinking is a social enterprise for which individuals are responsible. It can take place seriously only in a community where private thoughts can be made public and checked out. Where such a community does not exist, or where it is not healthy, thinkers have the responsibility of prodding it to life. The four chapters of Part 1 have presented certain problems of developing a community to reflect on the foundational problems of thinking. The arguments to follow constitute an offering to that community, an hypothesis for consideration, a guess at the riddle.

PART 2
IMAGINATION

A BEGINNING

Imagination is the beginning of experience. Creatures without imagination might at any given time respond to particular stimuli; but without imagination, they cannot respond at a moment from the perspective of many moments. With imagination, for instance, it is possible to respond now from the perspective of a whole judgment that began a few moments ago and which vaguely aims off into the future. Creatures without imagination may respond to especially forceful stimuli by suppressing responses to other stimuli. Without imagination, however, they cannot respond to both forceful and weak stimuli as coordinated in a common field. With imagination it is possible to locate different elements within a common field punctuated by diverse and coordinated levels of importance. It is imagination that makes it possible to respond to a subjective world with both spatial and temporal dimensions.[1]

Experience, therefore, begins with synthesis. The most elementary function of imagination is gathering so as to constitute experience in the form of a world present to a subject. In this sense, synthesis is a primordial value. Without synthesis, there is either sheer chaos or sheer immediacy; in neither case is there experience. Synthesis is the primordial experiential value on which all other experiential enjoyments and achievements are based.

Chapter 5 explores the character of imagination as synthesis in a four-section analysis. The groundwork is to provide a phenomenological review of the function of synthesis in imagination, taking the work of Kant as the starting point. ("Phenomenology" here and in the titles of the first sections of each of the chapters in Part 2 means "making issues appear," as the word says, not "pure description," in the technical Husserlian sense.) The neglected element in the Kantian analysis is that synthesis is a value, functioning normatively in experience. The second section, "The Kantian Synthesis," undertakes a critical review of certain of the consequences that the Kantian tradition has drawn from the fundamental importance of imagination as synthesis; in particular, any transcendental significance to synthesis will be rejected, leaving only a normative significance. The third section, "Synthesis in Experience," develops a positive theoretical interpretation of imagination as synthesis; this is a specification of the axiological cosmology introduced in Part 1. The fourth section, "The Value of Synthesis: Gathering," asks whether there is any sense in which the subjective world brought into operation by synthetic imagination is a public world. Must the foundational status of imagination as synthesis lead to the view that experience begins in private worlds and needs special help to become public? This is the result of Kant's interpretation. It is the purpose of his transcendental move to provide this special help in attaining publicity. If we reject the transcendental move, are we required to say that the foundation of experience lies in privacy? In fact, the publicity of imagination as synthesis is expressed in the foundations of religious consciousness.

Experience begins in imagination in another sense—namely, as perception. Maurice Merleau-Ponty, the great French practitioner of phenomenology, argued that perception is experientially and philosophically primary; Patrick Heelan has reformulated this thesis without objectionable commitments to transcendental phenomenology.[2] Although perception is not as primary as synthesis in the senses mentioned above, it is still primary in the sense that it provides an objective world. Imagination as synthesis is the foundation for a subject's having a world in a sense limited to subjective experience. With synthesis alone, the most one can say is that experience has the *form* of the world. With perception, however, *the* world—or perhaps worlds—enter experience. As Merleau-Ponty argued, perception is prior to critical questions about whether a perceptual judgment is a true perception. Even before criticism, though, perception relates an actual subject to an actual world. To be a subject beyond mere synthesizing imagination is to be a subject with presence to and within a world. To be a person is at least to be present in a world, as well as to experience the world as present to oneself. When gathering or synthesis is the primordial value of experience, perceptual presence is the next value.

Chapter 6 takes a four-fold approach, beginning with a review of the issues of perception and drawing heavily on both contemporary phenomenology and classical Taoism. It then considers the role of intentionality in perception. The question concerns whether the judgmental form in which perception is expressed in consciousness is a mirror of causal contact with the world, which allows perception to be the foundation of presence. The question is answered in the negative, with the result that the feeling tone of presence is acknowledged as experienced in nonassertive, intentional form. In the section

"Cosmology of Imagination in Perception," a theory of perception is added to the axiological cosmology, and the Section, "Responsibility in Imagination in Perception," demonstrates the social character of perception. At its most primitive, the world is grasped mythically.

Experience begins in imagination in a third sense—as appearance. An appearance is a speculative envisionment of part of a world in isolation from the larger, experienced world. An appearance, or image, is discrete; it is not homogenously related to its surroundings. It could be an imagined state of affairs, a sensible pattern, a feeling, anything that might enter experience. From a perspective beyond appearance, appearance might be true of a world, as when one fantasizes that a friend is coming when the friend is in fact coming; but the appearance is not causally connected with the world in a perceptual sense. The essence of an appearance is its formal integrity; whatever elements enter into the appearance, they must be formally integral. Appearance as fantasy is the origin of form itself.

The elementary function of appearance in experience is to contribute the forms by which experience can be organized. Synthesis requires appearance insofar as synthesis must take place according to some form or order. Perception requires appearance because, although real objectively formed objects are made available to experience through perception, they cannot be incorporated in the experience without being related to the other experiential contents. Appearance provides the forms for integrating perception into experience. As Charles Peirce would put it, synthesis abstracted from the forms of its operation is mere uniformity of Firstness; perception abstracted from its integration with experience is mere presence in duality—Secondness; appearance provides forms for mediating—Thirdness. Experience cannot begin without all three.

Chapter 7 explores this by first dealing with spontaneity and creativity, again reviewing the phenomenology of appearance. It is argued that the value involved in formal mediation is beauty. Second, it is necessary to criticize views which hold appearance to require that its influence on experience be subjective or conventional. Does the "human contribution" to knowledge mean merely that we read into nature our subjective forms of integration? This has often seemed the consequence of Kant's view that spontaneity is the source of form, that it is in need of transcendental criticism. Yet it is argued that the norm of beauty makes appearance a public enterprise, even though, from the perspective of this stage of the discussion, it is prior to questions of truth and falsity. The third section of Chapter 7, "Cosmology of Appearance," is yet another elaboration of the axiological cosmology, detailing a theory of appearance. The fourth section, "The Public Character of Image-Formation," is a discussion of the normative dimension of art, the primary expression of appearance in the cultural public.

The fourth beginning of experience is when one engages the world. The first three senses in which experience begins emphasize a kind of passivity with respect to the world, one in which the subject's activity is mainly responding internally to the flow of events. Genuine experience, however, involves participation in the flow of events. It involves responding to the values presented with evaluations based on one's own intentions and forming one's will, habits, and character through interaction with the world. Ideally, human experience is free, and freedom means creative engagement. Of course, engagement is far more than imagination, in all senses of the word. Imagination, however, makes engagement possible by supplying the images through which the world is taken up and in terms of which action is oriented. As experientially prior to assertions about the world, images form elementary recognitions and provide elementary orientations. In this sense, imagination is relative, both to the conditions mediated and to the character of the subject to whom they are mediated. The images prevalent in one's culture can foster relevant and valuable engagements, or they can foster alienation. Alienation at the level of imagination is not rejection; more profoundly it is disengagement, in the sense that the most important elements in the world are not mediated to the experiencer, that the greatest values of the experiencer cannot find expression in the world. The world is sour. The person is impotent.

After exploring the foundations of engagement, Chapter 8 examines the sense in which imagination has a moral obligation—namely, to provide the ground for engagement. As Plato saw, this has moral implications for art, though it need not be the case that art makes any moral assertions. One of the social functions of art is providing a culture with images for authentic engagement. The third section of Chapter 8, "Cosmology of Imagination as Art," develops a theory of the sociality of human nature based on the contribution of imagination to engagement, with particular reference to art. The fourth section, "Philosophy: The Critique of Critiques?", explores the obligations of philosophy to provide not only true views and interesting theories, but also images for proper philosophical engagement.

5

Imagination as Synthesis: Religion

Objects of thought and subliminal feelings, as well as causes of experience that we might not be aware of, are themselves diverse. Perhaps they have *no* important relations apart from being common elements of someone's experience. The elementary function of imagination is to relate these diverse objects so they can be experienced together. Through imagination, diverse objects are arranged in a *subjective* world, a world *for the experiencer*. This elementary function of imagination is synthesis.

PHENOMENOLOGY OF SYNTHESIS

The Kantian Syntheses

Immanuel Kant was the first philosopher to appreciate the fundamental importance of synthesis in imagination. Kant's concern in the *Critique of Pure Reason* was to show how knowledge is possible. His strategy was, first, to assume that we have actual synthetic a priori knowledge (*synthetic*, in that connections can be asserted that are not merely matters of definition; and *a priori*, in that the knowledge is valid regardless of the character of particular experiences). Kant then analyzed the conditions necessary for the possibility of synthetic a priori knowledge. Accordingly, his discussion of synthesis is set in the context of an attempt to define, a priori, how representations in a thinker are related to the objects represented. In the section "Critical Interpretation," we reject this strategy. Kant's demonstration of the necessity of synthesis as such is sound, however.

Kant distinguished three syntheses: "apprehension in intuition," "reproduction in imagination," and "recognition in a concept."[1] (All three syntheses

139

are performed by the *imaginative* faculty as the term is used here.)

By apprehension in intuition is meant synthesis of a field. For Kant, a field is a togetherness of many intuitions. How do we apprehend spatially related things as at once together and manifold? Kant's answer was that each intuition is unitary in the sense that it can fill a moment of time homogeneously. For the intuitions to be experienced together, they must "first be run through, and held together."[2] This "running through" is not serial but immediate and contemporaneous; it is a single synthesis, or gaze. Without intuition through synthesis, a manifold of representations could be experienced together only by obliterating their differences. Perhaps the metaphor of running through is unfortunate, since it seems to be ineluctably temporal. Kant can be amended, however, so that his point is as follows. The immediate synthesis of apprehension in intuition has a potential for later analysis that consists of running through the parts. At the moment, it is simply the case that things in the experiential field are synthesized so as to stand in a spatial relationship to each other—some in the foreground and some in the background, some side by side, up or down, left or right. As Patrick Heelan has shown, the precise form of the synthesis of apprehension in intuition is a matter of separate determination, whether it is a scientifically geometrical form, a phenomenologically idiosyncratic form, or something else.

The synthesis of reproduction in imagination is intended to deal with the following kind of phenomenon. When in my mind's eye I draw a line, I draw the "earlier" parts of the line first; then I draw the "later" parts. In order to have a complete line, however, the earlier parts must be reproduced as an immediate accompaniment of the later parts, or to continue Kant's example, to think the time from one noon to another, I must be able to reproduce the thought of the first noon with that of the second when reviewing the entire day.[3] In order to understand the present moment, it may be necessary to remember an earlier moment. The earlier moment must be reproduced, not as it was originally (which would be a regression lacking the advance of the succeeding moment), but precisely as something reproduced in synthesis with an object of present attention. Reproduction is required for the "running through" in the potential discrimination of spaces as well as for the discernment of continuous activity in time.

Synthesis of recognition in a concept completes Kant's syntheses. In synthesis, not only must an antecedent item be reproduced for serial progression to take place, the item must be recognized according to a concept that relates it to the present. For instance, we count "1," "2," "3." With mere reproductive synthesis, we could count only "1," "1," "1," because the earlier counts, though reproduced as prior, connected counts, could not be recognized as determining the later counts as higher numbers in the series. Synthesis requires that recognition of the concept of the number series be instantaneous.

Kant's point about synthesis can be extended far beyond the apprehension of space and duration. Suppose I have in my present experience nothing but the apprehension of a dog. I observe the dog with a quick glance that lasts perhaps no more than one second, sweeping from tail to head (the human eye can make about four focused stops per second). Synthesis of apprehension in intuition takes place at each moment of the glance. At no single moment do I see only a point of the dog's surface, nor do I see the dog's parts as undifferentiated wholes. Synthesis of reproductive imagination takes place because I sustain images of the spread-out parts at each moment of the gaze and because I apprehend the parts of the dog as continuous. The glance is sweeping, although physiologically my vision consists of four stopped moments. The synthesis of recognition in a concept happens because I integrate the whole glance according to the concept of dog; or if this is the first dog I have seen, according to recognizably connected parts—for example, head, feet, torso, coat, and so on.

Human experience, generally though not always, involves experience of movement. If the world experienced does not move, at least the attention required to experience does. The specious present—the sense of a present time—is characterized by a certain thickness, with the entire flow from earlier to later contained within the present. The leading edge of the present picks out emerging elements and the trailing edge drops elements into the finished past. Any sense of the specious present must therefore be built on Kant's three syntheses. Whereas the units of actuality in an experiential process may be smaller occasions than appear in any conscious "present," a unit with the quality of human experience must include a series of such occasions that have the structure of the three syntheses. Although occasions within a process of human experience must have the structure required to fit them into the process—including their individual contributions to the syntheses—the syntheses themselves are characteristic of the series of occasions taken as a unit, as an entire series.

There is a specious place as well as a specious present. Although Kant was concerned principally with the spatial dimensions of objects, an even more important consideration is the spatial dimension of the observer and his or her subjective world. Objects are always in space relative to other objects, and when experienced they are relative to the experiencer. Of course, the experiencer rarely apprehends the whole universe according to the dimensions spoken of by astrophysicists. But an experiencer apprehends objects in a world that has some spatial dimensions relative to his or her own body and with a centered point of sensation. Often the size of the world apprehended is limited by the range of the senses; sometimes it is as small as feelings internal to the body. At other times, it can be as large as the dimensions required by an object or a field that can be fantasized, including the dimensions speculated on in the imagination of the astrophysicist. The specious place, as well as the specious present, must meet the requirements of Kant's three syntheses.

The mathematical requirements of science aside, the phenomenology of experience may not require a sharp distinction between spatial and temporal dimensions. The multidimensional quality of living experience may have many structures in its field beyond those of space and time; also, the spatial and temporal structures ordinarily noted may be misleading abstractions. Whatever the dimensions of the field, their apprehension, reproduction, and recognition—to repeat Kant's syntheses—require synthesis.

We should note here that, whereas Kant spoke of synthesizing representations of objects, the present discussion speaks of the synthesis of experiential fields. Kant's objective in the passage under discussion was to define objects as they might be encountered in scientific or quasi-scientific knowing. Further, Kant was still in thrall to Newton's conception of the world as comprised of objects within the formal container of space. That Kant made the spatial container a form of sensation rather than an objective container did not, however, distort the Newtonian picture of objects in space. Because of recent scientific developments, as well as careful attention to experience, we have come to view space-time as a field of objects. The field's character is derived from the objects contained; the character of the objects comes partly from the necessity to define them, relative to each other, in a field. Kant's point about the need for synthesis, though, holds for both fields and Newtonian objects.

Synthesis in Experience

The discussion of synthesis concerns the function of imagination in isolation from its role in experience. Synthesis in imagination, however, is what gives experience its character of being in a world. This requires elaboration.

From an experiential standpoint, it is important to note that imagination is an active affair, not a passive one. Imagination occasionally seems passive, particularly when we cast our focal awareness on the play of images being produced. As the idea of synthesis implies, however, production of the images is an activity without which there might be some of the elements ready to be combined but not the combination. If we follow closely the flow of awareness, the activity in imagining itself can be discerned, inextricably bound up with the images. Indeed, perhaps some of the passivity or the ephemerality of images comes from the felt sense that they are contingent upon the imagining activities that produce them.

The activity of imagining, therefore, is something of an ontological, or existential, power. It is that power whereby the content of imagined aware-ness comes to be. An experiencing person is more than merely the content of an imagined world; there are levels of bodily life that cannot be called "experience" precisely because they lack the syntheses of elements that char-acterize experiential levels. On the merely bodily level there are integrating activities that express the same general principles as the synthetic activities of imagination, and imaginative activity is one aspect of a more general existen-tial activity.

That imagination does have such an existential quality is revealed in the psychopathologies in which people are said to be cut off from reality. For these people, the life of the imagination seems to have lost tangible connec-tion with the rest of life; it seems complete in itself. Yet, because it seems ephemeral simply as a life of the imagination, some people have a sense of panic about whether they can sustain themselves as sole creators of their universes.

Imagination, of course, is not the sole existential source of experience; there are all the objects felt from one's own past, as well as the past of other objects. These objects all have their own characters, and they all have various factual relationships to each other. The simplest epistemological hypothesis is that all these objects and relations enter into an occasion of experience in their full reality; they are felt just as they are. They are not, of course, compatible within a single experience just as they are; they must be trimmed and polished, cut and filed, ranked, coordinated, and, in many cases, eliminated. This reduction of the wealth of objects to a single harmony that can be experienced subjectively as a definite world is part of the work of imagina-tion. No matter how clever the synthetic imagination, however, it may work only with the material objectively given it. The *forms* according to which it synthesizes material may be novel, but the *material* given it is given objec-tively.

This does not mean that experience always begins with true perception. First, perception is a matter of intentional judgment, not one of feeling the objects out of which we imaginatively construct a world. Second, the word "perception" usually refers to perception of the outer world, whereas most of what is given in any experience are the imagined products of previous experi-ences, not necessarily the objects those experiences might refer to.

It now seems fair to conclude that synthetic imagination performs two functions for experience at the same time. On one hand, it establishes a connection between the experiencer and the experiencer's world: imagination creates the experiential relationship one has to the things of one's world, including one's own past and future, and other people. This is what Ray L. Hart, following Austin Farrer, analyzes as "discontinuous ingression."[4] Here it is worth stressing that imagining is not what goes on inside someone's mind separate from objects of imagination. This view, derived from the position which Hume assumed was a simple reading of the situation at the beginning of knowledge, is a metaphysical hypothesis; and not a very cogent one at that. From a phenomenological inspection of experience, the objects imagined are present in experience as imagined. The objects are taken as actually there. Any argument that it is not the objects but some disconnected representation of them should provide specific evidence of illusion. From a theoretical standpoint, it is not especially difficult to account for the presence of real objects in experience, but there is great difficulty in the theory that experience contains only representations. Imagining is the activity by which a new experience arises from a welter of given objects, but which, in that arising, establishes a context, or world, relating itself to the objects. An occasion that comes to be out of a welter of past occasions without imagining a context situating itself with respect to those objects would not be an experience.

On the other hand, imagination functions so as to provide the new experience itself, the new term in relation to objects in the world. We experience ourselves (though not always in focal attention) as being in the same world as the objects experienced—usually defining a spatial and temporal perspective with respect to the objects. This is not to say that we always make an object of ourselves in a grid with others. Rather, we make an experience-of-objects-being-present. The contours of the objects-being-present may define a perspective which is us rather than them. The "new reality," though, is the objects-being-present, the experience of the objects. Being "present" need not connote the temporal present; when we think of Caesar, he is present in our experience as an historical figure. Whitehead called this "presentational immediacy."[5] The new experience is the product of imagination and, perhaps, of other integrating activities.

What is the shape of the world of the imagination? What is the sense of self involved in the experiencing perspective? Our tendency is to assume that imagination naturally performs its syntheses in accord with the shape of the commonsense world, a world that presupposes some stable perceptions and that is interpreted by our knowledge of what things are, in relative independence of our experience of them. Thus the world of imagination is presumed to have three spatial dimensions and a temporal one; bodies are solid unless altered by mechanisms; and the experiencer is viewed as a more or less continuous consciousness whose experiential activity is a property of a body in the center of the temporal and spatial field, rather the way other activities are properties of other bodies. A person usually makes a fairly clear distinction between himself or herself continuously existing for a span of time and things other than himself or herself. From the standpoint of considering imagination alone, however, these assumptions cannot be made, since common sense, perception, and knowledge remain problematic.

There are important, positive reasons for not making these assumptions. First, consider dreams. In dreams, the structure of the world and the self is highly idiosyncratic, bizarre, and irregular; taking the commonsense world as paradigmatic, dreams are a distortion. Dreaming, however, occurs when the force of perception of external things is diminished and knowledge is used for purposes other than strictly knowing. Dreaming is much closer to what imagination does on its own than is waking life to the commonsense world.

Second, consider such esoteric spiritual experiences as those in mysticism or Tantric meditation. Unless one takes the commonsense, or scientific, world as a norm on which to base rejection of other articulations of the world, spiritual experiences present highly diverse articulations of the world—perhaps obliterating the spatial dimension or making the past and the future interpenetrate or viewing the world as *sub specie aeternitatis*. We know that, although spiritual experiences take place under the constraint of a discipline or of drugs, the imagination alone is capable of such experiences. Therefore, the contours of the imagination's shaping powers are at least this broad.

Third, consider the possibility that even common sense and common appreciation of theoretical knowledge are more limited than they need to be, in the sense that they tend to organize the world around a presumed feeling for a human subject with continuity, having meanings and relationships that are taken from the ego's need for meaning. This, at least, is the plausible thesis of Michel Foucault, who claims that the directions of current research are leading away from the self-oriented contours of the world of experience.[6]

The next section, "Value of Synthesis," begins a criticism of the Kantian thesis that the world is imaginable, meaningful, and knowable *because of* the transcendental unity of the self. Assuming for the moment that his analysis holds, how do we account for the shape of imagination? If imagination does not necessarily unify in order to make the world possible for a potentially unified self, why does it unify according to the forms it *does* employ? If this were a transcendental question in Kant's sense, it would have to be answered by assuming that there exists some established kind of experience (synthetic a priori knowledge, in Kant's case) for which the shape of imagination would have to be a condition. The only experience we have at this point in the agrument, however, is the content of imagination itself; thus the question must be treated phenomenologically. Can we uncover anything in imaginative experience that would account for such a synthesis?

The Value of Synthesis: Gathering

Whereas the *activity* of synthesis consists of putting things together, the subjective *feel* of synthesis consists of having things together. The lineaments of the imagined world constitute the "how" of how things are had together. John Dewey was one of the first philosophers to note the sense of appreciation involved in "having" things. In his work, Dewey spoke of valuational elements in "having" the qualities of experience, of "enjoying" them, of "suffering" them.[7] Further, his analysis talked about the gradations in value in terms of the degree to which an experience "had" is a consummatory experience, fulfilling numerous diverse hopes and expectations in an integrated way and initiating other, fruitful lines of development. Before Dewey, Peirce had argued that each experience is complex because it has the character of being a sign and that the signifying relation, though a complex containing at least three elements, has an "immediate" unity; that immediate unity Peirce characterized as an aesthetic element.[8] The suggestion from both philosophers and from many others is that complex experience—that is, synthesized experience—is valuable precisely because its synthesis is complex. Is this a valid point that will hold for imagination as synthesis alone?

This is a particularly difficult question to answer. It would seem that there are no differential experiences that can be compared—one experience imaginative and perhaps valuable and the other unimaginative and perhaps not valuable. There is no such thing as experience unformed by the synthetic imagination. An alternate approach would be to characterize the minimum universal imaginative activity in terms of a diminished limit of degrees of higher imaginative activity. We can easily distinguish levels of synthetic imagination, for example, that are more or less complex and elegantly integrated. From this perspective (defended later), it is apparent that the more complex and elegant integrations of the same material are appreciated immediately as better than less coordinated and mutually inhibiting integrations. Yet each level of integration, simply because it *is* an integration, is appreciated as having some value. At the least level—that characteristic of the minimal imaginative synthesis of a world—integration would still have some value because, however minimal it is, it would at least be a harmony. The difficulty with this approach is that it involves a complex theory of value; the approach also assumes that people might have the minimal syntheses as values without realizing it.

At the present stage in the argument, the best approach is to point out something about the nature of value, then determine whether by doing so, we uncover the crucial point in the experience of imaginative synthesis as such—in the bare achievement of a subjective world.

Every synthesis is a complex harmony of things; each of the contained things is also such a harmony.[9] The value in a harmony is that it is a *way* of possessing the things contained within it. The value in the contained things is that each of them also possesses its own components, and so on. Every act of synthesis is a gathering of the synthesized components, into possession by the imaginative act. The objects synthesized all have their own various values, whatever they be, independent of the synthesis, but the imaginative synthesis has the additional value of gathering those values together within itself. Imagination is the *taking possession* of the values of the world.

The price of synthesis is that, in order for them to fit together, the objects synthesized must be trimmed and cut. Put another way, the objects must be altered to conform to the overall form or pattern that integrates them. (As a Kantian philosopher might put it, objects must be altered so as to conform to a temporal structure.) Although some of the value of the independent objects is lost when the objects are synthesized within a person's experience, it is still a gain in value to have them with their remaining values synthesized. Indeed, it is an absolute gain. The values in the objects are in no way diminished by their playing further roles in synthesizing experience. A past fact reaches its full intrinsic value when its own internal process of synthesis ceases and it becomes past. What happens to it later in the way of being experienced does not alter that intrinsic value. What happens to the fact when it later functions as an object for others is sheer gain for those others. Of course, if a past object of experience is part of an enduring entity, a person may experience and respond to it in such a way that some potential of its later moments is destroyed. It is at this point that most moral questions arise. The intrinsic value of a past moment remains unchanged, no matter how it is trimmed and cut subsequently.

Phenomenologically, this means that the way in which an experiential act possesses objects and incorporates some of their values is by synthesizing them in a world. Imagination is enjoyment in gathering. That is its primitive value.[10] What is enjoyed depends on the content of imagination. Enough is now known about the physiological conditions that affect imagination for us to understand that even the most fantastic-seeming imagination involves synthesis, the very fact there is a synthesis means there is some value enjoyed. conditions that affect dreaming sleep. A person who dreams about a bell in order to sleep through a ringing alarm clock has included the real alarm within the imaginative synthesis. Whatever the level of quality in the imaginative systhesis, the very fact there is a synthesis means there is some value enjoyed. This is the same as saying that the synthesis achieves some existence.

The thesis that synthetic imagination by itself is the enjoyment of the valuable objects of which it takes possession, is limited. The above account has not attempted to explain value. Indeed, there is a circularity in saying that an imaginative synthesis enjoys the values of its components—each of which, in turn, enjoys the values of its components, and so on. The question of why harmony is a value is separate.[11] The present point is to note that harmony—at least, of the kind involved in synthetic imagination—is valuable.

Value in imaginative synthesis does not lie in the presence of an order as such, according to which the synthesis is formed (though the order itself may have value); rather, the order is the instrument for attaining the synthesis. Nor does value lie in the experiencing person's ability to appreciate things which otherwise would be alien (although this, too, may be true). Rather, the imaginative synthesis comes into existence itself as the harmony of values of which it takes possession.

Whether a particular imaginative synthesis is organized with other imaginative syntheses and other elements of experience to form a human person depends in part on the kind of imaginative synthesis involved. And the particular kind of imaginative synthesis determines just how the person as a whole stands related to the various things of which his or her imaginative acts take possession. This is another way of pointing out that just as the world of imagination includes determinations of the objects in the world, it also includes a determination of the contours of the experience. The self that takes possession of Bodhidharma's world differs considerably from the self of Proust's world. The difference comes about in part because of the structure of the imagination.

Another point must be stressed in the context of the phenomenology of imagination as synthesis. If synthetic imagination is where an act of experience constitutes itself by taking possession of things in the form of a world, then it is where the origins of mind, of appreciative feeling, and of will are present and undifferentiated. When a sage traces back the roots of his or her knowledge beyond theory, beyond assertion, beyond focal attention, the end point is the gathering in synthetic imagination. When a saint penetrates to the bottom of his or her heart, beyond comparative evaluations, beyond the importance of things for experiences, the end point is the presence of the world gathered in imagination. When the hero of will traces back the roots of intention beyond consideration of the consequences, beyond definitions of intentional objects, to the very springs of orientation toward the world, the end point is the synthetic activity of the imagination. This activity is the root of all three—knowledge, valuation, and will; it is only in subsequent manifestations of articulated knowledge, valuation, and will that they become different.

Tracing experience to its origins is not an everyday occurrence, however. It requires great discipline, perhaps even discipline resembling that of the occult. The philosopher who best understood this, and one who pressed the analysis far along, was Wang Yang-ming (discussed in Chapter 2). Wang's doctrines of the unity of heart and mind and the identification of knowledge with action make little sense if they refer only to the *separate* functioning of "faculties" in experience. If they refer to the origins, or roots, of experience, however, they become profound. Wang's point is that only through disciplined penetration to the heart can one find the source of the faculties that itself can be enjoyed as a norm for life. He believed that once we have done this, the higher levels of life—cognition, affection, and volition—can flow spontaneously. Determining whether this is so requires that we consider many factors besides imagination. At the very least, though, Wang was correct in pointing to the heart or to imaginative synthesis as the fountainhead of experience.[12]

CRITICAL INTERPRETATION

The naturalism of the preceding discussion of imagination stands in sharp contrast to the Kantian tradition of modern philosophy. In this, it would seem to find an ally in the tradition of British empiricism from Hobbes through Hume to contemporary philosophical analysis. Indeed, Hobbes may be read as a precursor of Whitehead's proposal that a person is to be understood as a bundle of perceptions actively forming themselves into a consistent judgment or resolve, although Hobbes's mechanistic theory prevented him from appreciating the role of spontaneity in the self-constituting activity of thinking. Empiricism's naturalism had turned to a very passive conception of imagining in the philosophy of Hume, however; and Hume did not present a view of imagination as synthesis in the sense discussed here. Hume's present-day heirs, by locating philosophy's principal concerns in the analysis of language, have accepted the main contention of the Kantians: that philosophy is second-order discourse, that things are to be considered as expressed in the medium of a unified knower-speaker. It is with Kant himself, that the present argument must come to terms.

Kant's discussion of imagination in the *Critique of Pure Reason* was embedded in his general concern for stating the limits of a priori knowledge of the world (a topic that does not properly enter the present discussion until we reach Chapter 6). This knowledge knows objects, not mere concepts; it knows them regardless of confirmation by experience. Kant began with the postulate that we have a priori knowledge in the founding principles of mathematics and physical science. He limited critical philosophy to spelling out the conditions under which the knowledge in hand is possible. He supposed that knowledge grows from two roots—the influence of outside objects and the spontaneous activity of the mind developing these influences in the form of knowledge.[13] The link connecting the two roots, he claimed, is imagination functioning at many levels. The basic level is imagination as synthesis. On a higher level, imagination has the peculiar synthetic task of schematizing the manifold of outside influences to the logical principles of mind.[14] The genius of Kant's strategy is his insight that thinking takes on identity and validity insofar as it conforms to principles. In other words, principles are norms; without some degree of conformation to principles, the activity of mind is chaos. Mind becomes thinking insofar as it uses concepts as rules for putting representations or thoughts together, and thought becomes perception by employing principles of empirical experience. Thought becomes knowledge to the extent that it conforms to conditions that make knowledge possible. These principles are universal principles of logic (principles of "transcendental logic," in Kant's terminology). People become thinkers to the degree that they conform their thought to these principles. Thus far, the axiology of thinking is not seriously in conflict with Kant's view.

Kant's theory cannot sustain the prima facie natural distinction between the two roots of knowledge—objects outside and spontaneity inside. The reason for this failing is not his cosmology of thinking as outlined above, but rather his insistence that there is certain, a priori, knowledge and, therefore, that the conditions of knowledge must be able to account for it. By a chain of brilliant, original reasoning, Kant provided an a priori definition of a possible object of experience (both actual and possible objects must be possible). Representations appear within the mind in a certain order; an order subjective in the sense that it depends, for example, on whether the subject looks from left to right or right to left. Certain elements in the order do not depend on the circumstances of the thinking subject; they are what they are objectively, as can be tested by an observer. A boat going downriver cannot be seen first as downriver and then upriver, no matter how much one turns one's head. An object, Kant said, is not something outside the mind; rather, it is a set of representations in the mind that are ordered objectively. Because an objective ordering can be tested publicly by a well-placed experimenter, the world of objects is a public one even though all experienced objects are constructs of individual minds conforming themselves to the principles of transcendental logic in the face of a mysteriously given manifold. Kant's philosophy is transcendental not only because it employs a transcendental method for philosophy but also—and consequently—because it provides a transcendental definition of the world.[15]

While our knowledge of physical objects admittedly involves a spontaneous ordering of the influences of the object according to the principles by which the influences can be integrated in our personal existence, it seems needlessly paradoxical to say that the existence of the object is nothing but these influences so ordered. The world seems naturally real. Furthermore, the way in which objects are "given" to thinkers should not be as mysterious as it must be on Kant's theory. On his view, a theoretical understanding of perception cannot possibly be an account of the mystery of givenness because the theoretical account is necessarily limited to relating the outside object—as an *object*, in Kant's use of the word—to the perceiver as an object, in the same use. On the other hand, the activity of giving must transcend both an empirical and a transcendental relationship between objects, because both the objects and the relationship are consequent upon it. Because of the great difficulty in providing an account of the original givenness of the manifold, most Kantians have abandoned the attempt and become idealists. The axiological cosmology provides a theory that preserves the sense of the world as naturally real in order to provide for the possibility of an account of the givenness of the manifold of sense.

Phrased in this way, the axiological cosmology of thinking offered here is an alternate hypothesis to Kant's, with certain, more attractive features. Kant, however, probably would have objected that a philosophical hypothesis, in contrast to a scientific hypothesis, is not knowledge. Anything claiming to be knowledge must be based on a nonhypothetical, a priori foundation that defines what objects are and what counts as evidence for or against hypotheses. Near the end of the *Critique of Pure Reason,* after the transcendental logic and in the "Discipline of Pure Reason," Kant considered the suggestion that knowledge *as hypothesis* might escape the limitations of reason imposed by his critique. This, in fact, is the suggestion developed at great length by Peirce and the pragmatists; it is also the foundation for the cosmology in the present theory. Kant rejected the possibility, however, with the following argument:

> If the imagination is not simply to be *visionary* [*schwarmen*], but is to be *inventive* [*dichten soll*] under the strict surveillance of reason, there must always previously be something that is completely certain, and not invented or merely a matter of opinion, namely, the *possibility* of the object itself. Once that is established, it is then permissible to have recourse to opinion in regard to its actuality; but this opinion, if it is not to be groundless, must be brought into connection with what is actually given and so far certain as serving to account for what is thus given.[16]

In answer to this, while it might be conceded that any hypothesis is meaningful only in a situation in which there is a conception of what objects for it might be, and what it would mean for objects to count against or for it, there is no reason why this situation cannot itself be created by living with a higher-level hypothesis. The higher-level hypothesis may state what it is to be an object and how objects enter into or are referred to by concepts. Not only is this sufficient for entertaining hypotheses on the lower level, it also, in the right context, makes possible criticism of the hypothetical character of the higher-level hypothesis itself. No theory need be anything other than an hypothesis subject to criticism when the occasion warrants and taken for granted when required. Remember that the life of believing and testing hypotheses takes place in the real world where natural structures continually correct our activities.

Why should there be anything certain in experience at all? Only if knowledge is defined in such a way as to demand certainty at the beginning are transcendental conditions necessary. Is it not the case, though, that thinking begins in confusion and error—or, at best, unwitting truth—and that we slowly back toward clarity, toward less error and more justification, through continual criticism and examination of presuppositions? There is no need for logic to be transcendental in the sense of defining possible objects, only normative in making thinkers real as thinkers over against objects. There is no logical necessity for any knowledge of objects a priori. A passion for certainty can be viewed seriously only when one presupposes a cosmology in which thought is locked in an isolated mind. In an alternate cosmology in which thought and action are one, however, certainty is not necessary for action to be initiated. With or without certainty, a person goes on living. When thought and action are continuous, however, what is necessary is recognition of norms that obligate both, that define a sense of responsibility which presses one toward rational justification. Thinking displays its responsibility by making itself available to be checked up on, not by claiming grounding in a transcendental norm. Kant's views on imagination are readily appreciated and used but only by recognizing that they must be extracted from the web of the larger transcendental theory.

Much that is said of Kant can be transferred to Husserl and the phenomenologists. Like Kant, Husserl wanted to establish a ground for certainty; he conceived phenomenological philosophy in order to provide a foundation for the possibility of science. This led him to make claims for the purity of phenomenological description that have unsettling analogies with Kant's claims for the possession of a priori knowledge in philosophy. Hardly anyone today believes that even the most carefully worked out phenomenological description is free of interest, hypothesis, and uncritical language. Such recent phenomenologists as Merleau-Ponty gave up the claim for certainty and recognized that there are many hypothetical elements in their description, and indeed argued for their points dialectically. But they asserted the interesting claim that the subject matter of phenomenological analysis itself is primary experience. For Merleau-Ponty, for instance, perception is the concrete experience out of which we formulate comparatively abstract conceptions— for example, those of discrete objects and theories by which to conceive of objects. In Merleau-Ponty's view, hypothetico-deductive science is so far removed from concrete experience that it occupies the naturalistic standpoint that necessarily falsifies the experience in its concreteness.[17]

While it is true that, in a sense, concrete experience is primary, the experience in concrete experience is more than is revealed in phenomenological description from the transcendental standpoint. Experiencing things concretely *includes* the application and criticism of categories. It *includes* concern for theories that might be related to these categories and to criticism of them. It *includes* spontaneity and unintentional feeling. Furthermore, experience may include efforts to experience responsibly. All of these elements, in turn, can be described; but the description of critical elements—elements that involve weighing things according to norms—cannot help but be dialectical. That is, the identification and description of a critical element requires the imaginative invention of descriptive categories, their critical application, and theories justifying their use and their long-range meaning.

The upshot is that phenomenological description is a very useful and revealing moment of philosophical thinking. At the same time, it is intrinsically incomplete, requiring appropriate critical discussion of the terms used vis-à-vis other descriptive systems, and a hermeneutical interpretation of the significance of the description itself. Because the question of interpretation leads to that of the values that control interpretation (as well as those that should), phenomenology intrinsically makes reference to the dialectic of value theory. Far from being a certain foundation, phenomenological description is a tentative venture waiting to be made more plausibile by other modes of thought. It is important to remember that phenomenological description may not be wanting more description but rather other kinds of thinking. At the same time, such description may be a crucial, indispensable mode of thinking. Indeed, the force of the phenomenological is often that more theoretically oriented modes of thought leave description behind and become irresponsible about the subject matter. This is a valid polemical point.

As to phenomenological contributions to the understanding of imagination, they do not say much about imagination as synthesis. Rather, they focus on the usefulness of imagination as a tool for phenomenological analysis, providing analyses of imagination itself considered as the act of imagining; this sense of *imagination* is, however, considered in Chapter 7, in the section "Phenomenology of Appearance."[18]

One more perspective needs to be considered at this point—that of Heidegger. Like the theory presented here, Heidegger took the notion of imagination as synthesis to be central to the concept of thinking. For the above discussion of synthesis as gathering, including the value of possessing or being valuable, is largely indebted to Heidegger's remarks on thinking as gathering and "thanks". Heidegger never sounded the theme of value in a positive way, however. In some measure this is a mere semantic difference. In discussing thinking and the experience of existing, Heidegger insisted on a kind of piety, as suggested for instance by his interpretation of thinking as *thanks*—that is, thinking which is not significantly different from the kind of valuing of synthesis defended above.[19] His rejection of explicit value language probably reflected his deep suspicion of philosophies that speak of values as high-level abstractions, a tradition that began with Plato and which, in Heidegger's view, set philosophy on an "unrighteous" course.[20] His position amounts to a challenge to any theory that asserts a continuity between the extremes of synthesis as the valuation of existence and deliberation as the discernment of highly reflected values.

Perhaps the difference can be put down to a primitive division over metaphysical intuitions. Heidegger believed that existence is to be understood in terms of actualizing, whereas the axiological cosmology suggests it is to be understood in terms of attaining the measure of norms. Such intuitions constitute no argument, however. The peculiarity of Heidegger's account is that he could not establish a continuity between fundamental ontological piety and more reflected forms of valuing. As a consequence he tended to reduce too quickly the more reflected realms to the ontological level, dismissing valid concerns about values intrinsic to them.[21] This seems to put Heidegger's approach at a theoretical disadvantage with the one presented here. Whereas a theory should not introduce continuities where there are none, it ought to recognize them when they *are* there. This means that testing the plausibility of what we can guess Heidegger's criticism of the project of the present book to be depends on explicit discussions of the values at each level of analysis and of the continuities between them.

COSMOLOGY OF IMAGINATION AS SYNTHESIS

The purpose of this section is to provide a cosmological scheme within which imagination as synthesis can be interpreted. To do this, we must add details to the hypothesis proposed in Chapter 3, where it is remarked that a thinking occasion is a natural occasion in which thinking elements are somehow important. Also, the synthesis of imagination is a form of synthesis characteristic of rare, higher occasions but continuous with more fundamental processes of synthesis characteristic of all occasions. First, the discussion summarizes the cosmology's general treatment of synthesis, following mainly Whitehead's view of categoreal obligations. The second part concentrates on imagination.[22] The reader should keep in mind that the argument here is neither criticism nor dialectic but explication of the cosmological hypothesis.

Synthesis in Process

An occasion constitutes itself through a series of synthesizing phases. The first phase contains only the previous occasions that are finished facts, unintegrated as yet by anything unique to the constituting occasion. The only thing distinguishing the given elements, or "initial data," of the first phase from the state of things previous to the constituting occasion is that they are compatible for being synthesized into a new occasion. "Compatibility" is such a minimal concept relative to initiating synthesis that two things are said to be compatible if one of them can be eliminated in the process of synthesis. The process of synthesis is called "concrescence," in the tradition of process philosophy, meaning "becoming concrete."

Interpreted developmentally, the initial phase of prehension contains only previous occasions as objects. There is little or no subjective form, that is, no form accruing to an object by virtue of integration with other feelings. Through successive phases, subjective form is added as the objects are brought together and harmonized and various elements of the objects are eliminated. In the final phase, called satisfaction, the objects left from the initial data and the elements of subjective form are perfectly integrated as a new physical fact and are called the "objectified datum." To call the end product an objectified datum is not to say that it lacks subjective form; rather, it is to say that the end product is the way in which the occasion objectifies itself as a physical being to be felt as an object by future occasions. The way an occasion objectifies itself is its way of influencing the future.

Only objectified data are physically real, because only they are completely definite. Consequently, only objectified data are in physical time. The prior phases resulting in the objectified datum are "in becoming," not "in being." Each subject occasion feels itself "coming to be"; it itself, however, is private and cannot be felt by another occasion.

The initial phase of an occasion's concrescence consists entirely of physical feelings. A physical feeling is one with a physical object or objects. A subsequent phase, however, can include "conceptual feeling." A conceptual feeling has as its object the forms, patterns, or qualities that give character to physical objects—but abstracted from the physical objects themselves. Most conceptual feelings are abstractions of physical feelings. The importance of the distinction between physical and conceptual feelings is enormous. The distinction allows that during the process of concrescence, a quality derived from one physical object can be synthesized with another physical object, it can be combined with another quality. Conceptual feelings are not so named because they are conscious; indeed, only a few are conscious—those that are objectified on rare, high-grade, intentional occasions. The name refers to the fact their objects are abstract properties. This is the basis of novelty in the world.

After the initial phase, an occasion coming into being must *value* what the initial data will mean for it. The occasion gives each datum a value or significant role in the occasion's self-constitution. Whitehead called this a "conceptual valuation." Each datum is felt to have importance relative to the concrete occasion. In succeeding phases, "evaluation" can take place, in which data are compared with each other as to their relative worth. Some—in fact, most—data are valued as inappropriate for synthesis in the new occasion and are eliminated, or "negatively felt." A datum negatively felt leaves no objective trace in the occasion; instead, it leaves the subjective form of its exclusion.

In view of the many past occasions that are relevant to synthesis in a new occasion, most must be eliminated from the simple occasions of the world. The loss of value presently enjoyed that this would involve is partially mitigated by transmutation. In transmutation, a group of objectified occasions is represented only by one of their number or by some other quality; then the group is eliminated, with the representation continuing some of the group's values. This allows for considerable simplification. For instance, the *feeling* of a blue tie by human beings involves transmutation of the electrical excitation of the perceiver's retina by the perceived quality "blue." The human mind apparently is such that it would be difficult for the electrical occasions to reach consciousness; yet under standard conditions they can be adequately represented by the feeling of "blue."

The mention of "value" above should be emphasized. Every occasion has an intrinsic value—namely, its own feeling of satisfaction or final integration, its own subjectively-aimed-at-harmony. The occasion's feeling of itself in concrescence is part of the subjective form it objectifies for future occasions. Therefore, an occasion's intrinsic value, or feeling of worth, can be felt objectively by another occasion. As mentioned above, the intrinsic value an occasion assigns itself is the sum of the values of the objects it feels, plus the special harmonies it contributes through its own subjective form. This conception of value is contrary to the usual belief that people experience facts only as given, that they introduce values into experience merely as subjective colorations. To say that all the emotional qualities of experience are subjective contributions is to indulge in prejudice. Nothing is objectified in consciousness without subjective contributions. It is also gratuitous to say that values are distinct from facts in their origin or that they are derived solely from unrealistic subjective projections.

The doctrine that values are felt objectively should not be mistaken for naive realism. There is a difference between the intrinsic values of the objects felt and the valuation placed on feeling them in a concrete occasion. I can recognize the intrinsic value of something as great, yet assign it trivial value in relation to my personal experience. And if I constitute my objectified presentations of myself to the world in such a way that the future occasions perceive the thing through me to be of lesser value than it intrinsically is, then I have done evil. For example, practically anyone would admit that human beings have such high intrinsic value that they possess "infinite dignity," yet racists find it impossible to accord this status to people who are the object of prejudice. We all ignore, or negatively feel, the infinite values of nearly all the people in the world, coping explicitly only with those near us. We do so, however, in ways that do not always feed back to the ignored people and hurt them. A racist mediates a person's value to the world so as to lessen it. Connoisseurs are people who feel an art object with its intrinsic value in their initial data and who maintain the value straight though their concrescence, including transmutations, objectifying it in their final judgment and appreciation. All appreciation of value involves both an intrinsic value in the objects felt and a subjective valuation of how the objects can be harmonized with other feelings in the occasion.

Among the elements of subjective form in an occasion, we can distinguish between those whose function is to determine the pattern and hierarchy of valuation within the occasion's satisfaction and those that merely reflect the pattern and hierarchy already determined. Although there may be borderline cases, the former may be called "essential" features because they are the ways in which an occasion determines itself. The latter may be called "conditional" features because they depend entirely on the combined determinants of essential features and initial data.

All conditional features of subjective form are derived by abstraction from physical feelings of past occasions. Some essential features of subjective form also derive from physical feelings of past occasions. These features are the grounds for continuity of character, for responsibility for past deeds, and even, in some respects, for regularity and physical law.

Other essential features of subjective form appear spontaneously; these are important for decisions involving the genuine adoption of forms not determined to be adopted by past conditions; the spontaneous essential features are necessary components of an account of personal freedom.[23] The citation of spontaneous features requires no denial, either of fact or of empirically verified regularity.

Still another group of essential features, one probably limited to higher organisms, derives from the anticipation of values to be attained in the future by virtue of the way in which the occasion objectifies itself. Moral obligation depends to some extent on these anticipation-derived essential features.[24]

By attaining satisfaction—that is, satisfying the concrescent process of attaining harmony—an occasion achieves a definiteness that makes it a physical individual. *Definiteness*, means "determinateness" and "position." An occasion is determinate when it clearly includes or excludes every possibility with potential for realization in it. Before satisfaction, there are still decisions to be made as to what is included and what is excluded. "Position" indicates that the occasion has occupied a place relative to other occasions in space and time, or in the worldly field. Before satisfaction, it is indefinite exactly where the occasion will be and what its time structure will be. The definiteness of an occasion allows it to be felt by its future successors in a pattern with other occasions. By becoming definite, an occasion becomes a part of nature. The definiteness of an occasion is its *being*; the concrescence prior to definiteness is its *becoming*. Change *in the realm of being* indicates only a difference of position and determinate quality; if this is the only respectable concept of change, then the existentialists are right in their criticism of the mainline philosophical tradition. Change *in the realm of becoming* is where things happen and where life is felt as a flux filled with decisions. Such a double meaning of change is in accord with the common experience of people.

The discussion in this section has concentrated so far on the internal constitution of occasions. An occasion as constituted—not as *coming-to-be* but as *having-become*—is an external, public matter of fact. It is objectified for future occasions to feel. Occasions by themselves, however, are not the only kind of public fact. The *relations* between occasions are equally matters of public fact, constituted by the occasions feeling each other, either directly and indirectly. The attainment of definiteness means that each occasion has a place in a coordinated framework of relations. Except for occasions having to do with the human mind, most actual, individual occasions may be neglected in favor of interesting patterns of relationships. Most things that exist in the mesoscopic order (smaller than the astronomer's world but larger than the particle physicist's) are not occasions but groups of occasions with relatively fixed identifying patterns in their relationships. A tree is not an occasion; it is an ecosystem comprising millions of occasions that are fleetingly existent, a pattern of relationships that slowly turn as the tree grows.

An ecosystem is a group of occasions with the following conditions: (1) there is a coherent pattern to at least some of the relations between the member occasions; (2) each member occasion feels this pattern, or at least some part of it, relative to its own position, and it objectifies itself as having a position or playing a role in the pattern; and (3) each occasion derives its feeling of the pattern from a feeling for other member occasions.

The significance of the first condition is that member occasions are related to each other by a pattern that touches them all; that is, any two member occasions are related by a pattern that also involves the places, or roles, of the other member occasions. *That an occasion is a member of an ecosystem does not mean all its feeling relations are exhausted in that system*; it can be a member of many ecosystems at once, and it can have feeling relations with occasions that are connected only trivially to it by ecosystems.

The significance of the second condition is that each member occasion must make itself definite in terms of the ecosystem's pattern. An occasion cannot feel and eliminate the pattern without first objectifying it. A member occasion *must* objectify itself as having a position or as playing a role in the ecosystemic pattern.

The third condition means the occasion is a member of an ecosystem because it feels other members in the ecosystemic pattern.

Most things with enduring identity in the world are ecosystems that contain subecosystems. The ecosystem of the human body includes all the occasions in that body; it also includes the patterns which arrange discrete sets of occasions in organs, circulatory systems, and so forth. What is important in the bodily pattern is not that all member occasions be flesh and blood parts of the body but that the patterned function of each organ and system be performed. It would be a mistake (and directly contrary to the word *ecosystem*) to think that all ecosystems are as tightly knit as a human body. Most ecosystems are loose confederations of subecosystems.

The most striking characteristic of a person's ecosystem is that its subecosystems are organically ordered with respect to each other according to the dominance of the nervous system. The nervous system consistently receives the effects of the other subecosystems, and consistently affects them, forcing them to respond in regular and consistent ways. Relations between occasions in the central nervous system are of various sorts. As an ecosystem itself, the central nervous system has physical properties of the sort studied in neurophysiology and neuropsychology. But there are also semantic relations between certain brain occasions such that there is continuity of thinking in imagination, in interpretation, and in other dimensions of experience. *Consciousness,* in the ordinary sense, is not a characteristic of single occasions but a characteristic of groups of occasions semantically ordered.

The continuity of consciousness required for ordinary imagination requires the following systematic addition to the above account of relations between occasions. Among the physical feelings that a thinking occasion can have of certain prior occasions are "hybrid physical feelings." A hybrid physical feeling is one in which the subjective content of the previous occasion is objectified. That is, the conscious experience and subjective feelings of the prior occasion are made available for being felt by a successor occasion, and the successor is able to feel them. In low-grade occasions, subjective feelings are not objectified for being felt. The reason that high-grade occasions can feel the subjective life of previous occasions is that they arise in the complex semantic-neural environment that makes them available and that allows them to be objectified in the occasions that feel them. The continuity of conscious life, such as it is, consists in the chain of semantic occasions that feel each other in serial and environing ways in terms of their respective internal subjective forms.

Synthesis in Imagination

The three imaginative syntheses for which we need a cosmological account here are, to use Kant's terms, those of apprehension in intuition, reproduction in imagination, and recognition in concept. Together, these syntheses organize the objects felt in a synthetic unity that can be experienced as a world by the subject. Such a subjective world is presented *immediately* in the subject's experience. Strictly speaking, this world contains no mediated claim that the world thus presented is "true" or that it corresponds to an objective world, to the concatenation of objects before they are experienced here, or to a real environment. In presentational immediacy the world presents itself as the world containing the experiencing subject; but it does so only immediately. The world of presentational immediacy is complicated by questions of perception, interpretation of external objects in terms of experience, and theoretical understanding. Although minimally subjective in status, the synthetic, imaginative experience of presentational immediacy is not necessarily false or distorted; rather, the issue of referential truth is merely irrelevant to it.

The subjective world of presentational immediacy may be indefinitely rich, by definition, containing within it everything that might appear in experience of any kind. At the very least, however, to be a subjective world, it must involve the activity of the three forms of synthesis in imagination, which are explained cosmologically below.

The synthesis of apprehension in intuition involves the composition of *propositional feelings*. A propositional feeling is a complex feeling that, at its simplest, has in its object two feelings in a propositional relation. One object-feeling functions as the "subject" in the propositional relation; an obvious example is the complex physical feeling of the objects making up a chair. The other object-feeling must be a conceptual feeling (of some complexity or other) that is proposed for characterizing the subject feeling. A propositional feeling can be symbolized by a propositional function, $f(x)$, although it must be remembered that this is a symbol of the feeling, not the feeling itself. The synthesis of apprehension processes real feelings even when feelings of symbolic notation are included.

The synthesis of apprehension involves the *composition* of propositional feelings. Most likely, the feelings themselves refer to structures or to ecosystems of objects. The imaginative world, however, is these objects composited into a field. In one sense, the mediational form of the field is determined by the objects combined within it; but in another sense, the unity of the field is more primordial than—and a necessary, prior condition for—comparison of the objects with regard to the compatibility of their natures. Kant pointed out the crucial element—namely, that the form must be a unified manifold with the potential for being run through serially, from one point to another. He thought that the form was space; indeed, this makes sense for most of experience that we recognize in terms of common sense: the apprehensive unity of our immediate experience usually is a surrounding spatial world defining a perspective center for our physical selves, according to which other objects can be distinguished and ordered. In this spatial sense, we relate to ourselves as objects. Kant, however, was premature in adopting geometrical space as a form to be used in apprehension. When we prescind from descriptions of what we know the world to be from common sense or from science and describe experience in its immediacy, spatial relations sometimes become inappropriate metaphors. Van Gogh and other painters have shown that ordinary perception sometimes grossly distorts spatial geometry.[25] In some dreams, the composition of the field of immediacy takes forms that can be called spatial only in the most metaphorical sense. Experience under the influence of psychedelic drugs is called "mind-blowing" because the conventional forms of composition of the field are replaced by forms which, by comparison, appear disorienting and bizarre. Experience in Hindu and Buddhist meditation contains incidents where the field of presentational immediacy is described in terms that explicitly deny the extensiveness of spatiality, separating the position of the subject from that of external objects. Just what the forms are that, in any presentationally immediate experience, order the composition of propositional feelings is an empirical issue that depends partly on deliverances of perception and imagery. The minimum requirement for any such empirically derived compositional form is that it allow the propositions to be felt as a whole in such a way that they have the potential for identification in an ordered relationship.

Synthesis of reproduction in imagination involves the serial ordering of propositional feelings. Serial ordering obtains when: (1) there is a conceptual feeling common to all propositional feelings in the series; (2) each propositional feeling feels the conceptual feeling by virtue of feeling some other propositional feeling in the series (rather than by abstracting it originally itself from physical feelings outside the series); and (3) for each propositional feeling in the series all the other feelings are divided into two classes—those that can be felt by the propositional feeling but which cannot feel it, and those that can feel the propositional feeling but cannot be felt by it. No two propositional feelings can occupy the same position in the series; if they did so, each would have to feel and be felt by the other, thus contradicting the third condition above. A given propositional feeling, however, can play roles in any number of serial orders. Suppose there are two serial orders, one containing propositional feeling M and the other containing M'. M can feel all the propositions in its series prior to itself and can be felt by those subsequent to itself. Suppose, however that M can feel all those in the series of M' except M' itself, and that it can be felt by all those that can also feel M'. M and M' are thus contemporaries in parallel series, with M belonging to both series (the series are different because they have different conceptual feelings as their unifying characteristics).

The synthesis of reproduction in imagination means that the world of presentational immediacy presents a flow. Propositional feelings are presented in orders such that later ones reproduce earlier ones. Even within the subjective immediacy of imagination alone, the flow can be felt as objective or subjective (although whether the world actually flows that way is another question). The flow is objective when the composition of serially ordered propositional feelings is felt according to the objective nature of the order; it is felt subjectively insofar as the conceptual feeling common to all the propositional feelings includes the subjective feeling of being in the process of conscrescence. If a propositional feeling feels itself as being in the process of a concrescing occasion, it may objectify this subjectivity to be felt by later occasions. With regard to the objective flow, each propositional feeling in the series must be located in different concrete occasions, for it is the occasions themselves that have objective serial order (even though the *experience* of them as being serial fastens on their contained propositional feelings). With regard to the subjective flow, however, a proposition may feel itself to be in a series of propositional feelings within a concrescing occasion; this phenomenon is necessary for the sense of subjective life, the life of seeking satisfaction in definiteness through integration. Except for the last member objectified in the satisfaction, the series of propositions within an occasion contains only partially indefinite propositional feelings. This indefiniteness may render somewhat vague the order in the series. The subjective sense of a flow of thought combines both the objective sense and the subjective sense of flowing. In each occasion is a propositional feeling that reproduces the propositional feelings of prior occasions in serial order; but the propositional feelings of these occasions also contain the feeling of their own subjective flow within the concrescence of the occasions themselves. Otherwise, there would be no continuity of subjectivity.

In ordinary experience it takes time to experience the flow of things because the flow of the world is conjoined to our sense of flow of our own subjective life. Strictly speaking, it is not necessary to take time to experience flow, since the proposition that reproduces the series can be felt in a moment, or single occasion. That this sometimes happens can perhaps be ascertained by noting those experiences in which entire episodes appear in a flash, as in dreaming where a sudden outside noise triggers a long, complex dream ending with a dream surrogate for the noise. People familiar with meditation describe experiences in which the past is imagined as present in its serial order in a single moment. In Hwa-Yen Buddhism it is argued that the future is present in the same way. It is quite possible that the future and past can both be *totum simul* in a moment of presentational immediacy, still serially ordered and experienced as subjectively flowing. One must take care, however, not to argue from this structuring of the *subjective* world of presentational immediacy that the objective world is truly structured this way; such a claim can be justified only through perception and the interpretive and theoretical tests that objectify imagination. Serious difficulties are encountered in attempting to believe that the future can be determinately present now when *now* it is not completely determinate.

Synthesis of recognition in concepts is explained cosmologically with the same categories as those used for synthesis of reproduction, with special attention given to the conceptual feeling in the series. In a concept, recognition involves not only reproducing the series with the common conceptual feeling, but also feeling the series as ordered by the relation of propositions to one another, relative to the common conceptual feeling. Here, the series is recognized as one that is relative to the feeling of the common conceptual feeling. Instead of merely reproducing the series 1, 1, 1, . . . , it is felt as 1, 2, 3, ...

Beauty: the Value of Synthesis

In the analysis thus far, some of the basic elements of synthesis in imagination have been discussed, and certain categories for understanding the imaginative process within a larger cosmological scheme have been suggested. But *why* is there such synthesis?

The answer has several dimensions. Insofar as the question asks for purpose served by imaginative integration in experience, the answer is in terms of evolutionary adaptability leading to more successful reproduction of the species. Insofar as it asks what value is accomplished in imagination, the answer as suggested in the first section, "Phenomenology of Synthesis," is that it preserves some of the values in the world and reproduces them in a new experience, perhaps enhancing them through a new conceptual organization. Insofar as the question asks for the value peculiar to imagination as synthesis, the answer is, beauty. Experience begins in beauty; without beauty, there is no world. This strong claim must first be explicated; then it must be justified.

Beauty. Beauty is a characteristic of the content of an experience. It involves a harmony with four dimensions, two pertaining to background and two to focal objects.[26] The first background dimension is bare synthesis of apprehension in intuition, whereby all objects of experience are felt as together but in such a way that the forms of togetherness add nothing to the objects. The only value in bare apprehensive synthesis is triviality; at this level of synthesis, nothing is more important than anything else, or bears upon anything else. By means of other forms of imagination one can run from one trivial object to another in the apprehensive synthesis without any implications arising from the route itself. The triviality assigned things in apprehensive synthesis is itself important because it provides a way to contain a host of objects within experience, which otherwise would have to be excluded if they were to be related to each other in important ways.[27] Most objects are sufficiently different that they can be contained within the same experience only by existing in some kind of contrast; but contrast is difficult to attain, and it requires that a complicated background be sustained. Through triviality, objects can be maintained together with minimal contrast. Furthermore, so long as the objects are maintained within the experience, it is possible for other forms of imagination to locate and lift them out so that they can enter into relations of intrinsic value and importance. The synthesis of apprehension allows, in principle, for any item in the synthesized to be located.

The second background dimension is bare synthesis of reproduction in imagination whereby many otherwise trivially related elements are vaguely unified in a common feeling. The feeling is one of the vague potential of sweeping over the multitude, or rather the vague unity of the potential manifold to be swept. The feeling of vagueness arises from the seriality of reproduction asserting a common character for all members of the series. Without vagueness there would be no commonality of feeling with which to orient experience to the trivial background and thus no possibility of locating items in the trivial multitude. With vagueness and triviality together, the harmony of experience has a feeling for one world with indefinite potential for alternate specifications.

The two dimensions having to do with focal objects are what Whitehead calls narrowness and width. They involve synthesis of recognition in concepts. Narrowness is the character of organization in objects of experience that produces intensity by multiplying factors in upon each other so as to achieve great density subsumed under simple, high-level, conceptual feelings. But experience might be filled with islands of narrow intensity unrelated to each other and therefore disharmonious overall. Width is the articulation of experience with the propositional feelings that allow for contrasts wherein narrow intensities are brought together. Considering—as far as we know empirically—that the world consists of tiny energetic occasions, only the organization of these occasions in width and narrowness allows for the experience of *objects,* in the commonsense usage. (Remember that organization within imaginative experience may or may not be true of the organization of the objective world.)

Narrowness, width, vagueness, and triviality give depth of harmony in experience, or beauty. By virtue of having a worldly background, the experience of objects or focal contexts contains not only its own density, but also the nearly infinite depth of the world. Precisely because the whole world, now mainly trivial, lies in potentially interesting contrast to anything now focused on means that the world of present experience has some depth, or beauty. Without narrowness and width, the beauty in the background would itself by only potential. Without vagueness and triviality, the beauty in the foreground would come at such price of exclusion that experience of objects of the usual recognizable sort would most likely be impossible. One can have those kinds of imaginative objects only because one can have our kinds of background world.

In imagination as in synthesis, there is no such thing as "bare" apprehension, reproduction, or recognition. Specific, concrete things are involved, both on the side of the objects and on the side of the concepts involved in recognition. Therefore, there will always be some focal elements as well as background elements; therefore there must always be some degree of depth or beauty. Imaginative experiences differ greatly in the mixture of these dimensions, however. An inadequacy of focal elements leads to a flat affect and boredom. An inadequacy of background elements leads to insane fragmentation and inability to hold an object continuously in focus. Any subjective world we can imagine requires minimal exemplification of these principles.

Justification. With regard to justification of the claim that experience begins with beauty, it is important to locate the issue of justification precisely. There are two principal questions. The first is whether, from a descriptive standpoint, all experience with imaginative synthesis (which is all experience) exhibits beauty in the sense described. The second, and more difficult, question is whether experience contains imaginative synthesis *because* that gives it beauty.

The first question can be answered by a review of the previous arguments. If it is the case that imagination as synthesis is the bedrock of experience, and if it is the case that the three elements in synthesis—apprehension, reproduction, and recognition—constitute the minimal exemplification of beauty in the sense described, then beauty is a transcendental property of *all* experiences. One may challenge whether the characterization given beauty is a good one, and more is said below in defense of the claim that it is; but even if it turns out that beauty is defined here in an ultimately idiosyncratic way, the claim is that beauty is pervasive *in the sense defined here*. One may also challenge the categoreal scheme according to which synthesis and beauty are interpreted. Indeed, there are values beyond those discussed so far, which enter into justification of the scheme. Again, this whole inquiry is involved in the justification of that scheme.

The second question refers to the metaphysical position mentioned in Chapters 3 and 4—namely, that the ultimate reason for a thing having the identity it has is because that identity embodies an appropriate value. Of course, diverse things are related to each other, and diverse values are embodied in multiple ways, competing with each other. The actuality of anything is the result of the extent to which its own value can be realized within the tolerance of an environment that sometimes has alien values. Thus, because of their biological and social background, human beings have the potential for "experience," and because "experience" is valuable as embodying beauty, human beings have beauty. Of course, the possibility for experience developed slowly through the interaction of individuals with their environment so as to produce progeny more susceptible to experience. One can analyze the development of experience with evolutionary categories, showing how experience is not only possible, but also beneficial in adaptive senses. Beyond this, however, one can show how, by embodying appreciation of beauty, experience actualizes a dimension of value which otherwise would be missing from the world, and that this dimension has an intrinsic worth of its own, capable of justifying claims of respect over against various other values. The decisive value of beauty in experience is illustrated by the Buddhist notion that sentient beings are holy and thus should be accorded infinite respect; although no one would say that the sentience of insects has *much* of the synthetic imagination recognizable in human experience, Buddhists believe there is enough there for insects and lower animals to have karmically interesting experience.

On the general principle that any value ought to be realized if it can be, other things being equal, experience with the synthesis of imagination and the beauty thus obtaining is justified in its existence. Further, its existence is a pervasive value. This does not mean that someone's life is unqualifiedly beautiful simply because that person has minimal imagination. The beauty of a life involves much more than mere imaginative experience (the "much more" can be dreadful). Nevertheless the struggle to stay alive and to maintain consciousness in the face of outrageous pain testifies to the intrinsic value of experiential beauty even at its lowest ebb.

RELIGION AND THE COMMONALITY OF THE WORLD

Synthesis and Commonality

In one sense, imagination as synthesis is entirely private. Its structures and values are what they are regardless of any veridical perceptions or interpretations of things other than the imaginative content itself. There are at least four senses, however, in which the synthesis of imagination undergirds and reaches toward the publicity of the world essential to the social reality of thinking.

First, even the most idiosyncratic subjective world is the image of a public world. One imagines objects as being in a common space-time with oneself, and one does this by objectifying oneself as definitely located. Where the spatiotemporal language is inappropriate for the forms of composition of the synthesized world, other kinds of commonality are required. By definition, *synthesis* guarantees this. Even when a person dreaming visualizes a scene as though the dreamer were an outside spectator, there is a public, mutual relationship between the scene and the dreamer. In all three senses, synthesis entails a public relation between objects and experiencing subject.

Second, in actual social experience the image of common worlds held separately by all participants is a necessary condition for the social interaction whereby the idiosyncratic subjective worlds can be corrected and transformed into a common public arena. If each participant did not form his or her experience as though it were, at bottom, a public world, it would be impossible for the critical tests to coordinate the subjective worlds. All high-level experiences of perception and social interaction presuppose an original synthesis that can be treated as an hypothesis about the objective world. As psychologists studying infants have shown, transformation of subjective worlds into objective worlds comes about because of the shocks and frustrations of reality, not from any consciousness that one's imaginative experience is only "hypothetical." The process of learning objectivity, however, can be understood by others as hypothesis-testing.

It is necessary at this point to insert a note about the integrity of imaginative experience as such. Although one's subjective world can and should be treated as an hypothesis about an objective world, the intrinsic worth of imaginative experience in its own subjectivity should not be neglected. This is not the utility of images, but rather the mere beauty of subjectively forming experience into a world. With cultivated attention to the immediacy in presentational immediacy, the sheer value of synthesis as the beautiful presence of experiential life is a delight and universally available joy.

Third, even without authority for saying that one's appreciation of objects in the world is objective, mere synthesis of imagination guarantees the possibility of identifying *with* the worth of any and all objects within that imagined world. Beauty in synthesis is converted to feeling for the beauty in anything in the synthesis, since, in principle, anything can become a focal object. In ordinary experience, we identify the focal *objects* rather than the gestalt of focus and background, as beautiful; yet the beauty in the focal object depends on the entire synthesis. Because anything imagined in the synthesis is enabled by its character to be in that synthesis, it exhibits elements of the beauty apprehended, reproduced and recognized in the experience.

The philosopher who best perceived this was Wang Yang-ming, who wrote:

> The great man regards Heaven, Earth, and the myriad things as one body. He regards the world as one family and the country as one person. As to those who make a cleavage between objects and distinguish between the self and others, they are small men. That the great man can regard Heaven, Earth, and the myriad things as one body is not because he deliberately wants to do so, but because it is natural to the humane nature of his mind that he do so. . . . Even the mind of a small man is no different. . . . Therefore when he sees a child about to fall into a well, he cannot help a feeling of alarm and commiseration. This shows that his humanity forms one body with the child. It may be objected that the child belongs to the same species. Again, when he observes the pitiful cries and frightened appearance of birds and animals about to be slaughtered, he cannot help feeling an "inability to bear" their suffering. This shows that his humanity forms one body with birds and animals. It may be objected that birds and animals are sentient beings as he is. But when he sees plants broken and destroyed, he cannot help a feeling of pity. . . . It may be said that plants are living things as he is. Yet even when he sees tiles and stones shattered and crushed, he cannot help a feeling of regret. This shows that his humanity forms one body with tiles and stones.[28]

Notice that Wang's criterion of what constitutes one body with oneself is not causality but empathetic affection. This is due not to similarity of value principles between other things and oneself but rather to continuity of value between oneself and other things. For Wang, the principal locus of this value is within one's own "heart-mind," as he called it. The heart-mind is the center of one's ontological existence. In it, knowledge and action are identical, and one's valuational responses to things are pure. Only when one moves from the heart-mind to the level of specific interpretations and wishes is an egoism, or selfishness, possible that would distort the continuity with other things. There are serious difficulties with Wang's theory if it is interpreted to hold in this respect for objective relations between the self and others. These relations are principally causal; cognitive responses depend on causal connections. If Wang's theory is interpreted as addressing the synthesis of imagination, however, the subjective world is indeed imagined as "one body" with the heart-mind of the imaginer. To cultivate awareness of this is to appreciate the beauty of synthesis in experience as such.

The fourth approach to publicity lies in the public applicability of the value of beauty as a norm for potential experience. If a value is a norm that ought to be realized wherever the conditions for it are appropriate, it ought to be realized in all such places. The norm is not adventitious. Even if there were conscious intentional control over imaginative synthesis, it would not make sense to say that one chooses that beauty ought to be realized by forming one's concrescence so as to have experience. Beauty is either relevant—and therefore, obligatory—or it is not. If a norm's embodiment depends on its being recognized and chosen, still its obligatoriness is independent of whether it is in fact recognized.

Not only is the subjective experience of a common world presupposed for the possibility of an actually objective common world, but its value is universally shared. Ordinarily, this is recognized in fragmented ways. We say this or that object is beautiful rather than saying that the world focused on this or that object is beautiful. Indeed, some senses of beauty apply to objects in contradistinction to their experienced background, as Chapter 6 shows. Beauty as a transcendental qualification of the subjective world-as-experienced, however, is felt as worthy and appropriate by everyone even when the beauty is obscured by what Wang would call selfish desires.

Religion and Imagination

That experience begins in imagination as synthesis is a profound anthropogenic condition. Not only is it the initial condition constituting human experience, it is the initial condition constituting reality as a *world* for experience. Experience is the synthesizing of reality into a world, relative to a perspective. The constitution of experience-world is logically antecedent to questions about the truth of the world construction, antecedent to questions about the objectivity or subjectivity of experience. The elementary condition for raising any of those critical questions is thinking formed as experience of the world.

The primordial status of world-building through imagination as synthesis is not apprehended solely through critical philosophical reflection, although chiefly philosophy would provide analytical categories such as imagination, synthesis, or even experience. Apprehension of this primordial status lies at the root of religious experience. Religions do focus on elements that are parts of the world; these focal elements usually center on ritual, cosmological expressions and on paths for personal cultivation. But these religious foci presuppose, arise out of, and are sustained as plausible through contact with apprehension of fundamental world-experience construction. The importance of this thesis, if true, is that beneath its special contingent expressions, religion expresses an apprehension of the founding character of human experience.

Contemporary sciences of religion support the view that religion has chiefly to do with world construction. The very phrase "world construction" is the central category for interpreting the sociology of religion in the work of Peter Berger. Following in the Durkheimian tradition, Berger has analyzed those aspects of religion having to do with giving meaning to the constituents of experience; indeed, he allows that things do not enter as constituents of experience except insofar as they have meaning, albeit problematic meaning, in terms of other elements of experience. Berger explains the actual process of world-construction with a dialectic of externalization, objectivation, and internalization.[29] In one sense, these categories are not as basic as those dealing with imagination, since they presuppose the experience-world synthetic activity in order to give meaning to internality and externality. In another sense, however, they reflect the basic point that both experience of things in a world and experience of oneself as experiencer originate in a common activity. Sometimes Berger loses sight of the fundamental religious character of world-construction and identifies religion with the special content of the world thus constructed; only world constructions containing sacred elements, he sometimes says, are religious, in contrast to consistently secular worlds.[30] This, however, misses the distinction between fundamental religious apprehension—that of the primordial quality of world-construction—and the content of constructed worlds, which may or may not represent religious apprehending.

The history of religions also supports the claim that religion arises from, and centers on, the formation of world. In his classic *The Sacred and the Profane,* Mircea Eliade shows how myths articulating the sacred represent the creation of the world. Sacred space is where one stands closest to the gods because it is the center of creations. Sacred time represents the moment of creation. When the myths of the sacred are demythologized by prescinding them from the etiological and geographical elements, they are found to articulate the composition of ordered worldly experience out of what would otherwise be a homogeneity of stimuli which, because of their very homogeneity, cannot be experienced as anything.[31]

In his profound study, *The Symbolism of Evil*, Paul Ricoeur argues that there are four types of myths of the origin and nature of evil. One, represented by the Babylonian legend of Marduk, shows the creation of order itself to involve violence and evil. The second, represented by the Adam story of the Hebrew and Christian scriptures, distinguishes the origin of evil as an historical event within the created order from the creation of the order itself, separating the sinfulness of mankind from the unsullied purity of the creator. The third, represented in Greek tragedy, accounts for evil through the creation of mankind out of a mixture of divine and titanic elements. The fourth, represented by Orphic myths of the exiled soul, articulates evil as the situation of souls being punished by lodgement in bodies, material bodies being a corrupted and corrupting end product of creation. In all the myths, creation of the world is the background for the origin of evil. In all of them, creation demythologized means the constitution of human experience in a world. Ricoeur argues for the primacy of the Adamic myth and shows how the truths of the other myths find some expression compatible with it. The situation of creation in the Adam myth is that the fundamental constitution of the human experience-world is without evil, that evil enters historically, when people make choices regarding the content of the experience-world.[32]

Berger and Eliade share the dubious methodological presupposition that the early, primitive forms are the authentic ones, that the advancement of civilization has caused the corruption and watering down of religious purity. For both, secularization is a direct threat to religion. One might as well hold the opposite methodological presupposition: that, with advancing history, religious forms are purified and articulated with greater clarity. This, indeed, is Ricoeur's view of demythologization. He points out that only modern, secular people can appreciate myth as myth, whereas the ancients confused myth with history and science. In contrast to both these views, it is necessary to distinguish apprehension of world construction from expressions of this apprehension within particular worlds. The former is the foundation of religion. The debate about the religious significance of secularization is a second–level consideration.

The clearest apprehension of the primordial status of experience-world construction probably is that of Paul Tillich.[33] Tillich believed that religion arises from ground prior to the distinction of subject and object. Although he perhaps underestimated the dynamic, creative element of synthesis, and spoke of the prior ground in static categories of being and nonbeing, Tillich saw that the elementary religious apprehension is of the contingency of the experience-world coimplication. Thus the religious quality of the content of experience—for instance, art—is not to be defined in terms of intraworldly symbolic meaning, but in terms of its capacity to articulate the apprehension of the primordial status of the experience-world constitution.

Another confirmation of the thesis that religion arises through apprehending the primordial status of world construction lies in the points made earlier about the character of the public world. Whether or not the mythological construction of the religiously apprehended world is "true," it is apprehended as being a common world with a place even for the barbarians. As Ricoeur points out, one function of a myth of origins is the presentation to consciousness of a way to conceive of a common nature and history with people whose direct origins are not connected to one's own. Furthermore, the religious apprehension grasps the world as valuable, as beautiful. As it noted above, the beauty involved in the synthesis of imagination is not beauty in opposition to ugliness. Rather, it is a kind of satisfaction in experiencing together things which, if they were not together, could not be experienced. Each thing has its own value because each itself is a synthesis. In this sense, beauty is the value of gathering; it is this sense of beauty that is present in religious apprehension. The attainment of cosmos over against chaos is the value of gathering. Explicit aesthetic recognition of this is religiously articulated in terms of the love of positivity in existence and of the "peace that passes understanding." Then, too, there is something awesome about the religious apprehension in the appreciation of the contingency of the gathering: were there no synthesis, there would be neither world nor experience—total loss of beauty.

The structure of religious apprehension involves much more than imagination, and it is premature to analyze it. Its content may be discussed, however, since the content is imagination as synthesis. Imagination as synthesis is a complex object for religious apprehension. It includes, in part, appreciation of the contingency of the synthesized content of experience. Religious apprehension might focus on the possibility that any finite item in experience cannot be synthesized with the other items, which means that it cannot be in the world-experience. "The grass withers, the flower fades." The focus might, instead, be on the contingency of the entire synthesized world-experience as it is expressed in wonder at the whole creation or in ontological anxiety about reality as such.

The act of apprehending contingency is existentially transposed into a focus on the abysmal ground on which the synthesis is contingent. From the standpoint of cosmology, *ground* may be taken in several senses. Imaginative synthesis is a natural activity continuous in various respects with other natural activities of complex animals. The biological ground on which imaginative activity rests, however, is not the abysmal ground that contrasts with the contingency of the experience-world; the loss of the experience-world would include loss of experience of biological grounds. Rather, the abysmal ground is the ground of the special differentia of the imaginative activity; the ground must be apprehended through the immediacy of the imaginative activity in which that activity differs from other activities. Yet the ground cannot be conceived except as productive of the synthesis itself. One cannot imagine a situation without imaginative synthesis, despite one's ability to appreciate the contingency of the synthesis itself. Religious apprehension, therefore, grasps its "object" not as an object but as an asymmetrical relation. One pole of the relation is the contingent world-experience, which can be appreciated alone; the other is the ground of that world, the creator, which can be appreciated only in terms of its creating, only within the creating relationship. Because the relationship is one of creation, however, world-experience is wholly dependent for its reality on this relationship, whereas the creator alone produces the relationship.[34] Fundamental religious apprehension can thus be expressed as a "feeling of absolute dependence" (Schleiermacher), as a feeling for the fragility of the givenness of the world (Eliot), as the uncreated fire whence the world arises (Boehme), as Brahman at once with qualities and without qualities, as the Emptiness of the world, at once such as it is and at the same time nothing transcendent—all are partial expressions of the basic religious intuition of the primordial status of world-construction through synthesis of imagination.

This interpretation of fundamental religious apprehension does not say as much as many would like. In particular, such an interpretation does not assert directly an apprehension of the genuine ontological grounding of reality. It might be the case that religious apprehension merely grasps the natural beginning of human experience. Then again, it might be the case that in grasping the beginning of human experience, the ontological foundation of reality is revealed. Whichever religious interpretation does is a matter of interpretation, not imaginative synthesis. Only with the aid of a critical ontological theory is it possible to tell whether imaginative synthesis has ontological significance, whether apprehension of the creation of the world is, as it seems, prima facie. Determination of the ontological significance of imaginative synthesis requires moving beyond the imaginative dimension of religion into philosophy proper.

If this conclusion seems too thin from the standpoint of ontology-oriented religion, it nevertheless presents an extraordinary conclusion. Even if the religious apprehension involves nothing more than a grasp of the primordial quality of the beginning of experience in imagination as synthesis, to that extent, the importance of religion cannot be minimized. Religious apprehension cannot be refuted because it makes no claims: it is the condition for all claims and interpretations of itself. The religious experience involved in the apprehension is not threatened by any advance of secularization or by the confusion of religions. Although the experience needs expression in conceptual frameworks that vary with secularization and religious traditions, the experience expressed is the condition for any expression. Religious apprehension may well be forgotten or denied within certain interpretive frameworks, but as the condition for interpretation, the apprehension must somehow always be ready for expression. This point may seem small comfort for those who want religious experience to be explicit and consciously expressed; surely apprehension alone does not entail organizing one's life around respect for what is apprehended. Furthermore, this interpretation of the nature of fundamental religious apprehension is itself only a hypothesis and may well be wrong. If the hypothesis is generally on the mark, however, the importance of religious apprehension is the most general, necessary condition for the importance of anything else, even the importance of the truth of interpretations.

In summary, this chapter advances four main contributions to the discussion. First, in describing imagination as synthesis, it is shown that even at this elementary level, value is involved in experience, and that experience as imaginative synthesis cannot be appreciated without noting the role of value. Specifically, synthesis is the elementary constituting of experience such that it contains value: to experience at the level of imaginative synthesis is to possess things of value, thereby being valuable in the possession. Second, the naturalism of the above point is justified over against the general claim that imagination as synthesis should be understood transcendentally. To this end, there is a critique of Kant's project of making philosophy transcendental. It is shown that among the contemporary phenomenological heirs of Kant, mere description without reference to value is intrinsically incomplete. Finally, it is urged that Heidegger shares the sense of the value found in imaginative synthesis but does not discuss it in language appropriate for value theory. Third, a cosmological theory adequate to explain imagination as synthesis is presented, which makes reference to the concept of beauty as that which is achieved in the coming-into-existence of imaginative synthesis. Fourth, it is suggested that, although imagination as synthesis is in one sense the most private act of self-constitution in experience, in several senses it is obliged to make reference to an objective, common, public world. This self-constitution of experience and the world is the foundation of religion.

The synthesis of imagination is considered in this chapter in abstraction from the possibility that the contents of imagination are valid feelings of real things, either from one's own past thoughts or from the more external world. Within the limits of this abstraction, it is necessary to speak of a subjective world only. The abstraction is false to real experience, however. Inevitably, our imaginations are influenced by things that impinge on them from the real world. Even in dreams, content is affected by such things as noise and temperature. In such cases, the contours of the subjective world are not, strictly speaking, made objective, since the noise of the alarm clock may be interpreted in the dream as the noise of a fire engine. Still, the determining feelings integrated in the synthesizing imagination are real feelings; they are merely misinterpreted. It is necessary now to expand our consideration of imagination and look at the role played by feelings about real objects. Imagination is formed, in part, by perception.

Imagination in Perception: Beauty

Although imagination in its most elementary form is synthesis, concrete imaginative experience cannot be understood in terms of the synthesizing activity alone. The nature and origin of what is synthesized must also be considered. In Western philosophy there have been two main schools of thought on the question of this nature and origin. One, perhaps best represented by Hume, claims that the content of experience, anything whatsoever that can be imagined, derives from perceptions. The other, exemplified by Kant, claims that all content of experience results from the capacity of the mind to represent things to itself, sometimes but not always by working up externally given material into a form that can be present in experience. The truth may lie more in Kant's view than Hume's. Nevertheless, Hume had a valid point, and its neglect has led to a denaturing of the relation of nature to experience.

Briefly, the thesis to be defended here is that perception is a judgment with an intentionality structure arising out of direct, nonintentional feeling, by way of a process of imagination. The topic of imagination in perception is not perception as such but the role of imagination in concrete acts of perceiving, in which it mediates between raw feeling and finished perception. Because of imagination's role, there are values in perception referring to the feeling side that are usually neglected when the judgment form of perception is emphasized.

PHENOMENOLOGY OF IMAGINATION IN PERCEPTION

Intention and Feeling in Perception

The experience of perceiving involves judgment and intentionality. To perceive something is to experience "that. . . ." As Husserl and others

177

pointed out, perceptive experience involves both a "turning toward" the object and an "apprehending" of it.[1] Turning toward means that the experience consists partly of reacting to the object, whereby the various experiential elements are organized and sorted to focus on the object. In perception, focusing attention means that perceiving is part of the process of aiming at some satisfaction in the experiential moment. Perception arises from the way the whole of an experience is organized. The latter factor, the apprehending, always takes the form of apprehending "as. . . ." Otherwise one would know no more after perception than before it. Perception is in part a function of the categories for classifying or recognizing things. Perceptive discriminations can be improved, for instance, by learning new categories. General sophistication in language, study of the arts, and specialized practical experience requiring discrimination lead people to perceive things in ways to which they would otherwise be blind.

To some people, the intentional and judgmental characters of perception are a disappointment. The intentional character entails that perception is not merely being in the right place looking in the right direction; because of intentionality perception is also a function of the whole of one's experiential processes. The judgmental character entails that perception is partly dependent on conventional and perhaps adventitious categories and that some perceptions require expertise. Anyone who looks for an indubitable beginning for thought cannot find it in perception. There are no infallible sense data or impressions, and Hume's hope of checking ideas by their sensible origin is in vain. Most philosophers are now reconciled to the fact that the "given" sought as an indubitable foundation is a myth.[2]

Nevertheless, perception is built from objects perceived as entering into experience, as well as from the categories and tissues of concerns which determine focus. We experience objects by feeling them, even though that feeling must be integrated with the rest of experience by taking on the forms of intentionality and judgment. Thus, the experience of perceiving has two poles. One pole is the entrance of the object into experience through being felt. This pole is dominant at the beginning of a perceptive experience and gradually is overlaid with the subjective form, integrating that feeling with others, until each occasion reaches a satisfaction. The entire process of perception can be discussed with reference to the feeling pole. Hume and his followers are mistaken in believing this is the only relevant pole.

The other pole is the issuance of the perceptive process in a definite, judgmental, intentional perception. The definiteness of the perceptual judgment arrives only in the satisfaction stage of a thinking occasion, although the process of perceiving can take many occasions to come to definiteness. The entire process of perception can be discussed with reference to the intentional pole, indicating how the early phases involve the accretion of the subjective form necessary to allow intentional focus and to bring the felt object into connection with the conceptual and semantic items involved in judgment. Kant and his adherents are mistaken in interpreting perception solely from the perspective of the judgmental, intentional pole. This error is understandable if one's dominant interest is in the *logic* of thinking, because only the judgmental pole of thinking—in perception or elsewhere—is subject to norms of logic. Yet it helps explain why the entrance of the given object into thought is such a mystery for Kant. For him, the object must be something constructed, when in fact only the experiential objectification of the object is constructed.

A fundamental question must be raised here. What is the experiential warrant for saying that there *is* a feeling pole in perception, if all experience is known only through its definite, judgmental objectifications? It would seem that the object of any judgment about experience (of the sort being made here, for example) must have experience-as-judgment as its object. One way to circumvent this problem is to admit that direct experiential warrant does not exist and to claim instead that the warrant is theoretical or dialectical. For instance, to avoid the difficulties of "one pole" theories, it is better to postulate "two poles." However, this argument overlooks the possibility that the later Kantians may be right in allowing perception with a given to be a mystery.

The situation requires defending the proposition that although experience is indeed judgmental or intentional in some sense, not *all elements* in experience are so. This is the position of Husserl who wrote:

> Under *experiences* in the *widest sense* we understand whatever is to be found in the stream of experience, not only therefore intentional experiences, *cogitationes* actual and potential taken in their full concreteness, but all the real (*reellen*) phases to be found in this stream and in its concrete sections.
>
> For it is easily seen that *not every real phase* of the concrete unity of an intentional experience has itself the basic *character of intentionality*, the property of being a "consciousness of something." This is the case, for instance, with all sensory data, which play so great a part in the perceptive intuitions of things.[3]

Although Husserl's account of the process of thinking differs from that given here, his sense of the "concrete" elements in experience is similar to the intentional or judgmental pole, and his idea of sensory data (and sensory feelings) refers to what is accounted for in terms of the feeling pole. But

what arguments can be given for this position? For Husserl, nonintentional
elements are abstractions from a more concrete unity. The claim made here,
however, is that the feeling pole, although not concrete, has a reality of its
own which is experientially present and deserves attention.

Whitehead, like Husserl, has defended this point. In his *Symbolism*,
he criticized Hume for claiming that only presentational immediacy (which
has judgmental form) is real, arguing that experience contains a sense of
"causal efficacy," a direct appreciation of the vector force of much of the
content of sense experience.[4] He argued that we perceive a red object not
only by an appreciation of the redness but also by an appreciation of the
redness coming into experience by means of our eyes. Furthermore, he
continued, one of the most pervasive traits of experience is the sense of
"conformation," namely, that the experience of the present moment is constrained to conform to the immediate past, illustrating its structures and inertia. Whitehead wrote in *Process and Reality*, that "the point of the criticism of Hume's procedure is that we have direct intuition of inheritance and
memory: thus the only problem is, so to describe the general character of
experience that these intuitions may be included."[5] Hume wanted to eliminate from experience anything that is not an impression or derivative from
an impression. However, the notions of repetition and memory, which are
needed to distinguish impressions from their copies, must refer to elements
which are directly in experience. As Whitehead said in criticism of this
view, "Hume seems to have overlooked the difficulty that 'repetition' stands
with regard to 'impressions' in exactly the same position as does 'cause and
effect.' Hume has confused a 'repetition of impressions' with an 'impression
of repetition of impressions.' "[6] Furthermore, said Whitehead, Hume's
account of memory was only that it differs from impressions in being faint-
er, and from ideas in being more vivacious. "This doctrine is very un-
plausible; and, to speak bluntly, is in contradiction to plain fact. But, even
worse, it omits the vital character of memory, namely, that it is *memory*. In
fact the whole notion of *repetition* is lost in the 'force and vivacity'
doctrine."[7]

Finally, we quote the following passage from Whitehead concerning
the reality of feeling in contrast to judgment.

> Anger, hatred, fear, terror, attraction, love, hunger, eager-
> ness, massive enjoyment, are feelings and emotions closely en-
> twined with the primitive functioning of 'retreat from' and of
> 'expansion towards.' They arise in the higher organism as states
> due to a vivid apprehension that some such primitive mode of
> functioning is dominating the organism. But 'retreat from' and
> 'expansion towards,' divested of any detailed spatial discrimina-

tion, are merely reactions to the way externality is impressing on us its own character. You cannot retreat from mere subjectivity; for subjectivity is what we carry with us.[8]

The following observations supplement Whitehead's argument. Although every feeling is involved in the process of becoming integrated with other feelings, in experience it is possible to focus attention on and *cultivate* a sense for the feeling pole. We can attune ourselves to be aware of the impingement of the past and the outer world on our immediate experience, and to objectify this awareness in our conscious, judgmental experience. Before explaining this, it is worth noting that the direction of this line of argument differs from Whitehead's. Whereas Whitehead shows that certain common experiential elements such as memory, repetition, and emotions directly refer to and exhibit the causal power of external agencies, and therefore must presuppose them, the argument here is that awareness of the external connection can be increased and developed. The acknowledgement of the feeling of real external things is not only for the sake of solving philosophical puzzles but also for the guidance of the responsibility to cultivate valuable experience.

Chapter 4 introduces the concepts of conformation and inclusion. Conformation is the necessity that any present moment of experience conform to the world out of which it arises. This takes two main forms: "embodiment" and "energy." Embodiment is the feeling of all our feelings in conjunction with feelings of our bodies and immediate environment. It is sensing external distant things with attention focused in part on the sensual qualities of the experience, qualities derivative from sensing with our bodily sense organs. It is sensing that our passing through daily affairs is a function of the movements and comportments of our bodies. It is sensing our own thoughts through memory and the continuity of consciousness in terms of the bodily sense that gives thoughts a location. Embodiment is a crucial element in being present, in having a location. It is crucial for being able to apprehend distant things accurately by factoring out the contributions of the media of our connections with them. People differ in their sense of embodiment, and individuals vary from one context to another. Nonetheless, people can learn to increase their sense of embodiment through training their sensual awareness and disciplining their attention to relevant feelings. T'ai chi ch'uan was discussed earlier as a method of cultivating embodiment.

The possibility of cultivation proves that judgments about distant things, about active affairs, and about our own thoughts—the judgments that inevitably constitute the concrete element in experience—can be supplemented by feelings which articulate their origin through the causal process of physical feelings. The point is not that the awareness involved in embodiment is nonintentional or nonjudgmental but that we can reach intentional awareness of the causal origins of judgment in feelings. Of course a Humean could argue that this is merely to juxtapose one kind of judgment (concerning sensation) with another (concerning the distant object, for instance). If it were only this, the content of the former—its assertion of the causal element in interpreting the latter—could not be taken seriously. Yet it is those sensible judgments that empiricists take most seriously.

What was said for embodiment applies to energy, the other element in conformation. With energy and embodiment combined, it is possible to feel oneself part of the flowing, ongoing processes of nature and society. One derives one's being from within the natural processes, and exhibits that being by responding to those processes. One's spontaneity arises by integrating the forces of natural processes into one's own comportment as a natural event.

Besides conformation, Chapter 4 mentions the elements of inclusion. The feel of external objects included in experience can be cultivated so that we are more sensitive to the intrinsic nature and importance of the objects felt. To some degree, this appreciation can be kept pure within experience in order not to be distorted by other feelings or by the direction of intentional development. Sensitivity and purity are difficult to attain, yet we recognize them as norms and cultivate them when the occasion arises. Their cultivation is a normative matter: experience is better when it is embodied and energized.

If these considerations make it plausible that there is experiential reference to the assertion of the feeling pole, a theory is needed to account for it. The account must deal with the connection between the feeling pole and the intentional pole, and that connection is made by imagination.

The Value of Imagination in Perception

The function of imagination in perception is continuous with several other functions from which it may be distinguished. On one hand, imagination in perception is continuous with the synthesizing, or integrative, activity in experience, physical as well as mental. It differs from the other functions within that broader activity by modifying initial feelings to form a final, perceptual judgment, whereas the broader activity includes all modification, from feeling to satisfaction. On the other hand, it differs from other mental activity, including other imaginative activities, because it always leads to perception. An experience, or series of experiential occasions, may find thinking satisfaction in a complex harmony of perceptual, reflective, volitional, evaluative, and other kinds of elements. All these may play background or foreground roles in the focus of consciousness; imagination is involved in all of them. Imagination as perception, however, is involved only in those elements which result in perceptual judgments.

Imagination in perception is spontaneous activity in which objects felt as initial data are, first, put in conjunction with descriptive terms so that they can be perceived "as . . . " and, second, thus conjoined, are related to other elements in intentional experience to play a significant role in the experience as objectified for further experience. These two products of imagination in perception can be analyzed as follows.

Schematism. In his discussion of the "schematism," Kant correctly saw that given data must be related to familiar categories and concepts in order for them to be perceived. Plato had already pointed out in the *Meno* that perception involves recognition. Perception of alien things, Kant saw, involves relating those things to the terms by which they or their properties might be recognized. Kant's solution was that the alien things must at least have the form of inner sense—time (some things also have the spatial form of outer sense)—if they are to enter experience at all, and that the concepts ready for recognition must also be capable of being interpreted as applying to things of a temporal (and sometimes spatial) form. Therefore, for Kant, imagination in schematism mediates between given content and general concepts by relating both to temporal (and sometimes spatial) form. This activity of the imagination does not necessarily produce images. In fact, Kant distinguished between a schema—a rule for constructing an image or representation—and a schema image. To use his example, five dots on a page, ... , constitute an image. The schema of numerical representation, however, constitutes the rule whereby the number five can be represented spatially. Although I cannot imagine exactly one thousand dots, I can represent them through the schema for putting dots on a page.[9] (Kant himself was interested in determining a priori schemata, to which any object must conform, in contrast to empirical schemata.)

Kant's general point is valid and can be adopted in the following way. In order to enter experience at all, it was argued in Chapter 5, the feeling of an object must be synthesized into a subjective world, with some forms or other constituting the patterning of this world arranged with some kind of beauty. Similarly, if any descriptive categories are to be applied to objects in perceptual judgments, they must apply to objects as they appear in the subjective world. Therefore, the forms of the subjective world are the links by which imagination in perception relates felt objects to the categories in which they can be perceived. And is this not just what we would expect? If I perceive someone's red scarf, I must perceive it in such a context that I can recognize it as an article of clothing and as the kind of thing that takes a "color" description; that is, I perceive it in the context of a world where there are clothes and colored objects.

Of the process of perceptive imagination itself, Kant said, "this schematism of our understanding, in its application to appearances and their mere form, is an art concealed in the depths of the human soul, whose real modes of activity nature is hardly ever to allow us to discover, and to have open to our gaze."[10] This process may not be as mysterious as Kant thought, however; in the section "Cosmology of Imagination in Perception" the process is discussed in detail.

Kant also was of the view that there is only one world, which there must be if there is to be a priori knowledge of it. Yet is there evidence that there is only one world whose forms are operative as the schemata for perceptual judgments? People's worlds take diverse forms, as noted in the preceding chapter; yet all or most subjective worlds have perceptual judgments in them.

Of course, not all perceptual judgments are true. Even in the commonsense world, our subsequent inquiries into the truth of perceptual judgments tell us we have sometimes seen mirages. An important distinction should be borne in mind between judgments which have the nature of perception (and can take place in dreams and in distorted perception) and judgments which are not only perceptual images of objects but also true. That a subjective world in experience contains some perceptual judgments does not necessarily mean that the subjective world is also the objective world. It does mean that objects in the objective world have entered experience, even if to be distorted from the natures we would see them have if our perceptions were sensitive, pure, and true.

Perception in a World. As noted earlier, an occasion of experience is never merely a perceptual judgment. Even if it is dominantly that, with consciousness focused upon the perceiving, many other elements are involved, elements that have come to intentional definiteness in the form of judgment. At the least, there is the determinate presentation of the subjective world as the background for perception; usually there are also bodily feelings, memories, and associations with the perception, and, frequently, purposeful intentions. Imagination in perception must clothe the perceptual judgment in such subjective form that it is congruent with those other elements. In this sense, imagination in perception blends with the imagination and other synthesizing activities involved in objectifying those other elements. In order to preserve the perceptual quality in the integrated subjective form, imagination in perception must observe the special qualities of embodiment and energy. Perceptual dominance requires an arrangement of experience such that the bodily routes of perception are clear and present.

Furthermore, experience has a receptivity to the world when it is incorporated with the energies of the world through perception. If either embodiment or energy is neglected, perceptual judgments will be difficult to integrate into the final satisfaction of any experience as important or as at the focus of attention. This function of imagination will be discussed further in connection with imagination as appearance.

A fundamental distinction grows out of this discussion of imagination in perception. The concept of value in experience has two roles, parallel to the poles of feeling and judgment or intention. Experience begins with valuing or appreciating the values objectified by the objects of feeling. It is an object's value which enters experience as an initial datum. But, because the feeling of that object must play a role vis-à-vis other feelings in experience, and because this role must be worked out through the complex process of integration which involves altering, eliminating, and substituting initially felt data, the object takes on a value within and for the subjective experience. Particularly, it plays a value-role in contributing to the ultimate satisfaction in the occasion. We may designate these two roles as "feeling the value of . . ." and as "valuing. . . ."

Feeling has a particular contribution to make to perception. It presents the initially felt value of the object for potential inclusion in the intentional process of coming to judgment. Whether or not the final judgment preserves the object's own beauty is a function of the integrity of the perceptive process. If the process observes the feeling norms of sensitivity and purity, and arranges its own intentional structure to acknowledge this, then the object's value can be maintained. This is not to say, however, that the norms of sensitivity and purity are the only obligatory norms for the process of thinking. Clearly, some objects should *not* be objectified in experience with anything resembling their intrinsic worth, and often even the best of objects needs to be sacrificed for other interests in experience—for example, that of vigorous action rather than observation and enjoyment.

Bearing in mind the distinction between "feeling the value of" and "valuing," it is possible to characterize the virtue of a person with a well-cultivated sense of initial feeling. Insofar as the person is perceiving objects, the person has good "taste." Taste is the cultivated capacity to maintain an object in its initially felt value, with purity and sensitivity, through the process of experience and to objectify it in its integrity. It is a combination of feeling and intention. Because of the feeling pole, it is not entirely a matter of logical judgment; because of the intentional pole, it is not entirely a matter of sensation.

It is possible to characterize the root value in perceptual imagination on a more general level. Chapter 5 demonstrates that the normative value in imagination as synthesis is beauty, which is characterized in terms of the harmony of triviality, vagueness, width, and narrowness. Yet the phrase *imagination as synthesis*, in presenting the worldly background of experience, refers primarily to triviality and vagueness. Imagination in perception presents the contrast of perceived objects with that of the background. Beauty is not only experiencing a world as beautiful but experiencing objects in a world as beautiful. With imaginative perception, one's subjective world is first seen as localized and particularized by virtue of conformation, with embodiment and energy. And it is then seen as punctuated by objects perceived with some degree of purity and sensitivity. Even in an experience in which all objects are severely distorted or eliminated, or in which the only objectlike content in the experience is the fictive product of fantasy, there is nonetheless a selective experience with objects focused against a background. And those fictive objects of focus have some perceptual beauty. Perceptual beauty exists when the worth of the real or fantasized object becomes an ingredient in the experience of that object against its worldly background.

In summary, imagination in perception is the spontaneous activity mediating between the *entrance* of objects through initial feeling and the *objectification* of objects in perceptual judgments. Prescinding from the value of the truth of the perceptual judgment, the values in feeling—embodiment, energy, purity, and sensitivity—are important for perception. Furthermore, the discussion of beauty begun in Chapter 5 has been made more complex by pointing out that perception constitutes an elementary focal element in beauty of the world and allows experiencing selected objects as beautiful. Before proceeding to give a more detailed account of these points, it is necessary to consider certain widely accepted philosophical views with which they are incompatible.

CRITICAL INTERPRETATION

All Thinking Is Interpreting?

In 1869 Charles Peirce published a classic essay entitled "Questions Concerning Certain Faculties Claimed for Man," in which he argues that every cognition is determined by a previous cognition.[11] This was understood as denying the thesis that we have a faculty of intuition, where an intuition is defined as a cognition determined not by a previous cognition but by something out of consciousness. On the basis of this early work, Peirce developed his well-known theory that all thinking is interpretation with signs. This may be interpreted as arguing that all thinking is judgment—nothing but judgment. Peirce was not an idealist. He believed that

we do have natural knowledge of external physical objects. In order to defend this belief he was required to interpret the process of perceiving a tone,
for example, as a train of signs interpreting other signs extending from the
physical source of the sound (namely, the vibrating violin string) through
the air, through one's body, and into one's mind. He interpreted causation as
a kind of interpretation.[12] In the course of his development, he was led to
abandon any commonsense notion of consciousness in which one's consciousness is subjectively continuous and in which objects are external to it.
Indeed, his mature idea of perceptive experience is similar to the one being
defended here.

There is a crucial point, however, at which Peirce's critical argument
challenges the distinction between feeling and judgment. If all cognitions are
determined by previous ones, what is there to understand about thinking
besides the form and material of semiotics? Thinking is, for Peirce, interpretation and nothing but interpretation, even though his theory of interpretation is broad. Peirce might say that beyond semiotics, thinking also
exemplifies the three general categories of being. "Firstness" is sheer quality, what a thing is in relation to nothing but itself. "Secondness" is sheer
duality, the being of a thing insofar as it stands related to another thing but
in brute opposition or contrast. "Thirdness" is the being of a thing insofar as
it mediates between two other things in some respect.[13] For Peirce, thinking
is concrete thirdness, the active process of mediating.

The process of thinking has an immediacy about it, which is its firstness. Secondness in thought is exemplified in two ways. Two thoughts can
be different from each other and be seen thus from the standpoint of some
mediating thought; this is degenerate secondness. A more genuine secondness is present when the flow of thinking is interrupted by the brute opposition of reality saying "No!" to some expectation. The process of interpretation involves the flowing continuity of habit and many expectations. Reality,
as something external to consciousness, can interrupt interpretation with its
opposition. For consciousness to recognize what happened is for thirdness to
be reasserted in a mediating interpretation. Peirce's view of the limited entrance of "external reality" has been reaffirmed by subsequent philosophers
of science, who point out that experimental testing asks whether experimental results will say "No!" to the operative hypothesis; reality never
enters positively, saying "Yes." This is a valid view if the nature of thinking
is comprehended completely in the semiotic of interpretation.

All this contradicts the view, however, that thinking has positive feelings of the world. We must be careful to locate the dispute accurately.
Peirce was right in pointing out that every cognition is determined by a
previous cognition, and that there is no radical opposition in kind between
mental elements and physical or other elements. According to the cosmolo-

gy presented here, each occasion feels previous occasions, which consist of the feelings of other previous occasions, and so on. Furthermore, each occasion in that process has or had a subjective process of coming-to-be and an objective finish or satisfaction. Within any person's experience, some present feelings can be traced to trains of experiential occasions within his or her own past; these constitute the continuity of consciousness. Others can be traced to trains of occasions extending out from the body, although possibly not objectifying any of the subjective elements that create continuity of consciousness.[14] All of this is consistent with Peirce. What is inconsistent is the claim that not everything coming from the past into present experience has an interpretive function.

Peirce was correct in seeing that experimental thinking can be told only "No" or "Not-no" in answer to its questions. Is there not, however, an existential presentation of reality in feeling? For Peirce, that could only be a sign calling for interpretation. But the sense in which the past calls for interpretation derives from the fact it must be taken up in an integrated fashion into present experience. Present experience constitutes itself by giving all its past influences a meaning within itself. Beyond this is the force of the past—its vector character, as Whitehead called it. Whitehead's examples of memory and repetition, cited in the preceding section, may be explained within Peirce's view by referring to interpretation. Can the same be said of the examples of strong emotion, or of the sense of physical compulsion? Of the feeling of continuity with the flow of nature? Probably not, although these experiences can always be interpreted as interpretive judgments themselves, because the interpretive element is present in them. To be seen in this way, however, is to lose their sense of continuity of compulsion and emotion. How can this element of experience be preserved in light of Peirce's arguments?

We may readily accept Peirce's arguments which show every cognition to be determined by a prior cognition in the sense he meant it. Yet we must distinguish two kinds of relations between sequential thoughts. Assume, contrary to fact, that each thought is, by itself, a whole occasion of experience. The first kind of relation between the thoughts is a semiotic one: the later thought interprets the earlier in some respect, anticipates a subsequent line of interpretation, and so forth. The second kind of relation is a genetic causal one, wherein the earlier thought enters into the later as one of the data out of which latter is made.[15] The genetic causal relation may carry elements with it other than those functioning semiotically. Remove the assumption that each thought corresponds to an occasion, and consider that the thinking of any thought takes many occasions which are experientially related in many ways, possibly bearing a multitude of simultaneous semiotic elements. From the perspective of the naturalistic cosmology, relations between the beginning and end of a single specified thought are themselves semiotic in whatever sense is necessary to account for the unity of a thought as sign. One thought blends into another through a process involving many occasions. The semiotic relations themselves are logical ones characteristic of the interrelationships of the objectified satisfactions of innumerable occasions. Yet the genetic causal relations between occasions underlie the semiotic ones. Sometimes the peculiarities of those genetic relations—for example, seeing with the eyes, a gut feeling, a sense of physical flow—lend their own characters to the content of the semiotic material.

The genetic causal element lends a depth to experience lacking in the Peircean view of thinking as solely a semiotic process. Depth is an important factor in the sense of inwardness and subjectivity, since it contributes the tone of our explicit experience arising out of more foundational elements.[16] The depth arising from the genetic causal relations is also crucial for establishing the continuity of inward experience *with nature*, and for noting that experience itself is a dimension of nature flowing from other dimensions.

The distinction between semiotic and genetic causal relations allows us to accept Peirce's claim that every cognition is determined by previous cognitions, while saying that not all determination is semiotic determination. Our cognitions arise from feelings, not only from prodding signs seeking interpretation. To repeat the point of previous chapters, acknowledging this allows us to focus on norms for elements in thinking other than those of semiotics, and to legitimatize the analysis of the bearing of those norms on thinking.

Bracketing?

The distinction between semiotic and genetic causal relations makes the Husserlian concept of phenomenological analysis ambiguous and problematic. If, as argued here, both the semiotic and causal elements show themselves in experience then both should be subject to phenomenological analysis. It is difficult to describe and distinguish between them, however, without a theory similar to the cosmology underlying this discussion. Furthermore, a hallmark of Husserlian phenomology is the methodological principle of phenomenological reduction, or *epoché*, supposedly bracketing out consideration of whether the objects experienced really exist independent of the experience.[17] Yet the entrance of items into experience by way of the genetic causal route—and everything enters that way, although some things have semiotic significance which experientially displaces genetic causal significance—makes such elimination, or bracketing, difficult, if not impossi-

ble. For bracketing must mean erecting an arbitrary limit for phenomenological considerations somewhere along the line of the vector of genetic
causal forces.

The notion of consciousness as a technical term is equally problematic
if it involves a distinction between what is inside consciousness and what is
outside. This distinction is important within the classical phenomenological
tradition, and it is possible within that tradition because it is rooted in transcendental philosophy. Transcendental philosophy can accept a field as
given—for example, the field of consciousness—and relate things to it, as
conditions for its possibility, matters of empirical inference, and so forth.
Since this is not unlike the way the concept of consciousness works for
Husserl, he could say that consciousness itself contains concrete experience.
However, the feelings of things entering experience know no boundaries
marked by the subjection of those feelings to the structures of intentionality,
such as focus. Thus it makes sense to acknowledge that we can extend our
conscious awareness (using that phrase in an ordinary, nontechnical sense)
into our experience to grasp deeper genetic causal connections with the
world. If we were to adopt the transcendental phenomenological theory,
bracketing considerations of existence, feeling an object would be more like
a Humean impression of it than the real presence of the object.

Noncognitivist Value Theory

Early in this chapter, a distinction is made between feeling the value
of an object and valuing the object for its role within one's own experience.
Of course one does not feel an object's value without the object; the object
is felt with its value, and the role it plays as valued within one's experience
must take account of the object's value character as well as the self-
composition of the experiencing subject. This distinction between the object's value as felt and the object as valued lays the foundation for seeing
one's way around several positions or dichotomies in value theory and ethics
which most philosophers would like to avoid but cannot.

First, the distinction undermines the dichotomy between cognitivist
and noncognitivist metaethical theories. That dichotomy depends on the
assumption that the world consists at least of facts and maybe (or maybe
not) values. Because of the imaginative contribution to experience, however, the world is experienced as having at least the value of beauty, both as a
whole including background and foreground, and as containing beautiful
objects as potential foci of narrowness and width. The experience of the
world this way is a valuable experience, and when that experience is objectified for subsequent experience, it is felt as having that value. And so it

continues: each object contains the values of those objects it preserves in its own existence and objectifies for subsequent feeling. Whether the value in a felt object is known depends on whether the person experiencing it feels positively according to the demands of his or her own integration, and whether it is perceived imaginatively in cognitive terms. But the potentiality for cognition is there. The only grounds for saying that an object is cognized without its value is that the perceiver must for some reason eliminate the object's own value in order for the object to play a valuable enough role within the experience as to be at the center of cognitive focus. Whether this is good or bad depends on the relative worth of the object compared with its cognitive role without its value, all seen in the context of the experiencer's needs for attaining definiteness of experience. A mystical experience may be interpreted in part as experiencing all or many objects according to their own values as felt, but without integrating them according to values unique to the experience. The price paid in such an experience is that the experiencer loses the cognitive focus on objects and understanding of their interrelations—a price sometimes worth paying, it appears.

To be sure, the distinction between feeling the value of objects and valuing those objects does not solve the problems of cognitive ethics. In the first place, ethics deals most immediately with directing actions rather than perceiving worths. Relevant values are those that are obligatory for the integration of experience itself. Furthermore, imagined ideals are not felt directly but must be imagined and examined for their relevance and worth. Yet those ideals tie in with the actuality of experience by reference to the real values in the components of experience they are supposed to measure. If the latter may be cognized, the process of criticizing ideals may be cognized, which is not merely a matter of imposing subjective values.

Second, the distinction between feeling the value of objects and valuing those objects militates against metaethical positions which argue that moral obligation stems from a self-justifying or transcendental purpose. Some people, such as the American idealist Josiah Royce (1855–1916), argue that the purpose of meaningful community is presupposed in any dispute about ethical values. Therefore, whatever underlies the realization of meaningful community must be presupposed as the underlying moral purpose. Although this position may or may not be correct about the importance of fulfilling meaning in community, it fails in making the determination of norms solely a matter of the intentional constitution of the experiencer (and his or her community). The intentional constitution determines how objects will be valued, yet they themselves have values which are felt and which are natural components of the experience of those objects. The natural values of the components of experience can be taken into account in determining the content of obligation.

Third, the distinction militates against hedonism—the view that people act solely to gain pleasure and to avoid pain. Like the previous view, this one assumes the only relevant locus of value to be objects insofar as they are valued, positively or negatively, by the subject. The objects themselves also have values which can be felt. There is a difference between a person who attends reflectively only to his or her likes and dislikes, and one who attends also to the objective values in experience, perhaps tempering likes or dislikes by the outcome of that investigation. Psychological hedonism may be defined as the theory that one always does or chooses according to the way one has come to value one's circumstances, and this is trivially true. Ethical hedonism concerns the way one comes to value one's circumstances, claiming that immediate liking or personal pleasure is the most important factor. The denial of ethical hedonism properly recognizes that the appreciated value in objects may outweigh any parochially defined liking or disliking. A simple example of this is food preferences. Children like or dislike certain foods based upon fairly simple physiological adversions and aversions to taste, coupled with strong psychological associations with the accoutrements of eating. As people mature, however, most of them learn to tell the differences among flavors and to distinguish food that is well prepared from that which is not. They cease judging food by whether they like it and pay attention instead to subtleties of flavor, to interesting qualities, to rarity, and to the difficulty of preparation. To have good "taste" in food is to pay attention to the food's value rather than to its value to the needs of one's own experience. A gourmet outgrows his or her infantile psychological associations with food and takes an interest in varied and exquisite flavors for their own sake. One may say that the gourmet comes to have more sophisticated likes and dislikes, but they are likes based on the values felt in the food rather than the values of the food for the drama of one's own subjective experience.

Fourth, these remarks about hedonism apply to any form of ethical egoism. A moral deliberator must take into account the values of all the objects in the world affected by potential judgment. If the egoist says that his or her own value outweighs that of other things in the world, this empirical thesis about experienced values must be substantiated by critical arguments. It seems a prima facie case that, if the world contains other people, at least sometimes the values of those others counterbalance one's own.[18]

In retrospect, this section demonstates three things. First, the challenge of Charles Peirce—that all thinking is interpretation and therefore can be understood solely in terms of semiotic without reference to feeling—was examined in detail. While affirming Peirce's positive claims, we may reject his negative ones in order to maintain, as the preceding section suggests, that experience has two poles, a feeling pole and an intentional pole, only the latter of which is properly subject to semiotic analysis.

Second, the section comments briefly on the significance of feeling, in the form of genetic causal properties, for phenomenology. If the importance of feeling is recognized, phenomenology cannot be merely the analysis of the content of given consciousness, as some phenomenologists claim. Phenomenology must be defined more broadly in referring to the contents of "experience" and its problems. This broader sense is characteristic of the discussions which this study calls phenomenological.

Third, the implications for value theory of the distinction between the feeling and intentional poles have been drawn through contrasts with some standard positions. Valuing and moral deliberation are empirical matters if one admits the direct feeling of value. The authority of this cannot be limited to the logical concerns of intentionality.

Whether the two-pole theory on which these points are based can be supported depends on the cosmological arguments of the following section.

COSMOLOGY OF IMAGINATION IN PERCEPTION

The purpose of this section is to provide a cosmological interpretation of imagination in perception by building on the cosmological theory already developed. The discussion has two main parts. The first elaborates the categories needed to understand the contrast between the feeling and judgmental poles, tracing their alternate perspectives on concrescence. The second deals with the cosmological structure of imagination and its function in perception, including the roles of norms in the function of imagination in perception.

From Feeling to Judgment

As we have seen, a distinction in the experience of thinking lies in the perspectival difference between looking at concrescence as coming from feeling and looking at it as leading toward judgment or satisfaction. From the former perspective, issues of conformation and inclusion predominate; from the latter, issues of intentionality and decisive judgment. The perspectives are obverse ways of looking at the process of concrescence. There is no neutral way to describe that process from the inside; only a larger view of the process between occasions allows the perspectives to be coordinated.

Whitehead held that concrescence can indeed be described neutrally. He believed that the description of concrescence, which he called a "genetic" analysis, takes the final objectified satisfaction as its beginning and infers how that satisfaction might have been generated from prior data, which might have functioned as initial data in the occasion.[19] This is the only sensible approach in dealing with occasions lacking the subtlety of human experience. Human experience, however, includes a subjective sense of the flow of experience. That is, some human experience has a perspective *within* concrescence, looking backward to its origin in feeling and forward to its satisfaction in intentional judgment. Although this perspective of looking at both ends from the middle is not "existent" in the sense that a thing is fixed in worldly coordinates, it is within the process of coming to existence, and it exhibits all the contingencies and ambiguities we find in the process of being conscious. In no way does this contradict Whitehead's observations about consciousness of the indeterminateness to be found within concrescence prior to satisfaction.[20] Any experiential perspective within concrescence immediately posits as further perspectives for analysis the feeling pole and the intentional, judgmental pole. These modes of analysis provide new angles for understanding initial data, subjective form, and norms of spontaneity.

Initial Data. From the perspective of the intentional pole, the beginning of an occasion of experience lies in initial data; the data are present in the incipient occasion as ready to be integrated, as ready to take on subjective form. From the feeling perspective, however, these initial data are rather the objects felt demanding a position in the incipient experience. The data are the inertia of the previous processes of the cosmos providing the energy, determinations, and directed movements that must find expression in the incipient occasion. Without the spontaneity of the occasion's own self-creativity, the momentum of the past would have no potential position in which to be expressed. This reflects the Zenonian point that the past cannot by itself cause anything, precisely because it is past and inactive. Neither can the present by itself cause anything, because there is nothing to be altered. Causation requires the determinations and momentum of the past and the self-creativity of the present to give it potential for definiteness.

Experience, as we are conscious of it, is a complex amalgam of judgments about feelings of objects near and far, in the foreground and in the background, important and trivial. Two classes among those objects must be acknowledged: physical objects occupying time and perhaps space (or their paraworldly variants), and objects which consist of previous thoughts that may be about things with worldly extension but which are not themselves extended. Any imaginative experience, from the lowliest synthesis to the most exalted artistic creation, involves propositions combining previous thoughts with physical objects or with other thoughts or with both. There is little difficulty in conceiving the feeling of an object which plainly has a physical character. The difficulty lies in conceiving the feeling of a past thought, a "hybrid physical feeling."

Any object for feeling, hybrid or otherwise, is a past occasion as that occasion has objectified itself; or the object could be a structured group of such occasions. Whitehead used the term *physical* to mean any occasion or nexus of occasions as objectified. The potentiality of an occasion for objectification consists in the various objects presented to it as initial data, plus all the elements of subjective form deriving from its own concrescent process whereby it integrates those initially felt data. A minimal requirement of definiteness in objectification is that the occasion take up a position for itself in the existential field of all the objects it feels: it must occupy a place and time, or the equivalent of that. This spatial and temporal character is among the elements initially felt when that object enters the experience of another. Our commonsense notion of physicality assumes spatio-temporal characteristics of things, characteristics that are represented spatially and temporally. Yet in principle there is nothing to require that the only elements in an occasion's concrescence that can be objectified are spatio-temporal. Elements in a concrescence that are not spatio-temporal include unrealized propositions about potential definiteness, propositions that take elements as signs of other elements, and propositions that exhibit various stages in integrating initial data through developing subjective form. These too may be objectified in conjunction with the spatio-temporal elements. Insofar as they are objectified, they must be called physical, as Whitehead uses the word.

All of this concerns what can be objectified in principle. But what is objectified in fact tends to be those elements that are well received in the environment and that tend to be reobjectified. If an occasion objectifies the elements which situate it existentially and its thoughts, both must be initially felt by the successor occasions. But both need not be maintained and objectified again by those successors. What the successors do depends on the variety and organization of all the data presented to them; or—expressed from the standpoint of the feeling pole—it depends on all the forces influencing them. In most of what we ordinarily understand to be the physical world, occasions eliminate from initial feelings everything except those characteristics that can be expressed on spatio-temporal coordinates. In our own experience, however, we have occasions which seem to do the opposite; sometimes we attend to and objectify past thoughts, such as memory, while we eliminate spatio-temporal elements or at least subordinate them to background triviality. In our thinking, we give great importance to hybrid physical feelings—feelings which attend to the nonexistential elements—in connection with what we feel and what we objectify. Experience is also bodily in all the senses discussed above. Yet it is not merely bodily, but also perhaps meaningful in the sense that propositions attach significant thoughts to feelings of physical objects, thoughts that carry semiotic weight, supported by other elements inherited within the occasion by hybrid physical feelings; consider the feeling of a printed word, for example. The subjective world of experience includes both physical objects in the ordinary sense and meaningful nonexistential thoughts; it can include them because the objective world presents them.

It might be suggested that Whitehead's definition of physicality as that which an occasion objectifies is perverse, solving the mind/body problem by sleight of definition. There may be merit in this accusation. It might be better to find another word for the totality of objectification and limit "physical" to spatio-temporal characteristics and whatever is expressed in them. Yet consider what has happened in physics as investigators hoping to find the building blocks of the universe have discovered ever smaller particles. Physicists say there are three kinds of elementary particles—photons, hadrons, and leptons—whose nature and behavior are described mathematically in ways that do not jibe with the characteristics of commonsense bodies which occupy commonsense space and travel across commonsense time in paths with commonsense continuity. Particle physicists say that commonsense bodies in a commonsense existential field are really aggregates of hadrons, leptons, and photons, aggregated by our human means of perception, interests, and capacities for manipulation. By the same token, the *nonextended* elements in our experience may be hadrons and leptons aggregated in different ways. Although it seems undeniable that thinking has a "physical" locus in the brain, and that the organs of the brain provide its environment, not since the nineteenth-century phrenologists has anyone suggested that the brain is the thoughts themselves. From the physicists' standpoint, neurophysiologists do not deal with the real "physical" material but with aggregates which bear the same relation to hadrons and leptons as a movie screen image has to the frames of film. Of course, it is possible that even hadrons and leptons are not the most elementary constituent particles of the things which bear the spatio-temporal characteristics of our commonsense world.

In discussing the reality of spatio-temporal characteristics, two referents must be borne in mind. On one hand is the existential field-character of objects which have objectified themselves as ready to be felt. On the other is the subjective character of the world through which they are integrated when experienced together. Philosophical realism is guaranteed because the objects present their own existential character (just as they present their own values) when they appear, from the standpoint of the judgmental pole, as initial data; and from the perspective of the feeling pole that existential character has a force to which the experience must conform either by carrying it along or by eliminating it. The subjective world may seriously alter the existential character of the objects presented. Indeed, it is only through the invention of highly sophisticated equipment that physicists can preserve and objectify the strange existential properties of hadrons and leptons; with the senses of sight, hearing, and touch, it has always been necessary to eliminate those characteristics and substitute grosser sense-data for the elementary particles. What other objectively existent elements are there that we cannot sustain in our experience because we lack the means to form our subjective worlds?

There is no legitimacy, however, in being suspicious of the category of hybrid physical feelings. To be suspicious of that would be to assert the authority of subjective commonsense experience over the empirical results of the scientific method. There is an objectivity to the commonsense world as well, but it is an objectivity that can be made critical when questioned only insofar as we recognize the relationship between the commonsense elements and the empirically ascertained elements that may be more basic. This is like saying that a stick half-submerged in water *should* appear bent when we know it is straight, because we know that water bends light rays.

From the perspective of the intentional pole, hybrid physical feelings provide the content by which past thoughts can, first, be made relevant to other feelings and, second, be objectified in intentional judgments. In speaking of human experience, physical feelings should include hybrid and plain physical feelings; indeed, there is no clear line between the two, since there is no reason to suppose that objects objectify *only* existential field characteristics or *only* subjective concrescence characteristics.

From the perspective of the feeling pole, physical feelings, hybrid or otherwise, convey the sense of continuous flow, the surge of movement and energy, the rush of consciousness and bodily awareness, the urgency of meaning seeking interpretation, the continuous grasp of a world at once perceived and rendered. From this perspective, we are our old selves thinking yet, we are the world reaching experience in us now.

For feelings at the initial stage, the norms of conformation—namely, embodiment and energy—express the excellence of concrescence from the perspective of the feeling pole. The norms of inclusion—namely, purity and sensitivity—express the excellence of concrescence of the later stages from the perspective of the feeling pole. It is at those later stages that the interests of the judgmental pole in the various norms of intentionality may subordinate the integrity of the continuity of experience with its felt objects to the integrity of the occasion's own satisfaction or judgment: only intentional beings can be selfish. The discreteness of an occasion's satisfaction, as intended through the process of concrescence interpreted from the perspective of the intentional pole, should be balanced against the continuity of the occasion with the objective world through feeling as interpreted from the perspective of the feeling pole.

Subjective Form. During the phases of concrescence moving from initial data to final satisfaction, there is the development of subjective form whereby the originally external objects of feeling are made internal to the occasion. Their objective forms are altered and supplemented by forms resulting from the activity of the subject occasion; these are called subjective form. The final phase of satisfaction consists in a completely definite integration of objective form and subjective form, objectified together.

From the perspective of the feeling pole, the process of attaining subjective form is to be interpreted in terms of the successive elimination of alternate potentials for integration, until the point of complete definiteness is reached. Definiteness consists of decisions having been made regarding the disposition of each element of form, force, and value present as a potential among the initial data. Every element must be either eliminated or positioned within the final harmonious satisfaction; if the latter, it must be put in some definite one of possibly several potential positions. Subjective form governs the move from indefiniteness of feeling to definiteness.

From the perspective of the intentional pole, the process of attaining subjective form is to be interpreted in terms of the novelties of a new being coming into existence. Whatever the contributions of felt data, their integration constitutes them collectively in a new entity, and the difference between old and new is made by the arising of subjective form.

From both perspectives, the development of subjective form is spontaneous. Though the forms may be derived from the felt objects, the deriving of them is sui generis. From the perspective of the feeling pole, the spontaneity seems fresh and original; from the judgmental pole, it seems the source of new being. The activity of imagination, from synthesis to the higher levels, is a spontaneous operation.

There appear to be four main kinds of operation in the development of subjective form: elimination, conceptual feeling, composition, and transmutation.

Elimination occurs when an object or any element of an object given among the initial data is rejected from potential objectification. Also, any composition of objects which may be made during the incomplete phases of concrescence may be eliminated. From the perspective of the feeling pole, elimination is interpreted both as the loss of an element of feeling and the development of the subjective form that results from no longer having to take account of that element. From the perspective of the intentional pole, elimination is interpreted as developing new potentiality for integration, which arises from the subjective form no longer having to take account of the lost element. Whereas there is no longer the potentiality of objectifying the lost element, there arises the new potentiality of integrating the rest, a potentiality that was lacking so long as the old element had to be included.

Conceptual feeling is Whitehead's term for the development within concrescence of new feelings whose objects are not the initial physical objects but rather elements of form expressed in those objects, and elements of form expressed in subsequent compositions of those objects. Frequently this has been called "abstraction." Whereas in elimination, a subjective form which excludes the eliminated element arises spontaneously, in conceptual feeling there is a novel feeling, which requires integration with the rest of the feelings, and whose object is an abstract entity—a pattern, for example. From the perspective of the feeling pole, conceptual feeling is the novel emergence of subjective sensibility, feelings of indefiniteness. From the perspective of the intentional pole, conceptual feeling is the emergence of novel potentials for decision.

Composition is the spontaneous activity of feeling diverse elements together, in a propositional pattern. Any things can be composited for which it is possible to find a harmonizing propositional pattern: physical objects, abstract entities, physical objects and abstract entities, propositions and physical objects, abstract entities, and other propositions. From the feeling pole, composition is the emergence of the world into novelty. From the intentional pole, composition is the potential advance toward definiteness. It is important to regard composition as a function in the real process of concrescence, not merely the development of ideal patterns which might be realized. Composition is the development of abstract patterns when its objects are exclusively abstract entities; but some of its objects are physical objects or their physical developments, and most propositional composition may have physical objects as some element in the subject term.

Transmutation is the development of a special subjective form whereby one element—either a physical object, group of such objects, an entity abstracted from such objects, or a proposition—functions in the subjective place of some objects which are then eliminated. For instance, in ordinary experience we transmute the occasions that, in aggregate, make up a distant visible object by substituting for them sensations such as color patches or tones; these substitutes are abstract entities derived through hybrid physical feelings from occasions making up our nervous system. The human race has learned pragmatically that this kind of transmutation helps to integrate experience, that under standard conditions of observation it does not lead to error, and that it allows for personal experiences of beauty, general interpretation of experience, and for public experiences of dealing with a socially common world. From the perspective of the feeling pole, transmutation is the spontaneous alteration of feeling. From the intentional pole, it is the creation of the novel content of the emergent occasion.

Elimination, conceptual feeling, composition, and transmutation are the operations by which the initial data are altered to take on such subjective form that they are integrated into a final definite entity.

But what *guides* this process, determining what is to be eliminated, which potential abstractions are to be felt, and so forth? There are two external limits on the process. First, the given initial data must be dealt with those data and no others except insofar as the concrescent process itself produces novelties. Second, the formal obligations for categoreal definiteness must be exhibited in the final phase of concrescence. These are general norms that must be exhibited if the new entity is to be existent as a definite entity. But there is no reason in principle to assert that the initial data for a given occasion can be integrated in only one way to satisfy the categoreal obligations of definiteness. Although this is factually possible, it would require a degree of rigid organization that seems unlikely for our world; surely some occasions have more options than others. If there is only one option, however, how would the occasion determine in its own concrescence what that option is?

Whitehead ingeniously attempted to resolve this problem with a doctrine of God.[21] He argued that God envisions a valuable path of concrescence for every potential occasion, and that the occasion feels this divine vision among its initial data. Unlike the other data, the divinely derived datum is felt as a lure, guiding the process of concrescence. Whitehead called the feeling of the divine lure a "subjective aim," since it aims the subjective development of the occasion. This also allowed Whitehead to explain why some occasions aim at things that manifestly are not in their own self-interest: God provides a more altruistic subjective aim. Since God's control ends when the divine envisioning enters as initial data, the occasion can do what it will with the divine lure during concrescence, sometimes disobeying the divine lure.

Several difficulties arise in Whitehead's solution. First, there is little experiential evidence for a divine lure that is distinguished from the feelings of worldly elements. Abundant evidence exists that divinity is felt within worldly things which, in turn, are made sacred, as attestified in the study of religions and in a multitude of personal experiences. All this is divinity incarnate, however; even those who claim experiences of God as Holy (wholly) Other find divinity expressed in a form of imagination—a vision, for example, or a voice or a heartfelt feeling. A divine lure, such as Whitehead's, in principle could not enter into an experiential world whose elementary form is imagination. Second, this hypothesis of the divine lure is theoretically inelegant; if all other objects in initial feeling are physical objects, as Whitehead defined them, then God's envisioning must be an idiosyncratic exception. Whitehead did not want to say God is physical; to do so would mean God would have to be somewhere or everywhere, in either case overlapping ordinary physical objects and thereby destroying the distinction between the divine lure and other physical feelings. Third, the conception of God has theoretical difficulties. If a divine envisioning is felt by an emergent occasion, it must have been the objectification of a divine occasion, because the only objects that can be felt (in the cosmological hypothesis shared with Whitehead) are the objectifications of occasions. If this is so, then God must be a series of occasions, as a person is. This view is espoused by Hartshorne.[22] If God is a series of occasions, there cannot subsist internal to God the necessary eternal principles by virtue of which every occasion can be anticipated in connection with the others and thereby envisioned for the good. Those principles would have to be external to every divine occasion and normative for it, and the principles rather than the divine occasion would be God. Fourth, Whitehead's view of the divine origin of subjective aim seems to be an unwarranted theoretical obstacle to human freedom. If God's envisioning is so powerful as to be an initial lure for subjective aim, then God becomes the dominant force in life, dominant in a sense comparable to other potential forces: of all the initial data, the divine datum can be least resisted. Yet what is more common, or more profound existentially, than the poignancy of a freedom which lacks a divine objective? So far are we from being bullied by God, as Whitehead's view implies, that we find God usually *not* manifest among the data of our experience.[23] Finally, Whitehead's hypothesis seems superfluous, considering the following account.

Each object present as an initial datum has a value of its own in the satisfaction it achieved in attaining its own definiteness. This value may be expressed through its physical form, energy, or the aesthetic or other semiotic elements in its objectification. As such, each datum contributes a value calling for a place in the emergent occasion's objectification, some values more insistent than others. To have an extra divine value does not by itself integrate the demands of the others, rather it just contributes one more, very powerful, value to be integrated.

Let us suppose that all the values presented among initial data are the values of natural objects. These diverse values differ in their significance, some having great intrinsic value, others less. If concrescence were a mechanical process, and if the values of the objects felt naturally could be ranked coherently, the structure of the emergent occasion's satisfaction would be determined by the objects felt. But the objects felt as initial data are not subjectively integrated into the new occasion. That is precisely what makes them initial data: decisions have yet to be made regarding *how* they can all be felt together. Therefore the process of concrescence *cannot* be mechanical; a mechanical process must have a definitely integrated beginning, as well as general laws and a definite outcome. Consequently, even a natural ranking among the values of initial data would not provide by itself the ranking necessary for those values within the subjective process of concrescence. Values felt individually must be valued subjectively by the emergent occasion in order to be brought into harmony. This distinction between feeling the values of things and valuing them arose earlier, and now the cosmological reason for it is apparent.

This initial indeterminacy means that there must be a process of norm-determination internal to concrescence; its function is to determine how the values felt in objects are to be valued within the concrescent process and provide the direction for the development of subjective form through elimination, conceptual feeling, composition, and transmutation. The importance of this is evident in recalling the distinction drawn in Chapter 3 between the essential and conditional features of a thing. Initial data, with their values, are the conditions from which an occasion arises. Unless the occasion develops its own principles for valuing those data, however, the occasion will never happen. What is essential to its existence is that it undertake its own valuing. Without that, it cannot appropriate its conditions.

The essential features of an occasion are the work of spontaneity within—indeed constituting—the concrescent process. They are the subjective forms for integrating the conditional objects according to the occasion's own values. The values are expressed in forms, but are not formal patterns themselves; values are simply a different kind of thing.[24] Values can be contemplated, however, only insofar as they are imagined as expressed in form. Part of imagination is to envision forms as ways of having various conditions together so that the value of those forms can be appreciated; we do this consciously in deliberation. Where do the essential features come from such that they provide the requisite subjective form?

Some essential features derive from past objects felt. That is, the values embodied in the occasion's subjective form are the values felt in the occasion's predecessors, or in propositions derived from those predecessors. To the degree that occasions exhibit features characteristic of other occasions, as is true of enduring entities and of the continuous thought of a person's life, important elements of subjective form are derived from the past. For reasons expressed earlier, that derivation cannot be mechanical. Instead, the past values felt must be transformed and given a new status; they must be *appropriated* as essential features determining the valuing of other conditional features within the occasion. Appropriating felt values as essential rather than conditional is an element of spontaneity.

In sophisticated human experience that can anticipate future consequences, some of the values functioning as essential features are derived from a potentially envisioned future. That is, what would be good to realize in the future if a certain action is taken now is appropriated as an obligation *if* that action is taken. Unlike conditional values from the past, however; those from the future are not always appropriated spontaneously in the present to function as essential features; some obligations fall on us regardless of what we do. Norms arising spontaneously in the present, as well as from the past and future, can determine subjective form. Wherever novelty or freshness is perceptible within the concrescent process, spontaneous value rather than spontaneously appropriated external value is felt. Since value is never expressed without form, spontaneous value has spontaneous form.

Hume claimed that all mental representations are derived from impressions, from something like initial data. And in apparent contradiction, he said that a person can imagine a shade of color he or she has never seen. While admitting this is a problem in his system, Hume passed over it. Whitehead criticized Hume's lack of systematic rigor and proposed instead that such experience could be accounted for by reference to the divine envisioning which presents itself as an initial datum.[25] Although a person may never have seen a physical thing with the missing color, the person could derive that color from the divine envisagement; Whitehead called this "conceptual reversion." We do not experience this, however. Because of this and the difficulties noted above with the doctrine of God and divine envisioning, it is simpler to say that some elements of form arise spontaneously within an occasion because they express some value subjectively essential to the occasion. While it is permissible to say that God or a divine ground is the ultimate source for what appears spontaneously within our cosmos, it makes little sense to say, as Whitehead does, that God functions *within* that cosmos.

Norms for Spontaneity. Spontaneity is the source, directly or through appropriation, of values expressed in the subjective form of an occasion, values which guide the development of subjective form through elimination, conception, composition, and transmutation. Are there general norms for spontaneity? It would seem so, since spontaneity has a specific task to perform, determined by the initial data, on one hand and the categoreal obligations defining definiteness of outcome, on the other. These, in fact, are the norms mentioned in Chapter 4.

From the perspective of the feeling pole, spontaneity is subject to the norm of novelty. If there is no spontaneous production of novel forms, there can be no advance in feeling from the disparateness of the initial stage to the objectification at the end. From the perspective of the intentional pole, spontaneity is subject to the norm of relevance. If the novel values and the various appropriated ones are not relevant to the prospect of attaining a definite harmony, no advance is made and the spontaneously produced forms are eliminated. When it occurs, spontaneity must exhibit some novelty and relevance; otherwise the occasion will not come into existence and cannot be said to happen. Spontaneity is "better," from the perspectives of the two poles, when it has greater novelty and relevance.

Another general norm for spontaneity is trivial, however, without the human level of experience: the norm of presence. "Presence" is the manifestation of spontaneity that contributes the tone of spontaneity itself to the occasion's satisfaction. Without presence, the occasion merely feels the past and drives toward the future. With presence, it enjoys itself; it values its existence for its own sake, in addition to fulfilling past urges and creating a valued future. The value of presence cannot fulfill the satisfaction of an occasion, however, unless there is imagination with presentational immediacy and imagination in perception. Without them, there would be no objects whose experience as present could be valued. This brings the discussion to the cosmology of imagination in perception.

Spontaneity as Imagination

A perceptual judgment predicates a special "perceptual" property of the intended perceived object. The judgment is itself a sign ready for interpretation. Potential interpretations include judging whether the perceptual judgment is true or false, whether it is indeed a perceptual judgment or something else, and in what respects the perceptual property characterizes the perceived object.[26] The intricacies of these issues of interpretation are left to the following chapters. The immediacy of a perceptual judgment, which will be treated here, is an experience of the content of presentational immediacy.

Simply stated, the cosmological account of a veridical perceptual judgment is that it is a proposition whose subject feeling has as its object either the cluster of occasions referred to in the judgment or some transmutation of them, and whose predicate feeling has as its object a form derived by conceptual feeling and transmutation from those same occasions to which the subject refers. A perceptual judgment, veridical or not, is one that is interpretable by subsequent judgments as having that form.

This account is too simple, however, because a perceptual judgment also locates its object and describes it in terms of the subjective world of the experiencer. This subjective location implies two things: first, that the basic structures of the subjective world mediate the transition from the objects felt as initial data to the objects felt in perceptual judgment; and second, that the

intentionality structure of the perceptual judgment arises through the mediation of the overall subjective form which determines the final phases of
experience in the occasions bearing the perceptual judgment. None of this is
to say that perceptual judgment idealistically imposes a form on objects that
are not worldly themselves. On the contrary, precisely because every past
occasion which may be the direct object of a perceptual judgment had in its
own time to locate itself definitely with respect to other occasions, each
object objectifies itself as located in a world, and the objectified worlds
must have at least enough common patterning as not to be mutually exclusive. The question of truth can be raised about perceptual judgments because
there is an objective world to which they refer.

Subjective Form: from Feeling to Perception. How do the basic
structures of the subjective world mediate the transition from the objects felt
as initial data to the objects felt in perceptual judgment? According to Kant,
the basic structures are the forms of space and time. We have seen in our
discussion of the three syntheses of imagination that something functionally
similar to space and time is required for the syntheses, although the characters of these subjective forms, observed empirically, are perhaps more
varied and less universal than Kant imagined. Nonetheless, based on the
previous discussion, the following can be said.

First, in the transition from initial data to perceptual judgment, the
original objects must be transmuted in order to take on as subjective form
whatever forms are involved in the synthesis of apprehension. This is to say
that both the feelings of the perceptual subject and the feeling of the perceptual object must be expressed in propositional feelings which themselves are
composited with the positive feelings of all other objects in the subjective
world. The compatible juxtapositions of the compositive feelings constitute
the formal structure of extensionality in the subjective world. If the perceptual judgment is veridical, in this context "veridicality" means that the occasions in the objects referred to perceptually are compatibly juxtaposed to the
other objects in the world they are in perceptually. The point here is that the
apprehension of both subject and predicate in a perceptual judgment must be
through propositional feelings which are composited with the feelings of the
other objects felt in the subjective world. It is the function of imaginative
spontaneity to provide these propositional feelings with the composited subjective form.

Second, the subjective form of perceptual judgments must similarly
exhibit the synthesis of reproduction. This means that the composited propositional feelings, including those apprehending the subject and predicate of
the perceptual judgment, must be ordered in a series that potentially can be
run through in successive fashion. Because a series requires a common con-

cept by which its members position themselves with respect to each other, requiring reproductive synthesis implies that the subjective form of the composited propositional feelings exhibit a coherent structure. Kant thought these structures to be the forms of space and time, which do illustrate the point.

Third, because at least some of the other objects in the subjective world are in the form of perceptual judgments, the composition in apprehension and common structure in reproduction require a concomitant development of their subjective forms. That is, all things occupying experience as perceived must undergo a coordinated development of subjective form, even though some are perceptually in the foreground and others in the background. Both requirements mentioned so far—synthesis in apprehension and synthesis in reproduction—are necessary in order to make a perceptual judgment compatible with the background elements of the subjective world.

Fourth, although the objects felt among the initial data have a worldly character, the traits of the subjective world of experience are apt to be simpler than their real referents. This is because human experience generally simplifies what it feels in order to include greater diversity through trivial composition and greater beauty through contrasting this with the narrowness of simplified perceptions. The selections of the relatively simple structures for vaguely integrating the subjective world serve many levels of experience, from the adaptive advantage of survival, to the more refined but no more important values of intellectual and aesthetic experience. The most complex human experiences treat as trivial certain structural elements which many of the felt objects themselves treated as important and defining. Even on the perceptual level, human experience does not mirror the world but simplifies it. Thus, definitions of truth in perception must deal with the values involved in simplification.

Fifth, the propositional feelings involved in both subject and predicate of perceptual judgments must develop by taking on subjective forms which express the concepts necessary to the synthesis of recognition in a concept. That synthesis transforms the structures, according to which synthesis in reproduction is a potential movement into a positive determinate characteristic of the perceived elements. This is to say that whatever perceptual properties are ascribed to the perceptual object must be recognizable as expressing the structure of the subjective world—as spatial and temporal, for instance. Space and time are only examples, however, because they seem to be the forms of vision and of the progressive articulation of vision. One's subjective world is structured by the forms of the sensations involved. They may have auditory, olfactory, tactile, kinesthetic, and other dimensions. Indeed, there must be basic structures of a unifing sense which integrates these and memories as well. Over the centuries, the school of philosophy that has made the deepest study of the function of imagination in supplying structures by which objects can be recognized in perceptual form is Yogacara Buddhism.[27] Its interpretation of the most basic structure of the perceptual imagination does not call on the metaphors of touch as in Aristotle, or of vision as in modern European philosophy, but on those of smell. The operation integrating sensation with memory to produce perception is called "perfuming." The description of the basic structures that make perceptual predicates perceptual is an empirical matter too complex to broach here, and Kant's a priori approach is inadequate for our purpose, although his visually oriented forms are a fair generalization about our commonsense world.

To summarize the discussion so far, a judgment is perceptual if both its subject and predicate propositional feelings have subjective forms conforming to the requirements of the three syntheses of imagination. In particular, by conforming to the conceptual structure required for the synthesis of recognition in a concept, subjects can be felt as being "in the world" and the predicates can be felt as perceptual ones, that is, predicates whose characters apply only to things having the forms of worldliness. Truth in a perceptual judgment, therefore, involves not only deriving the predicate from the same initial data as the subject feeling, but also mediating the transition from initial data to perceptual judgment by subjective forms of worldliness that "truly" simplify the objectified world.

Subjective Form: Perception in Intentionality. The preceding section states that the intentionality structure of the perceptual judgment arises through the mediation of the overall subjective form that determines the makeup of the final phases of experience in the occasions bearing the perceptual judgment. What does this involve?

Let us recall the distinction in concrescence between the feeling pole and the intentional pole. A propositional feeling (like any feeling) is a phase of concrescence viewed from the perspective of the feeling pole. Its structure is analyzed in terms of fitting the object felt into the overall structure of the experience. Viewed from the perspective of the intentional pole, however, a propositional feeling is a judgment. The emphasis here is not on its origin in the intentional object but on the overall satisfaction of the experience. The elements of subjective form in propositional feelings, analyzed as accretions to the data initially felt, may also be analyzed in terms of the intentionality structure, which incorporates the judgment with other elements in the satisfaction.

The satisfaction of an occasion does not delineate between the intentional and less refined elements of synthesis. For general purposes, however, we may say that those elements touched by the three syntheses of imagination are intentional ones, and the others are not, although the nonintentional elements provide a tone to our intentional awareness, a tone reflecting the origins of feelings.

What, finally, is the overall structure of intentionality which links a perceptual judgment with the rest of intentional experience? Only two observations are necessary here.

First, the experience which includes perceptual judgment, whether dominated by the perceptual element or formed in the background by perception, has the form of a subjective world. The preceding discussion points out that this is the case insofar as perceptual judgment arises out of initial data; the point here is that the form of the world must be the matrix of the entire experience. Although many extraperceptual elements in experience, such as abstract thoughts, might not have existential form illustrative of the subjective world, they are integrated with perceptions to the degree that their abstract forms are compatible with, although different from, the existential forms of the world. The intentional elements of experience are either existentially coherent in terms of the structure of the subjective world, or they are categorically irrelevant to that world.

Second, perceptual judgments are the means by which the subjective world, including its placement of objects and the location of its experiencer, is brought to awareness. The degrees to which perceptual elements dominate awareness vary from an intense consciousness of the setting, to a reverie which has no apparent awareness of the world or existential objects. The relative importance of perception in experience depends on the overall structure of the final complex intentional judgment.

One of the functions of imagination, then, is to clothe the perceptual judgments in subjective form in such a way that they cohere with the other judgmental elements in the satisfaction. This will be discussed in more detail in Chapter 7.

In his own way, Kant would have agreed that imagination relates the raw material of sensation to the concepts by which they become perceptual judgments through the mediation of space and time as the form of the world. But his concept of mediation was such that nothing in feeling could enter perceptual judgment unless it could be schematized by the forms of space and time. On the contrary, although what we regard as external physical objects may be spatio-temporal, memories and other semiotic elements are objects of feeling without being spatio-temporal. With his clear distinction between spontaneous representation and objects represented, Kant had grave difficulty with the concept of past thoughts presenting themselves as *given in continuity* with external objects, which also present themselves as given. For empirical psychology, in his view, thoughts associate regularly, just as physical entities have regularity of causation, but this occurs only on the level of constructed objects. It is important to emphasize, in contrast to Kant's view, that the "form of the world" cannot be solely spatio-temporal, but also must include all the elements which integrate felt objects usually identified as mental. After all, in direct experience, our world includes memories and abstract entities as much as—if not more than—physical objects. Thus, integrated mental entities must be compatible with integrated physical ones; the form of the world must make them coherent.

For Kant, the spontaneous roots of imagination are ultimately mysterious. Yet this mystery depends on the assumption that intelligible causation is only the regularity relating one finished object to another finished object. This concept of causality, possibly adequate for the verifiable claims of natural science, fails to address how one item arises out of another, which is the classical problem of causality. Earlier in this book is the argument that causation needs two elements: coordinate causality and genetic causality—or the readiness of the past to be a set of conditions for the present, and the readiness of the present to take them up. A necessary part of genetic causality is a concept of creativity. Creativity is more than moving old pieces around; it is the novel contribution of such subjective forms that the old pieces can be made coherent. From the standpoint of the causal process, creativity produces its novel products spontaneously, not out of the past, but out of nothing. Within the context of cosmology, creativity with spontaneity resembles a primitive notion, but it is not more primitive than notions such as regularity or order. It is no more mysterious than other cosmological notions; when it is expressed through imagination, it is no more mysterious than the idea of having something to imagine. Neither Kant nor Whitehead moved much beyond remarking on cosmological generalities. If one moves beyond cosmology to metaphysics or ontology and asks why or how there is spontaneity, one must also ask why there is order, and why anything is given. These are different from cosmological questions, being similar only in assuming that where there is complexity, there must be a maker of it. If one answers the ontological questions with a theory of God, one cannot construe God, as Whitehead did, as a member of the cosmos.[28]

Subjective Form: Beauty in Perception. The value which measures the overall intentionality structure is beauty. The preceding discussion notes that the elementary structure of beauty involves a contrast between background and focus, the former exhibiting trivial compatibility and vague comprehension, and the latter exhibiting narrowness of focus in contrast with a breadth of things focused on. The basic structure of the subjective world is the form of the background. The focus *might* be a perceptual judgment in which attention within the intentionality structure is directed at making a background element dominant. On the other hand, the focus might be on elements quite abstract with respect to the background or potential perceptual judgments. Most experiences are a complex joining of the two. It remains nonetheless, that the background of the subjective world is indispensable to any beauty in intentionality. Any form of focus, perceptual or not, must provide the contrast between background and the focus required for beauty. Whatever the nature of the focus, it is spontaneous imagination which produces the subjective form by which the satisfaction or intentionality structure can be made coherent.

Although we are explicitly aware of beauty in some abstract experiences—in contemplating mathematical proofs or in making certain kinds of decisions, for example—the paradigm of explicit beauty is perceptual beauty. In perceptual beauty, there is a clear progression from initial feelings to formation of intentional appreciation of the world, with worldly elements foremost. This makes explicit the connection between the value of beauty (characteristic of the structure of the intentional pole, with the norms of conformation and inclusion in the feeling pole) and the norms, for imagination, of novelty, relevance, and presence. Unless perceptual judgment has an important place in the intentionality structure, appreciation of achieved presence is apt to be lacking, as it is when we say we are "lost in thought." Presence requires a comprehension within experience of both the initial feelings and the final perceptual judgment of those feelings, because presence itself is the measure of bringing them together. If perception is suppressed in the intentional pole, it is possible to neglect presence and feelings of conformation and inclusion of the world as well.

We must remember that even the most abstract experience arises out of the feeling pole. Even if the feeling pole is not represented in perceptual judgments, it forms the unobserved background for abstract contemplation, to the point that if attention focuses on the quality of abstracted contemplation itself, the forces of the world—at least in the kinesthetic medium—are present in experience. Reverie terminates when numb feet, sore posteriors, or calls of nature grow increasingly evident until they break into the focus of attention. And of course, even the most abstracted reverie is guided by memory, which is merely the nether world to which we have access through hybrid feelings.

RESPONSIBILITY IN IMAGINATION IN PERCEPTION

Attunement and Taste

The fact that values are involved in the function of imagination in perception—the norms of conformation and inclusion for the treatment of the feeling pole, those of beauty for the judgmental pole, and those of novelty, relevance, and presence for imaginative activity itself—raises the question of responsibility. In a general sense, one has a responsibility if a value can be achieved better through one's attention and effort than by leaving the affair to other causes. If there are situations basic to human experience, and therefore common to all people, which could be improved by human agency, then they constitute universal responsibilities.

In the case of imagination as synthesis, viewed abstractly, the values associated with "gathering" are simply present and felt. At that level, there is little question of a responsibility toward beauty or any other value, for whether the values are realized does not depend on potential human agency. Extrinsic questions of responsibility, of course, arise in dilemmas where, for instance, one must decide whether a person with the beauty of imaginative synthesis should live, or should be kept alive yet without the possibility of imaginative experience. But what about intrinsic cultivation of the relevant values in experience?

In the case of imagination in perception, the question of responsibility does arise. It is legitimate to ask whether one has cultivated one's experience so as to realize the maximum of perceptual beauty. We all have met experiential philistines, and in fact most of us are remorseful from time to time because we are not as perceptive as we should be. We do have responsibilities for developing our aesthetic sensibility.

Aesthetics may connote a dimension of experience located among the refinements of life. The argument in this chapter, however, is that the aesthetic elements discussed here are not refinements of experience but the foundations of experience. Indeed, it is through perception that one first engages the world. If there is a problem in perceiving well, then there is a problem of engagement at *that* level, and whether one is engaged with the world is a matter of responsibility, not in the least refined.

This discussion of perception presupposes that generally we are speaking of veridical perception. That is, the function of imagination in perception is to mediate the real objects of the objective world given in initial data to perceptual places in the intentional structure of experience. Whether a given perception is veridical is a further mediation of the judgment itself, moving beyond presentational immediacy to interpretation. How this mediation can be made is a subject for discussion under the topic of interpretation. The question under discussion here is not whether the perception is true (although the question of truth is relevant to the best in perception), but whether imagination has formed intentional experience in a way to bring out the best in perceptual form, namely, its greatest beauty.

If we have responsibilities for imagination regarding perception, we can think of them as virtues. Virtues are the powers that can be developed in our characters, in our personal relations and in our ways of life, that allow values to be realized. Without these powers, norms cannot regularly be fulfilled. This does not mean that a person who lacks virtues fails to be obliged by the relevant values, for even without the virtues, that person has the capacity to develop them (or they may be developed within the group or culture). The virtues of aesthetic perception are themselves obligatory because the experiences they make possible are obligatory. After discussing the virtues themselves, we will return to this point.

With regard to feeling, we have noted that two principal values are involved, those of conformation and those of inclusion. Through feeling, our experience originally arises out of, takes its form and energy from, and maintains continuity with, the larger world. Through feeling, experience (indeed, all our being) conforms to the world. The value question is whether experience conforms well, for not only does the degree and kind of conformation vary from one context to another, but success at conformation also varies. Conformation consists of embodying the world's physical and mental contributions and appropriating relevant energies. A person who is well embodied and who shares the energies of the world may be called attuned. The first virtue of imagination in perception, then, is *attunement*.

The virtue of attunement has had an unhappy history in Western culture, which has generally neglected it. In recent years, the promotion of attunement by popular mystics, religious propagandists, and psychotherapeutic faddists has emphasized its anti-rational character. There is a reason for this. Dealing with feeling as conformation with the causal ground of experience, attunement stands at the opposite pole from judgment, where reason is an ideal for the intentionality structure. Where reasonableness might seem an ideal expression of human life, attunement might seem an ideal impression. Attunement is an ideal for attending to our origins, not to our productions.

Yet attunement is a virtue precisely because imagination mediates initial feelings to final judgment where ideals for judgment, such as reason might be relevant. If judgment were to arise anew, its origins might be ignored, and ideals such as rationality could be patterned on the pure intellect of the traditional Western concepts of God. Judgment is formed, among other things, by an imagination which mediates physical conformation to the world; it can be good or bad, depending on how well conformation arises through embodiment and energy. Examples of cultivation of conformation in Chapter 4 illustrate ways in which attunement can be a virtue.

Inclusion deals with how elements of the world fare within our own experience, in which they are subject to the demands of integration and are transformed to occupy positions within intentionality structures. As with the values of conformation, it is necessary that everyone responds to some degree to the things encountered in experience, although people rarely respond with the faithfulness that the term "sensitivity" connotes. Similarly, for pragmatic adaptive reasons, most people bring certain objects from feeling through to conscious intentional awareness with some attention to the objective integrity of the things, although seldom with the degree of integrity that "purity" connotes. Yet it is precisely through sensitivity and purity that perceptual judgments can grasp objects which stand against a vague background with narrowness and width. As this book mentions elsewhere, the virtue associated with the values of inclusion is taste.

Good taste is the foundation both of piety before the integrity of the world and of engagement with that world. Without good taste, narrowness and width in experience would be unrealistically connected with the world. Good taste and attunement are the foundation for good perception, and in that sense are they more basic than the virtue of perceiving truly. Truth in perception presupposes that the connection between initial data and formed intentional judgment is properly mediated by imagination.

It is now possible to reexamine the value of beauty. Beauty has been formally depicted as involving a contrast between background elements and focal elements, with imagination as synthesis providing the world which serves as the background. That subjective world is necessary and indispensable; therefore, there can be hardly any responsibility to beauty in the sense that it merely involves having a world. Yet since one does not have an imaginative world without also having some focal things in it, the elementary form of focal intentionality—perceptual judgment—does indeed impose responsibility. In perceptual focal elements, there should be aesthetic beauty; or rather, when perceptual judgments are well made, aesthetic beauty is the outcome.

The word *aesthetic* refers primarily to taking in the world, to perception and its roots; only secondarily does it refer to art. This secondary meaning will be important in the discussion of fantasy and art below. The word aesthetic refers to how to feel the world so as to perceive it well. Good aesthetic perception is a condition for engaging the world. Without good aesthetic perception, the intentionality structure of experience could not have the form of eros, the love of things for their worth. If eros does not derive from the direct feelings of things in initial data, our valuing of things would have to stem solely from will, a kind of love closer to agape, a love of things because of the lover's intent. Not doubting the virtue of love stemming directly from will, eros is the more basic form of intentionality that engages the world. The aesthetic imagination is essential for engagement.

The claim here is that the virtues of aesthetic perception—attunement and good taste—are necessary elements of good thinking. Without attunement and good taste, people think irresponsibly. We see such people as crass, boorish, and dangerous to the public weal. Their aesthetic insensitivity is expressed in ugliness and inattention to the general ecological aspects of conformation. This illustrates the important sense in which attunement and good taste are public virtues, to be required of everyone, in the same way that honest speech and reasonable inferences are public virtues.

There is a problem here, however, for these aesthetic virtues can be described without referring directly to the problem of the truth of perception. There are, in fact, two elements: beauty *and* truth. The value of beauty is universal only in the limited sense that everyone is responsible for realizing it insofar as it involves a mediation from initial feelings to perceptual judgment. It is possible for everyone's perceptual experience to be beautiful without agreeing about the same objects, because some beautiful perceptions are mistaken. The value of truth introduces a larger sense of universality, namely, common agreement in judgment as well as common excellence in forming judgment with beauty. It is the commonality of the responsibility to perceptual beauty which is the basis for engaging with the world, a world that is itself presupposed before questions of truth become meaningful.

Myth and Ritual

Myth and ritual are the cultural vehicles for attunement and taste. The "mythic consciousness" is the level of imagination at which feelings are rendered into judgments with a degree of attunement and taste. Rituals are actions whose symbolic meanings, according to the appropriate myths, engage ritualists with the world. To perform ritual actions is to practice orienting one's actions so that the world is imaginatively engaged with some degree of attunement and taste.

Myths and rituals are much more than this simple explanation indicates; they may be analyzed in ways that make no reference to the function of imagination in perception. Myths are images of the world for instance which present quasi-cognitive visions. They present cultural lore and operate on many symbolic levels. Rituals, too, are as complex as the myths interpreting them, and they function in roles of authority.

There is a component of myth, however, that should be understood in terms of imagination as perception, and following myth, ritual. Contemporary students of myths recognize that myths are not simply primitive scientific views and histories. If they were, then they could be replaced without remainder by genuine science and history. What does remain, however, is difficult to express as an addendum to science and history. The usual claim is that myths express something that seems paradoxical or contradictory at the intentional level, something that is at least without evidentiary warrant, but which nonetheless reveals important dimensions of life.[29] When they are interpreted as judgment, as intentional expression, myths exhibit an extraordinarily awkward status, one that can hardly be defended.

The suggestion here is that myths are not in the first instance to be viewed as functions of judgment but as functions of imagination. They are forms for organizing feelings into judgment. Myths do involve judgmental elements; indeed their formal properties are symbols woven into formal accounts and stories. But the worth of their function is not a matter of coherence, intelligibility, or the other criteria applicable to judgments. Their worth lies in how successfully they achieve attunement and taste. Does the myth bring feeling to judgment in a way to make the judgment attuned to important things in the environment? Does it make the judgment reflect what is important *as* important?

This function of myths encompasses a broader range of imaginative forms than what are usually called myths. For instance, the ancient Chinese concepts of the Tao, of yin and yang, as much as the legends of dragons and giant birds, form the Chinese imagination for feeling the world expressively. The axiological cosmology offers a way of making the point generally. In transforming feelings into judgments, imagination employs a mediating set of propositions. These propositions contain indicative subjects which can refer to the important elements felt. They also contain interrelating symbols which allow the subjects to be brought together. As far as their subjects are concerned, these propositions imply a selection from among the objects felt with regard to what is important. Thus they serve to screen the objects of feeling with respect to which a judgment might be attuned. As for the interlocking predicative symbols, the judgments issuing from imagination provide a scheme within which the objects felt can play roles of importance; the mythic structures make taste possible. These judgments are not to be confused with the mythic propositions. The function of the judgments is to intend. The function of the mythic propositions is to render the feelings into judgments with attunement and taste.

The statement of a myth is therefore different from the myth itself, for the statement involves an intentional reflection back on the ways intentions are formed below the surface of their intentional structure. As statements, the statements of myth, the telling of the stories, may be more or less accurate in reflecting the imaginative propositions, and there may be many ways of stating the same mythic structure.

The statement of a myth is not merely a second-order reflection of the mythic propositions in imagination, however. Myths are cultural entities, and their symbolic propositions enter imagination through the telling and hearing. Hearing myths, children come to possess them in their experiential environment so that they can function imaginatively. Genetically, for each individual, telling and hearing myths comes prior to the mythic function in imagination. Mythical rehearsal makes possible mythical experience.

Myth in this sense is close to ritual. Like myths, rituals have many functions and levels of meaning. Paralleling the imaginative function of myths, rituals rehearse a way of acting in the environment that fosters attunement and taste in the ways expressed in the myth. Although the ritual can be seen as an intentional action designed to produce some effect—honoring the gods or bringing rain, for example—the imaginative function of ritual is to channel action so that experience engages the world with attunement and taste.

A basic level of myth works to impose order on disorder. Chaos—undifferentiated initial data—destroys contentment and enjoyment and must be tamed. So Marduk the hero-king slays Tiamat, the mother dragon, allowing value to be achieved through order, yet always at the price of excluding other orders, other values. In the Chinese myth, the friends of Chaos drill holes in him so that he can experience and speak, but he dies. Imagination achieves value through dominating feelings, but at the price of destructive creativity.

At another level, myths articulate the extensionality of experience. The background against which perception takes place is the background for mythic action. Most primitive myths orient extensionality from a central place and time of creation. Extensionality might be oriented around a pattern of movement, however, as it is in the Chinese patterns of yin and yang. On a more sophisticated level, but equally basic to cultivated imaginative experience, some Buddhists attain experiences whose extensionality involves a mutual interpenetration of all parts.

Other levels of myth deal with locating the experiencer in the temporal and spatial environment, providing a frame for history and identity, and interpreting destiny. Ritual actions are related to myths in greater complexity than can be analyzed here. But it may be suggested that the most important forms of engagement vary with circumstances. Where food and survival are pressing needs, fertility rites are paradigmatic engaging actions. Where political organization is the greatest problem, rites celebrating order and hierarchy are most engaging. For both myth and ritual, their value is neither the truth of statement nor the legitimacy and success of intended result, but how effectively the experience that they form transforms feelings into judgment with attunement and taste.

If we are responsible for experiencing with attunement and taste, then we are responsible for the mythic and ritual life by which this might be accomplished. This is not the responsibility to have true myths or magically effective rituals. Nevertheless, the truth of interpretive elements involved in a myth might very well be related to its effectiveness in mediating attunement and taste. If those interpretative elements are false, then the attempted engagement might instead be alienating. Similarly, ritual actions are not independent in their actual accomplishments from their functions of engagements. How it is that interpretive elements in myth and the effectiveness of ritual relate to imagination is a topic that can be answered only with a theory of interpretation.

The discussion of myths suggests that the function served by art, that human achievement so prized in our secular consciousness, is at its foundation a religious function.[30]

Imagination as Appearance: Form

Imagination as synthesis was treated as the synthesis of a world as if the perceptual content and formal structure of the world could be neglected. Imagination in perception was discussed as if novelty in subjective form were not the creation of form. It is possible at this stage in the argument to speak of imagination concretely by including an analysis of form. Form is involved in every act of imagination, and imagination takes place through the formation of a perceptually oriented world. In this discussion of form, imagination is seen to be the activity by which the world appears in experience. Stated another way, experience arises insofar as natural processes are imaginatively appropriated as appearances.

PHENOMENOLOGY OF APPEARANCE

Forms

Kant wrote,

> That in the appearance which corresponds to sensation I term its *matter*; but that which so determines the manifold of appearance that it allows of being ordered in certain relations, I term the *form* of appearance. That in which alone the sensations can be posited and ordered in a certain form, cannot itself be sensation; and therefore, while the matter of all appearance is given to us *a posteriori* only, its form must lie ready for the sensations *apriori* in the mind, and so must allow of being considered apart from all sensation.[1]

Kant's definition of form and matter was not as arbitrary as his language suggests; it emerged from a long tradition, and his use binds together many levels of meaning. Although much of his theory is criticized in preceding chapters, it is apparent that the paragraph above can be understood in the following way, consistent with the axiological cosmology. Feelings entering any experience constitute the matter of that experience, and the way those feelings are taken up and integrated to be experienced is the form. With respect to the matter given, the form is all spontaneous, although it is not clear yet in what sense, if any, form can be a priori. For Kant, form is the result of *any* integrating spontaneity, not just what he terms imagination; in the axiology of thinking, by contrast, any production of form in experience is termed imaginative.[2]

What is form? It is that by which a manifold can be experienced as a unity. Kant defines this as a "rule."

> But a concept is always, as regards its form, something universal which serves as a rule. The concept of body, for instance, as the unity of the manifold which is thought through it, serves as a rule in our knowledge of outer appearances. But it can be a rule for intuitions only in so far as it represents in any given appearances the necessary reproduction of their manifold, and thereby the synthetic unity in our consciousness of them.[3]

What is a rule? It is a norm or value for an activity that should be manifested in the activity's product. By referring to the vocabulary of value in Chapter 3, we note that the various elements in any activity of experiencing are a manifold for which there is at least one normative measure. The normative measure obligates the activity, and any exercise of the activity exhibits the normative measure in some way and to some degree.

A normative measure takes its structure from the manifold it measures. Its structure is derived from the previously determined structures of the manifold elements it integrates, as integrated in its ideal way. If there is only one way the manifold can be integrated, the structure of the normative measure and the structure of fact are necessarily the same. When the manifold includes an activity, the normative measure obligates the process, whether or not the process as potential allows alternatives.

In this respect, normative measures can be either rules or goals. A rule measures a process, whereas a goal measures a static fact. Since a process can include any of its stages as products, rules are inclusive of goals. For many purposes of deliberation, however, it is more relevant to consider goals alone, and, as Dewey suggested, to remember that the de facto value achieved in reaching the goals must include the costs and benefits of the process of reaching them.

Fantasy can be defined as the activity of imagination which applies rules to the manifold of feeling so that the subjective world *appears*. The application of rules can be only spontaneous, although that spontaneity operates within limits. The limits are, first, the actual set of objects given to feeling, and second, the actual set of possible patterns for integration that might embody normative measure and that are included as potential suggestions within the initial data. There is no necessity in what is actually given that a normative measure, which may be eternally relevant to a particular manifold of feelings in the moment, be exemplified in a specific pattern. There is only the hypothetical necessity that *some* pattern be imposed on the initial feelings if the occasion of experience is to happen at all. Self-creativity in a moment of experience is the concrete application of a normative measure to a manifold of feeling in some de facto pattern. If imagination does not actually apply rules to the manifold, then the subjective world, an integration of the initial data, does not appear in experience at all. There can be no synthesis of imagination without forms or patterns by which the synthesis is made. There can be no perception in imagination unless the forms or patterns for organizing initial data into objects of perceptual judgments are applied subjectively. Because imagination applies rules to the manifold so that the subjective world appears, it can be called fantasy, with connotations of the Greek *phantasia,* or appearance. Fantasy is different from imagining, remembering, and similar activities; yet it underlies them all by meaning the appearance of a subjective world which all of them assume.

For a discussion in which the topic is supposed to be the appearance of the world, this has all been strangely abstract. The reason for this has been the necessity to develop the analytic components of appearance in imagination before the phenomenon of appearance itself can be explained. Let us consider a specific appearance within experience of a subjective world, filled with perceptual elements, arranged with a particular focus against a background. What is its form? It is particular, concrete: this landscape with that house there and this tree here, seen by me nuanced throughout with specific emotional qualities from under the tree. In the particularity of the appearance, the house is not so much related to the tree or to my emotions, insofar as "relation" connotes a universality such that there could be similar relations between other houses, trees, and emotion, as it is the case that the house, the tree, and my emotions are in a complex contrast. "Contrast" was Whitehead's word referring to the instance of two or more concrete, whole, actual things being together. In a contrast things fit together; they are not integrated by virtue of the contrast's providing some "third term."[4] On its face, the appearance of a subjective world in experience is a complex contrast.

The appearing world, however, is not a mere contrast; it also has form. Reflecting on the experience, I note that the house is over there and the tree here, and that my emotions are associated with the house because of childhood memories. In this reflection, the "over there" and "here" express geometrical relations with universal connotation, as they would have to be if the contrast is to be meaningful. Where do I find this formal relation? The simplest hypothesis is that certain elements in the contrast have *greater importance* than other elements, and that part of their importance is that they *give a position* to the other elements. For instance, if I were to make a line drawing of the landscape with house and tree, the lines on the paper would correspond to certain elements in the scene which I consider important—probably borders and shadows—and these relatively few marks represent, or convey the reality of, all those other elements for which there are no corresponding marks. The contour of the roof, for instance, suggests the interior of the house. Moved by a different sense of form, I might use charcoal to make a shade and texture drawing; in this case, other elements of form in the landscape scene would be represented. Or I could use colors, or perhaps paint textures, that correspond to emotional qualities in the house and tree. The point is that *the original experience of that appearing scene is a complex contrast which includes certain elements so important that a representation of them represents the whole scene.*

On the face of it, the juxtaposition of the house and tree is concrete and particular. But its importance is such that, in another scene, another house and tree could be juxtaposed *that way,* or a barn and a well, or other things. What is common to the several scenes is the relative importance of the juxtaposing factors to the other elements. For instance, those elements we represent as spatial geometry are of relative importance in all scenes of landscapey world, making it possible for other elements to be integrated into the appearance by virtue of their bearing on the spatial geometry. Granted, saying that several scenes of appearing worlds are landscapes is circular, because we refer to them by the very forms we are trying to define. That is the point, and it demonstrates a serious problem with the account given so far. A subjective world appearing in a particular experience is itself a concrete contrast, with some elements of the contrast being more important than others. The appearing world is particular, yet the important elements are universal because they would perform their ordering elements in any similar world. How is this possible? Kant made a suggestion which points to a solution. He wrote in his chapter on "Schematism," that

> The schema is in itself always a product of imagination. Since, however, the synthesis of imagination aims at no special intuition, but only at unity in the determination of sensibility, the schema has to be distinguished from the image. If five points be set alongside one another, thus, ... , I have an image of

the number five. But if, on the other hand, I think only a number in general, whether it be five or a hundred, this thought is rather the representation of a method whereby a multiplicity, for instance a thousand, may be represented in an image in conformity with a certain concept, than the image itself. For with such a number as a thousand the image can hardly be surveyed and compared with the concept. This representation of a universal procedure of imagination in providing an image for a concept, I entitle the schema of this concept.[5]

Four related elements appear in Kant's account. First, there is the *method* for representing a concept in an image; this corresponds to a structured normative measure. Second, there is the *representation* of this method, which Kant calls the schema; Kant did not always clearly distinguish the method from the representation. The third and fourth elements are undifferentiated in Kant's term "image." On one hand the particular five dots in some concrete appearance, ... ; this, the third element, may be called a *concrete appearance,* and the dots as appearance can enter into contrasts with other appearances. On the other hand, the five dots can be used universally as an image of the number five; this happens when they are printed in an edition of the *Critique.* In our common use of the word, this, the fourth element, is called an *image.*

The problem of deriving a universal structure from a particular concrete appearance concerns the relation between an image and a schema, as defined above. The image is abstracted from a concrete appearance. Yet, once abstracted, it cannot be a universal image for the number five unless it is experienced as being in agreement with its schema. In its genesis, the schema, representing the method, or, in the axiological language, the normative measure, might be abstracted from an appearance. Logically, however, its *normative reality* is prior to both appearance and image. The schema is what allows for a meaningful construction of an image or appearance. In Kant's terms, the schema allows an otherwise disorganized manifold to be integrated according to a concept; in axiological terms, it gives the appearance a structure, so that some elements are more important than others and, when abstracted from the appearance, they function as a universal image.

The relation between the image and the schema poses a fundamental problem in philosophy. Plato attempted to solve it with the theory of reminiscences and forms; Kant with the theory of concepts and imagination; Whitehead with the theory of eternal objects and conceptual prehension. A review of these apparent solutions and their inadequacies introduces the solution of the axiological cosmology.

Plato noted that one cannot perceive an object as colored, unless one already knows that color as a category for classification. He suggested then that a set of forms exists which are universal and in which particular things participate (or, which they particularize). Thus, an act of perception is a recognition of the thing's color in terms of the prior cognition in which one first learned the color. What could this prior cognition be? Plato told a myth of reminiscence according to which a soul in a previous state of being saw the color and could remember it later. But this explanation is flawed. If a soul could learn the color in a previous state, it could learn it now in the colored object; and if it cannot now, then it could not when it flew earlier around the heavenly showcase of forms. Furthermore, how would the soul know that the color seen previously was the same as the color now present in the object? Although this myth was persuasive to the participants in the *Meno*, Plato criticized its obvious flaws in the *Parmenides*. The form according to which one recognizes a color cannot itself be a color.

Kant construed the problem to be one of relating a concept to a manifold, resulting in an appearance which has the given contingency of the manifold as well as the intelligible structure of the concept. (For the moment, we may disregard the fact that he was speaking of a priori concepts, or necessary categories.) He believed his solution was helped by the fact that the structure of time is common to both the manifold and to possible representations of the concepts. Thus, the manifold has to conform to the structure of time in order to enter our field of subjective representations. But giving form to even the most elementary representations of a subjective world requires solving the problem at hand; we cannot assume that temporal formation is attained without also attaining conceptual formation. Imagination has the capacity to construct what the abstract concepts mean, if, according to Kant, time also structures representations of concepts. Abstract concepts have empirical validity only when they are applied as expressions of time. How do we know that what is abstractly normative for understanding the concept—for example, causality—is expressed by its temporal schema, "the succession of the manifold, in so far as that succession is subject to a rule"?[6] Why is succession in accordance with a rule the proper schematization of causality? For many philosophers, the normative element in the concept of causality, what makes it intelligible, is that the cause somehow *produces* the effect; this is precisely what is *not* rendered in the schematization Kant offered! Kant said,

> This schematism of our understanding, in its application to appearances and their mere form, is an art concealed in the depths of the human soul, whose real modes of activity nature is

> hardly likely ever to allow us to discover, and to have open to
> our gaze.[7]

This is an innocuous observation if it merely expresses surprise at the spontaneity of imagination. But it cannot be used to assert that any alleged schema is an authoritative schema simply because it is produced by the mysterious power of imagination.

For Whitehead, the problem appeared as the relation of eternal objects
to actual entities, and as the relation of conceptual feelings to physical feelings. In his theory every element of definiteness in an actual entity consists
of an eternal object, or universal form; eternal objects are what he called
pure forms of relatedness and they provide structure for the world. An actual
entity gets its structure by feeling its structural elements separately in the
previous objects it feels, and then integrating them into its own individual
structure. In human experience, the eternal objects felt in the initial physical
feelings can be isolated as objects of subsequent conceptual feelings. The
problem is, How can a conceptual feeling reduce the concrete particularity
of the contrasts in physical data to select those elements which are eternal
objects? It begs the question to say that eternal objects are simply there in
the physical datum and that, by nature, conceptual feelings have them as
objects; for the question then becomes, How are eternal objects resident in
concrete physical objects? When they are abstracted out by conceptual feelings, what is left? If a conceptual feeling had as its object the complete
complex eternal object which determined the satisfaction of a previous entity, would the conceptual feeling be different from the physical feeling of
that entity? Obviously yes, but how? Whitehead had no answer except to
employ Plato's strategy of preexistent forms, or eternal objects. That
strategy works only if the conceptual feeling somehow "knew" before finding its object what the eternal object is, thus "recognizing" it in the physical
datum. Whitehead's strength at this point is that he insisted on deriving the
components of experience from data given to experience; in doing so,
however, he could not acknowledge any "reminiscence" of eternal objects.

The solution to the problem rests on construing concepts as norms.
Kant's concept should be a normative measure. An appearance is a concrete
set of contrasts, some of its components more important than others. "Importance" means that the elements called important, fitting with the rest of
the manifold as they do, allow the rest of the manifold to be integrated.
Without those elements, the manifold could not appear. In general terms,
the important elements are those whose function it is to give the manifold its
harmonious complexity and simplicity. With reference to imagination in experience, the important elements are those which structure the manifold with

beauty, as Chapter 6 discusses. Some elements are important because they allow a vast background to be trivially present; others give the background a vague orientation; some provide narrow focus, and others comprehensive breadth. How each element functions depends on the particularities of the manifold; what allows vague orientation in one manifold might be a narrow focus in another.

In this interpretation, what is common to all appearances is the elementary presence of beauty; it is the general normative measure for appearances. *How* beauty is present depends on the particularities of the manifold. If several manifolds are similar in their particularities, that is, if different experiences feel more or less the same objects, then the elements in the concrete appearances organizing them beautifully will be similar. These elements constitute the images. An image is a set of elements that is important in an appearance because of its function of making that appearance beautifully harmonious. It is universal in the sense that it would perform that same function in any similar manifold. But its universality is not in any "nonparticularity" or "eternal objectness" that it has when it is in an appearance; rather, it consists in its *function* of organizing beautifully. That is, the element follows a harmonizing rule that can be followed by other elements in other appearances. An image is universal not because its particular character—these five dots, for example, ... —is the same in each copy of the book, but because five dots in one copy follow the same rule for organizing the appearance of the book as the dots in the other copies. An image, therefore, expresses a schema of the normative measure. It follows the schema by which that normative measure is structured in any of the similar manifolds that it makes to appear. The similarity in such manifolds consists of their components exhibiting the same normative measures for similar component manifolds, and so on.

Thus, an eternal object, or pattern, or image, is always a medium between an otherwise particularized manifold and a normative measure. Both sides are necessary. Without the normativeness of the measure, there would be no way to account for some elements in an appearance being more important than others, and for this same importance being found in other appearances. Without the antecedent particularity of the manifold, there would be no way of giving any definiteness at all to the normative measure, because only determinate things can be harmonized; pure harmony, or normativeness, is indeterminate.

Whitehead made a serious error, therefore, in claiming that eternal objects are separate relational essences in themselves and attain their value only when they are integrated as potential lures for particular occasions.[8] Without reference to the diversity of the occasions they are to measure, eternal objects are not determinate at all; one should say, rather, that there is only one eternal object, an indeterminate form of "the Good," as Plato called it. Furthermore, if eternal objects are not normative, independently from connection with what they measure, it would not be possible to say that they are normative when they are given structure by what they measure; for what would make the structure normative?

It appears that Whitehead was right, however, about the role that eternal objects play in experience. They are felt as values relative to the manifold they form, and their structure can be abstracted out by feeling just how they are important for their manifold.

Whitehead was also right in emphasizing that the concrete contrasts appearing in experience contain universality within them, although he did not stress the point that universality is contained through the structuring of appearances according to importance and the elements of beauty. How this is so is explored in the section to come entitled "Cosmology of Appearance."

Let us reconsider the appearance of the landscape scene. Although all the elements in that landscape are concrete particulars, some are so important that I fasten on them as organizing images; in reflection, I might draw them on paper to reproduce the landscape. Their importance is an importance they might have for other appearances. This would be possible because those other appearances are manifolds similar to the first and harmonized according to the same normative measure. To say that I see the same set of images from one glance at the landscape to the next is to say that the same things are important in the appearance of the landscape each time.

The appearance is a complex judgment resulting from my response to the manifold given in feeling. Separately, the feelings are not a subjective world; the subjective world is the frame in which I have those feelings unified. If I were able to focus on a single initial feeling, I would be able to appreciate its own beauty in its subjective world (something like this might happen in lingering over a thought through successive experiences); but I could make it appear to me only by integrating it with my other feelings and subjective contributions needed for complete integration.

As elements of importance in an appearance, images are found on many levels. The forms used in the syntheses of imagination, for instance, are fundamental. Imagery of focused perception—visual shapes and audible tones, for example—is also basic. Imagery of familiar objects and time spans may be less basic, but they are common to all except mystical and drug experiences. Despite Kant's arguments, there seems little reason to say that any level of imagery is a priori, although some levels might be universal. That they are universal and that they are presupposed as conditions for other levels and kinds of imagery, stem from the prior fact that the manifold contingently contains elements common to all or most experience. It is because so many of the objects we experience are spatial that our experience is invariably spatial, not the other way around. The description of fundamental imagery must always be phenomenological. It can never be seriously transcendental, because any "necessity" in the imagery comes from having to deal with the contingent realities of the world.

The contribution of the schematizing subject is not, as Kant thought, to organize the world according to a priori concepts. It is to gather in the world, however diverse, so as to constitute it an appearance, structured with importance. The source of the subject's contribution is the normative measure. In order to reveal the problems of this perspective, we must turn to the process of imagination itself.

Fantasizing Imagination

After presenting the complex problem of form in the preceding section, it seems necessary to ask how all this relates to experience. The problem of form is an extraordinarily abstract and dialectical issue. The outcome of the discussion, however, should be not only a demonstration of the dialectical superiority of the axiological concept to traditional alternatives, but a revisioning of experience. The question is, Does the axiological approach allow us to take our experience more straightforwardly, acknowledging the nature and modes in which its values are found, and giving clues to its underlying elements which, when we expect them, show themselves? In this connection, it has been argued that the work of imagination in forming feelings into appearances is to order them with respect to each other by means of organizing images. The images function within an appearance as the important elements according to which other elements are integrated. An appearance is thus a fantasy constituted around images organizing a manifold.

An appearance, in the sense used here, is a constitution of a subject's experience. It may be a "true" appearance of the real world out of which the experience arises, or it may be an "illusion" in reference to that real world. If it is the latter, it expresses the fact that much of a person's experience arises from feelings of memory, and that an appearance might be the representation of yesterday's world, or a world expressive of drives and needs which are out of phase with the person's real contemporary world. In any case, whether an appearance is truly or illusorily taken to be the way the world is, is the result of interpretation, not imagination. By itself an appearance is neither true nor false. Truth measures only the *interpretation* of appearance.

Nevertheless, a fantasizing imagination is the agent for *engagement* with the real world. A real world is given for experience, and imagination must make that world appear in experience. Regardless of whether the subjective world which appears stands in a "true" relation to the real world, it is the experiential engagement of the real world. It is the way the real world is taken up in experience. Appearance cannot help but be some kind of engagement, because appearance itself is the organization of data presented causally to constitute the experience of the data. The normative issue for imagination is whether the engagement is good as engagement. The topic of this section is the way that fantasizing imagination is measured by norms which constitute engagement.

A historical note is needed as background for this topic. The hermeneutical theory of Heidegger and Gadamer, precise as it is in seeing the problem of interpretive experience in the twentieth century, fails to distinguish the problem of interpretation from the problem of engagement.[9] In their discussions of questioning, these two philosophers point out that a person can come to experience a thing "in the open" only by a process of questioning. The function of questioning is to remove false prejudices and prepare a person to receive the object as it is. The result of discovering the true question is an openness that engages the object, and in that engagement establishes the being of the subject. Nevertheless, although this is the result of a dialectical, questioning hermeneutical process, the result is less hermeneutical than imaginative: the perfection of imaginative engagement requires correcting distorted interpretations. Heidegger and Gadamer follow the Cartesian tradition of taking philosophy's purpose to be the guidance of the will in order that intuition may do its work without distortion. Even with the dialectical openness of authentic questioning, however, the result is only engaged imagination. The question of truth still lies unanswered. The appearance of mysticism in Heidegger's writing comes partly from his seeming assumption that the thorny questions of interpretive truth have somehow been overcome in attaining open engagement. But, in Heidegger's approach, having struggled through a destructuring of interpretation to arrive at imaginative openness, a person must struggle back through interpretation to raise the *question* of truth, and beyond that to theory and vision, and beyond that to responsible life. Worse, describing this as a serial process is misleading: a person does all these things simultaneously; no single activity can be bracketed.

That fantasizing imagination engages the real world stems from the fact that fantasies or appearances are imaginative constructs made out of feeling the real world. This point is apt to be misunderstood, however, because of two common mistakes.

One error is that we do not commonly realize that the real world given as data to a present occasion includes the past experiences and biological and social structures of the person experiencing the world. We commonly think that only what is external to the person is the real world, and that past experience is part of subjectivity. This opinion stems from an inadequate cosmological model of the self and it is typical of dualistic substance metaphysics. In the substance view, what is internal to a person through time is regarded as subjective. The cosmological theory presented here acknowledges the relative independence of each present experience for which past experiences and past states of the self are among the real data to be integrated. There is a continuity of subjective feeling, accounted for by hybrid physical feelings. Furthermore, the structures of one's own past are likely to be the most stable and pervasive elements of one's environment and, therefore, to require greatest conformity from one moment of experience to the next. Nevertheless, those past states are as much a part of the real world as the so-called external elements, and fantasizing imagination must engage them as well. Any appearance, even if it is a landscape before one's eyes, is a way of engaging one's past experiences, biological drives including sexuality, and social realities. A "true" representation of some "external" reality is only a partial engagement; the "internal" realities also engaged may be more important. A critic of appearances might be on solid ground, therefore, in saying that although one's apparent experience corresponds pictorially to the landscape in the real world, it is alienated from one's sexual passions or cultural memory.

The second common misunderstanding is to confuse engaging the world with intending the world. An appearance is always a complex intentional judgment *about* something; if it is interpreted further, its object is specified. Intentionality in an appearance is not necessarily congruent with the reality the appearance engages and from which it is made. The illustrations in the preceding paragraph apply here, too. One may be thinking about the house in the landscape, with the rest of the space as background and the nearby tree as a marker for perspective and orientation. Yet that appearance is the result of engaging not only the perceptual objects in one's spatial field, but also one's memories, drives, and other predetermined forces to which present experience conforms. The intentional quality of the appearance is a function of attention. One may be paying attention to the house in its spatial relationship to the tree, or to the house as evocative of a memory; the entire landscape might recede into the background as one focuses attention on a memory or a theoretical concept. Whatever the focus of attention, that focus in its appearance embodies one's experiential engagement with reality. An analysis of appearance alone, therefore, is not sufficient to account for engagement. The analysis of engagement must include the entire activity by which imagination produces appearances by fantasizing on initial feelings.

Previous chapters discuss in detail the norms for feeling—those of inclusion and conformation, the norms for imaginative judgment—those articulating beauty, and those of spontaneity—novelty, relevance, and presence. It is now possible to indicate how they cohere in imaginative creativity.

The experiential activity of imagination takes place in the higher phases of integration which constitutes a person's life from moment to moment. In principle, any datum which is felt in any of the phases of integration, whether from a person's past life or from the "external" world, is available for integration into the higher imaginative phases. We may assume that most physical realities are excluded from imaginative feelings, given less value, transmuted with feelings of semiotic content, or composited in such a way as to become involved with other feelings in semiotic ways. When we think superficially about the content of our ordinary imagined subjective world—the "satisfaction" of the imaginative phases of experience—it may seem, as idealists have observed, that the whole of its intentional structure is a tissue of concepts and symbols.

Yet, generally speaking, the more sensitively and purely physical as well as personal and social data are preserved in feeling up to the satisfaction of imagination, the more imagination includes an embodiment of the subject with the energetic currents of the world, the richer the imaginative satisfaction. The beauty of the subjectively imagined world, integrating the data felt into background and focal elements, is *not* aesthetic in the nineteenth-century meaning of isolated, discrete experience. The beauty of subjective fantasy is not cut off from the world, but is made from the world and engages it. It is aesthetic in a sense which links beauty with feeling. The cosmology of subjective, imaginative fantasizing connects the fantasies directly to physical feeling; otherwise, the beauty of fantasies is "merely" phenomenal. If the beauty of fantasies is to express the feelings in initial data, then the norms for the imaginative process itself have enormous importance.

Novelty, relevance, and presence are the norms of the imaginative process, and together they are the norm of creativity. Creativity consists of inventing novel forms (in the sense of form described) which are relevant to a subjectively beautiful appearance which, in turn, maximizes conformation and inclusion, with an enjoyment of this process. The imaginative *process* is creative in the sense that its product is both the world experienced and the experiencer experiencing. The satisfaction of an occasion of experience includes both the subjective and objective poles of the experience. The objective pole in the case of imagination is the fantasy—the subjective world as an objectification of the initial data. The subjective pole is the experiencer entertaining the experience.

It may be tempting to say that in the satisfied experience only the experiencer is real, and that the world experienced is subjective, not only in being entertained by a subject, but also in being *merely* real for the experiencer. This overlooks the point made above that the real world is engaged and present in imaginative experience, even if the intentional direction of the fantasy is away from the world from which it arises or is false to it. On the contrary, the most deluded fantasy is a real product of an experiencer responding to real antecedents, and it is an objective datum for future experience. To deny this is to disconnect mind from the causal nexus of nature. The caveat to observe is that the real world intended in the fantasy may not be as the fantasy intends; this is to admit that imagination can be mistaken when we interpret it to be claiming a truth.

It may be equally tempting to say that, in the satisfied experience, only the experiential content is present, not a subject experiencing. This is true if the satisfaction is considered only after its present state, when it has become an objective datum for further experience. In its objective state, the experiencing subject is present in derivative ways. One such way is that the contours of the appearance in the satisfaction are formed by the perspective of the experiencing subject; indeed, part of the imaginative fantasizing of a subjective world is giving it form from a perspective which defines the place of the experiencer. Another way the subject is present derivatively is through the emotional and other subjective tones found in the appearance which are there because of the experiencing subject's own novel contributions to the process. When we consider the satisfaction from the standpoint of its being objectified for subsequent experience and from the standpoint of its own happening, its own concrescence, the experiencer is immediately present as the process by which the appearance is constituted. The concrescent process aims at a finished satisfaction. Or, to put the matter in terms of imagination, imagining an appearance bears with it an immediacy of the process of constituting the appearance out of initial feelings. This sense of immediacy can itself become the object of awareness. When it is, we are conscious not only of past appearances or of a nascent appearance, but also of the creative wreaking of the former into the latter. This is what it means to be imagining or entertaining an appearance.

Western culture has employed two metaphors for the state of being present to one's thoughts, which in its most basic and universal form is to have a world imaginatively. The first is the metaphor of *creativity* itself. As God creates a world by his own volition, so human beings in the divine image create their experience, both covert and overt, by their own volition. Whereas God creates out of nothingness, people create out of otherwise given materials. This metaphor has been expressed in philosophy, and in the arts and sciences, and may have its finest expression in Kant's philosophy. God's knowledge, according to Kant, is intellectual intuition, whereby he creates his cognitive objects by thinking them. Our intuition is empirical, which means we need the raw material of sensation. When that condition is satisfied, thinking rises out of our own spontaneity; in science, nature takes form from the questions we ask under the constraints of empirical experience. For Kant, it is in artistic creation that we seem most nearly divine, because the genius of the artist creates both the ideal concept and the material expression of the concept, although for Kant it is in morals that we are most autonomous, if not most creative. The axiological cosmology gives thorough expression to the concept of creativity.

The other metaphor for being present in one's thoughts is *eros*. People "are" insofar as they love; they are defined by what they seek as objects of love. As Plato expressed it, love is the god that relates people to what defines them and to what gives them their value. A person is a bundle of appetites disciplined by will and guided by rationality. It is clear from the axiological cosmology that experience is as erotic as it is creative, for in the creative imagination, the beauty of the nascent appearance is what orients the process. At any stage within the moment, the experiencing subject is driven by the values in the initial feeling which seek to be objectified in the world that is appearing, and seek fulfillment in the appearance itself. The immediacy of imagining is eros seeking not only fulfillment but definition in the appearance which its own activity is producing out of its erotically qualified drives.

That beauty is a norm for the intentionality of imagination means that the activity of imagining is eros. That embodiment and energy, purity and sensitivity, are norms for having feelings of given objects means that the activity of imagination is *driven,* as eros is driven. The two aspects of eros—that it feels itself incomplete and seeks fulfillment in the beautiful object, and that it feels itself driven by brute forces—are the characteristics of imagining.

Fantasies may be true or illusory intentional representations of the world from which they come. In either case, they embody the deepest passions that move us, the initial feelings that force themselves upon us. No wonder our fantasies express our sexual natures, even when those fantasies are true pictures of the external world. They express not only our appetites, but the contours of our physical and social environment. They are framed in the categories of the languages that color everything we imagine; they have as their images the ones our culture presents as important. By knowing the recurring features of the environment in which experience takes place, we can know the fundamental images through which the world appears.

Beyond the conditions to which imagination must conform, where the possibility of creative novelty exists, the quality of what appears in experience can be improved. For instance, through the creativity of imagination, it

is possible to have a true appearance, expressing the norm of truth in interpretation. It is possible to have vision and responsibility as well. Moreover,
from the standpoint of imagination, it is possible to increase the beauty in appearance. The principal power of fantasy is not to create distortions in what is
"plain vision," although under some circumstances that may happen. The principal power is to *have* the world given in initial feelings in a more beautiful
way. *Any* appearance must embody some beauty, insofar as it is formed with a
background, focal elements, and other attributes. The greater the beauty is,
the richer its complexity and more elegant its simplicity are; this becomes
possible when beauty brings more of the felt world into its own appearance.
Only through observing the norms of sensitivity and purity, embodiment and
energy, can the richness of the real world be engaged with the fantasies of
subjective experience. The norm of beauty thus requires the norm of creativity
in imagination to maximize the engagement. These norms lie so low in our
awareness that they are rarely topics for responsibility. But does it not make
sense to observe that, for the sake of its own mere beauty, imagination should
engage the richest possible feelings in its fantasies? If so, then not only was
John Dewey right to argue that art is experience, but he would also have
been right to say that imaginative experience itself stands under the obligations of art—deliberate creativity.

Recapitulation. The preceding argument has been a complex attempt
to solve the ancient problem of form by supplying successive waves of
analysis. The discussion began with an abstract exposition of Kant's distinction between form and matter in representations, and drew a parallel between Kant's "concept" and a normative measure. The argument then moved
to consider a particular experience of a concrete landscape. The analysis of
the particular experience drew out Kant's analysis of the schematism which
makes form definite in concrete experience. This gave rise to an amendment
of the previous account, now acknowledging a structured normative measure
to be Kant's method for representing a concept, a schema as the representation of the method, an image first as a concrete appearance, and then an
image as universal. The philosophic problem of universality and particularity in form can be formulated as the problem of the relation between a
schema and both meanings of an image. The solutions of Plato, Kant, and
Whitehead were considered and rejected. A solution was offered in terms of
construing concepts as norms. An image in a concrete appearance is that
which is important in the sense that the whole of the appearance is integrated by virtue of the structure of the image. The importance of the image
is that it expresses the normative measure. This theory, incomplete as it is,
was then set in a larger cosmological context and interpreted as an articulation of engagement. By giving formal importance to certain things, an occa-

sion can engage the world experientially as appearance. The distinction between engagement and interpretation was stressed, and the norms of the imaginative process—novelty, relevance, and presence—were defined in terms of imaginative fantasizing. Finally, creativity and eros, two grand themes of Western thinking, were employed to interpret the concrete process or imaginative experience. The treatment of form here is formally inadequate, however; it needs to be supplemented with the cosmological discussion of the section "Cosmology of Appearance."

CRITICAL INTERPRETATION

The preceding account of fantasy and appearance is distinguished on its positive side by an emphasis on normativeness. On its negative side, it is distinguished by a subtle denial of one of the central pivots of most theories of imagination, namely, the connection between imagination and personal continuity. Kant, for example, throughout his discussions of imagination as synthesis, focused on what he called the "transcendental unity of apperception" as a condition for the unifying logic of imagination. He believed that an appearance is not possible as a unification of a manifold unless there is a logical unity, a transcendental unity of apperception, to which all subjective thoughts must be conformable: without a potentially unified self, there is no unified appearance. Although this transcendental unity is not identical with continuity of the empirical ego for Kant, it is the condition for it. The present interpretation of imagination in terms of norms, however, makes no appeal to preconditions of unity, other than those of the causal conformations found in feeling and the integrity of the norms in imaginative appearance. Personal continuity, therefore, is more problematic in this theory than in Kant's and some others. As will become evident in the axiological cosmology, personal continuity is *desirable* only in the senses involved in being responsible for the norms and values of life.

In the meantime, however, it is important to highlight the differences between the themes of the axiological cosmology regarding continuity in imagination and the main approaches in Western tradition. The first of the traditional approaches, derived from Aristotle, says that a person is continuous by virtue of being a single substance. The second, derived from Kant, articulates personal continuity in terms of the conditions necessary for unity of consciousness through time, for unity of moral life, and for applying the ideal of happiness. The axiological cosmology instead allows personal identity to be interpreted in terms of the self-creativity of occasions of experience with reference to norms.

Aristotelianism

Aristotle. For Aristotle, a person like any natural substance, is an irreducible unity. There are in principle four ways, corresponding to Aristotle's four causes, to understand a person's unity, although the intrinsic substantiality of the person cannot be reduced to any one or be a composite of all four abstract perspectives of understanding (see *Physics,* Book 2, Chapter 3). With respect to efficient causes, one may understand how people have the form they do in the matter that constitutes them, here and now; this is one kind of unity of identity. With respect to final causes, one may understand how people's lives are meaningful, part by part, as contributing to their generic and special purposes. With respect to formal causes, one may understand how the essential properties of human life and the accidental attributes deriving from the contingencies of time, place, relations, and movement cohere to describe the shape of personal lives. With respect to material causes, one may understand how all the changes in people's features take place as alterations of form in their basic material components. No single cause explains human life without reference to the other causes. Nevertheless, a kind of priority is given to material cause as an explanation of personal continuity. It is one's "matter" (1) that individuates what otherwise would be mere universal features; (2) that endows efficient causes with potentiality for action; and (3) that allows final causes to be realized rather than to remain merely ideal. Objections to Aristotle's view may be framed in terms of these three contributions of matter.

With regard to the relation between matter and form (1), if matter individuates, is it possible to know an individual person? For Aristotle, to account for knowledge is to say that the form of the object is in the mind of the knower (*De Anima,* Book 3, Chapter 5, 430a). The form is universal, and it can be in the person known and the person knowing. Since matter is particular, it can only be simply located, that is, located in one place. The person knowing has his or her own matter which makes him or her different from the person known, even when they share common forms. And the person known can be known only with respect to form, because his or her individuality is precisely that which cannot be transferred to the substantial reality of the knower. Aristotle attempted to mediate the separation of people's knowable forms from their unknowable matter or individuality by saying that empirical knowledge takes place through the particularistic sense of touch (interpreting vision as a kind of mediated touching) (*De Anima,* Book 3, Chapters 12–13). But then if this is so, it is difficult to understand how the physical alteration of the knower can represent the physical nature of the known; and if it could, how could a knower's particular sensation—individuated by his or her own matter—be related to forms that are supposed to be the same as the forms of the known person? Finally, from what perspective could one compare the forms in the known person with those in the knowing person to see that they are identical? These questions constitute the complex issue of representative perception. One result of three hundred years of debating the issue has been the suggestion that we do *not* know other individuals as individuals, and perhaps do not even refer to an external world, although we may think we do.

With the axiological cosmology, a whole person, individuality and all, can be the object of a feeling, and thus enter a knower's experience. That the person, having entered as a complex initial datum, *appears* to the experiencer is made possible by the structure of imagination. Whether that happens depends on the structure of reference in the intentionality of the appearance. Since the nature of an appearance is to be a concrete contrast, the individuality of the person appearing poses no special problem.

The relation between efficient causes and matter (2) is equally problematic in the Aristotelian theory. Since the rise of modern science, most thinkers have given up the view that an antecedent cause produces its effect by actualizing a potential; instead, they have interpreted efficient causality as a regularity between events which might be ontologically unconnected. Even within the bounds of Aristotle's premodern view there are difficulties, however. Consider the situation if cause and effect are temporally distinct. The activity of the cause has ceased to exist when the potentiality of the effect is being actualized: what has ceased to exist can no longer be the actualizing cause of something. Consider the contrasting situation where the actualization is a conceived unitary process within which no temporal distinctions are made. If the activity is not temporal, how does it relate things which are in time as cause and effect? Since the actual cause has ceased to do anything when the activity of causing takes place in the effect, the causing activity must be in the effect rather than in the cause. Such a process of self-creation cannot be interpreted on the Aristotelian model of an antecedent efficient cause actualizing potentials in the matter of the effect.

The axiological cosmology says that the actualized satisfaction of each occasion is potentially an ingredient in subsequent occasions, but that the existential activity of those successors is what integrates the potentials together into new actualized occasions. Thus the activity of causation takes place in the present in which the objectified past is contained; the present itself has no determinate temporal duration, however, until it has realized itself as a finished fact. Only after it is finished can its stages be distinguished as earlier and later according to a superimposed time frame. In its present immediacy, an occasion has no distinctions of earlier and later.

The way matter functions (3) to realize final causes is most problematic. In Aristotle's theory, a final cause is normative, not because it is a
normative measure for some manifold which happens to be real, but because
the nature of some substance is to find its completion or fulfillment in it.
The final cause depends on the prior nature which requires completion or
self-sufficiency. Ethics, then, is an affair of self-realization, the realization
of an antecendently given self.

Why is it normative that an acorn grow up to be an oak tree rather
than perish as an acorn to become food for squirrels? The material reality of
the acorn serves both ends equally well. In fact, the normative claim of the
oak tree can rest only on some greater value in its being an oak tree than in
being squirrels' food. Yet, because of the interdependence of nature, which
Aristotle fully recognized, it is not clear that, with respect to every acorn,
mature oaks are more deserving than fed squirrels. The normativeness of a
final cause is relative to what is ready to be measured by it, not to independent substantial entities. Rather than defining norms by individuals, or personal selves, who need to be "realized," it is better to define "selves" by
reference to norms that require personal coordination.

Objections to Aristotle's own analysis do not necessarily mean that his
basic position is not capable of being developed in a contemporarily viable
way. Two contemporary philosophers may be cited as representatives of
certain aspects of Aristotle's approach: Peter Strawson, author of *Individuals: An Essay in Descriptive Metaphysics,* and Paul Weiss.

Peter Strawson. Strawson's work is generally regarded as a defense of
the Aristotelian view that the world is filled with particular material bodies,
including people, extending in space and enduring for a period in time. That
Strawson shows some of our ordinary suppositions about the world to presuppose conceptions of bodies and persons is undeniable. But what does this
amount to? That question turns on the significance of Strawson's claim to be
doing only "descriptive metaphysics," which, he says, is "content to describe the actual structure of our thought about the world."[10] The subject
matter of descriptive metaphysics is the "massive central core of human
thinking which has no history—or none recorded in histories of thought;
there are categories and concepts which, in their most fundamental character, change not at all."[11] His view of the nonhistorical character of basic
categories and concepts is dubious: Homeric persons are not persons in the
same sense that Aristotelian-Strawsonian persons are. Let us suppose,
however, that he means to describe only the actual structure of his contemporaries' thought.

His argument comes down to showing that, in the ways we refer to
and describe the world, we assume it consists of material bodies and persons. He cannot infer that we might not also actually refer to and describe

other sorts of things; for to argue that would be to engage in what he calls "revisionary metaphysics," urging that we ought (not) refer to certain kinds of things. Suppose Strawson has described the world as we commonly refer to it. How could it be inferred from this that our everyday references are philosophically important? Perhaps the very commonality disqualifies such reference from the philosophical accuracy and perspicacity required of considered metaphysical reflection; after all, common references in ordinary discourse are precisely those that are not the result of disciplined philosophical reflection. It is wrong for any philosophy after Hegel to believe, without deliberate consideration, that metaphysics expressed in ordinary language is serious in itself.

It is possible, however, that references in ordinary language not only describe what we assume about the world, but also have a normative status about what is metaphysically important. Possibly, too, Strawson's descriptive metaphysics gives a thorough and persuasive account of the nuances of reference by which we interpret this world of material bodies and persons. A further question immediately arises and requires an answer: What is the nature of the world that we can refer to it in terms of material bodies and persons? The claim that it is material bodies and persons is tied to the account of how we refer to it, and what we naively believe in so referring. But how can we account for the material bodies and persons to which we refer? In any *normative* metaphysical view, an account of the world includes material bodies and usually persons. In the *Timaeas*, for instance, Plato explained enduring and interacting material bodies with the likely story of the receptacle and the forms of a demiurge. Aristotle provided the account of substances with four causes. Spinoza accounted for enduring material bodies and persons as modes of the Divine Substance. Leibniz explained them as modes of perception by which monads mirror each other. Process cosmology presents its account in terms of feelings and the repetition of forms. Each of these metaphysical views accounts for a world *that can be referred to in terms of material bodies and persons.* Yet to evaluate these competing views requires moving beyond Strawson.

At best, then, Strawson gives an account of where metaphysics should *begin,* although his insistence on description rather than normative discussion prevents him from inferring that metaphysics *ought* to begin there. As philosophers since Hegel have usually known, no mere description can serve as an innocent field for metaphysics to explain. Whatever Strawson has undertaken, it does not amount to a successful defense of Aristotelian substance philosophy in contemporary terms.

Paul Weiss. A clear, straightforward defense of substance philosophy has been presented by Paul Weiss, in explicit reaction against the process philosophy of Whitehead. Unlike philosophers, including Strawson, who have taken a linguistic approach, Weiss sees the relation between natural objects and our knowledge of and reference to them as thoroughly dialectical. That is, we cannot describe the objects of the world directly from the perspective of the structure of our reference to them because the natures of our cognitive faculties cannot be understood in themselves alone, but only in connection with the nature of what is known. Further, natural objects cannot be described or explained without accounting for the way they relate to their appearances within human experience.

In his early (1939) *Reality,* Weiss presents his first major criticism of Whitehead and writes favorably of substance philosophy:

> The fundamental temporal fact is not the passage of events, but the occurrence of changes in persistent substantial individuals. It is the denial of this doctrine which is characteristic of the modern approach to the problem of a temporal world. The denial assumes that to be temporal is to be a completed being at every moment of time, perishing with the passing moment because inescapably contained within the span of that moment. But to suppose that entities either have non-temporal boundaries and are thus eternal, or that they have the temporal boundaries of the present and thus perish with the passing moment, is to commit the *fallacy of essential completeness.* Though Whitehead has pressed home the point that it is a fallacy of "simple location" to suppose that there are entities which occupy places in space or time and do not essentially refer to other regions, he has not acknowledged the fundamental fallacy of essential completeness of which his own was a specialized instance. . . .
>
> An avoidance of the fallacy of essential completeness permits of an escape from the absurd result that temporal beings can last only for a moment, and involves a return to something like those pre-Cartesian philosophies which hold that there are features essential to the individual which are not present in it as actual and active. *To be is to be incomplete*; an actuality with its equilibrium outside itself; a reality whose boundaries lie somewhere in the future; an existent possessed of a virtual region vectorally extending indefinitely outward.[12]

In the years since that statement Weiss has elaborated his theory of substantial reality in extraordinarily complex and subtle ways. In *Beyond All Appearances* (1974), he distinguishes between individuals, such as people, and what he calls *Finalities*. A person (and every physical object) is an instance of the Finality Substance; Substance individuates, which means that each instance of Substance is an individual over against each other instance. In another sense, each instance is over against Substance itself; that is, each instance has its own core of privacy. Human beings are not only instances of Substance, but they internalize Substance in the form of psychic depth. The other Finalities are Being, which a person internalizes by exercising reason; Possibility, which a person internalizes by developing mind; Existence, which a person internalizes by possessing sensibility; and Unity, which a person possesses by cultivated spirit. The personal self is a rough harmony of psyche, reason, mind, sensibility, and spirit, which are dominant at different times and varying conditions. Continuity of the self—its combination of actual and virtual elements, to use the language of *Reality*—is derived from the interaction of an instance of Substance with temporally and spatially extended Existence, ordered with respect to other things by Possibility, unified through time by Unity, and connected with all these and their amalgams by Being.

Weiss's early views seemed to involve an assertion of surd interiority and persisting continuity, which he had named substance. But this appearance may have been mistaken. For the actual interaction of an individual with the Finalities is an achievement, not something that happens automatically, or, as a strict Aristotelian would say, "by nature." At each present moment of existence, a person must act to take possession of the past and must internalize possibilities to have a future; a person contingently actualizes himself or herself as having a past and gaining virtual powers. Weiss says:

> Since the individuality of an actuality depends on its internalization of the qualification [of Substance], the individuality could be said to be the result of an act of self-individuation. But one might just as well say simply that every actuality is a private, self-maintained substance.[13]

If one stresses the expressions having to do with acts of self-individuation, Weiss's theory is a species of process cosmology. On this interpretation, privacy would consist in each act of self-individuation being isolated until it results in an individual which could be publicly related, and self-maintenance would be an individual's own creativity. But if one stresses the expressions having to do with privacy and self-maintenance, the paradoxical result is a substance with private continuity (for process philosophy, continuity is only public) and with surd self-assertion.

Responding to critics in "Process and Substance: A Reply," Weiss aligns himself *against* process philosophy with a belief in substance philosophy. He details his view that if events are the ultimate realities, and if they perish in their own time, they cannot act beyond themselves; therefore, it is inconceivable that a person is a harmony of events. His response neglects the elements typical of process philosophy which emphasize continuity through feeling and reiteration of form: the subjective coming-into-existence of an occasion is continuous with the past which it feels with conformation and inclusion, and its objective reality must be involved in future events. The most interesting part of Weiss's argument, however, is not the direct metaphysical considerations, but his view of the way metaphysics should relate to the world of common experience.

> It is not possible for a reflective man to accept the world of everyday without making some changes. It is too disjointed and incoherent to satisfy one who would know what is present and why. Science, mathematics, logic, history, art, as well as philosophy, move away from it in order to better understand what is objective, real, steady, and basic, and what is not. But one should move away from it only if and so far as one must. Its distinctions, components, courses, and lessons should be accepted until the presence of borderline and difficult cases, error, ambiguity, superstition, prejudice, contradictions, incompleteness, and new discoveries force one to modify, supplement, and sometimes to reject what is commonly held. I suggest that what then be done is to see if there are steady, controlling, intruded factors there, use of which will allow one to reach what clarifies, rectifies, and extends what had been originally accepted.
>
> It is not the objective of philosophy to portray a new world, no matter how neat, noble, simple, or arresting. One of its tasks is to hold on as much as possible to what is daily known while making its grounds evident, thereby giving one a better hold on most of it than one had had before.[14]

How similar Weiss is to Strawson! While avoiding the limitations of Strawson's linguistic approach, and remaining more dialectical than Strawson about the relation between experience and explanation, while recognizing that experience is not as tidy as it has to be for ordinary language philosophy to be plausible as a norm, Weiss believes that one ought to stay as close as possible to the daily world.

The argument against this viewpoint is developed in the section "The Public Character of Image-Formation," which contends that the function of theory is to provide vision, which is not reducible to a rationalized common sense. Before proceeding to that, however, we will reintroduce two arguments.

First, contrary to what Strawson and Weiss believe, daily life is not prima facie normative as that for which philosophy should render an account. Certain kinds of experiences—in the arts, morality, and religion, for instance—can be cultivated to reveal experiential nuances and values which do not appear in daily life and which make powerful claims for orienting philosophy. In order to judge competing claims for importance in the need for philosophic accounting, arguments about the value of various experiences need to be given. And for the sake of these arguments, to assert the centrality of daily experience is to beg the question. That things have value in experience is a function of the imaginative structure of elementary experience before it is a function of any commonality resulting from interpretive interactions.

Second, norms for the form of theories—that they be simple, fecund, elegant, and the like—make the distance between philosophical theory and daily experience greater than Weiss thinks. Instead of gerrymandering a commonsense view and rationalizing terms whose virtue is their irrational sensitivity to disjointed segments of experience, the formal considerations of philosophical theory-making suggest that one should move dialectically between unrationalized experience and theoretical terms developed in abstract consonance with neatness of explanation. In this way, as long as all experiences illustrate the abstract theory, their real incongruities can be represented. The danger in rationalizing common sense is that experientially sensitive terms are generalized, distorted, and nudged out of the contexts in which they have precise meaning. One loses more of the vividness of experience by trying to make its diverse self-representations fit together than by deliberately maintaining the distance between abstraction and concrete expression. Although this is a fault from which Weiss's philosophy is not free, the point is somewhat paradoxical in that, *in practice*, few philosophers are as architectonically elegant as Weiss.

In contrast to the Aristotelian or quasi-Aristotelian approaches to personal continuity, the axiology of thinking embraces these views:

In Causation. Causally, the continuity of a person's life consists in each moment of experience arising out of feeling the past, including the person's own past states, and out of presenting an objective personal experience to be felt by following occasions.

In Experience. Experientially, the continuity consists in experiential occasions possessing hybrid physical feelings of the subjective experience of prior occasions; these are integrated with all the other feelings that, moment by moment, make up a person's grasp of the world.

In Imagination. Imaginatively, each moment of experience is structured by the appearance of a world. This appearance synthesizes the manifold of initial feelings; it presents the world as having perceptual form; and it presents the world *as formed* around elements that punctuate the world with value. Regardless of whether the imaginative appearance is true, it presents the experiencer among the appearances, although not necessarily in the foreground. Being among the appearances, the experiencer appears relative to other things with a temporal and spatial continuity.

In Normative Measure. More important than any of these is the fact that the experiencer's own personal identity is among the forms within the imaginative appearance of a world means that it is related to a normative measure, or many normative measures, for that personal identity. For a person to experience himself or herself as obligated by a normative measure, however, is to include within the appearance of the world an added element, that something in the world is truly obligatory, truly related to a normative measure.

Kantianism

Like any systematic philosopher, Kant had many approaches to the problem of personal identity and continuity. From a religious approach, for instance, a person must have enough continuity to enjoy the perfect happiness deserved if life were lived with perfect virtue. From a moral standpoint, Kant argued that the ideal, or type, of one's continuity must be imaginable in order to consider the morality of promises, rewards, and punishments. From a cognitive standpoint, Kant argued that a transcendental unity of apperception must be presupposed as a norm which, if followed by thought, allows categories to be applied to the manifold of sense so that appearances are possible. It is this last with which the argument is concerned here.

Kant observes that it must be possible for what he called the "I think" to accompany each representation making up appearances. The representations are not necessarily consistent with each other, and they need not come in any rational order. If it is possible that they do make sense as the appearance of a world, or as appearances of worldly objects, it is possible for the "I" which thinks to think according to rules that produce consistency and sense. The forms of judgment are such rules—since thinking is judgment—and thus they may be treated as categories by which representations must be ordered if appearances are possible. But, even the categories schematized to the manifold of sense would not give rise to empirical appearances, Kant argued, if the consciousness which thinks according to those categories is not unified. If one person thinks the "cause" representation and another thinks the "effect," neither has an empirical experience or appearance, for neither one is thinking the whole manifold of representations according to a rule which can be verified objectively.

It is a brilliant stroke to employ, as Kant did, the concept of an ideal unitary self to justify a claim that the empirical world can appear in experience. That stroke reinstated the conception of the unified self, which Hume's skeptical criticisms had made problematic. It allowed Kant to assert that the self is unified only as a transcendental ideal for the possibility of experience, without having to assert that any particular person has fulfilled that ideal or is empirically conscious of his or her own unity.

Kant supposed, however, that the transcendental ego or transcendental unity of apperception is justified as transcendentally real because actual experience itself presupposes it. What happens if this is not true? What happens if the knowledge we are slowly gaining, contrary to Kant's anticipation, is moving in radically incoherent directions, if the knowledge of an affair divides into the contours of different sciences that simply are incommensurate? This is Michel Foucault's position. He says that the present tendency of historical research to pay attention to documents reveals more discontinuities than continuities. Of the previous emphasis on continuities he writes:

> Continuous history is the indispensable correlative of the founding function [constitution of appearances through the imagination guided by transcendental ego] of the subject. . . . Making historical analysis the discourse of the continuous and making human consciousness the original subject of all historical development and all action are the two sides of the same system of thought. In this system time is conceived in terms of totalization and revolutions are never more than moments of consciousness.
>
> In various forms, this theme has played a constant role since the nineteenth century: to preserve, against all decenterings, the sovereignty of the subject, and the twin figures of anthropology and humanism.[15]

The burden of Foucault's argument is to show, in opposition to Kant, that *dis*continuous scientific knowledge is possible. Without trying to assess

Foucault's argument, we see that it can open thinking to new foundations. Whereas before, Kant and Kantians could argue that the world cannot appear unless it conforms to categories that make it amenable to being "totalized" in human consciousness, fitting into a coherent world appearance, now that argument begs the question. For perhaps the world appears discontinuously so that the unity of the "I think" is trivial. Perhaps the unity of the world, such as it is, comes from the content of the world rather than from the demands which the subject imposes on the world.

It is at this level, more foundational than Kant's, that the axiology of thinking presents an account of appearance. All that is presupposed in imaginative appearance (and all appearance is at least imaginative) is feelings of objects, beauty in the form of appearance (formal structure constitutes the beauty), and spontaneous creativity that makes the subject an erotic emergence. There is no necessity for the form of beauty in the appearance to reflect human meaningfulness—only aesthetic coherence, and that perhaps at a minimal level. From the side of the subject, there is no necessity that the world appear identical from one moment to the next; the necessity of continuity comes entirely from the character of what is given in feeling, from similarity in the things given for experience, and in the leeway those things allow for being integrated. From the side of the subject, there is no necessity for judgments to be logically coherent from one occasion to the next; *that* necessity comes entirely from the norms relevant to the occasions, because the occasions present judgments to which norms apply. There is no moral necessity to be consistent from one moment to the next, except the obligation which comes from the normative quality of consistency; nothing is presupposed from the side of the subject for the possibility of appearances.

Assuming that Foucault has indeed presented a problem, if not an answer, and assuming that the account of imaginative appearance presented here is plausible, then Kant's transcendental constitution of the human subject is at best a regulative ideal. To defend it as such would require an argument that such unity as it entails is *desirable* relative to other things, an argument antithetical to Kant's procedure. At worst, Kant's transcendental ego would be a transcendental illusion, an attractive ideal that *mistakenly* leads us to distort the appearances of the world so as to make them reflect an interest at transcendental unity.

COSMOLOGY OF APPEARANCE

A cosmological account of appearance has two principal topics. The first is the nature of form itself: what form is, from a cosmological perspective, and how it enters the process of imaginative concrescence. The second is the nature of presentational immediacy as it is constituted by imagination, that nature being a fantasy in which imaginative creativity, or eros, mediates the passions of feelings to the beauty of intentionality.

Form

Elements of Form. With regard to the problem of form, Whitehad had one term, *eternal object*, comprise four elements that are categorized in the previous section "Phenomenology of Appearance," namely, normative measure, schema, concrete appearance, and image. Whitehead did draw a clear distinction between the concreteness in an appearance, which he called a *contrast*, and the abstractness of an image, which he called pattern or relation. But the definiteness in both he said was due to the ingression or presence of eternal objects, which he called forms of definiteness.

Whitehead's failure to distinguish the other elements perhaps stemmed from his neglect of the normative element in form. This is ironic. Far more than any preceding philosopher, he was sensitive to the ways in which form acts as a lure for creativity. Propositions, which most philosophers see as "forms of facts," to use Wittgenstein's phrase, Whitehead saw as proposals for passion.[16]

Had he asked more fundamentally about what there is in form that makes it attractive, Whitehead might have developed more completely the insights he suggested in his discussion of order and value.[17] This would have entailed a serious revision, however, of his doctrine that eternal objects are diverse, multiple, and preexistent to what he called the "divine envisagement." Unless they relate to a determinate multiplicity, eternal objects are indeterminate, indistinguishable from nothing and indistinguishable from each other; they are not good for anything. All we can speak of apart from connections with a determinate world is what Plato called the form of the Good, which is neither objective nor itself good, though it is valuable to know.[18]

Whitehead, however, attempted to hold that eternal objects are real existents, an Aristotelian version of Plato's Forms. Because abstractions do not exist by themselves, Whitehead was compelled to say they exist by being in the mind of God, who is an actual entity. Yet if their determinate existence is an abstract part of the nature of God, the eternal objects cannot be normative *for* God; they must be treated as mere structural forms of definiteness. It is a miracle then that some forms of definiteness are more alluring to God and finite creatures than others are. What Whitehead could have said, in order to save his theology, is that his God conceptually entertains the schemata of normative measures relative to the world; the schemata are reproductions of normative measures in a conceptual medium, their presence for conceptual feelings. The determinateness of the normative measures themselves would harmonize a given multiplicity. That determinateness has no independent existence; it is rather an obligation. If there is a multiplicity to be measured, the reality of its measure is whatever would best harmonize it. The subjunctive mood required to speak of determinate normative measures independent of specific multiplicities testifies to the irrelevance of applying the category of existence to them.

What does exist, however, are *objectifications* of normative measures for experiencers, that is, schemata. If God is an actual entity, as Whitehead claimed, then his mind would provide the actual ground for the existence of eternal objects *as schemata*. But God would not be needed to create determinate normative measures through primordial envisagement *if* there were a world containing actual multiplicity. The existence of that world would be enough. Finite occasions could conceptually reproduce normative measures in schemata as well as God, and as well without him. Whitehead's concept of God, therefore, can be dropped from the axiological cosmology.

Concerning appearances, it is pointed out above that they are concrete contrasts embodying a certain value. The value they have derives from their form, which harmonizes their components. The coming-to-be of an occasion requires it to find a form for its feelings whose concrete embodiment will be the occasion's satisfaction. Each of the initial data in an occasion is also an objectified satisfaction, or a complex of such satisfactions. If the data are experiential occasions, they objectify their own appearance, with its value in form. The physical feelings of a concrescing occasion grasp their data-occasions separately but concretely. It cannot be overemphasized that this is concrete physical reality with which the emerging occasion is continuous, and that it is reality with its own value which is felt as such.

For the concrete physical data to be integrated into the new physical reality of the emerging occasion, however, their separate values must be related to each other; they must be valued by the emerging occasion in order to contribute to it. This means that the forms of the data must be reconciled so that they constitute one complex form allowing all their multiplicities to be together. Such reconciliation may be looked at as a cutting and pasting of structures, as a kind of mechanical rearrangements, with the easiest manipulation being plain rejection of the data from further embodiment in the process. Put another way, the reconciliation of forms is a new valuation of the initially separate given values. For, *valuation is the establishment of forms by which some components are rejected and others kept, and those which are kept are related in a way which produces a concrete harmony.*

Whitehead was extremely sensitive to this point. For him, the first move away from physical feeling within concrescence is conceptual feeling. A conceptual feeling is one which has an eternal object as its object, and which arises as the feeling of an abstract component of a datum physically felt. Whitehead also characterized conceptual feeling as "conceptual valuation," and this is where his sensitivity lay. He recognized that conceptual feeling is giving a physical datum some subjective value for the emerging occasion by abstracting out its form; that form, then, is a candidate lure for the way the data shall be reconciled in the final satisfaction which would objectify the initial datum if, and to the extent that, it is sustained.

However, Whitehead failed to capitalize on what this means about form in the objects of physical and conceptual feeling. A physical datum has a value in that some of its elements are such as to allow the other elements to be present in harmony; these former elements have special importance and are the datum's form. A conceptual feeling, or valuation, eliminates from the original object all except the important or formal elements, or parts of the formal elements. Thus, the conceptual feeling or valuation is an appreciation of what is important within the datum. If the initial datum is an objectified appearance, on the level of conscious imagination, the conceptual feeling of its form is a valuation of it with respect to what is important in it. The object of a conceptual feeling is therefore, an image as defined above in the section "Phenomenology of Appearance." In this way is preserved the empiricist principle that forms are derived in mind by abstraction from concrete experiences.

This does not explain, however, how conceptual feeling, or valuation, arises. Since the feeling of the importance of the datum's form is already contained in the physical feeling, why should any conceptual feeling arise which contains less than the physical feeling? The answer is that conceptual feelings (valuations) serve the concrescence of the feeling occasion. They are oriented in one sense toward the objects they feel but in another sense toward the incipient satisfaction. Therefore, the arising of conceptual feelings (valuations) has its own normative measure, which is to advance toward satisfaction, given the initial data. Since the satisfaction is intended as the greatest achievement of value, conceptual feelings (valuations) seek what is valuable in the data. By its own normative measure a conceptual feeling is looking for how the datum expresses the datum's normative measure. *Its object therefore is an image which reproduces the datum's normative measure, or, schema.* Conceptual feelings are valuations which identify images with schemata. A physical datum presents itself with a valuable form; this much is noted in a physical feeling of that datum; a conceptual feeling isolates that form *because* it is valuable. Conceptual feeling is not merely a passive reaction, but a creative act of feeling whose normative measure is to possess what makes the datum valuable, because it is the way that datum expresses its normative measure. The spontaneity in a conceptual feeling is thus the "production of the reproduction" of the normative measure. This is not free invention, however, since the conceptual feeling has no access to the datum's normative measure except through its expression in the datum. But its activity is a recognition of the importance in the datum's image as itself a schema of the datum's normative measure.

Let us recapitulate the elements of form uncovered. There are the normative measure of the datum, the concrete datum appearing, the image which is the important elements in the datum (or its form), and the recognition or schematization of the normative measure in the image by the conceptual feeling.

A normative measure is a form in the sense that Plato spoke of Forms. It is an ideal way for a specific multiplicity to be harmonized. It does not exist, although instances of it may exist in the sense that multiplicities have harmonies schematizing it. A normative measure obligates, normatively measures, any multiplicity to which it is relevant. The relation of a normative measure to its relevant multiplicity is eternal in the sense that its normativeness does not come into being and then pass away. Its multiplicity may be temporal, however, so that the relevance of a normative measure to the world comes into being and passes away.

A concrete datum has a form in the sense that its manifold parts harmonize because certain of its parts order the rest coherently. The circularity of this statement is unavoidable in saying what concrete form is. A physical feeling of a concrete datum grasps all the parts, including those important for harmonizing the whole, and it appreciates the importance of the formal elements without separation from the others. To say that a concrete datum has form is to speak relatively. The form of the whole datum is the select, important elements that allow its components to cohere—its essential features. Each component is or can be derived from preceding data, which in turn contain formal elements organizing the rest. The regression to find formed components of formed data might continue infinitely, or it might diminish gradually in the triviality of homogeneous parts or in the chaos of minimal integration.

An image is a form in the sense that it is the set of important elements in a concrete datum or appearance which is abstracted from the rest. An image itself is concrete, though incomplete: it requires a physical context outside itself in order to exist. An image is universal if it is experientially grasped in connection with a schema.

A schema is a form in the sense that it is a representation of the way a manifold is best harmonized. The representation can be literally in the medium of an image. A discussion above states that conceptual feeling is the selection of a specific concrete datum's form as an image, because that image is recognized as schematizing the normative measure to the manifold. The medium of representation can be other than a direct image of the manifold, however. It may be a rule, as Kant suggests, for constructing an image. For example, "with a radius of four inches, describe a complete arc around a point" is a verbal schema for an image of an eight-inch plate which is not derived from looking at a plate; in this example, the normative measure is partly fixed by the will to create an image of an eight-inch plate. Where the medium in which the schema represents the normative measure is other than an image, there is always a problem of identifying the two. In the example of the plate, one might have to measure the image produced by a compass with a line drawn around a plate laid on a piece of paper.

Normative measures and schemata are both normative for the relevant manifolds, each in their own ways. Concreta data and images are values, although not necessarily normative. An image becomes a universal form only when it is identified with a schema as normative for *any* manifold which the image could order.

The discussion in this section is formal, selecting out the philosophical problems and concepts that apply in any involvement in form. It is necessary now to apply the discussion specifically to form in imaginative fantasy.

Sources of Form. An occasion of experience arises out of formed initial data. The imaginative synthesis of this data involves the conceptual feeling (valuation) of various formal elements as image-schemata. Image-schemata can be refined further by conceptual feeling (valuation) of their own more important elements, and this process of abstraction can continue indefinitely. As conceptual feeling moves toward greater abstraction, increasingly more of the fullness of the original concrete manifold is left out. For example, one can move from a physically felt house to an imagined silhouette, to an outline representation, to an idea of rectangularity, to an idea of geometrically formed space, to the idea of extension, to the idea of external relations, to the idea of otherness. As one progresses, the concreteness of the image diminishes and the normative-stipulative character of the schema increases; the result is that one loses sight of the concrete origin of the trail of feelings. Instead, it becomes evident that the direction in which the process of abstraction proceeds is determined by intentional interests. The silhouette, for example, could be abstracted by a contrast of light and dark, rather than by an outline representation; the reason for the direction is not to be found in the tangible house, but in the intentionality of giving rise to an appearance guided by schemata as reproductions of the house's normative measure.

Conceptual feelings may be combined in propositional feelings. A propositional feeling is one whose form combines a conceptual feeling as predicate with another feeling, either conceptual, physical, or propositional. The form for a propositional feeling can come from two sources.

In an elementary way, form derives from physical feelings through conceptual feelings; that is, the form of the proposition is felt conceptually from images of the initial data through a process of abstraction. In this case, any propositional feeling differs from the conceptual feeling presenting its form by virtue of the fact it applies the form to components different from those in the form's original concrete embodiment. The formal image (or more abstract representation) is treated as universal and used to harmonize a set of components different from its concrete presentation. This occurs in transmutation, for instance, where the form of a pattern, or a part, is used to harmonize a larger whole. Because propositional feeling involves the transference of an image from its source to a new manifold, it is not a passive reaction. It is an activity with its own normative measure—in this case, the integration of material otherwise unintegrated, or not integrated that way. As a conceptual feeling does, a propositional feeling applies its form to its subject-predicate manifold—or, said another way, feels its subject-predicate manifold with its propositional form, recognizing that the form schematizes the proposition's normative measure to the manifold.

The second source for the form of a propositional feeling is through composition of forms derived separately from conceptual feelings. Propositional form deriving from this source can be called subjective form because its first appearance is in the present subject, and it arises because of its relevance to that subject's potential satisfaction. Subjective propositional form is more creative than copied propositional form. It is an image (or more abstract representation) not merely recognized by reference to a scheme, but produced as an expression of the scheme. Its formal parts derive empirically from physical feelings; its formal integrity derives from the propositional feeling's own normative measure.

The imaginative process proceeds through physical, conceptual, and propositional feelings, with transposition, composition, and elimination, until a schematic form is found which allows the initial data to be reconciled with complete determinateness. This is the satisfaction of the demands for definiteness in existence. It is a physical result in which the physical initial data constitute a new physical being with a reconciling form; that is, the satisfaction has the value of reconciling the initial data, and that reconciliation may be more valuable than the sum of its parts, as, similarly, a harmony enhances its components.

The foregoing account combines the perspectives of the feeling and intentional poles discussed in Chapter 6. From the feeling pole, each conceptual and propositional feeling was seen moving away from multiplicity toward a more manageable, simple set of elements. From the perspective of the intentional pole, each conceptual and propositional feeling was seen as actively contributing forms which schematize the initial manifold to a normative measure for the occasion's own satisfaction. In other words, the spontaneous activity of the occasion is the production of a schema for the normative measure of its own satisfaction, where the manifold is its initial data. Its spontaneity is value-producing in the objective sense of harmonizing previously formed values and in the subjective sense of normatively schematizing the initial data with its own normative measure. In experiential occasions, consciousness is a quality of a feeling whose object is a propositional feeling combining a schema with an appearance which it schematizes; that is, consciousness is a feeling of the contributions of subjectivity.

With this discussion in mind, it may be helpful to review the preceding analysis of norms in imagination. There are norms of feeling—embodiment, energy, sensitivity, and purity; norms of intentionality—the various features of beauty; and norms for spontaneity—novelty, relevance, and presence. How do these relate to the normative measures in data, in feelings, and in the final appearance in satisfaction?

When they find expression, norms are schemata: reproductions or representations of normative measures. Normative measures are made definite only in reference to manifolds to be harmonized. The norms for feeling, for instance, measure what is important in feeling-as-such in concrescing occasions. These norms are general, applying to any occasions of experience. They are always relevant to concrete manifolds, for among the most general formal or important elements in any physical feeling are those properties which make it a physical feeling. Similarly, beauty as the norm of intentionality applies to all experiential intentions that are potentially concrete appearances. The norms for spontaneity apply to all concrescences because of the nature of concrescence, but they apply to each specifically. That the norms of feeling, intentionality, and spontaneity are among the most general normative measures does not mean they are more or less important than less general norms presented directly by an occasion's initial data or newly developed regarding its satisfaction. For the most part, the norms of feeling, intentionality, and spontaneity do not show up directly through images in the concrete appearances of daily life. Their importance lies in governing the processes by which things appear in daily life—the function of imaginative fantasy.

Presentational Immediacy: From Eros to Art

The result of an imaginative concrescence is an appearance, nested in the broader physical satisfaction of the natural occasion. The imaginative act

is not only its own result; it is also its happening and, because of the conformation and inclusion of feeling, it is a development of the past. As objectified for subsequent feeling, an imaginative act is only the appearance in
which it results; as an occasion itself, it involves feeling and spontaneity, as
well as its intentional appearance.

Because of this, it is appropriate to describe imaginative life as erotic,
in the extended sense that Plato used that term. The chief marks of eros, as
mentioned in the first section, are that it is an activity that takes place under
compulsion, a *passion*, and that it seeks to make itself one with or to become something beautiful that attracts it. Compulsion in imagination stems
from the force of feeling, from the necessity of conforming to the world it
apprehends, and from the power of including that world within the imaginative process. The creativity of eros, making itself one with what attracts it,
is its intentional orientation to satisfaction in an appearance which is
beautiful.

Classical accounts of eros occasionally have had difficulty reconciling
its passionate compulsion and its creativity, although most have acknowledged both sides. Plato, for instance, emphasized the seductiveness of the
attractive object (see *Phaedrus, Symposium*). His account is successful in
articulating how lovers orient themselves in pursuing the beloved, but it
does not explain what is in the lovers to be motivated by the beauty in the
beloved. Plato showed that eros is rational, given attractiveness; he also
showed that differences in character may be understood by differences in the
kinds of beauties people pursue. From one point of view, in fact, the entire
content of people's lives is the mixture of appetites or erotic passions that
they have, from sexual and physical pleasures, through domestic and civic
attachments, up to the "higher" passions of art and philosophy. Plato never
explained adequately, however, what a person is, such that beautiful objects
have the power of attraction. Responsiveness to the attractive is, for Plato, a
given; while this may be experientially accurate, it is philosophically unsatis-
fying.

Appreciating this difficulty, Aristotle clearly distinguished final
causes—the ends pursued—from efficient causes—the energetic movers.
This depicts the way a person can be compelled and yet intentional. Yet
precisely because of the separateness of efficient and final causation. Aristotle's picture failed to capture the undivided nature of eroticism. Eros is at
the very heart of a person, and it comprises both the compulsion and the
attraction that orient its internal creativity. By assimilating creativity to the
efficient causes, Aristotle's account abandoned the possibility of showing
how creativity itself mediates compulsion and attraction.

Whereas Aristotle balanced efficient and final causes, the modern
tradition focused its account solely on efficient causes. Freud's account of

eros, for example, represents it as a mechanical or hydraulic pressure seeking release. Although this provides an easy explanation for the sense of passion or compulsion, it leaves the original choice of erotic object, or object of cathexis, a mystery. With regard to sexual orgasm itself, Freud saw it as a sudden release of tension, whereas Plato took it to be but a reinforcement of increased involvement with the beloved and with what is best in the beloved.[19] For Freud, eros is indirectly, rather than directly, creative in the sense that people create civilized structures within which to settle their erotic pleasures. Furthermore, in Freud's opinion, unfulfilled sexual longing can be sublimated into artistic pursuits. Yet he did not explain why beauty in the arts is attractive, and thus he left unexplained the intentionality in sublimated sexual creativity.

The axiological cosmology not only balances the passionate and the attractive in eros, but shows how they both are intimately involved with creativity. On the imaginative level, a person's subjective existence is creative eros, and his or her objective existence is the appearances or fantasies resulting from this.

The objects out of which imaginative feelings arise reflect the entire structure of people and their environments. Sexual feelings, for instance, originate partly from feelings of biological states, the actions of hormones, tactile sensations, and so forth; but these alone do not account for the pervasive sexual coloring of experience. These bodily feelings enter the imaginative levels of experience combined with feelings of symbolically important past experiences. Stated simply, bodily feeling of soft warmth is propositionally combined with memory feelings of the security of the womb or of being nursed. Suppose Freud were right about the development of sexuality through the oral, anal, and genital stages. In each of those stages, people imaginatively combine purely physical bodily feelings with other feelings that come to have symbolic meaning, although perhaps not at the level of conscious awareness. As all of these accrue in richer and richer mixtures in mature adults, coloring more and more experiences of seemingly diverse situations, sexuality becomes a part of every experience. Because sexual feelings are propositionally combined with so much of our experience, it may be impossible to take possession of that experience without taking the sexual feelings, too. This may be true of most bodily feelings, or feelings of common elements of the environment, such as temperature, air pressure, the scale of nearby physical objects, perhaps even preponderances of certain colors. Eros is a good metaphor for imaginative creativity because sexual feelings seem to be the most pervasive and insistent feelings.

Sexual creativity in eros values sexual feelings for their contribution to beauty in appearances, quite apart from whether attention is paid explicitly to sexual orgasm. This is because the forms in sexual feelings have come to be consistent with the forms of the many diverse experiences which have received sexual coloring; giving importance to sexual feelings brings in countless other elements. Sexual coloring in appearance is itself a form-value that gives a vague orientation over a host of data which might otherwise have to be eliminated. Within human experience, sexual forms may be as important as extensional forms of space and time for providing the imaginative synthesis of the background in beauty; without doubt, they function earlier in childhood development.

The focus of attention in an appearance is a function of many things, including personal interests, social demands, and unexpected stimulation. It is not a function solely of the need to reconcile the initial data into a satisfaction, precisely because appearances arise through imagination. Imagination involves levels of experience in which it is possible to distinguish between background and foreground elements within the satisfaction. While the background elements solve the problem of massing the initial data in appearance, the foreground elements are more subject to free play. Although sex may color all appearances, people need not attend to sex exclusively, or have sexual stimulations be the overriding orientation to imagination. The more that beautiful appearances contrast background and foreground, the more the composition of the appearance lies within the license of the experiencer.

When this consideration is taken into account, art arises. Whatever else it may be, art is the manipulation of the foreground and background in order to enhance beauty. The point is clear in speaking of artists' works. Although anything may inspire an artist—a water pot, a decorative painting, a building with public spaces—art comes in manipulating the elements so as to attain a harmony with narrowness and width in the object relative to vague and trivial orientations for the background world. This applies as well in speaking of the creation of appearances. An appearance, although it constitutes an experience of the world, does so fantastically. Fantasy connotes the freedom to focus the appearance around the creative interest of the experiencer. The appearance must be a way of reconciling the forceful objects of the world, and it may be a true representation of the world. If it is so, the fantasy involved in its construction is still fantastic in the sense that the experiencer is self-constituted with a particular focus. If that focus is forced upon the experience—a sudden loud whistle, for instance—the fantasy may have very little option for control by the subject in contrast to the conformational necessities of the initial data. The connotations of fantasy may be somewhat misplaced here. Yet the connotations are not entirely misplaced, because the appearance, though antecedentally determined by forces to which the subject must conform, is still the creative product of the subject imagining. The limitation is that the imagination could not be any other way.

The discussion has proceeded to this point as if experience could be simplified into a single occasion of experience. This is not so, as the mention of memory and symbolization indicates. A given bodily feeling may be purely a physical feeling in one occasion, and in succeeding occasions come to be associated with other feelings, until some time later it takes on the form of a sexual feeling. As a sexual feeling, it plays increasingly more important roles in succeeding occasions until it begins to color the person's orientation to the world. All the while, the person's occasions have slowly shifted their attention from one object to another. The appearance in each occasion remains much the same as in the neighboring occasions, except that some of the appearing objects may move in relation to one other, causing the subject's attention to shift. Possibly a sexual feeling with its accrued associations moves toward the center of attention, and the subject begins to focus his or her appearances around it. The person could initiate overt sexual activity, or could fantasize about the sexual feeling rather than about the physical world. If the latter, the fantasy would not be representationally true, and the experience would have to relegate to the distant background those feelings, such as physical sensations, which are dominant when one is having a perceptual experience of the present environment.

Edward Casey has documented a number of ways in which one can imagine things other than one's perceptual environment.[20] All of these must be possible ways of integrating one's initial data, although none of them need be ways in which the physical world is truly represented. Casey distinguishes imagining from perception, memory, and even fantasizing, by which he perhaps means quasi-involuntary daydreaming. In all of these distinctions, however, he refers to the nature of the attention involved in the appearance, not to the process of imagining by which subjective experience is formed. For reasons apparent in Chapters 4 through 6 here, the axiology of thinking uses a more general and basic language of imagination.

Because appearances are fantasies, and because the elements of a given appearance can be developed in their formal subjective importance through a process involving many moments, imagination is art as well as eros. It would be a mistake to minimize the importance of the nature of external materials and their manipulation for artists who work with pliable materials. Even these artists must have a prior art to their imagination, and their imaginations must respond artfully to the experimental effects of manipulating the media they work in. Feelings themselves are the media of imaginative art, and beautiful appearances their products. There is a continuum from eros in the sexual sense to eros as the art of imagining. At the former pole, creativity is expended in coming to terms directly with the sexual forces entering experience through feeling. At the latter pole, creativity is expended in transforming the given material so as to have greater beauty than was possible in the physically felt forms themselves. In imaginative art, beauty in the appearance is itself at the center of attention. Between eros as sexuality and eros as art lies a multitude of concerns in which eros mediates passion to satisfaction without either the passion or the attractiveness of the satisfaction dominating attention. What dominates most of these in-between experiences is concern for meaning, truth, and specific values.

THE PUBLIC CHARACTER OF IMAGE-FORMATION

The Universality of Beauty

Imagination is the cognitive point at which experience begins. Through imagination, a person has at least "an experience." To discuss imagination as such is to prescind from whether the experience is true about the objective world or whether the experience is shared with other people. Imagination is simply the activity by which a person has a world appear. This is not to say that private fantasies develop prior to objective fantasies, nor is it to say that private experience is prior to public experience. On the contrary, it is possible that in animal life the dull reiteration involved in brute true perceptions is easier and more immediately pragmatic than imaginative flights characteristic of private fantasy. Rather, the claim is that imagination is the experiential foundation on which our more critical interpretive and moral faculties are erected. The hypothesis of the cosmology is that imagination is universal in human experience. Thus, beauty at some level or other is common to everyone's experience. As the norms of beauty apply universally, so do those of feeling and spontaneity. An important characteristic of the public world can be indicated even before considering the problem of how to distinguish the objective from the merely subjective in appearance: each person relates to the public world by experiencing it imaginatively. Beauty is a transcendental property of all appearances.

This understanding of beauty claims, paradoxically, both less and more than is ordinarily understood about beauty. It claims less in that it is oriented solely toward beauty in experience. There are contexts in which it is important to speak of the beauty of objects or natural conditions in terms of their own characters, apart from any reference to experience; although these contexts are obviously related to the question of beauty in experience, it would be a mistake to confuse the two. The understanding of beauty in imagination should not exclude the possibility of understanding that beauty is in objects prescinded from experience. The following chapter examines this in detail.

Beauty in imagination involves more than is readily apparent. Because beauty is a norm which governs the beginning organization of experience, it is normative in some way for all experiences. At the least, every experience is imaginative; that is, it involves the appearance of a world and thus is marked by some beauty. In most forms of intentionality, the imaginative element is not dominant, although it is necessarily the foundation. In interpretation, for example, the world which appears is interpreted regarding its truth; in remembering, musing, questioning, doubting, anticipating, and other interpretative activities, the imaginative structure measured by beauty is not at a high level of awareness or at the focus of attention. In desiring, willing, feeling obligated, guilty, responsible, being moved, angered, excited, depressed, in loving and countless other experiential modes, one would not think to call the experience beautiful or based on imagination. Yet the basic constitution of any experience involves having a world appear, and this is a function of imagination, for whose activity beauty and the other values discussed are normative. It would seem that Kant is right in his perception of the basic universality of imagination.

To treat imagination by itself requires abstracting imagination from richer dimensions of experience. Perhaps the only common experience in which the imaginative dimension lies at the center of attention is that of explicitly subjective imagining or fantasizing, in the sense that Casey treats it. In these cases, we imagine things that are not objectively there. In the psychoanalytic sense, our fantasies are precisely what we are not acting out. The images washing across our minds when we turn our imaginations loose are those whose organization is determined by elements of our feelings which are cut off explicitly from the objects those fantasies might be taken to represent. Yet even in the case of subjective fantasizing, the structure of intentionality usually is governed by interests beyond those of imagination alone. Beauty in imagination, though universal, is not a strong attraction in setting the direction of attention.

Nevertheless, the fact that every experience has an imaginative base means that imagination's norms are among those norms which apply universally. Therefore, every kind of experience has a certain responsibility toward beauty, however dominated this responsibility might be by other responsibilities.

There can be more or less beauty in imagination. The variation comes partly in differences in the initial data which distinguish one occasion from another and one person from another. And the depth of beauty depends partly on the art with which one exercises imagination. The art of imagination can be cultivated, and some people cultivate it better than others.

It seems difficult to know scientifically how artful imagination de-velops, or even how to establish clear criteria for discerning the difference between highly artful imagination and restricted, plodding imagination. Art-ful imagination develops through experiences which provide a variety of data and images; it helps to have one's flights of fancy encouraged by a tolerant environment rather than punished by an environment that constantly demands pragmatic truth. Imagination is also aided by a self-consciousness about one's habits of thought, about cultural expectations, and about the presuppositions within which one allows a world to appear.

Noting the responsibility to imagination's norms, it does not help much to say that one should concentrate on imagining well in every experi-ence. The intentionality of most experiences is deflected from the specifical-ly imaginative. From this we may infer that responsibility to imagination's norms is cultivated best in specific spheres, for example, that of art. (John Dewey, one of the first to recognize this since Plato, articulated the point in *Art as Experience*.) "Art" has two senses, one narrow and the other ex-tended. The narrow, more common, sense means producing works of art. A work of art transcends the imaginative experience of the artist and occupies a public place. If it is genuine art, it provides an important image to be felt by those who perceive it or participate in it, an image which contributes to novel beauties in their experience. Art has an extraordinary cultural impor-tance as the conveyer and inventor of the images providing depth and rele-vance to cultural experience. In this narrow sense, art is the public agent of imaginative engagement with the world. This is one of the principal themes of the following chapter.

In the extended sense, art is the practice within experience of culti-vating imagination. Its dominating intention is to perfect imaginative pow-ers. In this respect, it aims to deepen imagination's expression of the norms of feeling—embodiment, energy, purity, and sensitivity; of the norms of spontaneity—novelty, relevance, and presence; and of beauty, the norm of imaginative intentionality. The activities that cultivate these are not merely imaginative ones. People can improve their imaginative powers through making works of art; through exercises for movement and feeling; through conversation, travel, and many other endeavors. The objective expression of all these efforts should be the production of new and worthwhile images that themselves free the imagination.

Perhaps too few people are aware of the need for art in experience, believing that art can be left to the professionals. Its importance is under-valued by schools and media which more often reward truth or some desired behavior to the exclusion of imagination. For people lacking their own artis-tic cultivation of imagination, this means that the worlds which appear to them are dominated by the routine images reinforced throughout a society's culture. Not only is this impoverishing aesthetically, it inhibits people from truly interpreting those elements of life which are not rendered by routine images; it inhibits their inventiveness in will; it limits the senses in which they can engage the world.

How important are responsibilities to imagination's norms? Aside from the intrinsic quality of beauty, imagination is the means, the medium, by which people engage the world. Consider action, for example. If a person feels the forces of the world but does not feel them imaginatively *as* the forces of the world, any response is only a movement, not an action. An action occurs when a person transforms movement according to an intention regarding the world. Without imagination, there can be only movement, not action. Or, consider knowledge. If a person is in causal contact with the world, imagination is needed to form intentional judgments about what is contacted. As always, the basic question is, What is most important to be and to do. To discover what these things might be requires engaging the world where the important things might lie. And to be and to do are themselves ways of engaging the world. Imagination is the medium by which the world may not only be reacted against but engaged.

Religious Cultivation of Experience

Whereas art is judgmental attention directed at the imaginative formation of appearance; religion houses the indirect attention imagination pays to itself. One of the most important elements of religion is the *cultivation* of the imaginative structure by which the world's appearing constitutes experience. Religious images, used artfully, can form imagination so that the world appears, or experience is constituted, in such a way as to realize the religious value in the subjective act of transforming feelings to judgment. Religious value is less a value to be achieved in some intentional outcome than a norm for the subjective existential process of experiencing.

Consider this hypothesis: By repeated rehearsals and meditations upon significant religious images, a person can bring those images to dominate the basic structures in which the world appears. The domination may not be explicit, or even thoroughgoing, but those images come to color all appearances. In light of the foregoing discussion, it appears that the elements selected for importance in experience are what they are because of the basic experiential images. Some examples will illustrate this.

In Jewish religious life, the story of the exodus with the establishment of the covenant is a basic image told and recited in many contexts. Its metaphors color the Sabbath and feast day rituals, and the story provides the intellectual framework for understanding the concept of law. As the complex image of exodus and covenant becomes ingrained through the devotions of Jewish daily life, the "Jewish experience" is formed at a level more basic than any interpretations claiming to be truth. Not only do the Jewish people who are so formed regard themselves as special because freed from the Egyptians and bound to God by the Torah, they *become* that in their imaginative construction of the world. Jewish experience is, in fact, different from non-Jewish experience, or from the experience of other Jews who may be relatively uninfluenced by the exodus-covenant imagery. The fact of this difference is not the same as the interpretive claim that the Jewish people are special, or that real relations to God are involved, or that the imagery reflects a true story; these claims are meaningful only on a higher level. Rather, the world appears in special ways to devout Jews. The cultivation of religious Jewishness involves, therefore, devotional practices to embed the central imagery in experience. The religious values are implanted in experience by making the imagery expressing them the imagery by which the world appears.

For Christians, meditation on the life of Jesus can play a similar function. Insofar as the imagery of Jesus' life becomes the imagery by which the world appears, Christian experience is special; or, experience can be made to appear in a special Chrisitan way. So, too, respect for suffering, for poverty, and for powerlessness can be ordering principles for the appearance of the world. Consciousness of the working of these principles may exist only in consciousness of the concrete picture of Jesus, or it may exist at a highly reflective interpretive level. Nevertheless, the precritical appearing of the world can be formed by those images. One measure of faith is the degree and extent to which Christian imagery forms experience at its level of mere appearing.

An even more striking illustration of this hypothesis is found in Tantric Buddhism. By meditating on a mandala, a person forms experience wholly by the world-structures of the mandala. All other elements are turned to emptiness or transformed into the structures of the mandala. In that mandalic world, the "personality" of the mandala's "god" becomes the personality of the religious seeker. His or her own ego-image is lost and the image-structure of the mandala replaces it. The most striking characteristic of this religious practice, however, is the fact that no mandalic world is "true." Tantric Buddhism shows its followers that worlds can be entered at will, that experience can be structured any number of ways, that there are as many worlds as can be imaginatively formed. Its purpose is not to claim infinite worlds exist and assert that truth, but to form direct experience which, when interpreted, exhibits the claim.

The axiological cosmology makes it possible to present a crucial distinction about religious claims that is often obscured by the assumption that the whole of experience is judgmental. Every theologian acknowledges that there is a difference between a religious dogma, or claim to truth, and the existential value of religious truths. Usually, however, the existential "truths" are reduced to the subjective appropriation of claims otherwise intended in the objective mode; or the objectivity claims to truth in religion is reduced to matters of private, subjective "attitudes." Employing the categories of the cosmology, it is possible to represent both the objective and the existential sides, at least with regard to religious claims about imagery.

On the objective side, the imagery involved in experientially structuring a world does express itself in the intentional structure of the experience. Among other things, the imagery constitutes the intentional claim that this is the way the world is, or that this is a valid way to organize experience. As such, the imagery is subject to interpretation and to questions about its historical accuracy, demythologizing, moral rightness, and the religious, moral, aesthetic, political, and cognitive worth of the imagery. Imagery whose interpretation is approved becomes transformed into religious doctrine, canonical symbol, and story.

On the subjective side, the imagery functions within the process of concrescence as the complex normative measure by which the initial data are sorted into an appearing world. Although the imagery can be recognized and reflected upon only after the fact by interpretation of its final disposition in intentionality, its immediate function is to be essential features within the coming-to-be of appearance. Inherited from the past, the imagery functions essentially to order the experiential elements, distinguishing important foreground elements from trivial background ones. Although this function can be criticized after the fact, and the imagery changed for the future, the function itself underlies and is prior to the intentional structure that can be interpreted. This is one of the reasons religious imagery is "religious": It constitutes the important orders of experience itself. It is at the heart of the world. The imagery may be that of divine figures such as Buddha and Jesus, or the inspiration of the exodus and covenant; it may also function in the place of the "creation of the world," in the "creation of living experience." When it is said that God is closer to us than we are to ourselves (Augustine), or that we are atman and atman is Brahman (Upanishads), part of what can be involved is that the imagery of the divine makes the most important discriminations in the constitution of experience itself.

Reacting to Hegel's triumphant rendering of all reality in the form of dialectical judgment, Kierkegaard asserted the apparently opposing claim that (religious) truth is subjectivity. What this means is there must be a subjective appropriation of religious judgments, and this appropriation may not be bound by, and surely is not defined by, the canons of good interpretation. Although Kierkegaard's is a further dialectical move beyond Hegel, showing yet another dimension to judgment, it misses the humbler, prior reality of religion: that its imagery forms the experience which makes interpretation possible. Recognizing this draws attention to the process of cultivating religious experience—not experience of the religious object, but experience of the world formed by the imagery of religion.

In personal spiritual cultivation, acquisition and deepening of religious imagery are the goal of devotional practice. By invoking imagery in ritual, by meditation and contemplation, through reflecting and pondering on texts and doctrines, religious imagery comes to achieve importance in the imagery-forming experience. And the basic formative imagery that is not religious is understood as not-religious, as demonic.

It is useful to classify the imagery of the major world religions in three general categories, each defined by a spiritual "hero."[21] Spiritual discipline is imaged in the model of the warrior; integrity, loss of the selfish ego, and the capacity for action and attainment have imagery associated with warriors and kings—with Moses and David, Arjuna and Krishna, with the Buddhist kung fu fighters and the Zen samurai, with St. Paul donning the breastplate of righteousness and with the Jesuits' spiritual exercises perfecting obedience to the Father General. Spiritual wisdom is imaged in the model of the sage who feels the world in both its relative and absolute aspects, appreciating the ontological significance of that contrast. Amos and Isaiah, Buddha and Bodhidharma, Augustine and Aquinas, Lao tzu and Confucius—all are heroic figures whose lives and thoughts embody the imagery of sagacity. The saint is the third model, whose imagery involves transformation of the heart so that the most basic desires are perfected. The rabbis of the Torah, Jesus, Ramakrishna, Hui-neng, and the Sufi master present characteristics to serve as models for transformation of the heart. The images of these figures overlap, and, from the religious point of view, the spiritual perfection in each is a relevant ideal for every person.

The content of religious imagery is not devoted exclusively to personal spiritual cultivation. Whatever the content, insofar as the imagery is basic to experience, it serves to cultivate. As much as patterns of behavior, as belief and as psychic content, imagery of origins and destiny organize the religious dimension of experience. In a reflective concern to organize the several dimensions of imagery, religious thought often refers to the types of organization illustrated in the heroic persons of soldier, sage, and saint.

That imagery is religious in constituting the basic structures by which the world appears, and that it functions at a level which is a condition for interpretable experience rather than the experience itself, does not mean it is immune to criticism. On the contrary, since religion is concerned with the most basic imagery with which we engage the world, it is vital that it be criticized. The juncture of art and religion in the process of imagination embodies an awesome beauty that ought not be forgotten when imagination itself is subjected to interpretation. That awesome beauty is the fundamental, though often hidden, quality by which we engage the world.

8

Imagination as Engagement: Art

That imagination is the medium by which people engage the world in experience is paradoxical. It runs contrary to the dominant interpretation of imagination in the Western tradition. Aristotle, for instance, carefully separated imagination from sensation on the one hand, by virtue of which the world is engaged passively, and from judgment and appetite on the other, by virtue of which the world can be engaged actively (*De Anima*, Book 3, Chapters 3–11). Yet running alongside the dominant tradition is the theme stemming from Plato's discussion of the Divided Line (*Republic,* Book 6, 509D–511E) that imagination is basic to all the other thinking faculties, a theme surfacing in Kant's philosophy for which imagination is the condition for representing the world. Engaging the world nevertheless is a more meaty relation than representing it.

Only Wang Yang-ming seems to have seen the importance of the primordial composition of the heart-mind. At the center of this composition there is no question of truth or falsity, or of good or bad, only of self-constitution relative to the world. This constitution is potentially in harmony with the world, on his view, and can be distorted only in the functions between its center and the world it reaches. For Wang, the question of responsibility has to do only with reaching and clarifying the heart-mind. But the problem lies deeper: should we ourselves not take responsibility for the composition of the heart-mind? Or, to put it in modern language, are we not responsible for imagination?

This is neither a rhetorical nor an academic question. Although the previous chapters have insisted on a positive answer to it, the question must be pressed afresh in connection with engagement. If the positive answer can be sustained, then certain important practical consequences follow for taking responsibility with respect to imagination.

The first section, "Phenomenology of Engagement," explores some of the more important ways in which imagination is the medium of engagement on the personal and social levels and with respect to the depth dimensions of life. The second section, "Criticism of Images," raises the critical question, Can we be responsible for the role of imagination in engagement? The answer is, We can be through art. The third section, "Cosmology of Imagination as Art," provides a cosmological interpretation of the role of art in imagination and the pervasive contribution of art to life. The fourth, and final section, "Responsibilities of Imagination," discusses the cultural role of art in the twentieth century, as well as the role of those critical enterprises by means of which art makes it possible to render imagination responsible.

PHENOMENOLOGY OF ENGAGEMENT

In some obvious senses one's engagement with the world is a seamless whole. The ways one engages nature affect one's engagement with other persons; engagements with people and with social structures and habits affect each other; and engagements with the particular things of life affect and are affected by one's engagement with life as such. In equally obvious senses the fabric of one's engagements is rent along the flaws in each of those areas.

For purposes of analysis it is feasible to make the following abstract division. Engagement can be explored with reference to a person's natural connections with the environment—that is, engagement in feeling, in intentional action and in the immediacy or play of life. The discussion in the chapters above lays the groundwork. The *natural* qualities of engagement, however, seem abstract compared to the social dimension of life. The concrete embodiment of natural engagement is engagement through participation. Like natural engagement, participatory engagement involves feeling, intention, and spontaneity; its ideals have to do with appropriating roots and tradition, with moral fulfillment, and with the happiness of life which, as Aristotle remarked, is activity conducted in accordance with virtue. Engagement is not only with particular things, as the natural and participatory dimensions indicate, it is also with life itself. This, as a quality of spiritual engagement, provides perhaps the most fundamental role for imagination.

A beginning of the discussion must be made, however, with an analysis of the role of images in imagination. In Chapter 7, images are distinguished from concrete appearances, schemata, and normative measures—all of which are involved in imagination and all of which play a role in engagement. Yet it is images that we bring to experience in order to facilitate engagement; they are the elements the control of which makes it possible for us to be responsible for imagination. Concrete appearances are the final product of imaginative experience. They can be controlled imaginatively only by first controlling images. Schemata are accessible through criticism; their grasp is essential to any critical assessment of images, although they too are abstract and are not to be found in imaginative presentations. Finally, normative measures are discernible only through highly abstract procedures of dialectic. The imaginative formation of experience deals directly with images.

Images

Critics and artists speak of images in senses that are popularly understood and meaningful to their crafts. There are images of sight and sound, and of dance, and of a turn of phrase. Images are spoken of as grouped together so as to be imagery, and imagery is discussed in terms of style and theme. Although these and related senses of images are perhaps too specific and professional for a general meaning of *image* relative to engagement, they deal with the topic, and our discussion needs to be able to connect with them.

But before attempting to make that connection it is possible to underscore the wider meaning of *image* by reformulating the conclusions reached in Chapters 5 through 7. Chapter 5 shows imagination to be an activity of synthesis in which objects of feelings are combined in presentational immediacy. This synthesis expresses beauty, in that the combination harmonizes the objects with a contrast between background and foreground. Things in the background are combined in a way that makes them trivially relevant and vaguely orienting. Things in the foreground are broadly organized and narrowly focused. Chapter 6 shows how imagination provides a perceptual structure for elements in the foreground, mediating objects of the world to intentional awareness. By the formation of perceptual propositional feelings, imagination mediates the experience of beautiful objects. Chapter 7 shows how the element of form, employed in both synthesis and perception, itself is an expression of value. In any experience, form is present in four dimensions— as: de facto contrasts in the concrete appearance, image, schema, and normative measure. All are involved in providing experienced multiplicity with value by organizing it normatively. The cumulative argument of these chapters is that experience has the form of a world and that this form is a gathering of objects of feeling in which the focal importance of certain elements makes possible the harmonious presence of the other elements in trivial, vague contrast.

An image is a hybrid entity. On the one hand it is always particular, occurring in the appearance of some experience. Images therefore are always bound up with the media in which they occur. A musical image, for instance, must be heard to be felt. The musical image may be expressed in musical notation, and it may be mentally hummed through in the mind's ear, as it were. But the notation and the mental melody are themselves images, similar to the sounded musical image but different in medium; they are images because they are particular events. The same holds true for images in sight. The landscape discussed in Chapter 7 is available to experience by virtue of the images of the house, the tree, and the perspectival point of view. A painting of the landscape is a similar image; so is a line drawing.

On the other hand an image is always universal. It is a set of elements that could give structure by being important in any appearance with similar components. Part of apprehending a scene through its organizing images is the recognition, though perhaps unexpressed, that those images potentially could organize other scenes. In fact, insofar as the scene is apprehended as meaningful, part of the meaningfulness is that the image could be repeated in the interpretation of the meaning. In the case of the musical image, part of apprehending the sounds heard is structuring it with formal elements one could recognize again, perhaps by humming to oneself. In a more complex experience, the image is apprehended as one that can be written down and perhaps played on other instruments, even on other kinds of instruments. In the example of the landscape, apprehension of the actual scene includes grasping that it has a structure that can be represented in a painting or drawing.

The sense of universality involved in apprehending through images differs from that involved in interpretation. In the latter there is an explicit recognition of universality. To interpret the tree as being green, for instance, includes a reference to the universal character of greenness. Apprehending in imagination, however, does not involve explicit recognition; one simply images the scene with a green tree susceptible to interpretation. Yet even in imagination there is a subjective feeling of universality in the elements of the experience selected out as important, as the image.

Every concrete appearance is particular and unique. The universality of its image, therefore, must be vague universality. Any other expression of the schema in a "like" image must be somewhat different because the components of the other experience to be organized by the image are somewhat different. One of the crucial elements in discussing images, therefore, concerns the degree and kind of shift from one instance to the next. At one extreme is the near identical reproduction of Kant's five dots, ... , in each copy of the *Critique of Pure Reason,* or the many copies of the same recording, or many glances at the same landscape from the same perspective. Although slight differences are evident in each case, they are not differences that require close scrutiny. At the other extreme is the transfer involved in moving from one medium to another. From landscape to paint and canvas, or to pencil and paper, or to reproduction in memory; from a symphony in a concert hall to variations in the grooves of a record, to reproduced sound through an amplifying system, to a musical score printed in many copies. Because the elements in various media are different in some respects and similar in others, the transfer of the image is possible, but only with alterations. The painted image of a scene shares with the drawn image the elements of spatial arrangement, though the images differ in texture and color. For purposes of interpretation, as opposed to imagination, the differences between an image moved from one medium to another are crucial, for it is partly through seeing what the image involves when so transferred that understanding consists. Most criticism involves "transferring" the image from its original medium to the verbal medium.

Since writers use words and struggle most with verbal imagery there is a tendency to overemphasize the importance of images in the verbal medium. Genetically the oldest, most pervasive, and most fundamental media of our biological modes of apprehension have to do with smells, sounds, sights, and movements. Verbal images are usually piggyback on nonverbal ones. Yet overemphasis on verbal imagery can never be too far off the mark because we possess experience mainly by appropriating it verbally. The nuances and vast range of interconnection in verbal imagery, as well as its capacity for immediate, noninterpreted self-reference, give verbal imagery a special place. But it is a place that is significant mainly in the context of interpretation, vision, and responsibility—not imagination alone. To perform the function of imaging, verbal imagery requires interpretation.

Where do the images that arise in experience come from? Because this is a highly obscure, empirical question, it is possible to address it only programmatically. At the most basic level lie the fundamental modes of extensiveness which must be congruent with the way in which experienced things are related to the environment. Space and time are highly abstract images of extensiveness; feelings of extension themselves are images, but they are usually so trivial that they go unnoticed. The human body is the immediate neighborhood of most experience; thus extension is felt through mediation by the organs of the body. For instance, there is the spatial structure of vision and the temporal character of observed motion; and of course these depend on the objects seen in the extensive field. The extension of a sound-space-time has different characteristics. The images that coordinate these, like those in a drama, are so complex as to lose most of their interest when translated into a verbal medium. As neuropsychologists learn more about the workings of the brain, the nodal points of physiological experience will be available for greater understanding. Finally there are the many layers of imagery that are built up through social contact. The images of warmth and comfort, for example, are nearly universal because of the experience of the womb and early nurturing. Images of conflict may arise through early frustrations. Speech, in its turn, becomes a basic imagery: we learn to harken to the environment for its *logos*. And with speech comes all the imagery of culture, of cooperation, planning, and understanding.

It is important to remember that images are the means by which imagination constitutes experience. There is no imageless concrete appearance on which we later impose images (although images can be imposed in subsequent interpretation, when the interpretation, not the original appearance, has the image). To have experience at all, rather than mere physical synthesis, it is necessary for images to be among the objects felt. The most basic images are those constituted by the objects felt as mediated through the dominant structures and functions of the body. An occasion of experience feels the visual and auditory apparatus of the body, and through them, feels other things. Whereas the eyes and ears feel with little or no imagination (hence with no experience), experiential occasions can feel the eyes and ears as providing images, hence as elements of experience. Because experiential occasions themselves can be felt by subsequent occasions, images themselves can be objects in experience; they can be developed and given meaning. What steadiness and order human experience has comes about largely because of the continuity of images through time. The imagery of spatial and temporal orientation is similar through most places and times, although of course experiences differ greatly concerning how important such imagery is, and some experiences may lack the images completely. Cultural images, particularly those of language, of the gestures of social relations, the architectural contouring of space, and the culture's habits of using colors, also provide continuity. Through personal experience, each person develops important images. For most people, there are occasions in which they are uncertain about how to achieve images that will allow them to have what they consider appropriate experience. Each of us has been in situations with a vague awareness that something important is being missed or distorted because of our failures of imagination.

One final general feature of images may be brought out at this point. In a concrete appearance, the images consist of those elements which are important because they enable the appearance to be harmonious. Suppose one were to focus on a portion of the appearance not contained within the image structure, the bush midpoint between the house and the tree. If that can be made the object of focus, then it too has an image structure. Its overall shape and color, for instance, as rendered in a painting of the landscape, would be its image, while its individual leaves would be relatively trivial, vague background that can be experienced only as within the image shape. Then again, if one focuses on a leaf, its outline and veins are its image structure, with its cells relegated to the background.

The point can be expressed from the opposite side. It is by virtue of the vaguely and trivially perceived cells that the outline image of the leaf has its concrete density. Because of the leaves, the bush is felt as having weight. Because of the bush, the spatial relation of the house to the tree is given reality. One of the chief differences between a concrete appearance of nature and that of a work of art is that, whereas the former is indefinitely rich in terms of its trivial, vague background, the latter, being constructed for the purpose of imaging the schema in the art medium, soon lapses into homogeneity or irrelevance in its background. A line drawing of the landscape, for example, fills the space between the house and the tree with white paper, which, for a line drawing, is exactly what is needed. But in contrast to the scene in nature, the internal image-structure of the blank paper does not support and reinforce the images of the house and the tree in the landscape. Whereas in nature the house and tree constitute the landscape (partly because of the bush)—which is what it is because of its leaves, because of their cells, and so on—in art, the sketched house and tree are mediated by an homogenous space.

Natural Engagement

Like most important human realities, engagement with the world is a mixture of actual achievement with unfulfilled possibilities. With respect to some particulars, engagement itself may be good or bad; embracing one's toothache may not be as wise as analgesic alienation. But with respect to engagement generally, to be engaged is to be alive, to be responsive to the possibilities for value, and to be concretely beautiful in the sense suggested in the chapters above.

Although suggestive enough, "engagement with the world" is not a precise expression. In the first place, *world* is ambiguous. As noted, imagination constitutes the subjective world of experience, in contrast to the objective world. Yet "engagement with the world" refers to the objective world, since imaginative experience *is* the subjective world for a person.

The relation between the subjective and objective world is both causal and normative. It is causal in the sense that "feeling" is the fundamental mode of causation; the subjective world is a special, imaginative way of feeling the objective world. Some aspects (but only some) of the subjective world *refer* to the objective world descriptively; in these highly abstract ways, the subjective world can be said to mirror the objective world with varying degrees of distortion. But in most aspects, the subjective world is the way the objective world is possessed and responded to, and the subjective world of any moment is an element in the objective world of the next. The relation between objective and subjective worlds is normative precisely because the objective world can be incorporated experientially and modified by experience in ways whose worth varies. How to take in the world, how to order oneself though incorporating the world, and how to have public consequences on the world—all are processes subject to norms.

Engagement, then, can be defined initially as the normative relation between subjective experience and the objective world, between the subjective appropriation of feeling and the objectivity of the data felt, between the freedom of spontaneous imagination and the independent forces of the environment, between the subjectivity of one's intentional thoughts and actions and the objectivity of their consequences. The relation between the subjective world and the objective world has many layers which are dependent on particular elements of both—for instance, objects about which one's experience should make true descriptions, obligations to particular people, formal proprieties, and special enjoyments. Under these layers of particular relations are the layers of engagement itself whereby the very structure and function of imagination makes possible special connections. Deficiency in engagement is alienation. The question of engagement is not one of the truth of claims, the morality of actions, the fulfillment of responsibility, or the richness of one's vision. It is a question, rather, of the intensity and worth with which subjective experience relates to the world.

Alienation is deficiency of engagement. Generally this is a situation in which the causal connections between the world and a person make for life in some sense, but not for imagination, not for experience; engagement involves an experiential response to one's causal matrix. Alienation, in particular, is a situation in which experience is organized so as to distort or suppress various modes of experiential connection with the world. The images with which one subjectively experiences, form the ways by which causal influences are received and the structures by which one's experience objectively affects the future. These images, therefore, make the difference between engagement and alienation.

There is no known fixed structure of human engagement. It can be analyzed according to many schemes, each of which has its place. The scheme employed here, which can give no more than illustrative suggestions about engagement, derives from the axiological cosmology. It begins with a discussion of engagement through feeling, action, and play (the imaginative face of spontaneity); in succeeding sections it moves to social participation and then to engagement with life itself. Throughout, the role of images is highlighted best against the background of alienation.

Engagement through Feeling. The chief modes of engaging the world through feeling are pleasure and pain. Alienation of feeling is anesthesia. The question here is not whether a pleasure one feels is a function of the worth of an object or whether the pleasure has implications for one's subjective grasp of the object; rather, it is whether one engages the object with pleasure or pain. Both pleasure and pain are complicated psychological phenomena. One may observe one's pain but not be pained by it, as is the aim of certain neurosurgical procedures used for analgesic purposes. The issue of engagement is whether one responds to the world with pleasure and pain, or whether one merely observes.

The role of images in pleasure and pain is to form experience so that the affective elements may have importance. In general, this means having images of oneself-in-the-world relative to the various affective objects that include affective responses. In some measure, these images are derived from the objects themselves. There is an immediacy to irresistible joys and sorrows not to be derived in any other way. Because life is complex, however, the affective elements never occupy experience alone. People who are alienated from their own feelings, as psychologists say, may grasp the content of their feelings, but they allow the affective elements only trivial places. That is, the images in their alienated experiences consign the affective elements more to the background than to the foreground. Freud and his followers have shown how both pleasure and pain can continue to be operative even when they occupy trivial positions in awareness; their "operations" clearly are not trivial in some other senses. Because feeling pleasure and pain depends so much on complex neurological structures which themselves can be distorted, in many respects, alienation cannot be interpreted as a symbolic matter. That is, the images of pleasure and pain may have much less symbolic content than many other kinds of images. Even the pleasures that derive from symbolic objects such as contemplated future states or abstract conversation have a strong physiological component in the way they appear. Pleasures and pains issue in sighs and groans even when they are completely cerebral.

Thus affective imagery must be multilayered. It has levels of physiological sensation, of symbolic representation as pleasurable, and of formal elements connecting it with the rest of experience, perhaps as the outcome or the initiation of processes, in contrast to elements of differing affective character. For genuine engagement, these layers must be integrated, as the cells are in the leaf in the bush in the path between the house and the tree.

Alienation occurs when distintegration takes place, for instance, when the physiological feelings of pain or pleasure are denied on the higher symbolic levels, or when the higher symbolic levels signify an affective content which, in fact, is missing physiologically. At the higher symbolic levels, which lack deeper roots, affective feeling is mere sentiment. At the physiological levels, which lack symbolic integrations, feelings of pain or pleasure, if they are felt at all, are inhumane. Sexual imagination illustrates the point. It is possible for some people to make love while their minds are elsewhere; the sexual feelings of excitement and orgasm amount merely to a dull perturbation of awareness. Most people make love with a phantasmagoria of sexual and other images that more or less bring to awareness what they are feeling physically and how they are feeling with the other person. A well-engaged imagination presents the pleasures as unique to the relationship with the real sexual partner. Even more engaged is the imagination that presents one's feelings about the whole relationship with the other person, not just the immediate sexual contact, particularly when that relationship is rich with various affective overtones.

Engagement in the content of feeling can be distinguished from engagement in the affective tones of feeling because of the phenomenon of being able to observe the affections without being affected by them. Something of an opposite phenomenon is also possible—namely, that one can be responsive to affective elements while viewing the content as trivial. The pleasures of love-making can be enjoyed while objectifying or even ignoring one's partner. The question of engaging the content of feeling is not to be confused with the related question of feeling with embodiment and energy, sensitivity, and purity. True, the norms of feeling must, to some degree, be fulfilled if engagement is to be possible. Without embodiment, energy, sensitivity, and purity, experience would not be inclusive of the world. The question of engagement, however, has to do with how important the well-felt content is in experience. That is, do the images forming the appearance of the world lend much importance to what is felt? Is the content of feeling relegated to a background of triviality? Of course, *some* feelings must be given importance, or there would be no experience at all. But the feelings that achieve importance might be those deriving from a person's prior experience which seriously distort some object apparently in the foreground. For instance, a bigot might see a member of a despised race merely as an example of the race, not as a person. If the two people work together for some time, the bigot's experience inevitably is penetrated by the evidence of the other person's uniqueness and humanity, a penetration that might be sensitive and pure in its way. But if the prejudice remains strong, the prejudicing image may force recognition of the other person's uniqueness and humanity to remain in the background of trivial awareness. Perhaps only a crisis that upsets the image of prejudice would allow for a new image that lends importance to what was known on a lower level.

Another dimension of engagement through feelings needs to be stressed—fear. Fear and the responses of fleeing or fighting are basic physiological components of experience. Their genetic base in the human organism is among the oldest biological systems. Fear itself is often a crucial element among the feelings making up experience; therefore, engagement with the world requires an image in which fear can be registered as important. When one denies one's fears by forming experience in ways that make them trivial, the roots of the necessary avoidance behavior cannot be appreciated. The world *is* fearsome and can be engaged well only by recognizing this quality. Perhaps this point runs counter to the understandable tendency to want to image the world only in pleasant and secure ways. Of course it is an empirical question as to the extent of the world's fearsomeness, and as a question of truth the topic goes beyond a discussion of imagination. It appears from a casual survey, however, that avoidance of an image of fear, which is the denial of fear itself, results in distortion of many other feelings by which the world is engaged.

Throughout this discussion it should be remembered that the role of images is not to implement feeling as such but to integrate feelings in the world as experienced. Imagination has to do with the way in which one constitutes oneself an experience of the world. At the elementary level, to engage the world is to make the important elements in the world important in one's subjective grasp of the world. The question of being able to engage feelings comes before that of the interpretive truth of the feelings or of judgments about what is really important.

Engagement through Action. Images also allow one to act in the world, to engage the world by making a difference to it. In part, action is a reaction to feeling; the quality of one's active engagement depends on the quality of one's passive feeling. The bigot who cannot feel other people's uniqueness and humanity will, most likely, act inhumanely toward people. But another part of action involves appreciating the normative qualities of action. For better or worse, actions have effects. Through anticipatory imagination, one can feel consequences and then evaluate them. More often, we feel the worth of actions in immediate reaction to the actions themselves, changing course as the experience progresses. This does justice to the spontaneity and play of experience far better than does the moral-deliberation paradigm. But even in actions immersed in immediacy there is a triangular integration: the need to objectify forces which are integrated in experience from the past, the necessity of objectifying oneself according to opportunities provided by the larger environment, and the normative quality that comes from the fact that actions make a difference to the worth of the world.

Images, therefore, affect engagement of the world through action in three distinguishable ways. First, they present as important what really is important in oneself that needs active expression. Roughly speaking, images that involve repression are alienating because they do not allow one to deal with certain important feelings with awareness and integration; when the results of repressed feelings are expressed in actions, it is often in ways that are unrecognized and usually disintegrated, counterproductive, and irresponsible. Second, they form an overall sense of oneself as capable of relating causally to the real opportunities of the world. Images of oneself as incompetent, and images of the world as determined completely apart from oneself, are alienating because they result in impotence. Images of competence for engaging the world in action are prior to specific judgments about being able to perform specific actions. Third, images allow for an appreciation of the worth of things apart from the ways those things affect one's own self-definition. Appreciation of norms that might guide action requires a kind of objectivity of appreciation, the opposite of narcissism. Narcissists are alienated from action because their images of the world are functions of what their personality needs to believe. True engagement suspends, at least in part, the *need* to believe and attends to what the world presents. The issue comes to a head in the normative component of action, because the distortions of narcissism have less to do with noting the existence and general characters of things than they do with appreciating the values things have in themselves in contrast to their values for the narcissist.

Engagement through Play. Both engagement through action and engagement through feeling are abstractions from a more concrete engagement with the world, though they are abstractions that can be given some independence through genuine stresses. The concrete engagement perhaps can only be called life itself; alienation of all its abstractable parts can be called death, at least in the spiritual sense. When engagement through feeling and action are abstracted, however, there is a significant remainder: engagement through play.

Play is the engagement of spontaneity with the process of life. As described in the axiological cosmology, spontaneity does not directly engage objects other than oneself; it requires the mediation of feelings and intentions. But feelings and intentions are two poles of the integrating self-constitution of experience, and spontaneity is the heart of that process. Play, therefore, is engagement with the process of life itself.

The materials of play are the feelings. But the insistence of the feelings is not the only determining factor in life; there is also the factor of appropriating the feelings and coming to be a new person through this appropriation. Intentions and their consequent actions are the result of play. But the norms for action—the opportunities and the drives for expression—are not the only factors determining these results. There is also the factor of delight in novelty and chance, of decision without a reason. Play saves action from overbearing moral seriousness. It makes life life and not mere value production.[1]

The images that alienate one from play are those that stress too much the importance of feeling or of the norms of intention. The proper stress for play is seasonal; there is a season for feelings, a season for intentions, and a season for play. How do we discern the season, though? That is the question. Engaging images of life are sensitive to the importance of the season at hand. The Taoists call this problem the task of returning to the Original Mind, of attaining nonaction, nonknowing, nonbeing. Original Mind does not mean an earlier mind but rather the primodial container and fount of mental activity— spontaneity itself. The spontaneity is not empty, however; it is immersed in the demands and materials of life, though it is not reduced to them.

Images of play and spontaneity are extremely problematic, since they so often seem irresponsive to the real demands of life and irresponsible regarding life's norms. Their function, though, is to set limits on the effectiveness of feelings' force and the good's commands. Proper images of play are probably rooted in a deep sense for the process of the universe, paralleling the way images of feelings are rooted in images of component feelings ad infinitum and the way images of action are rooted in the triangulation of need, opportunity, and norms. This is why play seems essentially a religious phenomenon, a frequent characterization of the gods, and a scandal to both the naturalist who overidentifies with feelings and the moralist who takes norms too seriously.

Participatory Engagement

All of the above issues of imagery are abstractions from concrete life when its social dimension is considered. Although some feelings may be so biologically based that their social components are negligible, images that integrate these feelings with others are not. Central to the concept of sociality is the experience of things as having roles in the experience of other people as well as in one's own.[2] Although language is paradigmatic here, it is no more basic than are useful artifacts, the gestures and practices of nurturing, homemaking, work, and the celebration of life's milestones. Following the distinction between feelings, action, and spontaneity, the images of participation can be analyzed from three points of view:

Feelings. As a matter of feeling, engagement through social participation involves appropriating the experience of others. This means: empathy with individuals and with the experience of classes; the appropriation of human tradition; and the constitution of oneself as having a history and tradition by adopting certain features of the past as definitive resources and identifying marks for oneself.

Identification and appropriation of the experience of others is a two-sided engagement in which both sides need to be integrated. If our images foster too much identification, there is a loss of the integrity of the self. Some people imagine their place in the world in such a way that they become preoccupied with other people's lives. They treat other people's problems and careers as if they were their own. As a result, they lose the sense of their own independent identity and behave as though other people's successes and failures were their own. Identification needs to be balanced with images of appropriation, in which the experience of others is given a caring role in one's experience in ways attendant upon one's own responsibilities, feelings, and process of life.

Similarly, images that emphasize appropriation without identification alienate others by engulfing them emotionally. Rochester's image of Jane Eyre as the pure, honest elf sent to bring him to life is merely a consumptive image. He does not identify with Jane from her perspective; he can engage her only as a machine of his own redemption.[3]

Less subtle than the alienating images whereby we seek to live through others, or to let them live only through us, are those that bind us to or separate us from our past, from our ancestors and traditions. The people who think themselves somehow superior because their ancestors achieved something of worth are foolish when observed directly, though perhaps most of us fall prey to this sometimes. Similarly, people whose images involve denial of heritage are alienated in their own ways.

Images properly engaging the experience of others need to combine both identification with the others from their standpoint and appropriation of the others' experience from one's own standpoint. Perhaps the problem can be expressed as one of establishing images with proper ego boundaries. But this does not connote the dynamic quality of personal relationships, which requires an imagery of interchange, of life together.

Action. Participatory engagement also requires an imagery of action that sets the context for moral life. Imagery for moral action should not be confused with moral judgment as such. Images for engaging the moral life are not themselves moral in the sense that actions are, yet they, too, set the context in which the world can be engaged morally and thus have their own kind of moral content.

The subtleties of images for moral engagement cannot be classified quickly. In general, good images for social action combine a sense for one's own responsibility with respect for the joint participation of others in social intercourse—all subject to norms and the bearing of greater or lesser worth. The joint participation of others itself has at least two aspects. One is Kant's famous point that the other people involved should be treated as persons, as ends in themselves, not as means only. The other is the recognition that others, too, are agents in social activity, that they are also involved in acting according to moral norms; images help distribute the original sense for those whose responsibility it is to attend to various responsibilities, as well as for the definition of "joint effort."

Alienating images are those that might represent oneself as not involved morally in the social processes in which one is involved physically. Consider the images of social life held by the Germans who acquiesced in the forces that brought on the Holocaust. Images that objectify other people as mere elements in the social process are alienating. Consider the imagery in the analyses of social institutions by systems analysts. Images that present the affairs of social processes as all one's own responsibility are equally alienating; feminist consciousness-raising has pointed out how the imagery shared by many men and women presents the world as if significant action were open only to men.

Spontaneity. Images not only provide the context for sharing experience and sharing activity, they provide the context for sharing the process of life together. Whereas, on the merely personal level, the spontaneity of life integrates feeling and intention with an imaginative sense of playfulness, on the social level it integrates sharing experience and sharing activity with shared life. On one hand, it seems arbitrary that we should be here together with such and such parents, with the contingencies of geography, politics, and history, while, on the other, it seems somehow fated, determined by antecedents, Further, though we are here together, this is the context in which we work out our individual lives. The imagery of shared social process combines a sense of freedom with arbitrary fate; it cannot be reduced either to shared experience or to joint moral action.

Perhaps alienating imagery is more common than adequate imagery regarding shared life. In times of great crises, people are sometimes forced to image their joint careers on earth. The American Civil War was such a time for many people, as was the battle for civil rights in the 1960s. Space flights to the moon and photographs of earth from space have also created a powerful sense of joint life. Devotees of the great religions which present human life as essentially contained within the history of salvation have long traditions of imagery for the social unity of life.

Alienation from engaging life as a joint social process involves images that focus too much on either shared experience or shared moral activity. Perhaps the heart of such alienating imagery is that which suggests a profound division between "us" and "them," between Greek and barbarian, Jew and Gentile, between those in the group whose experiences we do share and whose activities we respect with our own, and those outside that group. With the imagery of "us" and "them," shared experiences take on the extra meaning of setting off oneself in one's group from the rest of the world. That imagery gives moral activity the added dimension of distinguishing one's partners from those who we imagine do not deserve equal respect. But what imagery is there that does not, at bottom, reflect the division between "us" and "them"?

Engagement in Depth

It is one thing to engage life in the sense that follows the contours of a cosmology. In this sense, engagement is a matter of imaginatively integrating oneself so as to be experientially related to things. It is another to engage life in the sense that relates one to the basic fact of existence itself. The contours here are not cosmological relations between things but the relation between things and their ground, the relation of things to their existence. The great philosopher Kierkegaard explored the experience of the immediacy, or absoluteness, of life, and showed that the relation here is ontological and that it cannot be interpreted in cosmological terms.[4]

Ontological engagement with life is at the heart of religion, and the imagery for such engagement is religious imagery and its alternatives. Peter Berger has argued that the defining traits of religions are their contributions to an image of the world that makes life meaningful.[5] This is a delicate and problematic point, since it seems to interpret religion in terms of its function in the sociology of knowledge, a reductive account. Yet this account might be true as far as it goes if philosophy can make sense of such concepts as the "meaningfulness of life." The point here is not to discuss life's meaning but of relating to the fact of it. The claim does not involve a particular way of relating; instead, it involves the imagery that provides the context for relating.

Authentic religious imagery seems to need two aspects to engage one with life itself. One is that it needs to shock or disorient one from exclusive preoccupation with the cosmological elements of experience. Part of the *depth* of experience is the appreciation of the contrast between the ordinariness of most of our feelings, actions, and play (as well as our social lives), and the utter strangeness of the *fact* of them. Experience is ordinarily concerned with the *what* and *how* of life; but religiously it is concerned with the *that* and *why*. This is not to say that religion does not deal with shared experience or morality or with any of the aspects of personal life; it deals with them, however, with a special seriousness that comes from seeing that, *whatever* life is, its existence is an absolute fact. Religious imagery, therefore, needs to render the world strange.

The other aspect of religious imagery has already been alluded to— namely, that it returns one to ordinary cosmological affairs with a new appreciation of their depth. Religious experience involves a contrast between appreciation of the world and one's perspective within it, together with the appreciation of it as simply real. Neither, alone, is the genuine sense of depth.

Allegedly, religious imagery can be alienating by emphasizing either transcendence of the mundane cosmos or immersion within it. The imagery of popular mysticism often does the former, leading people to experience the world as only an obstacle to be transcended. The moralistic imagery of popular religion often does the latter, leading to moral fervor not tempered by depth. Many images of the great religious traditions seem now to have lost their power to engage at all, even with alienation. As a result, most imagery for engaging life as such is secular, even for people who consider themselves religious and who fervently hold religious beliefs and theories.

The testimony of the civilized traditions, if not that of the culture-shapers now, is that engagement with life has a depth not exhausted in feelings, intentions, and play. Interestingly, the great images of religion have often focused on analogs of the images of spontaneity. For instance, some Indian imagery of Shiva likens the world to a divine dance, or playing.

Western religions employ metaphors of brotherhood and contemporaneous life together. Perhaps this is because the images relative to spontaneity suggest something of eternity more than do those of feeling the past and intending the future. Not that existence as such is an instantaneous present, but that the temporal flow itself is what enjoys existence. Also, spontaneity itself is perhaps the most direct locus in experience of the grounding or absoluteness of existence.

In the present discussion, the role of images in engagement is presented in terms of a rough classification of kinds or aspects of engagement. An attempt has been made to illustrate various points with commonly recognized images. But as the discussion has proceeded, it has become apparent that in many cases our culture seems to lack commonly accepted authentic images. Engagement with life as a shared process, for instance, and religious engagement in depth, only rarely exist for most people, and perhaps not at all for some. Thus the argument that imagination underlies this kind of engagement is not persuasive. Neither is the argument that the images we have of these aspects of life are alienating.

On the other hand, suppose that life is to be engaged in these respects, that our images are simply inadequate. Suppose, also, that the images underlying the more commonly accepted forms of engagement are also inadequate, at least in everyday life. Can we say that there *ought* to be better images?

In its ordinary sense, "ought" is a moral word. The problem with imagination is not exactly a moral one except where a person fails to meet moral responsibilities because of a failure to grasp the world in adequate images. Rather, morality deals with the norms by which we order the world that, antecedently, is grasped imaginatively. Experience of the world begins with engaging it imaginatively. In what sense, if any, is there a norm for engaging the world?

The argument throughout much of this book is that beauty is the norm for imagination. It has been claimed in that argument that beauty is an ingredient of the imaginative formation of experience. Another dimension to beauty may now be elicited—namely, that it is the norm for engaging the world experientially.

The argument is a simple extension, on a theoretical level, of the previous claims about beauty. Beauty is analyzed as a harmony of appearance with background and foreground, the former involving triviality and vagueness and the latter, narrowness and width. Beauty is the contrast between such a background and such a foreground. But the state of the previous argument assumes that the elements in experience need only be subjective, that they be contained within one's imagination in contrast to the objective world. But the cosmology developed throughout maintains that feelings are feelings of real objects, not representations of the objects except in cases of abstraction. Similarly, the reality of an intention is itself a datum for future experience. Therefore, the true nature of beauty is not to harmonize a merely subjective fantasm but to harmonize one's grasp of felt objects so they can be experienced harmoniously. A concrete appearance is not an appearance in contrast to a reality, but the appearance of the world itself.

Beauty, then, is the norm for the beginning of realism. Experience *ought* to engage the world because beauty is its norm; beauty means the harmony in experience of things felt and intended, which is engagement. The special modes of engagements—for instance, in description, moral action, enjoyment, personal relations, and so forth—are formed by norms over and above (but presupposing) beauty.

The critical question is whether we can gain control of experience to *take responsibility* for making it beautiful.

THE CRITICISM OF IMAGES

There is a continuum of imagery in experience beginning with those levels of experience so rooted in the bodily processes of nature that the relevant organizing images are functions mainly of physiological structures. For instance, sensory experience has imagery derived mainly from the physiology of the senses. Also, basic experiences of position, atmospheric pressure, pervasive forces of nature, and bodily states such as temperature,

responsivity, anxiety, and aggression are functions mainly of physical factors. At the other end of the continuum are levels of experience formed by
images which we are conscious of creating. For instance, one returns home
after an absence of many years and, becoming suddenly conscious of the
discrepancy between one's childhood image of the place and the way it now
appears, asks what images are really appropriate and attends to developing
them. An artist, confronted with the staleness of images in a medium, strug-
gles to develop images. Perhaps the artist asks what images can be embodied in a new medium. Experience at this end of the continuum is relatively
more creative, sensitive to problems of imagining, and deliberate in its
attempt to grasp the world in terms of authentic images.

Few would argue with the claim that artists in some sense are responsible for the images they create, although the responsibility may not be
of the usual moral kind. Similarly, when people deliberately enter into
fashioning images to handle such special situations as a delayed homecom-
ing, their imaging is responsible because some images are better than others
and people can have some measure of control over the images they produce.

If, however, we can control images at the level of art, as well as
control the conscious formation of our capacity to experience, can we then
control images for better or for worse further along the continuum toward
the physiological pole? How far? Ordinarily, image formation is not the
object of special attention except in special cases. Can we achieve control
over a greater extent of the continuum of imagination? How much of experience can be made artful? What disciplines deal with the media of imagination in experience?

The kind of control that artists exercise over their images is extraordinarily subtle, too subtle to be treated with much theoretical accuracy. Nevertheless, it differs in certain gross, recognizable ways from the control involved in moral, intentional activity. Intentional activity guided by moral
norms involves some conception of the goal, with an understanding of
which possibilities within the process accord with or depart from pursuit of
the goal. Intentional activity does work to produce the desired goal, realizing it through actualization of the potential of the environment. (Intentional
activity is more subtle than is indicated here, since conceptions of the goal
change through activity and work itself produces a definiteness that cannot
be conceived in advance.) Artistic production of images is controlled in a
different way, with two phases. First is the comparatively spontaneous production of an image, either mentally or in the physical medium itself;
second is the reflective criticism of the image. Art involves considerable
random arranging and rearranging of pieces with after-the-fact criticism. A
painter makes a variety of sketches; actors try their lines many ways. The
more experienced the artist is with the context, problems, and media, the

more the artist can arrange and sort mentally. Whether mentally or overtly expressed, however, control over the products of creative imagination comes by the subsequent application of critical judgment.

One might think that once an artist has learned a technique, it would be possible to represent the subject matter (in representational art) by simply drawing what is seen. But that would not address the problem of images. Part of what is meant by an artist's *technique* is the selection of those elements that make the image important; technique embodies imagery. Precisely because of its universality, an image is not limited to a particular scene; it can be extended to many scenes. A skilled technician can produce many watercolors of the same landscape. If the technique is not varied, the paintings do not vary in imagery. If the artist is a genuine artist attempting to develop the best possible image, although the paintings may look the same to the tourist who compares them with the landscape, the critic sees that each successive painting is an experiment in making something else important—the line of the trees, the texture of the shade patterns, the alteration of perspective. Cezanne's landscapes and Monet's garden scenes are experiments in perfecting imagery.

The difference between art and experience in most of the rest of the continuum of imagery is, first, that the artist's image is more abstract, relatively speaking, and second, that the artist is more conscious of the "problem" of making images.

Consider the concrete images of my audial world. I can name the sound of the typewriter, the creak of the chair, the roar of the neighbor's lawn mower, the sounds of traffic in the street, the sound of birds and the buzz from the wasps' nest by the window. But all these sounds are related to countless other sounds of which I am at best vaguely aware but which give the nameable sounds their concreteness. Consider, then, a composer preparing a score that directs musicians to produce various sounds. Although the composer can order any number of sounds, a far richer mixture perhaps than could be described verbally, the composition consists only of the sounds called for. The infinite richness of the concrete sound image is not there, or rather, since the music will be played in some natural setting such as a concert hall, the intended musical sounds will not intentionally be integrated with the concrete infinity of natural sound in the auditorium. Many composers prefer that their music be performed in concert halls with as few extraneous sounds as possible. Against this, recent musicians (and parallel claims could be made for visual artists, sculptors, and dancers) have tried to make their music concrete by incorporating the sounds of concrete life—street sounds, for instance—or they have composed music intended for playing in a sound-rich environment. This only recognizes the point that intentionally produced images are abstract in comparison with the imagery of concrete experience.

An artist abstracts certain elements from a concrete setting and arranges them in a certain way—that is, with images. The excellence of a work of art, it is argued in the section "Cosmology of Imagination as Art," lies in its being a double contrast. Within the work is a contrast between the important elements constituting its images and the other elements harmonized by the images. There is also a contrast between the selections in the work of art itself and the potential in the background, out of which the selection is made consisting in subject matter, if any, the nature of the medium, the experiences of the artist, and the audience.

Artistic control—hence, responsibility—arises because the artist can make a critical judgment about both contrasts. On one hand, the question is whether the work has formal integrity, with the important forms genuinely harmonizing the rest; while, on the other, it is whether the work has imagic authenticity: Is this a good way to image the background? To rephrase the question: Does the imagery in the work of art provide a good way of experiencing the world? (Remember that, for an artist, *relevant world* includes the art media, the cultural state of the arts, personal intentions, and other factors beyond a subject matter that might be represented.)

If responsibility is to be taken for images at levels of experience other than the artistic, it might be possible with analogs of the artist's contrasts. That is, one would have to develop ways of selecting certain experiential elements for experimental trials as images. The explicitly constructed images would have to have formal integrity of their own, but they would also have to be judged for their authenticity relative to their background. The background might consist, in the first instance, of the concrete image that needs criticism. They newly invented image then might be a way of abstracting that concrete image so as to discern what is genuinely important in it. Or the newly invented images might be abstract ways of imaging reality that are alternative to the one originally presented in the concrete image. That is, one must learn to see in a new way in order to grasp the imagery in one's old way of seeing. One must go home after an absence in order to appreciate how one first saw one's neighborhood.

The second difference between artistic experience and concrete experience is that in concrete experience we are usually not conscious of the images employed or of the processes by which we come to form those images, whereas the artist is. But this difference is only relative. A newly blind person, for instance, can come to understand vision better in some respects than a sighted person by having to image the world through other senses. Through science, for another example, we come to understand the functions of images in various aspects of experience otherwise unnoticed. Once noticed, the images perhaps can be contrasted with alternatives. Far more profound than the sciences in their present state, literature, poetry, philosophy, and history can raise images to consciousness.

When raised to consciousness, the question about images then becomes one of responsibility: How do our images stand under critical judgment? What are their alternatives? What is gained and what is lost by grasping the world with this imagery rather than with some other?

It is possible to take responsibility for an image by identifying it as forming one's grasp of the world; critical distance on it can be gained by imaging alternatives and comparing them. Artists come to see how they perceive by attempting to create images for seeing; they create images through spontaneous trial and error and through a cumulative appreciation of the problems of imaging. But how much can this be done throughout the other levels of experience?

The identification of images, the first step in imaging alternatives, involves two things. First, one must come to recognize their content. This might be done through various forms of social and artistic criticism; it might also be done through one's own reflection on personal experience or family or friends. Second, one must arrive at an understanding of *how* the images form one's experience. The images are universal and may be employed with many different functions. How individuals or social groups employ an image is a function of larger aspects in the structure of their experience. A kind of existential understanding, therefore, is necessary of the *way* one images, *how* one's images play roles in constituting concrete experience.

To push responsibility for images down from the level of explicit art to the more profound and concrete levels approaching physiological experience requires coming to recognize facets and functions of experience that are ordinarily ignored. Ordinarily, we recognize only the content of interpretations expressed through images, not the images themselves or how they function. Yet this deeper recognition is possible to a greater extent than is often realized. On one hand, critical tools for reflection—for example, historiography, literature, poetry, philosophy, and the psychological disciplines, including psychoanalysis and its cognates—all provide a means for identifying both images and their imaging functions. On the other hand, disciplines of body awareness and sensitivity training, as well as yoga, t'ai chi ch'uan, and meditational practices of the religious traditions, offer ways of altering our usual modes of imaging, even at the bodily level, so that we can perceive real alternatives. An hallucinatory state offers an alternate way of imaging the perceptible qualities of the world. Although this does not, by itself, mean that a drug-induced state has greater authenticity or greater perceptual truth, it does make possible an objectification of the images in ordinary perception and bodily feeling. *Then* critical judgment is possible. As an artist must master a medium well enough to make alternative arrangements and to try things out spontaneously, even deep layers of everyone's imaging can be rendered capable of critical judgment by altering and so objectifying our bodies.

To take responsibility for images involves the two points mentioned, an intentional critical evaluation based on the intellectual tools of analysis developed through culture and the invention of concrete feelings of alternative images. To have only the last, yogic disciplines, without the former is to have merely uncritical alteration of imagination. To have only the critical objectification without the experimental alteration of imagination is not to be in touch with the crucial contrast between images and their backgrounds.

Identification of one's images and a critical comparison with alternatives is not enough for responsibility, however; responsibility requires control. To be responsible for one's images and engagements with the world, one must be able to change them. To change one's imaging is extraordinarily complex and difficult. For those images with semantic meaning, simply arriving at new and better meanings often is enough to effect the change. To be told to notice the beautiful shapes of a city skyline may be enough to enable one to see the city with a new beauty. Besides content is the existential function of images. One may know that certain humane images are the right way to see people but, in fact, not be able to see Jews except through anti-Semitic images.

To alter images requires altering one's character insofar as that establishes a context for images. This entails a thorough and continuous analysis of the images reflected in one's behavior and experience, and the regular willing of the best imagination. "Willed" imagination is not quite the same as concrete imagination. All products of imagination are intentional and in that sense are "willed"; but most concrete imagination, particularly at those levels reflective of the physiological components of experience, is itself the condition for deliberate willing. To alter's one's imagination thus requires introducing distance in one's imagination, making the conditions of the rest of interpretive experience complex in a new way. The critically chosen image must be fitted into the position of imaging the basic ways one engages the world. And part of its own form is that it is critically chosen.

Imagination cannot be innocent, although it functions prior to the kind of interpretation needed for critical evaluation. To further complicate things, the way in which new images are incorporated in experience, enabling new kinds of engagement, is by altering the rest of experience so that those new images can function. The reason the old images functioned as they did is that the rest of experience made way for them. To adopt a new image, therefore, means transforming the rest of one's character to allow for it.

How far one's character might be transformed is a difficult, empirical question. Many relevant variables have been noted here, although how they bear on an individual or on society's life is almost impossible to say. The possible kinds of cultivation of imagination through critical reflection and spiritual discipline have not been investigated popularly and hardly studied at all under the kinds of controlled scientific conditions that would allow one to determine the limits of responsible imagination. Surely more is possible than we ordinarily realize, though.

The project of cultivating imagination may be conceived of as a work of art itself. Perhaps the better analogy is that with an artist's entire body of work, since imagination has so many dimensions to cultivate, shifting in their focal awareness. The tasks involved in cultivating imagination for the sake of authentic engagement are similar to the artistic tasks of identifying the elements of one's media, arranging and rearranging them in alternative forms, and critically evaluating the results.

In two respects, however, the analogy is closer to that of morality than to art. On one hand, the artist can choose materials; in both moral life and in imagination the materials are given; whereas, on the other, the cultivation of images, like morality, needs to effect real changes in experience, not rest with experimentation, as sometimes happens in art. The body of an artist's work, however, is not an experiment but an achievement. This is so even if the achievement consists entirely of experiments. Similarly, one's imaging need never be settled or perfect. Although we have been speaking of cultivating the images for an authentic engagement of the world, that engagement is, in fact, a two-way transaction in which the world is also altered so as to be better experienced.

The best analogy with art is that cultivation of imagination and art both seek beauty. Art can then be seen in a new role with regard to the responsible cultivation of imagination. Art characterizes certain higher levels of experience and is something of an analog for cultivating imagination. It may also be seen as a tool for *altering* imagination, for it is through art that we gain access to our concrete imagery, both for understanding and for altering.

The means by which art does this is its re-presentation function: a work of art is an abstract image of concrete images in experience. That is, the artist selects certain elements as important from the background of experience and organizes them so they have formal integrity, leaving aside the other elements as trivial. In concrete experience, the imaging elements are the most important, but they are not singled out as the image-form unless abstracted by art and so noted. Furthermore, because of the universality of images, an artist can transfer an image from the medium of concrete experience and re-present it in a new medium where, by contrast, its imagic elements are noticeable. Perhaps an artist does nothing more than hang a shovel on a museum wall—the shovel is seen for its imagic elements. A shovel in a painting may not be very dramatic because one somehow expects a painting to be filled with recognizable objects. "Re-presentation" here, does not mean "representative" in the sense of looking *like* an object, as in realist painting, programmatic music, or dramatic ballet. Rather, it means that the image through which part of the world is engaged in experience is presented again in another medium, in conceptual imagination or in a physical or verbal medium. The artistic image may focus mainly on the objects being engaged—in which case, the image may look the way the object does when experienced. Or the artistic image may focus on the *manner* of engagement, on the subjective form of the engagement in the person's experience. Abstract expressionism has more to do with feelings than with objects. An artist would say the object depicted is more the *manner* of engaging than anything engaged.

If one takes a broad enough view of art, it can be seen as the principal tool by which individuals and cultures take responsibility for images for engagement. Art not only gives access to images by re-presenting them, it creates better images or at least alternate ones that may be assessed critically. In re-presentation, art need not aim for *truth* in what is presented; rather, it should aim for beautifying—that is, producing a re-presenting image that is schematized closer to the normative measure than is the original image. By making art pervade concrete experience, one might then engage the world better, more harmoniously, and more beautifully.

Art must, however, be taken in a broad enough view for this point to hold. The fine arts deal with images as defined according to fairly rigorous traditions—images of vision, sound, physical feeling in movement, drama, verbal interpretations of life, poetic experience of image-making itself. But there are other activities for investigating experience which, however scientific they might be in some sense, are matters of art in the sense that they create alternative imagic experiences for engagement. These include all the humanistic disciplines, the social and natural sciences, and the disciplines of psychology and physical training. If these disciplines are interpreted according to whether they give true knowledge about experience, they may well qualify as sciences; but if they are interpreted with respect to whether they lead to a greater beauty of engagement with the world, they are arts. In this sense, they have the potential for negating specific cultural forms in ways that undercut any assertive defense. And they are the source of salvation.

From a practical perspective, the relation between art and imagination suggests the possibility of taking responsibility for imagination at levels far broader than those usually addressed by art. But to ascertain the extent of this, it is necessary to represent the issue in cosmological terms.

COSMOLOGY OF IMAGINATION AS ART

The axiological cosmology may now be elaborated to treat three major points. First, it may be shown how to envision the role of images in experiential engagement of the world, including the normative function of beauty. Second, a theory of art may be sketched in which it is shown to involve creative abstraction, interpreting the remarks made about representation in the section "Criticism of Images." Third, the cosmology may be summed up in a discussion of intentionality in the artistic cultivation of imagination.

Images as Experiential Engagement

The distinction between the subjective world and the objective world drawn in Chapter 5 has only preliminary validity. In the context of questions of truth, the structures of imagination are only subjectively descriptive. Imagination alone makes no claim to truth. As a norm for interpretation, truth involves reference. The engagement of the world in imagination need not be referential or interpretive. With regard to truth, then, the full life of imagination may be only subjective—that is, characteristic of the experiencing subject. Objectivity does involve reference to the world independent of the experiencing subject, but it is a problem only in connection with the truth of assertions. In the discussion of imagination alone, it is not appropriate to ask whether the world of experience is objective as well as subjective, or whether it is subjective alone.

From the standpoint of an analysis of imagination which attempts to give a true interpretation of the situation, it is, indeed, possible to speak of the real world of objective data given, to be experienced, and of how these data are engaged experientially. So whereas we cannot speak of objective experience, we can speak of experiencing the objective world. This is the sense in which "engagement" of the objective world is meant.

The importance of this distinction is vast. On one hand, there is the temptation (too often acceded to) to regard imagination as dealing with its own contents in contrast to objects to which its contents might refer. What makes the temptation plausible is that imagination is the basic constituent of the experiencing subject; the act of imagining is the life of the subject as such. Kant phrased his theory of imagination in such a way as to make it problematic whether the representations formed in imagination refer to an independently real world. For him, objectivity is simply the order of representations *within* mind, which could be validated universally by experimental inquiry—a position of transcendental idealism. Kant's problem arose because of his view that all contents of subjective experience are representations. Experience, indeed, contains representations insofar as it refers to things through propositions. But the objects referred to may themselves

be *in* the experience and yet not have lost the character they had independently. The naturalistic position of the axiological cosmology offers an
alternative to Kant, in which experience is allowed to be inclusive of both
real objects and their representations. Instead of independent objects being
represented in mind, they are, at the least, causal factors within mind. Instead of causation being a regularity or sequence of representations, as it
was for Kant, or an activity of earlier things to bring later things into being,
as it was for Aristotle and most of the naturalistic tradition, the axiological
vision of causation shows the spontaneous activity of the present to take up
the past into itself as formative conditions. In terms of experience, a subject
constitutes itself by engaging the past world experientially.

On the other hand, it is an even more subtle temptation to assume that,
if objective things enter experience causally, the way they are experienced
(imaginatively, interpretively) is the way they are independently. This
assumption stems from the view of naive realism that the "kind" of causation
that puts things into experience, puts them there unaltered. But, in fact,
something entering experience must be reconciled with all the other things
that enter experience. Further, the structure of experience is intentional,
whereas our best intentional understanding of the world is that many of its
causal elements are not intentional. Descartes concluded from this that there
must be two kinds of substance, each with its own kind of causality—one
kind intentional and the other mechanical. By and large, the empiricist and
idealist traditions concluded from the naiveté of realism that experience involves only representations. The axiological cosmology, however, shows
how the causation involved in imagination is the same kind of causation—
that of feeling—as is involved in nonexperiential natural processes. It
shows, too, how the special structures of intentionality—so far, at least,
those of imagination—are special cases of feelings being integrated into a
novel concrete datum.

Causation enters experience through engagement. Engagement is a
grasping of the independent objects of the world in experience. A person, of
course, grasps many objects on physical levels that never enter experience,
or that rarely do so. For an object to contribute to experience, it must be
engaged, and this means it must enter imagination. Engagement is having
the objective world as part of subjective life through imagination.

Perhaps the decisive contribution of twentieth-century philosophy, in
all its main branches, has been the demonstration that experience includes
more than mere descriptive awareness. The world is experienced through
gamelike activities, according to what Wittgenstein called forms of life. The
world presents many modes, some objects ready-to-hand, others as naked
beings constituting the knower, yet others as constituting a world wherein

things can be objects, as Heideggerians say. Dewey's adherents would say that experience of the world is having, doing, enjoying, and suffering. Surely, imagination is this rich!

Imagination, though bearing intentional structure, is not all 'imagining that . . .'. It is imaginatively taking part in the activity of running, talking, appreciating, sensuously enjoying, deciding, building, loving, playing, and working. These are the connections through which we engage the world in imagination. Some imagination is, indeed, descriptive awareness and can be assessed, more or less, as true interpretation. This is the kind of imagination most often discussed by philosophers; it is expressed as 'imagining that. . .' . The element of descriptive awareness is supposed to grasp independent objects as they are or as they are from the perspective of the experience of the knower. Regarding these elements of imagination, in some sense, the way objects are causally engaged reveals the way they are or the way they are as engaged with the experiencer. For the rest of imagination, and the greatest part, the roles of images are to engage the experiencer in the processes of life that extend far beyond a local perspective. Imagination engages the world so that in experience it is had, done with, enjoyed, and suffered. The experiencer's own self is part of the world.

The beauty-norming imagination now must be understood in a new dimension. It applies not only to experience considered subjectively, not only to the show of experience from the perspective of the experiencer; it applies to the activity of experiencing itself. That is, harmonizing the world with background and foreground, with vagueness and triviality in the former and narrowness and width in the latter, is the foundation of experience. Experience may do more than that—for instance, attain truth, vision, and responsibility; but at least it contributes beauty to the world, albeit in a special sense. A world without experience would have many kinds of causal feelings; yet without experience, the world would not contain the peculiar kind of integrated process of feeling that harmonizes components according to the norm of beauty.

Chapter 5 characterizes beauty in terms of its form as a norm for synthesis of imagination, allowing experience to have the appearance of the world. Here, beauty is seen to characterize the subjectivity of experience. Chapter 6 characterizes beauty in terms of objects experienced as beautiful, analyzing perception as a form of valuation of the worth of objects within the larger background of synthesis. In this sense, we call *objects* beautiful. Chapter 7 characterizes beauty in terms of form, that is, of those things in experience that have the peculiar importance of together being able to harmonize a much larger field of objects; here, beauty is shown to be a special kind of value. Chapter 8 reveals beauty to be a foundational value of experience as a natural object. This is to say that experience itself has at least the positive value of beauty.

The question has been asked: Why should one improve one's images so that engagement with the world will be more beautiful? The answer is, beauty of experience is a value greatly worth enhancing. Why should one be engaged rather than alienated? Because the beauty of engaged experience makes for a better life. Where engagement is alienated, one's experiential background is blighted in some way, or one's focus of experience lacks coherence or intensity, or a host of other unaesthetic properties obtain. When another question is asked, Why should one enhance basic values?, the questioning has moved to the moral sphere: because a person should do the best that a person can.

The point of this chapter is that human imagination—hence engagement—has something of a moral quality to it, precisely because it is, in part, the product of human freedom; to some degree, for better or worse, it can be controlled. Therefore, in having a cultivated imagination—which humans have had to some extent since the beginning of culture—one's imagination is ruled by norms governing intentionality. Morality is the governance of intentionality by norms. The specific norm for imagination is beauty.

At this point we should recall that the function of a theory is to allow the subject matter to be envisioned. Its chief arguments, then, are persuasive definitions of words that enable envisionment. The word *beauty* has been pushed far beyond its commonsense connotations in this discussion, although there is solid precedent in the Western philosophical tradition for most of the special connotations suggested here. The plea for extending the meaning of the word this way is that to do so carries connotations that lend themselves to envisioning the role of values in imagination. The difficulty with this strategy is that, in order to gain a rich sense of the envisioning theoretical concept, one must trace the piecemeal defenses of accretions of meaning to the concept. This is a difficulty philosophy is designed to confront.

Art as the Organ of Responsibility

It is argued above that art is: (1) a higher level of experience involving deliberate creativity of images; (2) an analog for responsible control of imagination at levels more physiological in imagery; and (3) an instrument for cultivating responsible imagery. How is all this to be viewed theoretically?

Artistic activity is an intentional activity dealing with the subjective development of the image structure of experience (it may also involve much more than this). As is true among the higher levels of experience, artistic activity involves a complex process of abstraction whereby propositional feelings act as lures for the development of concrete imagery. The artistic propositional feelings are those that assert of the experience to be formed imaginatively a set of elements as the important forms for harmony. A host of such propositions can be formed for the same experience; this is why art presents alternate ways of imaging. The subjective form of artistic propositions is not to assert a truth about the experience to be imaged, but to assert a judgment of what might be important for harmonizing the experience.

A person's experience can be formed imaginatively without artistic propositions. In this case, the pattern of experience with the formative elements is simply inherited from previous experience, or it results from some combination that is adventitious with respect to a deliberate attempt to image well. When a person's experience is formed in part by means of artistic propositions, the process of forming the experience has itself, not merely the inherited antecedents, as a relevant, responsible cause. The resulting imagery involves a contrast between artistic propositions present in their subjective form as specially created as potential lures, and the rest of the material imaged, which would have a different form were it not for artistic propositions. When this occurs, the experiencer is partly responsible.

Most images are the result, not of the sheer creativity of the individual experiencer in the moment, but of previous experience—often experience by others. A sculptor, for instance, creates a sculpture whose form presents an image. A person living with the sculpture then slowly can take on the image in the art as one of the components in his or her repertoire of images for engaging the world. What the individual necessarily contributes, however, and which does not derive from external artists, is the existential function an image plays in personal experience. To be sure, part of the form an image has is its readiness to fit into some experience but not others. To adopt an artist's image for seeing the world itself, however, requires some artistry; the old claim has merit: that appreciating a work of art requires something of a recapitulation of the experience of producing it.

Most of the images employed in experience are inherited by individuals from culture; perhaps the bulk of them are from language. For most people, perhaps, the imagery of their experience is so reflective of the culture that it can be understood only in terms of cultural experience. Because of this, it is possible to speak of the imagery of a group as well as of individuals. But the *critical* use of images comes from art, for art is the activity that creates alternate images and presents them as worthy. One of the major social functions of art, therefore, is the creation of alternate images so social imagery can be recognized and judged. Asking whether an artistic creation replaces an old image is one of the social functions of morality, based on judgment about the vitality of the engagement. Art's social function alone does not lead to judgments about the appropriateness of images for adoption in experience, although individual artists present their work as containing vital images.

That an image deriving from art (or elsewhere) is adopted means that the adopting experience contains a complex proposition whose pattern includes a contrast between the artistic image and the form in the concrete appearance. The contrast involves this subjective form—namely, that the artistic image expresses a worthy schematization of the normative measure for the components in the experience and that the concrete appearance has the image because it is worthwhile to have it. That is, the experience includes a concrete appearance with an image whose subjective form includes taking responsibility for the imagery in the appearance. Once an image has been adopted and made part of the way one engages the world, the subjective form of responsibility may fade into the background; henceforth, the image is simply inherited until called into question.

It is argued above that art is a higher level of experience, an analog for responsible control of imagination, and an instrument for cultivating responsible imagery. Artistic activity is a higher level of experience in the sense that it involves the development of abstract propositions that may be examined as potential lures for engagement, comparing the freely wrought propositions as alternatives and judging their fitness. Artistic activity is an analog for responsible control of imagination at other levels because, as artists must find alternate images in their media, so responsibility requires experiencing engagement with the world in alternate ways. As art produces its images not according to rules or compulsion but with significance measures of spontaneity, so does the discipline of cultivating alternate experiences. And as art involves judgment of the aesthetic fitness of its alternate productions, so taking responsibility for images in general requires judgments, normed by beauty, about how to engage the world, given alternatives.

Art is an instrument for cultivating responsible imagery, in the sense that responsiveness to art can show us how we image the world for engagement and what some of the alternatives are. The response to art as such, however, need not involve the actual transformation of our imagery, even when we see that it should be transformed; such transformation might involve altering the whole rank of factors inherited from past character, moment by moment. One might be tempted to say that if the art is genuine, the proper response to it is to make that transformation. But that probably demands too much of the artistic response. After all, the connoisseur is one who has cultivated the capacity to experience a work of art in protection from the rest of his or her personality; otherwise, one could not make a pure response to the art or to its own value.

From the theoretical standpoint of cosmology, art is defined in a broader way than that ordinarily compassed by the phrase "fine arts." For, art would be any activity that intentionally creates alternate images and offers them as worthy means of engaging the world. Besides the fine arts, this includes any critical discipline that exercises creativity regarding images, as well as the disciplines of self-knowledge and transformation.

The fine arts do occupy a special place. More than the other arts, fine artists are conscious of the task of image-making and how it alters experience. The other disciplines are more apt to confuse the image-making function with other aspects of their task—for instance, analysis, explanation, critical evaluation, or other forms of interpretation. The fine arts, therefore, are the epitome of the civilized effort to criticize imagination.

RESPONSIBILITIES OF IMAGINATION

In this argument is presented a theoretical statement of what experience is, as a natural phenomenon, such that it engages the world through imagination and such that we can take responsibility for engaging the world as well as possible. What does this mean concretely? What is the character of imagination in the twentieth century. What is the critical role of art?

Twentieth-Century Art as Critic of Imagination

Western art, as it often was in the past, is, in the twentieth century, an extraordinarily complex tissue of movements. Many movements seem at the time to be continuous with and an extension of the main currents of European art through the ages; others seem to be fairly radical innovations. From our own perspective, it is difficult, if not impossible, to determine which will ultimately be the dominant and determinative movements in this century. There has been little enough unanimity about what is perceived as dominant within its own time. But certain fairly common features do stand out as indicative of the role of art in criticizing images. The discussion here is directed primarily at the imagery within Western civilization and its art.

The First Feature: Revolt against Technocracy. First is the rebellion against the imagery of industrial society that has grown into giantistic, technological forms of life. *The Education of Henry Adams,* a work solidly within the image life of Western tradition, essayed to understand the twentieth century by replacing the image of the Virgin with that of the dynamo, the electric power generator.[6] Contrast this with the music of Charles Ives, a younger contemporary of Adams, which largely rejects industrial, technological imagery and builds an image from a collage of small-town, religious, and patriotic themes. Ives's music is thoroughly part of the twentieth-century, innovative and prophetic in its handling of the themes, radically inventive in its own musical imagery, but insistent that the worthy twentieth-century image must be wrought from elements of the past that were not caught up in industrial-technological development. French painting of the late nineteenth and early twentieth centuries transformed itself by adapting the images of primitivism and Oriental art. Witness Gaugin and Picasso. The "fauves" in painting were followed after the First World War by *Les Six* who, in the words of John Tasker Howard and James Lyons, "led a reaction against the 'eloquence' of Cesar Franck, the impressionism of Debussy, and what they termed the 'scholasticism' of Vincent d'Indy. They adopted American jazz and imitated the music-hall style," idioms considered alien to "serious music."[7]

Primitivism in early twentieth-century music found a responsive feeling in dance with the Stravinsky–Diaghilev collaboration in *The Firebird, Petrouchka, The Rite of Spring*, and *Les Noces*. Modern dance developed primitivistic movements among its primary images in the long career of Martha Graham. Choreographers such as Alvin Ailey have developed American primitivism, and Kazuko Hirabayashi has combined the Graham technique with images from Japanese dance theater. Dramatic theater itself has perhaps been slower than other arts to rebel against the images of a developing industrial society and its problems. With Ionesco's theater of the absurd, however, this tradition has been purged of its seriousness, and with Artaud's advocacy of pagan violence, primitivism perhaps reached its most extreme artistic expression. Fiction has explored the insanity of the dominant images of twentieth-century technological, bureaucratic culture. One thinks of the imagery of Kafka's cockroach, of Sartre's nausea, and of Camus's images of sheer affirmation bringing meaning to a world in which he could find no authoritative worth.

Even in many cases the lifestyles of artists came to be associated with a rejection of traditional culture, with Bohemianism, "beat" wandering, and generally, with a stance of social criticism. It is a fairly common feature of the art of this century to reject the imagery generated by the development of industrial-technological culture and represented by dominant nineteenth-century movements in art.

The Second Feature: Modernist Abstraction. The second feature is a characteristic tendency of twentieth-century art toward modernist abstraction. Here, 'abstraction' means the isolation and treatment of a specifically limited set of images compared with the richer imagery of the art against which twentieth-century art has reacted. The clearest examples are in painting, beginning with the impressionists' interest in color and texture in contrast with 'realistic' portrayal. Cubism abstracted the images of spatial planes, surrealism the element of unconscious imagery in artistic representation, abstract expressionism the elements of emotion, Albers and the Hard Edge school the elements of color. Dance has moved from the romantic representationalism of nineteenth-century ballet dramas to abstract painterly movements a la Balanchine and the focus on emotions and the physicality of movement itself in Graham and Cunningham. Even the dramatic, realistic choreography of Jerome Robbins in *West Side Story* presents a narrowly focused prism of dance idioms. Primitivism itself leads to a kind of abstraction when considered against the background of nineteenth-century European art, for it disassembles the sense of totality formed by a story line and related to cumulative meaning in terms of the human ego. Twentieth-century temporal arts—dance, music, and drama—employ the imagery of collage more than they do images with a story form; even when there is a story line, the flashback is a prominent image for ordering, an innovation made popular through film (though used by such novelists as Faulkner).

The artistic importance of abstraction comes from the sense on the part of artists that, because concrete life is nonhistorical, images themselves must be isolated and explored before they can be related to concrete life.[8] One is tempted to say that twentieth-century art represents the fragmentation of contemporary life—and this may be true. But beyond this is the artistic sense that images of worth are those that can be explored on their own terms. If the gestalt of imagery in the industrial-technological trend of society is corrupt or alienating, what are the resources for a better alternative? The post-modernist answer can only be: the *parts* of that traditional gestalt and the images of other cultures; yet both must be held up for judgment about how to engage the life we have, which, indeed, is predominantly technological.

The Third Feature: Media. The arts have exploited new media and expanded the uses of old media. Paints are troweled, poured, or blown onto canvases. Pianos have their strings plucked by hand or damped by sticks or sheet music. Sculptors build with steel, reconstruct found objects, drape cliffs with cellophane, run fences from the mountains to the sea. In *Density 21,* Edgar Varese broke the image of the flute's tone as continuous in timbre from the lowest octave through the middle to the highest, replacing it with a cellolike quality in the lower register, a whistle timbre in the upper, and a conventional sound in the middle. Contrast this with the continuity in octaves of Debussy's *Syrinx.* The revival of small-ensemble music in this century has coincided with an exploration of the nontraditional sounds instruments are capable of. In musical composition the traditional tonal sense has been altered by the polytonic music of Ives in his *Over the Pavements* and Stravinsky in *Petrouchka.* It has been altered more by Schoenberg's twelve-tone row and by the even more radical sense of musical syntax in Elliot

Carter, Karlheinz Stockhausen, George Crumb, and, most of all, Krzysztof Penderecki, whose *Kosmogonia* is the most serious advance in religious music since Bach.

Perhaps architecture, more than any other art, has had new vistas opened by the development of new media. Many things are important in the development of new media. The new media are often technological innovations which themselves form an important part of the environment. Therefore, the artistic epitomization of the images they can express is a way of humanizing and interpreting them. Also, new media can be used to express old images; in so doing, one comes to understand something of the universality of the images involved. Further, the development of new artistic media adds to the richness of life. As would be expected, artists working with new media or new combinations of media are often accused of lacking the depth available to traditional media. While this accusation may be well taken as regards some intrinsic quality of the art, it may miss the point of the importance of exploring new media. Because their medium is new, and despite their universality, the images expressed in new media show new possibilities for the images of engagement.

The Fourth Feature: Warm and Cool Art. There seems to have been something of an oscillation between what may be called the warm and the cool. The warm in art presents the human sensibilities as involved and immediate, and its image expressed in art—no matter how abstract—involves a passionate engagement of the world. The cool is somewhat detached, in control, self-moving but unmoved, and analytic. Stravinsky's early primitive work exemplifies the warm, his later neoclassical work the cool. Jackson Pollack is warm, Joseph Albers cool. Frank Lloyd Wright's architecture is warm, Bauhaus buildings cool; Graham's dances warm, Ballanchine's cool.

This oscillation expresses what must be a characteristic of the imagery of the twentieth century—namely, the tension between engaging the technological world with an embrace or with detachment. From the standpoint of imagination, both are engaging. With respect to content of imagination, the warm imagery suggests that, however we react to the world, we are part of it and potentially at home. The cool imagery suggests that the contemporary world is habitable only if we somehow rise above it through control and "playing it cool."

This oscillation raises the question, Can people live in the world *they have made*? This differs from the question of the Renaissance: Do people reflect in themselves all the dimensions of the cosmos? And from the question of the Middle Ages, Does the universe provide a place for human kind in which the fleeting joys and ever-present suffering and spectre of death have transcendent meaning?

The Fifth Feature: Scale. Much of twentieth-century art has been concerned to provide an image of human life in a technological and natural
environment that seems out of scale. How can people fail to be dwarfed by
buildings as large and impersonal as the Lever Brothers Building or the
World Trade Center? The response has been to fill the public spaces with
ten-feet-by-thirty-feet abstract paintings that declare the images of human
experience—its emotions, color, and spatial senses, its controlled arrangement of nature—to be the patina of technology. The sculptures of David
Smith and Louise Nevelson do the same thing. The music of Stockhausen,
Crumb, and Penderecki images human life in the sounds of technological
society. Existentialist drama provides a way of engaging the contemporary
world; though nihilistic, it has the effect of domesticating alienation.

Relativity is an essential feature for imagery in the environment of
twentieth-century science. A cubist painting presents an object whose visage
is not unified by the perspective of the observer but whose integrity is the
unification of what it is from many perspectives; the object is a sum of
perspectives, not a single entity to be grasped from a single perspective.
Musical sound is also a process combining many perspectives.

The lesson of relativity, of constant change and shifting of the relations that give position to life, has been learned not only from physics but
from politics, religion, and now art. If any one thing stands out as important
in the artistic images of this century, it is that life is in process, that the
lineage of things irregularly shifts, and that perspectives are all relative. The
heroic position which in the nineteenth century determined the contours of
meaning is now the antihero *whose position can determine nothing*. One of
the messages of twentieth-century art, if we may speak that way, is that the
world cannot be engaged authentically with an imagery whose coherence
comes from an absolute perspective for the subject. Rather, an adequate
imagery must engage both the fluxes of the world and the strands of the self
as interweaving in an ever-changing harmony.

One may not like this conclusion, and one may lament the passing of
vitality in images of stable perspective. But if the movements of twentieth-
century art are genuine, there is something wrong with the images of stable
perspective.

Responsibility in Critique of Art

There is an element of criticism built into the artistic process, for the
imagic alternatives produced are compared and appreciated. At the same
time, there may be a kind of amorality in what is otherwise an authentic

artistic process. An artist can produce a work that images the world with worthy engagement in one respect but which in other respects is unworthy. T. S. Eliot and Ezra Pound, for instance, were peers in poetic power, yet they expressed ideologies that are poles apart. Perhaps those aspects of their poetry in which they disagreed ideologically are irrelevant to the ways their images engage the world; perhaps those differences are "merely" moral and can share complementary imagic bases. It is the critic's function to determine whether this is so.

A critic is one who objectifies a work of art as art and assesses it in various relevant dimensions, distinguishing, as the case may be, the imagic qualities of art from didactic content or usefulness for social programs. Criticism has various levels. The most basic, perhaps, is that a critic "describes" a work of art by saying what is important in it; that is, the critic lifts out the imagery in the work. Description of imagery is usually a re-creation of the image in another medium, that of discursive prose. Because images are universal, this is possible. Because images are also particular, however, there is something lost in the move from a medium of one character, the visual field of a painting for instance, to the medium of prose. There are two special advantages to the prose medium. One is that most people are comfortable understanding in that medium; the other is that its structure allows for quick connection with other relevant considerations. For instance, expressions of visual imagery can be related verbally to didactic content, to moral considerations, to a discussion of the history and genre of the painting, to social meaning. Description of a work is, in a sense, an artistic activity because the critic is stating the imagery of the work of art in a new medium. Critical description is a form of re-presentation.

Beyond description is the critical level of judging whether the artistic image in fact engages life vitally. In part, this judgment can be made in terms of proximate experiential responsiveness to the art. This is a necessary part; but precisely because engagement with the world is problematic, the critic must ask what valid engagement consists in, and this inquiry must move through countless corridors of explanation, psychological and social interpretation, and moral judgment. Although one's images constitute the means through which one engages the world experientially, and although this is a precondition for questions of truth, morality, and the other values of life, these values are affected by one's images. Therefore, the interpretation and criticism of those images must bring those values to bear on the question of the beauty of engagement. From the critical viewpoint, art cannot be for art's sake but for life's sake, and life's values are multifarious.

To be responsible for our images, then, requires that we engage in criticism of the arts for the purpose of changing images. As a society, we require and support critics. Individually, we may learn from them. On a

personal level, criticism must be a self-reflective, individual function if we
are to be responsible for our own images. That is to say, responsibility in
imagination requires interpretation of images and of the process of improv-
ing them. Imagination needs critical interpretation to be responsible as imagination. Responsible engagement has the detachment of interpretation
built in.

The concreteness of art and imagination should not be obscured by the
observation that responsibility requires interpretation. Interpretation is a process that involves moving away from something and replacing it by a sign
from which one then moves to find meaning. Imagination, by contrast, is
having the world immediately; it is the world itself being experienced in
activity, appreciation, and play. Whereas it might contain interpretive elements, as is the case if one engages with images for which one has taken
responsibility, the interpretive elements have been re-incorporated in the
concrete image. If one's activity is interpreting, then one's relevant image is
the material reality of the interpreting, not its meaning. Taken together,
one's images constitute the important parts of the concrete world being experienced.

Philosophy: The Critique of Critiques?

Whitehead said that one of philosophy's roles is to be the critic of
abstractions.[9] In the present context, this can mean that philosophy is the
critic of critics, the need for which is a natural extension of the critical
process itself. But in its function of critique, philosophy is also a peculiar
way of engaging the world. Images in philosophy, then, are of crucial importance for a culture's responsibility to its imagery. This raises the question
of what philosophy's own imagery has been in this century.

Contemporary philosophy has been divided into camps separated by
gulfs in imagery. Although a fairly traditional range of doctrines—idealism,
materialism, nominalism, realism, and so on—are represented within each
major contemporary tradition, the separation of traditions is more important
than the doctrinal options they share. Philosophers find it difficult to communicate with colleagues in other traditions, to take their positions seriously, to engage their arguments as if they made a difference to one's own
view, or even to consider that the others are doing philosophy as one defines
the term. The reason for this is that with different imageries, the traditions
engage the world differently. Philosophy, then, must indeed be different in
each case, different forms of engagement. This is a deeper gulf than can be
bridged with arguments about truth claims or about theories, for the arguments themselves are different kinds of activities according to different im-

ageries for engaging the world. Even when there is apparent verbal agreement about arguments or theories, the agreement is deceptive when it crosses traditions. The way an analytic philosopher engages the world with an argument is simply different from the way a phenomenologist engages the world with the same verbal argument.

The diversity of philosophical imageries presents a serious problem for any attempt to speak to the professional philosophical public about issues of thinking. To argue for a theory of imagination, as many chapters in this book do, is to imply that the imagery employed in engaging "imagination" is the best philosophical imagery, or at least better than the understood alternatives. The implication can be supported by reflecting, as critics, on the imagery of analytic philosophy, of phenomenology, and of process philosophy.

Analytic Philosophy. Despite great variation in approach and doctrine, most analytic philosophers fix on the image of the "statement" or proposition, for engaging the world. Statements are analyzed for their formal logical properties, their status within theories, their relation to the world. When analyzing concrete moral problems, analytic philosophers say, "We would say X about Y; we wouldn't say $X_1{}^1$." The analysis then shows its quickest explanatory tie to be to language and speaking rather than to the causal or moral contours of the subject matter. The existential justification for this is simply that it is the imagery of the analytic tradition of philosophy, and that this imagery is the most genuine philosophic engagement of the world; that is, modernism in style is *true,* analysis asserts.

By and large, the five features noted for art in this century hold for its philosophy, and analytic philosophy is no exception.

Analytic philosophy was, first of all, characterized by a rebellion against the imagery of earlier philosophy. Moore and Russell in Britain, Frege and the Vienna Circle on the Continent, and Lewis and Quine in America all construed the preceding idealist establishment in philosophy to be disengaged, alienated. "Gassy" is the word frequently used. The early analytical philosophers believed that the imagery of the idealists was too fraught with linear arguments that led far away from what, in fact, can be known. The idealist concern with system, necessity, and the "whole" bespoke a frictionless slippage of thought over the path of concrete knowledge. The imagery of knowledge itself had to be close to science, the analysts thought, and to reflection about the process of making moral judgments.

Like the artists, analytical philosophers moved to abstraction in developing their imagery. Here, *abstraction* does not refer to concepts (the idealists had very abstract concepts), but to problems. The analysts believed that engagement is genuine when it takes on one problem at a time, separating that problem from the others. The idealists thought a person cannot deal with one problem without dealing with them all. The imagery associated with "analytic" in "analytic philosophy" means that philosophic activity is engaged when it is analyzing the problem at hand, rather than when it is interpreting the problem in terms of the rest of life. The abstraction of analysis went hand in hand with imagery's focus on statements, for statements are supposed to have meanings that can themselves be understood. More recently, analytic philosophers have focused on statements *within* theories or special languages.

The new medium for analytic philosophy is logic. Although serious divisions remain between ordinary and formal-language analysts, generally, both may be said to concern themselves with expressing philosophical problems, arguments, and positions in logical terms. It is often suggested that a philosophical problem is not engaged unless it can be expressed in a logical statement; sometimes even expression in symbolic logic is thought helpful.

The significance of the above statement can be grasped by noting the kinds of philosophical engagements that are excluded by this imagery. It is not that other philosophers might want to say something logically contradictory; rather, they might use philosophical language poetically to bring experiences to the fore, or suggestively and analogically to create continuities of thought, or speculatively to establish a different perspective on the world. Analytic philosophers would tend to see these alleged linguistic engagements of the world as nonphilosophical because they do not necessarily employ the virtues of logic—that is, clarity and inference. Of the many kinds of philosophical engagement advocated in this book, analytic philosophers would tend to approve only theoretical inference, where an abstractly formulated theory or a language construed as a system is presupposed as the ground within which statements can be judged to be well formed. To be sure, analytic philosophers use many older media of philosophy as well as symbolic logic, as they must when arguing for the worthiness of logic.

Whereas twentieth-century art has oscillated between cool and warm engagements with life, the imagery of analytic philosophy has generally been cool. Philosophy is a detached, public engagement ready to change course with significant arguments and subject to professional discipline. The cool professional is the analytic image of the philosopher. The striking feature of this imagery, however, is that it divides the life of the philosopher into professional activity, on one hand, and the rest of life on the other. In nonprofessional contexts, analytic philosophers can be passionate devotees of the arts, ardent lovers, political advocates; Bertrand Russell was the stellar cool professional with the hot-blooded lifestyle. Separation like this of philosophic professionalism from the rest of life is rare in the history of philosophy. For most periods, philosophy has been thought to require a lifestyle integral to the philosophy. Whereas some analytic philosophers engage the philosophic issues only in the public realm of language, subject to what counts for speaking well, most other philosophers believe they must transform their whole lives to engage the world philosophically, or at least that philosophical engagement would lead to their own personal transformation.

Analytic philosophy's images of human life in technological society are striking. There is, first, the sense that a person can engage the real philosophic issues only as a professional, with disciplinary and psychological boundaries around one's craft. There is the correlative sense that other disciplines engage the world in other ways, and that those ways may greatly overshadow philosophy. Science, for instance, is often viewed as the kind of engagement philosophy used to think it had itself but to which it must now attach itself parasitically. Whereas philosophy engages through the analysis of statements, it depends on others for the development of the statements—at least, for its first-order business to begin. More than any other contemporary school of philosophy, analysis believes that people best engage life in a technological society *as professionals*. For analytic philosophy, the relativity of life means that no discipline, especially philosophy, can hope to engage the whole of things and that the best course is a division of labor. What is true of analytic philosophy is true of all schools that press professionalism as a comfortable style.

These remarks about analytic philosophy—and those to come, about phenomenology and process philosophy—are crude generalizations with many exceptions. Surely, many analytic philosophers hold to doctrines that contravene what is expressed here as a commitment of imagery. But even when such philosophers as Wilfrid Sellars advocate the importance of metaphysical systems, they do so in a mode that engages system abstractly. To put it technically, the analytic approach through statements is extremely vague, leaving out most information for determining concrete things. Ask Kripke, "But what about Napoleon?", and he would say that is an irrelevant and nonphilosophic question; Hegel, however, would have a ready philosophical answer.

Phenomenology. By contrast with analytic philosophy, consider the imagery of phenomenology, the other main school contending for dominance in America. The main sense of engagement in phenomenology seems to be "getting back to basics." This is expressed most clearly perhaps in Husserl's attempt to find a presuppositionless foundation for the sciences. It is pursued in different ways by Heidegger, for whom the search for a foundation was a search for being.

To treat philosophy as the search for a foundation is a way of rebelling against what is perceived as the unsubstantiated imagery of the past. Whereas analytic philosophy, by and large, identifies its past with professional philosophers, Husserl and his followers rebelled against the imagery of European culture. Along with the analytic philosophers, Husserl believed that science was the source of close-at-hand, tactile knowledge; but he thought that science's self-presentation was ungrounded and that its claims could not be taken at face value without philosophical underpinnings. Heidegger was more radical, claiming that the imagery of the developing culture of science does corrupt human life if not shown to have a finite place with respect to a more basic experience of being. For Heidegger, getting back to basics meant a destructuring of the historical Western tradition. For Husserlians, a preoccupation with statements is not genuine engagement because it is not reflective of the activity of grounding the statements in a plain description of consciousness. For Heideggerians, such a preoccupation would not be philosophical, because it merely reflects the outcome of rootless technological culture: "professional philosophy" means the abdication of philosophy to the image of technician.

Phenomenology moved to abstraction by insisting that its philosophical engagement bracket off questions most other philosophers had found important, namely questions about existential reality and theoretical explanation. After transcendental and empirical descriptions of consciousness had been given, existential and explanatory questions could be referred to science. For Heidegger, this line of abstraction took a peculiar turn, for what is bracketed out are the questions of evaluation that suppose a distinction between the real, the opined, and the normative. Philosophy is engaged when it attempts to open up a level of experience prior to this distinction. Although phenomenology and analytic philosophy disagree about the proper content for philosophic engagement, they agree in distinguishing philosophy's proper engagement from that of science.

If one can speak of a new medium for phenomenology, it is that of the method of pure description, that is, the bracketing of existential and explanatory considerations and the simple description of the essences making up the content of consciousness on transcendental and empirical levels. (Heidegger did not share in this new medium; instead, he developed his own method of historical analysis.) Since Husserl, the notion of a pure description has received some severe criticisms; but without making claims for purity, phenomenologists have engaged in the journeyman work of description.

Because of their sense of the importance of history for philosophical engagement, some phenomenologists have tended to be warm rather than cool in their engagement. Perhaps because Husserl identified with the sciences, he is considered the coolest of the major phenomenologists. But Scheler was as warm as philosophers come. Heidegger wrote with such a passionate conviction that one is what one knows (or is not insofar as one knows not) that philosophy for him *is* the transformation of character attendant upon arriving at an encounter with being. For Heidegger, it may be said that one engages life fully only insofar as one engages it philosophically.

Phenomenologists agree with analytic philosophers that the most important challenge for human engagement in the twentieth century is the humanization of technological society. There is little agreement among phenomenologists about the direct merits of technology, but there is agreement that the way to humanize it is to see it in light of what is more fundamental. For Husserl, this is primarily epistemological, whereas, for Heidegger, it is profoundly moral. For most phenomenologists whatever the foundation they seek, the philosophic engagement with the foundation is a crucial underpinning for the rest of life. Since this affects everyone, they cannot accept the division of labor into professional philosophers versus others but must argue that everyone must attend to the philosophic dimension of life. Of course, only professional philosophers might be genuinely creative in the field, but everyone in a culture should attend to experiencing themselves relative to their foundations.

Process Philosophy. Process philosophers, the third group whose imagery is discussed, agree with both analytic and phenomenological philosophers about the need to overcome the imagery of the past. They agree with the phenomenologists that the relevant object of rebellion is the imagery of industrial-technological culture, not merely of nineteenth-century philosophers. Their dominant image of philosophy, however, is that one should engage the world with the contrast of aesthetic feeling and abstract theory. Whatever the object of one's philosophic analysis, it is engaged philosophically when attended to with both an aesthetic sense of continuity with all experience and a cosmological theory of which the object can be shown to be an example. This somewhat misstates the image, however; keeping aesthetics and theory together requires the philosophic process of criticism. As mentioned above, philosophy for Whitehead is the critic of abstractions. It does this by exaggerating (from the viewpoint of other traditions) the concrete immediacy of aesthetic feeling and the abstraction of cosmological theory. There is a tendency in recent process philosophy to neglect the aesthetic side and indulge in a kind of scholastic interpretation of Whitehead's cosmology. There is also a tendency in a different group to neglect the sharp categoreal thinking of cosmology in favor of poetic statements of the aesthetics of process. But Whitehead's own philosophic engagement, generally honored by process philosophers, binds aesthetics and abstract cosmology in the critical process of interpretation. Although one may occasionally employ language peculiar to cosmology or aesthetics, such discussion is not fully engaged philosophy unless it is situated in a dialectic connecting it with the rest of the matter.

Whitehead's rebellion against previous imagery, then, was two-sided. On one hand, both philosophy and culture had lost the sense of concrete immediacy needed to prevent technology from cheapening life; philosophy engages life by criticizing this. On the other hand, both philosophy and culture had assumed that the most general and authoritative abstract theory was that in science. Philosophy engages the technological world by developing a cosmology that itself embraces science and its limitations. Philosophy cannot engage in these two ways without incorporating them in a general critical process relating both to concrete affairs.

Like much twentieth-century art, process philosophy involves abstraction, abstraction of cosmology; but it does so in a contrast with expressions of aesthetic experience. It values the abstract for its capacity of showing what is concrete about concrete experience. Process philosophy takes the focus on the logic of statements, particularly the language of symbolic logic, to be a false abstraction. The crucial philosophical engagements have to do with how language stands in between the near ineffability of aesthetic feeling and the empty purity of abstract cosmology. Language is used to broaden experience so that it embraces both poles. Similarly, process philosophy looks on description as a false abstraction. The relation between the aesthetic field and the categories in which it is described is always dialectical, subject to a host of considerations including those of existential reference and explanation. Consciousness itself was not an important category for Whitehead and most process philosophers.

Process philosophers would probably disclaim much interest in new philosophical media, arguing that the immediacy of concrete feeling and the synoptic vision of cosmology should include all new media between them (else they are deficient). The practice of process philosophy reveals that it employs the medium of argument by collage. This involves in Whitehead's arguments, sections on the historical development of materialism followed immediately by an analysis of poetry, followed by a technical exposition of the cosmological categories of change, value, eternal objects, endurance, organism, and interfusion.[10] There is neither a logical nor a dramatic order to this exposition. Rather, the parts are different aspects of philosophical engagement that must be juxtaposed. Philosophical thinking is ordered not by the sequences of argument but by the cumulative effect of different dimensions of the philosophic task. In this sense, the medium of process philosophy bears close resemblance to the artistic media of assemblage practiced in so many twentieth-century art forms, and stands somewhat opposed to more traditional forms of philosophical argument which it views as partial philosophic engagements.

The complexity of levels of abstraction in process philosophy runs the gamut from the cool to the warm as modes of engagement. Technical discussions of the categories in cosmology is a cool professional task, requiring expertise and unfortunately being accessible only to those willing to think their way through technical materials. One's discussion of cosmological matters is thoroughly public and open to criticism by one's peers. On the other hand, the aesthetic dimension of experience as embraced by process philosophy is extraordinarily nontechnical and warm. As Whitehead put it, one's honest response on first seeing Niagara Falls should be "Ohh, isn't it beautiful!" Most philosophical activity is a movement between these extremes of temperature. This image of philosophy cannot fix a single temperature for engagement; it suggests engagement is a multifaceted affair spread out in time, with more juxtapositions than continuities.

The image of life in technological society that guides engagement in process philosophy is that of professional life with aesthetic culture. Rationality can deal with technology if rationality is an art and employs the culture of art. With a cultivated aesthetic sense, individuals can grasp the continuities of the world. With their disciplined professional skills they attain the limitation and narrowness required for intensity of life. Agreeing explicitly with the main drift of twentieth-century science and art, process philosophy construes all positions, including philosophical positions, to be relative. Therefore, the approaches to the world from the perspectives of different disciplines add richness to experience, not fragmentation, unless the continuities of aesthetics are also lost. Process philosophers tend to engage the technological world optimistically, though with a Promethean sense of the integrating task of philosophy.

The imagery of this study so far is closer to process philosophy than to the others. This is particularly true in its use of a dialectical medium of presentation: phenomenology, criticism, theory, and public responsibility as essential modes for the treatment of the main topics. There is also agreement with process philosophy, in the theory of what philosophy's imagery should be. That is, the emphasis on the phenomenological presentation of problems corresponds roughly to the aesthetic moment for Whitehead, and the cosmology corresponds to his cosmological theory in intent if not in doctrine. But there are two major points at which the approach taken here stands apart from process philosophy.

First, although Whitehead made some remarkable observations about value in aesthetic, theoretical, and moral contexts, he did not develop extensively those notions when they applied to philosophy itself and its imagery. These eight chapters argue, on the contrary, that philosophical activity itself has a complex value and that philosophers have special responsibilities. Part of the imagery of this book, therefore, is deliberative and hortatory, as if it were a moral process. This may seem like preachment or like a politiciza-tion of philosophy; the intent of the imagery, however, is that philosophic inquiry engage the world as a special form of responsibility.

Second, the rather simple image of human life as professional, on one hand, and aesthetic, on the other, is seriously deficient with regard to the problems of constituting a community. One need not swing to the near-totalitarian extremes of Peirce's or Royce's notions of community to appreciate their point that neither aesthetics nor abstract theorizing can exist without public transactions. This is what is missing from Whitehead's image of life in the technological world. Part of the imagery of these chapters is the invitation of alternate positions to engage in dialog concerning the issues. The attempt has been made to criticize philosophers whose approaches are radically different in the hopes of establishing a wider community and to state positions in as vulnerable a way as possible. For vulnerability is of the essence of truth.

Notes

1. This highly focused simplification of the approach of the ancient Greeks to thinking stands out from a background of primary texts and modern commentaries too vast to mention. A general orientation to this literature can be found in, for instance, Newton P. Stalknecht and R. S. Brumbaugh, *The Spirit of Western Philosophy* (New York: Longmans, Green, 1950); brief summaries of the Greek philosophers, supporting the point, are found in Brumbaugh's *The Philosophers of Greece* (New York: Crowell, 1964; Albany: SUNY Press, 1981). For the simplified focus on qualitative and quantitative thought, and its relation to valuational thought discussed below in the text, I am indebted to conversations with Dr. Robert M. Veatch.

2. This comparison within Shakespeare was pointed out to me by Prof. Judah Stampfer. The Renaissance story can be told many ways. For a fascinating study of these issues in the representative thought of Robert Boyle, see Eugene M. Klaaren, *Religious Origins of Modern Science* (Grand Rapids: William B. Eerdmans, 1977).

3. For the former point, see Daniel Bell, *The End of Ideology* (New York: Free Press, 1962); for the latter, see Jürgen Habermas, *Theory and Practice,* trans. by John Viertel (Boston: Beacon Press, 1973), Introduction, chaps. 1, 7; also his *Legitimation Crisis,* trans. by Thomas McCarthy (Boston: Beacon Press, 1975), part 3.

4. Popular views about the status of philosophical ethics are usually a confusion of genuine relativism and subjectivism with cynicism and ethical dogmatism in certain areas. For a survey of philosophical opinions, see Joseph Margolis's anthology, *Contemporary Ethical Theory* (New York: Random House, 1966); for a detailed analysis of ethical theories focusing on this point, see Brand Blanshard, *Reason and Goodness* (New York: Macmillan, 1961).

5. This distinction is derived from Kant. See his *Critique of Judgment,* trans. by James Creed Meredith (Oxford: Oxford Univ. Press, 1928), part 1. Concerning claims to knowledge, there is always the possibility of dispute; but there is no disputing taste, it is said.

6. Wittgenstein, *Tractatus Logico-Philosophicus* (London: Routledge & Kegan Paul, 1922), p. 183, paragraphs 6.4–6.421.

313

7. For Peirce, see, for instance, "An Outline Classification of the Sciences" and "The Normative Science," both in *The Collected Papers of Charles Sanders Peirce*, ed. by Charles Hartshorne and Paul Weiss (Cambridge: Harvard Univ. Press, 1931–35), vol. 1, paragraphs 180–202 and 573–677, respectively. For James, see *Essays in Radical Empiricism* (New York: Longmans, Green and Co., 1912), chap. 5, "The Place of Affectional Facts in a World of Pure Experience." For Dewey, this theme pervades his corpus; see, for instance, *The Quest for Certainty* (New York: Minton, Balch & Co., 1929), esp. chaps. 8–11; *Experience and Nature* (2d. ed.; LaSalle, Ill.: Open Court Publishing Co., 1929), esp. chaps. 2–4, 9–10; *Theory of Valuation* (Chicago: Univ. of Chicago Press, 1939); *Art as Experience* (New York: Minton, Balch & Co., 1935).

8. See Whitehead's *Science and the Modern World* (New York: Macmillan, 1927), chaps. 5, 9, 11–13; and his *The Function of Reason* (Princeton: Princeton Univ. Press, 1929); also his *Modes of Thought* (New York: Macmillan, 1938).

9. See, for instance, Husserl's *Ideas*, trans. by W. R. Boyce Gibson (New York: Macmillan, 1931), esp. chap. 5. For Heidegger, see, for instance, *Being and Time*, trans. by John Macquarrie and Edward Robinson (London: SCM Press, 1962), div. 1. For Merleau-Ponty, see *Phenomenology of Perception*, trans. by Colin Smith (London: Routledge & Kegan Paul, 1962), part 2.

10. See Foucault, *The Archaeology of Knowledge*, trans. by A. M. Sheridan Smith (New York: Harper, 1976), where he asks:

> And now I should like to ask you a question: how do you see change, or, let us say, revolution, at least in the scientific order and in the field of discourses, if you link it with the themes of meaning, project, origin and return, constituent subject, in short with the entire thematic that ensures for history the universal presence of the Logos? . . . What is the fear which makes you reply in terms of consciousness when someone talks to you about a practice, its conditions, its rules, and its historical transformations? What is that fear which makes you seek, beyond all boundaries, ruptures, shifts, and divisions, the great historico-transcendental destiny of the Occident? (pp. 209f.)

Or see Derrida's *Of Grammatology*, trans. by Gayatri Spivak (Baltimore: Johns Hopkins Univ. Press, 1977).

11. Kline, *Mathematics: The Loss of Certainty* (New York: Oxford Univ. Press, 1980), pp. 4, 6.

12. Derrida writes:

> There are thus two interpretations of interpretation, of structure, of sign, of freeplay. The one seeks to decipher, dreams of deciphering, a truth or an origin which is free from freeplay and from the order of the sign, and lives like an exile the necessity of interpretation. The other, which is no longer turned toward the origin, affirms freeplay and tries to pass beyond man and humanism, the name man being the name of that being who, throughout the history of metaphysics or of ontotheology—in other words, through the history of all of his history—has dreamed of full presence, the reassuring foundation, the origin and the end of the game.

("Structure, Sign, and Play in the Discourse of the Human Sciences," in *The Languages of Criticism and the Sciences of Man,* ed. by Richard Macksey and Eugenio Donato (Baltimore: Johns Hopkins Univ. Press, 1970), pp. 264f. He also writes:

> This moment was that in which language invaded the universal problematic; that in which, in the absence of a center or origin, everything became discourse—provided we can agree on this word—that is to say, when everything became a system where the central signified, the original or transcendental signified, is never absolutely present outside a system of differences. The absence of the transcendental signified extends the domain and the interplay of signification *ad infinitum.*

(Ibid., p. 249.)

13. Gewirth, *Reason and Morality* (Chicago: Univ. of Chicago Press, 1978); see, for instance, p. 22:

> I use 'reason' in a strict sense as comprising only the canons of deductive and inductive logic, including among the latter its bases in particular sense perceptions. I also construe conceptual analysis on the model of deductive logic, in that when a complex concept A is analyzed as containing concepts B, C, and D, these concepts belong to A with logical necessity so that it is contradictory to hold that A applies while denying that B, C, or D applies. The concept of action, while representing actual phenomena of human conduct, will be obtained and used by such conceptual analysis. Although difficulties may be raised about the general justification of both deduction and induction, in the present context it must suffice to note that, because they respectively achieve logical necessity and reflect what is empirically ineluctable, deduction and induction are the only sure ways of avoiding arbitrariness and attaining objectivity and hence a correctness or truth that reflects not personal whims or prejudices but the requirements of the subject matter.

14. For representative works, see Weiss, *Modes of Being* (Carbondale: Southern Illinois Univ. Press, 1958), and *You, I, and the Others* (Carbondale: Southern Illinois Univ. Press, 1980); Hartshorne, *Creative Synthesis and Philosophic Method* (LaSalle: Open Court Publishing Co., 1970); and Buchler, *Metaphysics of Natural Complexes* (New York: Columbia Univ. Press, 1966).

15. See Putnam's *Meaning and the Moral Sciences* (London: Routledge & Kegan Paul, 1978); Saul Kripke's *Naming and Necessity* (Cambridge: Harvard Univ. Press, 1980); Toulmin's *Human Understanding: The Collective Use and Evolution of Concepts* (Princeton: Princeton Univ. Press, 1972). See also, Rozin, "The Evolution of Intelligence and Access to the Cognitive Unconscious," in *Progress in Psychobiology and Physiological Psychology,* vol. 6 (New York: Academic Press, 1976), 245–80.

16. For Scheler, see *The Nature of Sympathy,* trans. by Peter Heath (London: Routledge & Kegan Paul, 1958); see also, Ihde, *Listening and Voice: A Phenomenology of Sound* (Athens: Ohio Univ. Press, 1976).

17. See David L. Hall, *The Civilization of Experience* (New York: Fordham Univ. Press, 1973), and *The Uncertain Phoenix* (New York: Fordham Univ. Press, 1981).

18. See note 7 above. Richard Rorty, in his *Philosophy and the Mirror of Nature* (Princeton: Princeton Univ. Press, 1979), directs Dewey's critique against Anglo-American philosophy's development of the quest for certainty. Anglo-American, or "analytic", philosophy is not to be confused with American pragmatism and systematic philosophy.

19. Of the many studies of Hegel's concept of reason, perhaps the most succinct and historically well grounded is Quentin Lauer's "The Phenomenon of Reason," in his *Essays in Hegelian Dialectic* (New York: Fordham Univ. Press, 1977). Hegel's own text is the *Phenomenology of Spirit*, trans. by A. V. Miller (Oxford: Oxford Univ. Press, 1977).

20. This discussion of cosmology, and the more detailed one in Chapter 2, build on my earlier defense of "axiological cosmology" in *The Cosmology of Freedom* (New Haven: Yale Univ. Press, 1974), chaps. 2 and 3.

21. This is Foucault's main point in his *Archaeology of Knowledge* and one of Rorty's points in his *Philosophy and the Mirror of Nature*.

22. The bearing of the community on the distinction of reality from merely subjective experience, replete with an interpretation of Peirce, is incisively analyzed by John E. Smith in "Charles S. Peirce: Community and Reality," in his *Themes in American Philosophy: Purpose, Experience, and Community* (New York: Harper, 1970).

23. See, for instance, Toulmin, *Human Understanding*, pp. 85–96 passim; also Rorty, *Philosophy*.

CHAPTER 2   (Pages 33–66)

1. For a brilliant discussion of the historical category of "modernism," see Carl E. Schorske's *Fin-de-Siecle Vienna: Politics and Culture* (New York: Knopf, 1980).

2. Whitehead, *Process and Reality: An Essay in Cosmology* (New York: Macmillan, 1929), p. x. As will be apparent in what follows, the cosmology to be developed here builds on many of Whitehead's basic categories. Its deviations from Whitehead take three main directions. First, it thematizes the problem of value to a much greater extent than he did; thus it may be called an "axiological cosmology." Second, it rejects Whitehead's doctrine of God (for reasons largely irrelevant to this book), and therefore must provide alternate accounts of the functions God was supposed to perform in Whitehead's system; specifically, an alternate account of the development of subjective unity must be provided if Whitehead's notion of subjective aim deriving from God is rejected. Third, a distinction between essential and conditional features plays an important role in the present cosmology, a distinction that is lacking in Whitehead's cosmology. In this book, the cosmology is developed with a specific orientation to thinking. For a more general discussion with reference to Whitehead, see my *Cosmology of Freedom* (New Haven: Yale Univ. Press, 1974), part 1: "Freedom and Cosmology."

3. Kenneth E. Boulding, *The Image* (Ann Arbor: Univ. of Michigan Press, 1956). See also, Paul Rozin, "The Evolution of Intelligence and Access to the Cognitive Unconscious," in *Progress in Psychobiology and Physiological Psychology* (New York: Academic Press, 1976).

4. Patrick Heelan, distinguished philosopher, physicist, and theologian at SUNY Stony Brook, analyzes a fundamental kind of image, the basic geometries of

perception, in his *Space, Perception, and Science,* forthcoming.

5. The spatial dimensions of an image vary by so many factors that they are almost impossible to list. Art historians, psychoanalysts, perception psychologists, theologians, and journalists all interpret important variables of spatial dimensions of images.

6. See, for instance, John Mbiti's *African Religions and Philosophies* (Garden City: Doubleday Anchor, 1970; original ed., Praeger, 1969); also, Mircea Eliade's classic *The Sacred and the Profane,* trans. by W. R. Trask (New York: Harper, 1961), chap. 2.

7. The term *scheme* is an ordinary word to which a sharpened and somewhat special meaning is given in the text. A highly technical historical consideration lies behind the distinction between images and schemes, however. Kant (*Critique of Pure Reason,* B 179f.) distinguished between schema images, schemas, and concepts. By "concept" he meant an intellectual notion, for instance, that of a triangle. By "schema image" he meant a representation of that concept in consciousness, for instance, the mental image of a triangle having angles of certain degrees. A "schema" itself is the representation of the method for constructing an image (which is always particular) on the basis of a concept (which is always universal). It is a device of the imagination by which the concept of an enclosed plane figure with three angles can be represented by a mental image of a figure with three particular angles. In reverse, the schema allows us to see that a particular figure is a representation of the universal concept, even though figures quite unlike it, with very different angles, could also represent the concept. The schema of the concept triangle is the complex rule for drawing a triangle on a piece of paper with a straightedge. For Kant, it was a mystery how the imagination constructs and uses such schematic rules, although he was certain that it does.

The distinction in the text between images and schemas does not repeat Kant's exactly. Most of the content of images would be particular spatial, temporal, sensible, and emotional elements—for example, schema images. This particular content functions in something approaching universal ways for sorting information: they work similarly to analogies. Furthermore, images may include concepts that are clearly universal. A scheme, as the text explains, is made up of universal concepts, or categories. Taken in isolation, they are rather like Kant's "concepts." But a scheme functions as Kant's schemas do, to connect the multiplicity of particular experiences with the concepts that unify thought. A scheme is *expressed* through definitions and categoreal principles. It may even be *pictured* by vivid images and metaphors. A scheme is *understood,* however, in the mind's ability to interpret certain elements of experience—concrete or abstract—in terms of other elements and according to schematic rules. The rules are provided by the scheme's categoreal connections. Understanding the scheme is not the mere contemplation of the categoreal connections but the mental ability to connect experiences according to the scheme. The technical, philosophical difference between schemes and images, on one hand, and schemas, schema images, and concepts, on the other, probably lies in the text's adherence to abstractionist metaphors characteristic of the empiricist and rationalist traditions. Kant's "transcendental" philosophy was a conscious attempt to repudiate these traditions. Chapter 7 elaborates on Kant's notion of image.

As used here, "scheme" is a specialized kind of "theory," with the connotations not only of its intellectual content but of that content's relation to experience. The notion of theory is discussed in various places in the text. Instead of "scheme" or "theory" the term "model" could have been used. The current vogue in philosophical literature for "models" confuses the fairly general points raised in the text with debates arising out of a special history of philosophy over the last twenty years; see May Brodbeck's article on models in her *Readings in the Philosophy of the Social Sciences* (New York: Macmillan, 1967), pp. 579–600. The term "paradigm" could also have been used in the sense made popular by Thomas Kuhn in his *The Structure of Scientific Revolutions* (Chicago: Univ. of Chicago Press, 1962), namely, a theory plus all the assumptions about investigating the world according to it. The text, however, limits the use of paradigm to the meaning "prime instance or example." Besides its history in the Kantian distinction, the word "scheme" was used by Whitehead in almost the exact sense intended here; see *Process and Reality,* chap. 2, "The Categoreal Scheme."

8. See Peirce's "Issues of Pragmaticism," in *Collected Papers of Charles Sanders Peirce,* ed. by Hartshorne and Weiss (Cambridge: Harvard Univ. Press, 1934), vol. 5, paragraphs 447–50; and his "Consequences of Critical Common-Sensism," ibid., 505–506.

9. In Whitehead's cosmology, the basic unit of existence is an "actual occasion"; this is a vague concept because, without further information, it is impossible (even after the concept is explained) to apply it to individuals. For instance, is the bird outside the window an actual occasion? No, the bird is a certain system of such occasions. We would need information from common experience and ornithology to explain how the bird illustrates the category of actual occasions.

10. Wittgenstein, *Philosophical Investigations* (New York: Macmillan, 1953), trans. by G. E. M. Anscombe; paragraph numbers are given within the text of the quotations.

11. See, for instance, his *Tractatus Logico-Philosophicus* (London: Routledge & Kegan Paul, 1922), propositions 1, 1.1–1.21, 5.6–5.641, 6.373–7.

12. See the lucid account of Wittgenstein's intellectual context in Allan Janik and Stephen Toulmin, *Wittgenstein's Vienna* (New York: Simon and Schuster, 1973).

13. Citations of classical works are given in the text, referring to the standard book, chapter, or page rubrics that are common to all modern editions. Citations for direct quotations are by footnote.

14. This use of the word *society* is Whitehead's, who counts himself a modern Platonist in this regard. See his *Process and Reality,* part 1, chap. 3, sec. 2., passim. See also, Karl Popper, *The Open Society and Its Enemies* (5th ed.; Princeton: Princeton Univ. Press, 1966), vol. 1, *The Spell of Plato.*

15. Trans. by Francis MacDonald Cornford, *The Republic of Plato* (Oxford: Oxford Univ. Press, 1941), p. 356.

16. In *The Basic Works of Aristotle,* trans. by W. D. Ross (New York: Random House, 1941), ed. by Richard McKeon, p. 1104.

17. Speaking of the small remnant of philosophical souls who preserve their integrity, Plato said:

> And those who have been of this little company and have tasted the sweetness and blessedness of this possession and who have also come to understand the madness of the multitude sufficiently and have seen that there is nothing, if I may say so, sound or right in any present politics, and that there is no ally with those whose aid the champion of justice could escape destruction, but that he would be as a man who has fallen among wild beasts, unwilling to share their misdeeds and unable

to hold out singly against the savagery of all, and that he would thus, before he could in any way benefit his friends or the state, come to an untimely end without doing any good to himself or others—for all these reasons I say the philosopher remains quiet, minds his own affair, and, as it were, standing aside under shelter of a wall in a storm and blast of dust and sleet and seeing others filled full of lawlessness, is content if in any way he may keep himself free from iniquity and unholy deeds through this life and take his departure with fair hope, serene and well content when the end comes. . . . *He would not have accomplished any very great thing either,* I replied, if it were not his fortune to live in a state adapted to his nature. In such a state only will he himself rather attain his full stature and together with his own preserve the common-weal. (*Republic,* Book 6, 496c f.; italics added)

In *The Collected Dialogues of Plato,* trans. by Paul Shorey, ed. by Edith Hamilton and Huntington Cairnes (New York: Bollingen Foundation, 1961), p. 732.

18. Bernstein, *Praxis and Action* (Philadelphia: Univ. of Pennsylvania Press, 1971), p. x. For Bernstein's view, see also his *The Restructuring of Social and Political Theory* (New York: Harcourt, Brace, Jovanovich, 1976).

19. See Peirce's essays, "Questions Concerning Certain Faculties Claimed for Man" and "Some Consequences of Four Incapacities," in the *Collected Papers of Charles Sanders Peirce,* ed. by Charles Hartshorne and Paul Weiss, 6 vols. (Cambridge: Harvard Univ. Press, 1931–35), vol. 5; also, Wildrid Sellars's "Empiricism and the Philosophy of Mind," in *Science, Perception and Reality* (New York: Humanities Press, 1963).

20. See Peirce's "Neglected Argument for the Reality of God," in the *Collected Papers,* vol. 6.

21. *The Yellow Emperor's Classic of Internal Medicine,* chaps. 1–34, trans. with an introduction by Ilza Veith, New Edition (Berkeley: Univ. of California Press, 1966), pp. 10–25.

22. Chang Chung-yuan, *Creativity and Taoism: A Study of Chinese Philosophy, Art, and Poetry* (New York: Julian Press, 1963; Harper & Row, 1970).

23. *Creativity and Taoism,* pp. 66–67. Other than the citation from Whitehead, Chang's quotations are from *Tao Teh Ching.*

24. Translated by Wing-tsit Chan in his *Source Book in Chinese Philosophy* (Princeton: Princeton Univ. Press, 1963), pp. 86–87.

25. See, for instance, the discussion by Han Fei Tzu in the forty-ninth chapter of his book, called the *Han Fei Tzu,* trans. by Wing-tsit Chan in his *Source Book,* pp. 259–60. The problem of the relation of legalism to Taoism is discussed at length in Herrlee G. Creel's *Shen Pu-hai: A Chinese Political Philosopher of the Fourth Century B.C.* (Chicago: Univ. of Chicago Press, 1974), chap. 11.

26. Wang's "Inquiry on the *Great Learning*" is translated by Wing-tsit Chan in his *Source Book* and in a more comprehensive edition of Wang's work, *Instructions for Practical Living and Other Neo-Confucian Writings by Wang Yang-ming* (New York: Columbia Univ. Press, 1963). An excellent commentary on the points discussed here is Julia Ching's *To Acquire Wisdom: The Way of Wang Yang-ming* (New York: Columbia Univ. Press, 1976).

CHAPTER 3   (Pages 67–91)

1. The cosmological concepts are discussed in detail in my *Cosmology of Freedom* (New Haven: Yale Univ. Press, 1974), esp. chaps. 2–6. Readers interested in the cosmology for its own sake are urged to begin there. For those interested in the Whiteheadian background, the basic source is Whitehead's *Process and Reality: An Essay in Cosmology* (New York: Macmillan, 1929; Corrected Edition ed. by David Ray Griffin and Donald W. Sherburne, New York: Free Press, 1978). An excellent, general exposition of Whitehead is Elizabeth Kraus, *The Metaphysics of Experience: A Companion to Whitehead's Process and Reality* (New York: Fordham Univ. Press, 1979).

2. An historical account of the importance of this distinction for twentieth-century philosophy can be found in my "Metaphysics," *Social Research* 47/4 (Winter 1980), pp. 686–703.

3. The commonsense theory of knowledge as representation has found expression even in contemporary philosophers. As such, it is brilliantly criticized by Richard Rorty, in *Philosophy and the Mirror of Nature* (Princeton: Princeton Univ. Press, 1979).

4. This characterization of metaphysics has been developed most fully in our time by Charles Hartshorne in his various writings. See esp. his *Creative Synthesis and Philosophic Method* (La Salle: Open Court Publishing Co., 1970), chap. 2.

5. For Kant's distinction between "transcendent" and "transcendental," see *The Critique of Pure Reason,* B352f.

6. Chapter 5 presents arguments to this effect.

7. These highly abstract considerations are defended at length in my *God the Creator* (Chicago: Univ. of Chicago Press, 1968), chap. 2 and Appendix.

8. I examine this in detail in *The Cosmology of Freedom* (New Haven: Yale Univ. Press, 1974), chap. 3. I present the thesis here only as a suggestion; later chapters develop it in an application to the concepts of thinking.

9. See the debate between Lewis Ford and myself on this point in the *Southern Journal of Philosophy,* 10/1 (Spring 1972), pp. 79–86.

10. Toulmin, *Human Understanding* (Princeton: Princeton Univ. Press, 1972). I doubt, however, that Professor Toulmin would appreciate the systematic use I am making of his historical point.

CHAPTER 4   (Pages 93–132)

1. John Dewey, *Theory of Valuation* (Chicago: Univ. of Chicago Press, 1939), *International Encyclopedia of Unified Science,* vol. 2, no. 4.

2. Robert S. Hartman, *The Structure of Value* (Carbondale, Ill.: Southern Illinois Univ. Press, 1967).

3. See Brumbaugh's "Education and Reality: Two Revolutions," in *Thought,* 48/188 (Spring 1973), 5–18; also "Formal Value Theory: Transfinite Ordinal Numbers and Relatively Trivial Practical Choices," in *Journal of Human Relations,* 21 (1973), 211–15; and "Robert Hartman's Formal Axiology: An Extension," *The Journal of Value Inquiry,* 11/4 (Winter 1977), 259–63.

4. A splendid, scholarly discussion of the practice and philosophy of yoga is Mircea Eliade's *Yoga: Immortality and Freedom*, trans. by Willard R. Trask (Bollingen Series 56; Princeton: Princeton Univ. Press, 1958).

5. Cultivation of Taoistic powers is described and beautifully illustrated in terms of Chinese art by Philip Rawson and Laszlo Legeza, *Tao: The Eastern Philosophy of Time and Change* (New York: Avon Books, 1973). See also, Lu K'uan Yu's *Taoist Yoga: Alchemy and Immortality* (New York: Samuel Weiser, 1973).

6. The best of many books on *t'ai chi ch'uan* in English is Sophia Delza's *T'ai Chi Ch'uan: Body and Mind in Harmony* (New York: David McKay, 1961). A large potpourri of Chinese arts related to and including *t'ai chi ch'uan* is Wen-shan Huang's *Fundamentals of T'ai Chi Ch'uan: An Exposition of Its History, Philosophy, Technique, Practice and Application* (Hong Kong: South Sky Book Co., 1973).

7. See Edward De Bono, *New Think* (New York: Basic Books, 1968).

8. See Peirce's "Neglected Argument for the Reality of God," *Collected Papers of Charles Sanders Peirce*, ed. by Hartshorne and Weiss (Cambridge: Harvard Univ. Press, 1935), vol. 6, paragraphs 458–65.

9. The value of "presence" is discussed more thoroughly in my *Soldier, Sage, Saint* (New York: Fordham Univ. Press, 1978).

PART 2. "A BEGINNING"   (Pages 135–138)

1. The term "imagination" is used here in a broad sense, running from the metaphysical foundations of experiential synthesis in any form to the production of specific images and the existential function of imagining. The basis for this range of meaning lies in both the philosophical literature—for example, Kant, *Critique of Pure Reason,* B 103—and the intrinsic connections of the concepts discussed in this book. It should be pointed out, however, that "imagination" is also used in a more restricted sense, as a particular mental act in contrast to perception, memory, and sometimes even fantasy. Edward S. Casey treats the term in the last sense in his *Imagining: A Phenomenological Study* (Bloomington: Indiana Univ. Press, 1976). By "imagine," he means something like the experience referred to in "let me imagine a mermaid, first one with a human head and torso and a fish-like bottom, and then one with a fish top and a human pair of legs." Casey's use of "imagination" is one of those discussed below under the notion of appearance. For the discussion, I am considerably indebted to Casey for his illumining analysis.

2. See Merleau-Ponty's *Phenomenology of Perception,* trans. by Colin Smith (London: Routledge & Kegan Paul, 1962). See also Patrick A. Heelan's *Space, Perception, and Science,* forthcoming.

CHAPTER 5   (Pages 139–175)

1. These categories are taken from Kant's chapter on the transcendental deduction in the first edition of *Critique of Pure Reason,* trans. by Norman Kemp Smith (London: Macmillan, 1933), A 98–110. Although this chapter was completely rewritten for the second edition, the points discussed in the present work are not contradicted by the later edition.

2. Ibid., A 99.

3. Ibid., A 102.

4. Hart, *Unfinished Man and the Imagination* (New York: Herder and Herder, 1968), pp. 156f.

5. See Whitehead's little book, *Symbolism: Its Meaning and Effect* (New

York: Macmillan, 1927; New York: Capricorn, 1959), chaps. 1, 2; see also *Process and Reality* (New York: Macmillan, 1929), part 2, chap. 8. Hart's discussion of this aspect of presentational immediacy centers on what he calls "continuous ingredience," *Unfinished Man*, pp. 138f.

6. See Foucault's *The Archaeology of Knowledge*, trans. by A. M. Sheridan Smith (New York: Harper Colophon, 1976), parts 1, 2.

7. Among Dewey's numerous works emphasizing these themes, see, first, *Art as Experience* (New York: Minton, Balch & Co., 1935).

8. See, for instance, Peirce's essays on speculative grammar in *The Collected Papers of Charles Sanders Peirce*, ed. by Charles Hartshorne and Paul Weiss (Cambridge: Harvard Univ. Press, 1931–35), vol. 2; also the essay on normative sciences in vol. 1. Peirce's most general early statement of his view is found in "Questions Concerning Certain Faculties Claimed for Man" and "Some Consequences of Four Incapacities," in vol. 5.

9. The reference to theory here and in the discussion that follows builds on the preliminary statement of a theory of value in my *Cosmology of Freedom* (New Haven: Yale Univ. Press, 1974), chap. 3.

10. See an interesting, parallel discussion of this point in Martin Heidegger, *What Is Called Thinking?*, trans. by Fred D. Wieck and J. Glenn Gray (New York: Harper & Row, 1968), esp. part 2, lecture 3.

11. The question of the value of harmony is discussed at length in my *Cosmology of Freedom*.

12. See *Instructions for Practical Living and Other Neo-Confucian Writings by Wang Yang-ming*, trans. by Wing-tsit Chan (New York: Columbia Univ. Press, 1963) and the commentary by Julia Ching, *To Acquire Wisdom* (New York: Columbia Univ. Press, 1976). See also, Tu Wei-ming, *Neo-Confucian Thought in Action: Wang Yang-ming's Youth (1472–1509)* (Berkeley: Univ. of California Press, 1976), esp. chaps. 3, 4. For an analysis of the concepts of *sage, saint,* and *hero* in terms of will, see my *Soldier, Sage, Saint* (New York: Fordham Univ. Press, 1978).

13. *Critique of Pure Reason*, A 50, B 74. For a discussion of the significance of Kant's supposition, see Martin Heidegger, *Kant and the Problem of Metaphysics*, trans. by James S. Churchill (Bloomington: Indiana Univ. Press, 1962), p. 40 passim.

14. Kant, *Critique*, B176–87.

15. See Kant's discussion of the "Second Analogy," *Critique*, B 232–56. See also my analysis, "Specialties and Worlds," in *Hastings Center Studies* (January 1974), 2/1, pp. 53–64.

16. Kant, *Critique*, B797–98.

17. See Merleau-Ponty, *Phenomenology of Perception*, trans. by Colin Smith (London: Routledge & Kegan Paul, 1962), intro.

18. For a review of the literature, as well as an example, see Casey, *Imagining: A Phenomenological Study* (Bloomington: Indiana Univ. Press, 1976).

19. In addition to the reference in note 10 above, see Heidegger's "The Question Concerning Technology," in a book by the same title, trans. by William Lovitt (New York: Harper Colophon, 1977), esp. p. 35.

20. See Heidegger, *Introduction to Metaphysics*, trans. by Ralph Manheim (New Haven: Yale Univ. Press, 1959; Garden City: Doubleday Anchor, 1961), esp. pp. 164–67 in the Doubleday edition.

21. In "The Question Concerning Technology" cited above, Heidegger interpreted technology as a way of bringing things to presence, of revealing them; tech-

nology differs from other forms of relevatory presencing by virtue of its mathematical ordering and its capacity to put what it reveals in a "standing reserve" ready for human use. Like Whitehead before him, Heidegger pointed out the danger in this limited form of envisionment, arguing that the fine arts must provide a counterpoise that will drive understanding to a deeper appreciation of both art and technology. He separated this discussion from consideration of the merits of specific technologies, making it impossible, in his thought, to assess his claims when they come in conflict with each other—for instance, the claim of better health technology and that of independence from medical support systems.

22. See Whitehead's *Process and Reality,* part 1, chap. 2, section 3; and part 3.

23. If spontaneity seems offensive from the standpoint of scientific explanation, a doctrine of divine creation will give an account of the origin of what appears as spontaneous within time. This is discussed in my *God the Creator* (Chicago: Univ. of Chicago Press, 1968); see the Appendix for a detailed discussion of the distinction between essential and conditional features. For a discussion of this theory in connection with determinism, see *The Cosmology of Freedom,* chaps. 5, 6.

24. The doctrines of these last paragraphs mark a significant departure from Whitehead, who would not recognize the second or third kinds of essential features of subjective form, or even a distinction between essential and conditional features. Instead, in order to derive the novel features necessary for real decisions in the occasion, Whitehead held to a doctrine that among the initial data is a prehension (feeling) of God's envisagement of possibilities for the occasion. This prehension in ordinary occasions provides a lure for a certain pattern in the satisfaction. For many reasons, this is overcomplicated and involves God's interference in the cosmic process in a way destructive of freedom. The reasons are detailed in *God the Creator* and *The Cosmology of Freedom,* as well as in *Creativity and God* (New York: Seabury Press, 1980). These issues are not important for the present book.

25. See Heelan's *Space, Perception, and Science,* forthcoming, Chapter 5.

26. Whitehead was the first to articulate this general point. See *Process and Reality,* part 2, chap. 2, secs. 1–2. He somewhat overgeneralized the point, however, not limiting it to experience involving synthetic imagination but ascribing it to the integration involved in any concrescence whatsoever. Although I believe he was correct to see that the structures involved in lower organisms must be the ones from which those of higher organisms arise, it is not necessary that all the characteristics of experience be ascribed to all occasions. Indeed, there are some values that are not relevant to lower occasions, only to higher ones, and only the higher ones can therefore be characterized in terms of those values, for instance beauty. Goodness in some more general sense may apply to all occasions, however; in fact, the argument made in the first section in this chapter about the value involved in mere synthesis has an analog for any kind of synthesis, imaginative or not.

Whitehead's own best discussion of beauty is in *Adventures of Ideas* (Cambridge: Cambridge Univ. Press, 1933), chap. 17, where he defines it on p. 324 as the "mutual adaptation of the several factors in an occasion of experience." He explicated *mutual adaptation* to mean that feelings take on subjective form by virtue of contrasting with each other, and that "variety of detail with effective contrast" constitutes massiveness. Massiveness, together with intensity of feeling, gives "strength," "harmony," or "beauty." This view is compatible with the claim to be developed here—that beauty consists in maximizing narrowness and width against a background both trivial and vague.

27. As John E. Smith aptly declares:

Conjunctions are notoriously promiscuous; the connective "and" is without restriction ("numbers *and* angels *and* nations," etc.) and even existential conjunctions, as bare conjunctions, may connect almost anything under the sun. For two realities, however, to be *with* each other as body is with mind, meaning is with language, husband is with wife, the two cannot be "wholly other."

(in *The Analogy of Experience: An Approach to Understanding Religious Truth* [New York: Harper & Row, 1973], p. 20). My point is that, since it is so hard to make marriages work, bare conjunctions themselves provide an elementary enrichment of experience; further, bare conjunctions, like the bare contrast of female and male, provide a background out of which true marriages become possible and have meaning.

28. See Wang, *Instructions,* p. 272.

29. See Berger, *The Sacred Canopy: Elements of a Sociological Theory of Religion* (Garden City: Doubleday Anchor, 1969), chap. 1.

30. Ibid., p. 25.

31. See Mircea Eliade, *The Sacred and the Profane* (New York: Harper Torchbook, 1961).

32. Paul Ricoeur, *The Symbolism of Evil,* trans. by Emerson Buchanan (Boston: Beacon Press, 1969), chap. 6.

33. See Tillich's "Two Types of Philosophy of Religion," in *Theology of Culture,* ed. by Robert C. Kimball (New York: Oxford Univ. Press, 1959); *The Courage to Be* (New Haven: Yale Univ. Press, 1952).

34. This analysis of the experience of contingency in the world and relative to its creative ground is expanded in *God the Creator,* chap. 8; the implicit ontology is explained in chap. 4.

CHAPTER 6   (Pages 177–217)

1. See, for instance, Husserl, *Ideas: General Introduction to Pure Phenomenology,* trans. by W. R. Boyce Gibson (New York: Collier, 1962), chaps. 4, 8, esp. pp. 109–11.

2. See the discussion of Wilfrid Sellars in his *Science, Perception and Reality,* the essay entitled "Empiricism and Philosophy of Mind" (New York: Humanities Press, 1963); see also Richard J. Bernstein's discussion in *Praxis and Action* (Philadelphia: Univ. of Pennsylvania Press, 1971), p. 72.

3. Bernstein, *Praxis,* pp. 108f.; Husserl's italics.

4. Whitehead, *Symbolism: Its Meaning and Effects* (New York: Macmillan, 1927), chap. 2.

5. *Process and Reality* (New York: Macmillan, 1929), p. 253.

6. Ibid., p. 204.

7. Ibid., p. 205.

8. *Symbolism,* p. 45.

9. *Critique of Pure Reason,* trans. by Norman Kemp Smith (London: Macmillan, 1956), B 179.

10. Ibid., B 180f.

11. The paper originally appeared in *The Journal of Speculative Philosophy*, vol. 2 (1869), pp. 103–14; it is reprinted in the *Collected Papers of Charles Sanders Peirce*, ed. by Charles Hartshorne and Paul Weiss (Cambridge: Harvard Univ. Press, 1931–35), vol. 5, paragraphs 213–63 (cited as 5.213–263).

12. Ibid., 5.119. Peirce himself argued that perceptual judgments are incorrigible and the first premises of our reasoning (ibid., 5.116), a position to which the axiological cosmology does not subscribe. His argument, however, was not that perceptual judgments are intuitive in his technical sense, as Hume or Morris Schlick would have held, but rather that we cannot control them and that we cannot criticize what we cannot control. The counterargument is that perceptual judgments in various senses can indeed be controlled and ought to be controlled responsibly, as this chapter attempts to establish.

13. This formulation is from his correspondence with Lady Welby, published in *Collected Papers*, vol. 8, ed. by Arthur W. Burks; CP 8.327–341; esp. 328. An extended discussion is in CP 5.41–179; the theme reappears at many places throughout Peirce's work.

14. This way of expressing the cosmological point is developed in detail in my *Cosmology of Freedom* (New Haven: Yale Univ. Press, 1974), pp. 110–15.

15. The two words of the phrase "genetic causal" are not redundant. Sometimes causality refers to the pattern exhibited in the sequence wherein one kind of event regularly follows another kind; this may be called "coordinate causality," following Whitehead's distinction of coordinate analysis from genetic analysis. Genetic causality refers to the sense of causality in which a later thing arises out of an earlier thing. Sometimes it is claimed that natural science must limit itself to the study of coordinate causes, or causation as regularity; this is Kant's position.

16. Richard Bernstein rightly criticizes Peirce on this point; see *Praxis*, p. 313.

17. See, for instance, Husserl's *Ideas*, chap. 3.

18. Process philosophers have neglected this line of argument in defense of altruism. Hartshorne, for instance, in his defense of altruism, appeals mainly to the disinterestedness of direct anticipations of the future; see his *Creative Synthesis and Philosophic Method* (La Salle, Ill.: Open Court Publishing Co., 1970), pp. 198–204.

19. See *Process and Reality*, part 4, chap. 1; also p. 335.

20. He said, for instance: "the triumph of consciousness comes with the negative intuitive judgment. In this case, there is a conscious feeling of what might be and what is not. The feeling concerns the definite negative prehensions enjoyed by its subject. It is the feeling of absence, and it feels this absence as produced by the definite exclusiveness of what is really present. Thus the explicitness of negation, which is the peculiar characteristic of consciousness, is here at its maximum." Ibid., pp. 417f.

21. Throughout *Process and Reality*, but see esp. part 3, chap. 3.

22. See, for example, Hartshorne, *Creative Synthesis*, and his many other writings. For an extended discussion of the criticism being made in the text, see my *Creativity and God* (New York: Seabury Press, 1980), chap. 4.

23. For an extended discussion of these criticisms, see ibid., chap. 1.

24. For a more systematic presentation of the present point, see my *Cosmology of Freedom*, chap. 3.

25. *Process and Reality*, p. 381.

26. This discussion and others of the propositional form of experience owes much to the work of Peirce and Whitehead. Peirce's theory of signs is found

throughout his works, but particularly in volumes 1 and 5 of the *Collected Papers*. Whitehead's best-focused discussions are in *Process and Reality,* part 3, chaps. 4–5.

27. Yogacara is an ancient form of Mahayana Buddhism founded by the brothers, Asanga and Vasubandhu. Vasubandhu's "Treatise in Thirty Verses on Consciousness-Only," along with an influential commentary by the Chinese monk, Hsüan-tsang, can be found in *A Source Book in Chinese Philosophy,* ed. and trans. by Wing-tsit Chan (Princeton: Princeton Univ. Press, 1963), chap. 23. Perhaps the most interesting expression of Yogacara is in the novels of Yukio Mishima, esp. the four books comprising the *Sea of Fertility.* Yogacara's description of the perceptual elements of the subjective world is shrewd; the question whether it applies to the objective world, or whether objectivity can be asserted within Yogacara, is complicated and confused.

28. For a criticism of Whitehead on this point, see my *Creativity and God,* chap. 3. For a conception of a noncosmological God, see my *God the Creator* (Chicago: Univ. of Chicago Press, 1968). God as the source of spontaneity in human experience is discussed in my *Soldier, Sage, Saint* (New York: Fordham Univ. Press, 1978).

29. See Ricoeur's *The Symbolism of Evil,* trans. by Emerson Buchanan (Boston: Beacon Press, 1969), pp. 3–24, 161–74, 347–57. For a general treatment, see G. S. Kirk's *Myth: Its Meaning and Functions in Ancient and Other Cultures* (Berkeley: Univ. of California Press, 1970).

30. This thesis is supported by T. R. Martland's *Religion as Art* (Albany: SUNY Press, 1981).

CHAPTER 7   (Pages 219–265)

1. *Immanuel Kant's Critique of Pure Reason,* trans. by Norman Kemp Smith (London: Macmillan, 1933), B 34.

2. Ibid., B 103.

3. Ibid., A 106. Kant distinguished universal concepts from the "individual" forms of space and time; so, for him, the term "form" had a wider extension than the term "rule." This is not, for the moment, an important distinction for our problem, which handles universality and particularity differently.

4. For Whitehead's discussion of "contrast," see *Process and Reality* (New York: Macmillan, 1929), part 3, chap. 5, pp. 206–28.

5. Kant, *Critique*, B 179f.

6. Ibid., B 184.

7. Ibid., B 180f.

8. Whitehead, ibid., pp. 63ff.

9. For the following points, see, for instance, Heidegger's essay "On the Essence of Truth," trans. by R. F. C. Hull and Alan Crick, in *Existence and Being* by Martin Heidegger, ed. by Werner Brock (Chicago: Regnery, 1949), pp. 319–51; and Hans-Georg Gadamer, *Truth and Method,* trans. ed. by Garret Barden and John Cumming (New York: Seabury Press, 1975), pp. 235–41.

10. Peter Strawson, *Individuals: An Essay in Descriptive Metaphysics* (New York: Anchor, 1963; orig. Methuen, 1959), p. xiii.

11. Ibid., p. xiv.

12. *Reality* (New York: Peter Smith, 1949), pp. 208f.

13. Weiss, *Beyond All Appearances* (Carbondale: Southern Illinois Univ.

Press, 1974), p. 312. Relaxing his concern for a metaphysics of Finalities, in *You, I, and the Others* (Carbondale: Southern Illinois Univ. Press, 1980), Weiss provides an absolutely brilliant phenomenology of internalization, self-individuation, and privacy.

14. Weiss, *First Considerations: An Examination of Philosophical Evidence* (Carbondale: Southern Illinois Univ. Press, 1977), p. 226.

15. Foucault, *The Archaeology of Knowledge,* trans. by A. M. Sheridan Smith (New York: Harper & Row, 1976; orig. Tavistock Pub., 1972), p. 12.

16. Streetwalkers, not logicians, grasp what Whitehead understood about *Principia Mathematica.*

17. See *Process and Reality,* part 2, chap. 2, secs. 1–2; see also, Whitehead's "Mathematics and the Good," published in *The Philosophy of Alfred North Whitehead,* ed. by Paul Arthur Schilpp (New York: Tudor, 1941), Library of Living Philosophers, vol. 3, pp. 666–81.

18. On this complex point, see the exchange between Lewis S. Ford and myself, as follows: Neville, "Whitehead on the One and the Many," *Southern Journal of Philosophy,* 7 (Winter 1969–70), 387–93; Ford, "Neville on the One and the Many," ibid., vol. 10/1 (Spring 1972), 79–84; Neville, "Response to Ford's 'Neville on the One and the Many'," ibid., pp. 85–86. Since this exchange, my views have departed even farther from Whitehead, although along lines indicated in the discussion.

19. See Rollo May's interesting contrast of Plato and Freud on the subject of eros, in his *Love and Will* (New York: Norton, 1969), pp. 74–96.

20. Casey, *Imagining: A Phenomenological Study* (Bloomington: Indiana Univ. Press, 1976).

21. These classes are developed as universal ideal types in my *Soldier, Sage, Saint* (New York: Fordham Univ. Press, 1978).

CHAPTER 8   (Pages 267–312)

1. For an alternate approach to the axiology of thinking, see David Hall's *The Uncertain Phoenix* (New York: Fordham Univ. Press, 1981). Although Hall's account may be a touch overdrawn, it presents a response to most of the issues discussed here from the dominant standpoint of spontaneity or play, a thoroughgoing Taoist metaphysics.

2. John Dewey has made the most thorough case for this point in his *Experience and Nature* (2d. ed., 1929; reprint ed., New York: Dover, 1958), pp. 173–80. I analyze this point in detail in *The Cosmology of Freedom* (New Haven: Yale Univ. Press, 1974), chap 10.

3. See Helene Moglen's *Charlotte Bronte: The Self Conceived* (New York: Norton, 1978), chap. 3.

4. See particularly, Kierkegaard's *Sickness Unto Death,* trans. by Walter Lowrie (Garden City: Doubleday Anchor, 1955), part 1. See also my *Soldier, Sage, Saint* (New York: Fordham Univ. Press, 1978), chap. 3.

5. Peter L. Berger, *The Sacred Canopy* (Garden City: Doubleday Anchor, 1969), chaps. 1, 2.

6. Adams, *The Education of Henry Adams* (New York: Modern Library, 1931; private ed., 1907).

7. John Tasker Howard and James Lyons, *Modern Music* (rev. ed., New York: Mentor, 1958), p. 77.

8. For a definitive interpretation of modernism, see Carl E. Schorske's *Fin-de-Siecle Vienna* (New York: Knopf, 1980).

9. Whitehead, *Science and the Modern World* (New York: Macmillan, 1927), p. 126.

10. Ibid., chap. 5.

Bibliography of Works Cited

Aristotle, The Basic Works of. Trans. by W. D. Ross. New York: Random House, 1941. Ed. by Richard McKeon.

Bell, Daniel. *The End of Ideology.* New York: Free Press, 1962.

Berger, Peter L. *The Sacred Canopy: Elements of a Sociological Theory of Religion.* Garden City: Doubleday Anchor, 1969.

Bernstein, Richard J. *Praxis and Action.* Philadelphia: Univ. of Pennsylvania Press, 1971.

———. *The Restructuring of Social and Political Theory.* New York: Harcourt, Brace, Jovanovich, 1976.

Blanshard, Brand. *Reason and Goodness.* New York: Macmillan, 1961.

Boulding, Kenneth. *The Image.* Ann Arbor: Univ. of Michigan Press, 1956.

Brodbeck, May. *Readings in the Philosophy of Social Science.* New York: Macmillan, 1967.

Brumbaugh, Robert S. *The Philosophers of Greece.* New York: Crowell, 1964; Albany: SUNY Press, 1981.

———. "Education and Reality: Two Revolutions," *Thought,* 48/188 (Spring 1973).

———. "Formal Value Theory: Transfinite Ordinal Numbers and Relatively Trivial Practical Choices." *Journal of Human Relations,* 21 (1973).

———. "Robert Hartman's Formal Axiology: An Extention," *Journal of Value Inquiry,* 11/4 (Winter 1977).

Buchler, Justus. *Metaphysics of Natural Complexes.* New York: Columbia Univ. Press, 1966.

Casey, Edward S. *Imagining: A Phenomenological Study.* Bloomington: Indiana Univ. Press, 1976.

Chan, Wing-tsit. *Source Book in Chinese Philosophy.* Princeton: Princeton Univ. Press, 1963.

Chang, Chung-yuan. *Creativity and Taoism: A Study of Chinese Philosophy, Art, and Poetry*. New York: Harper & Row, 1970.

Ching, Julia. *To Acquire Wisdom: The Way of Wang Yang-ming*. New York: Columbia Univ. Press, 1976.

Creel, Heerlee G. *Shen Pu-hai: A Chinese Political Philosopher of the Fourth Century B.C.* Chicago: Univ. of Chicago Press, 1974.

De Bono, Edward. *New Think*. New York: Basic Books, 1968.

Delza, Sophia. *T'ai Chi Ch'uan: Body and Mind in Harmony*. New York: David McKay, 1961.

Derrida, Jacques. "Structure, Sign, and Play in the Discourse of the Human Sciences," in *The Languages of Criticism and the Sciences of Man*. Edited by Richard Macksey and Eugenio Donato. Baltimore: Johns Hopkins Univ. Press, 1970.

―――. *Of Grammatology*. Translated by Gayatri Spivak. Baltimore: Johns Hopkins Univ. Press, 1977.

Dewey, John. *Reconstruction in Philosophy*. New York: Henry Holt & Co., 1920.

―――. *Human Nature and Conduct*. New York: Henry Holt, 1922.

―――. *Experience and Nature*. 2d. ed.: La Salle: Open Court, 1929.

―――. *The Quest for Certainty*. New York: Minton, Balch, 1929.

―――. *Art as Experience*. New York: Minton, Balch, 1935.

―――. *Theory of Valuation*. Chicago: Univ. of Chicago Press, 1939.

Eliade, Mircea. *Yoga: Immortality and Freedom*. Translated by W. R. Trask. Princeton: Princeton Univ. Press, 1958.

―――. *The Sacred and the Profane*. Translated by W. R. Trask. New York: Harper Torchbook, 1961.

Fisk, Milton. *Nature and Necessity*. Bloomington: Indiana Univ. Press, 1973.

Ford, Lewis S. "Neville on the One and the Many," *Southern Journal of Philosophy*, 10/1 (Spring 1972), pp. 79–84.

Foucault, Michel. *The Archaeology of Knowledge*. Translated by A. M. Sheridan Smith. New York: Harper & Row, 1976.

Gadamer, Hans-Georg. *Truth and Method*. Translation edited by Garret Barden and John Cumming. New York: Seabury Press, 1975.

Gewirth, Alan. *Reason and Morality*. Chicago: Univ. of Chicago Press, 1978.

Grünbaum, Adolf. *Philosophical Problems of Space and Time*. New York: Knopf, 1963.

Habermas, Jürgen. *Theory and Practice*. Translated by John Viertel. Boston: Beacon Press, 1973.

―――. *Legitimation Crisis*. Translated by Thomas McCarthy. Boston: Beacon Press, 1975.

Hall, David L. *The Civilization of Experience*. New York: Fordham Univ. Press, 1973.

———. *The Uncertain Phoenix*. New York: Fordham Univ. Press, 1981.

Hart, Ray L. *Unfinished Man and the Imagination*. New York: Herder and Herder, 1968.

Hartman, Robert S. *The Structure of Value*. Carbondale: Southern Illinois Univ. Press, 1967.

Hartshorne, Charles. *Creative Synthesis and Philosophic Method*. La Salle: Open Court, 1970.

Havelock, Eric. *Preface to Plato*. Harvard Univ. Press, 1963.

Heelan, Patrick A. *Space, Perception, and Science*. Forthcoming.

Hegel, Georg. *Phenomenology of Spirit*. Translated by A. V. Miller. Oxford: Oxford Univ. Press, 1977.

Heidegger, Martin. *Existence and Being*. Ed. by Werner Brock. Chicago: Regnery, 1949.

———. *Introduction to Metaphysics*. Translated by Ralph Manheim. New Haven, Conn.: Yale University Press, 1959.

———. *Being and Time*. Translated by John Macquarrie & Edward Robinson. London: SCM Press, 1962.

———. *Kant and the Problem of Metaphysics*. Translated by James S. Churchill. Bloomington: Indiana Univ. Press, 1962.

———. *What Is Called Thinking*. Translated by Fred Wieck and Glenn Gray. New York: Harper & Row, 1968.

———. *The Question Concerning Technology*. Translated by William Lovitt. New York: Harper Colophon, 1977.

Howard, John Tasker and James Lyons. *Modern Music*. Rev. ed. New York: Mentor, 1958.

Huang, Wen-shan. *Fundamentals of T'ai Chi Ch'uan: An Exposition of Its History, Philosophy, Technique, Practice and Applications*. Hong Kong: South Sky Book Co., 1973.

Hume, David. *A Treatise of Human Nature*. Edited by L. A. Selby-Bigge. Oxford: Oxford Univ. Press, 1888.

Husserl, Edmund. *Ideas: General Introduction to Pure Phenomenology*. Translated by W. R. Boyce Gibson. New York: Collier, 1931.

Ihde, Don. *Listening and Voice: A Phenomenology of Sound*. Athens: Ohio Univ. Press, 1976.

Janik, Allan and Stephen Toulmin. *Wittgenstein's Vienna*. New York: Simon and Schuster, 1973.

James, William. *Essays in Radical Empiricism*. New York: Longmans, Green and Co., 1912.

Kant, Immanuel. *Critique of Pure Reason* (1st ed., 1781; 2d. ed., 1787).

Translated by Norman Kemp Smith. London: Macmillan & Co., 1956.

———. *Foundations of the Metaphysics of Morals* (1785). Translated by Lewis White Beck. Indianapolis: Liberal Arts Press, 1959.

———. *The Critique of Judgment* (1790). Trans. by James Creed Meredith. Oxford: Oxford Univ. Press, 1928.

Kirk, G. S. *Myth: Its Meaning and Functions in Ancient and Other Cultures*. Berkeley: Univ. of California Press, 1970.

Kierkegaard, Søren. *Sickness Unto Death*. Trans. by Walter Lowrie. Garden City: Doubleday Anchor, 1955.

Klaaren, Eugene M. *Religious Origins of Modern Science*. Grand Rapids: William B. Eerdmans, 1977.

Kline, Morris. *Mathematics: The Loss of Certainty*. New York: Oxford Univ. Press, 1980.

Kraus, Elizabeth. *The Metaphysics of Experience: A Companion to Whitehead's Process and Reality*. New York: Fordham Univ. Press, 1979.

Kripke, Saul. *Naming and Necessity*. Cambridge: Harvard Univ. Press, 1980.

Kuhn, Thomas. *The Structure of Scientific Revolutions*. Chicago: Univ. of Chicago Press, 1962.

Lauer, Quentin. *Essays in Hegelian Dialectic*. New York: Fordham Univ. Press, 1977.

Lu K'uan Yu. *Taoist Yoga: Alchemy and Immortality*. New York: Samuel Weiser, 1973.

Margolis, Joseph. *Contemporary Ethical Theory*. New York: Random House, 1966.

Martland, T. R. *Religion as Art*. Albany: SUNY Press, 1981.

May, Rollo. *Love and Will*. New York: Norton, 1969.

Mbiti, John. *African Religions and Philosophies*. Garden City: Doubleday Anchor, 1970.

Merleau-Ponty, Maurice. *Phenomenology of Perception*. Translated by Colin Smith. London: Routledge & Kegan Paul, 1962.

Moglen, Helene. *Charlotte Bronte: The Self Conceived*. New York: Norton, 1978.

Neville, Robert. *God the Creator*. Chicago: Univ. of Chicago Press, 1968.

———. "Ford on Neville on the One and the Many," *Southern Journal of Philosophy*, 10/1 (Spring 1972), pp. 85–6.

———. *The Cosmology of Freedom*. New Haven: Yale University Press, 1974.

———. *Soldier, Sage, Saint*. New York: Fordham Univ. Press, 1978.

———. *Creativity and God*. New York: Seabury Press, 1980.

————. "Metaphysics," in *Social Research,* 47/4 (Winter 1980), pp. 686–703.

Peirce, Charles Sanders. *The Collected Papers of Charles Sanders Peirce.* Vols. 1–6 edited by Charles Hartshorne and Paul Weiss, 1931–35; vols. 7–8 edited by Arthur Burks, 1958; Cambridge: Harvard Univ. Press.

Plato, The Collected Dialogues of. Various trans. New York: Bollingen Foundation, 1961. Ed. by Edith Hamilton and Huntington Cairns.

Popper, Karl. *The Open Society and Its Enemies.* 5th edition; Princeton: Princeton Univ. Press, 1966. Vol. 1: *The Spell of Plato.*

Putnam, Hilary. *Meaning and the Moral Sciences.* London: Routledge & Kegan Paul, 1978.

Quine, Willard. *From a Logical Point of View.* Cambridge: Harvard Univ. Press, 1953.

Rawson, Philip and Laszlo Legeza. *Tao: The Eastern Philosophy of Time and Change.* New York: Avon, 1973.

Ricoeur, Paul. *The Symbolism of Evil.* Translated by Emerson Buchanan. Boston: Beacon Press, 1969.

Rorty, Richard. *Philosophy and the Mirror of Nature.* Princeton: Princeton Univ. Press, 1979.

Rozin, Paul. "The Evolution of Intelligence and Access to the Cognitive Unconscious," in *Progress in Psychobiology and Physiological Psychology,* vol. 6. New York: Academic Press, 1976.

Scheler, Max. *The Nature of Sympathy.* Translated by Peter Heath. London: Routledge & Kegan Paul, 1958.

Schorske, Carl E. *Fin-de-Siecle Vienna: Politics and Culture.* New York: Knopf, 1980.

Sellars, Wilfrid. *Science, Perception and Reality.* New York: Humanities, 1963.

Smith, John E. *Themes in American Philosophy: Purpose, Experience and Community.* New York: Harper, 1970.

————. *The Analogy of Experience: An Approach to Understanding Religious Truth.* New York: Harper & Row, 1973.

Stalknecht, Newton P. and R. S. Brumbaugh. *The Spirit of Western Philosophy.* New York: Longmans, Green and Co., 1950.

Strawson, Peter. *Individuals: An Essay in Descriptive Metaphysics.* New York: Anchor, 1963; orig. Methuen, 1959.

Tillich, Paul. *The Courage to Be.* New Haven: Yale Univ. Press, 1952.

————. *Theology of Culture.* Edited by Robert C. Kimball. New York: Oxford Univ. Press, 1959.

Toulmin, Stephen. *Human Understanding: The Collective Use and Evolution of Concepts.* Princeton: Princeton Univ. Press, 1972. See also "Janik."

Tu Wei-ming. *Neo-Confucian Thought in Action: Wang Yang-ming's Youth. (1472–1509)*. Berkeley: Univ. of California Press, 1976.

Wang Yang-ming. *Instructions for Practical Living and Other Neo-Confucian Writings by Wang Yang-ming*. Translated by Wing-tsit Chan. New York: Columbia Univ. Press, 1963.

Weiss, Paul. *Modes of Being*. Carbondale: Southern Illinois Univ. Press, 1958.

———. *Beyond All Appearances*. Carbondale: Southern Illinois Univ. Press, 1974.

———. *First Considerations: An Examination of Philosophical Evidence*. Carbondale: Southern Illinois Univ. Press, 1977.

———. *You, I, and the Others*. Carbondale: Southern Illinois Univ. Press, 1980.

Weissman, David. *Dispositional Properties*. Carbondale: Southern Illinois Univ. Press, 1965.

———. *Eternal Possibilities*. Carbondale: Southern Illinois Univ. Press, 1977.

Whitehead, Alfred North. *Principia Mathematica* (to *56), with Bertrand Russell. Cambridge: Cambridge Univ. Press, 1910.

———. *Science and the Modern World*. New York: Macmillan, 1927.

———. *Symbolism: Its Meaning and Effect*. New York: Macmillan, 1927.

———. *The Function of Reason*. Princeton: Princeton Univ. Press, 1929.

———. *Process and Reality: An Essay in Cosmology*. New York: Macmillan, 1929.

———. *Adventures of Ideas*. Cambridge: Cambridge Univ. Press, 1933.

———. *Modes of Thought*. New York: Macmillan, 1938.

———. "Mathematics and the Good," in *The Philosophy of Alfred North Whitehead*. Edited by Paul Arthur Schilpp. New York: Tudor, 1941.

Wittgenstein, Ludwig. *Tractatus Logico-Philosophicus*. London: Routledge & Kegan Paul, 1922.

———. *Philosophical Investigations*. Translated by G. E. M. Anscombe. New York: Macmillan, 1953.

The Yellow Emperor's Classic of Internal Medicine. Chapters 1–34. Translated with an Introduction by Ilza Veith. New Edition; Berkeley: Univ. of California Press, 1966.

Index